THE FLIGHT INTO THE UNCONSCIOUS

An Analysis of C.G. Jung's Psychology Project

The Collected English Papers of Wolfgang Giegerich

The Collected English Papers of Wolfgang Giegerich makes the work of one of archetypal psychology's most brilliant theorists available in one place. A practicing Jungian analyst and a long-time contributor to the field, Giegerich is renowned for his dedication to the substance of Jungian thought and for his unparalleled ability to think it through with both rigor and speculative strength. The product of over three decades of critical reflection, Giegerich's English papers are collected in six volumes: *The Neurosis of Psychology* (Vol. I). *Technology and the Soul* (Vol. 2), *Soul-Violence* (Vol. 3), and *The Soul Always Thinks* (Vol. 4), *The Flight into the Unconscious* (Vol. 5), and *Dreaming the Myth Onwards* (Vol. 6).

For a full list of titles in this series, please visit *www.routledge.com/The-Collected- English-Papers-of-Wolfgang-Giegerich/book-series/CEPWG*

Titles in this series:
The Neurosis of Psychology: Primary Papers Towards a Critical Psychology (Volume 1)
Technology and the Soul: From the Nuclear Bomb to the World Wide Web (Volume 2)
Soul-Violence (Volume 3)
The Soul Always Thinks (Volume 4)
The Flight into the Unconscious: An Analysis of C. G. Jung's Psychology Project (Volume 5)
"Dreaming the Myth Onwards": C. G. Jung on Christianity and on Hegel (Volume 6)

THE FLIGHT INTO THE UNCONSCIOUS

AN ANALYSIS OF C.G. JUNG'S PSYCHOLOGY PROJECT

COLLECTED ENGLISH PAPERS
VOLUME FIVE

WOLFGANG GIEGERICH

Routledge
Taylor & Francis Group
LONDON AND NEW YORK

First published 2013 by Spring Journal Books

Published 2020 by Routledge
2 Park Square, Milton Park, Abingdon, Oxon OX14 4RN
52 Vanderbilt Avenue, New York, NY 10017

Routledge is an imprint of the Taylor & Francis Group, an informa business

British Library Cataloguing-in-Publication Data
A catalogue record for this book is available from the British Library

Library of Congress Cataloging-in-Publication Data
A catalog record has been requested for this book

ISBN: 978-0-367-48519-1 (hbk)
ISBN: 978-0-367-48520-7 (pbk)
ISBN: 978-1-003-04142-9 (ebk)

Cover design and typography by:
Northern Graphic Design & Publishing
info@ncarto.com

THE FLIGHT INTO THE UNCONSCIOUS

AN ANALYSIS OF C.G. JUNG'S PSYCHOLOGY PROJECT

COLLECTED ENGLISH PAPERS
VOLUME FIVE

WOLFGANG GIEGERICH

Routledge
Taylor & Francis Group

LONDON AND NEW YORK

First published 2013 by Spring Journal Books

Published 2020 by Routledge
2 Park Square, Milton Park, Abingdon, Oxon OX14 4RN
52 Vanderbilt Avenue, New York, NY 10017

Routledge is an imprint of the Taylor & Francis Group, an informa business

British Library Cataloguing-in-Publication Data
A catalogue record for this book is available from the British Library

Library of Congress Cataloging-in-Publication Data
A catalog record has been requested for this book

ISBN: 978-0-367-48519-1 (hbk)
ISBN: 978-0-367-48520-7 (pbk)
ISBN: 978-1-003-04142-9 (ebk)

Cover design and typography by:
Northern Graphic Design & Publishing
info@ncarto.com

Contents

Acknowledgments

Versions of the following chapters have previously been published elsewhere:

Chapter 2, "Psychology as Anti-Philosophy: C. G. Jung" was first published in *Spring 77 (Philosophy and Psychology)*, June 2007, pp. 11–51 and appears here in a slightly expanded version.

A slightly different version of Chapter 3, "The Disenchantment Complex. C.G. Jung and the modern world," was an invited paper delivered at the Inaugural Regional Conference in London, July 2011, of The International Association for Jungian Studies on "Enchantment and Disenchantment: The Psyche in Transformation" and appeared in print in *International Journal of Jungian Studies* vol. 4, no. 1, March 2012, pp. 4–20.

A considerably shorter, rudimentary oral version of Chapter 6, "The Flight Into the Unconscious," was presented September 2, 2000 at "An International Symposium of Archetypal Psychology" organized by Pacifica Graduate Institute at the University of California, Santa Barbara, and was made publicly available through audio tapes as well as later, in 2009, in the Internet at http://www.rubedo.psc.br/artingle/flight.htm. The present text of Chapter 6 is based on parts of several different longer and very long versions both in German and in English written between 1999 and 2002, presented at lecture series extending over several semesters at the C.G. Jung Institute, Zurich as well as at the Neresheim Seminars, and was augmented by the inclusion of a new paradigm, the mytheme of Pan and Echo.

Chapter 7, "*Liber Novus*, that is, The New Bible. A First Analysis of C.G. Jung's *Red Book*" first appeared in *Spring 2010, Vol. 83 (Minding the Animal Psyche)*, Spring 2010, pp. 361–411.

The original version of Chapter 8, "The Opposition of 'Individual' and 'Collective' – Psychology's Basic Fault. Reflections On Today's

Magnum Opus of the Soul" was presented orally to The Guild of Pastoral Psychology, London, in May 1996, and published both in *Harvest. Journal for Jungian Studies* vol. 42, No.2, 1996, pp. 7-27 and as *Guild of Pastoral Psychology Lecture Pamphlet No. 259*, 1997, as well as in Italian translation by Anna Accogli in *l'imaginale 21*, ottobre 1996, pp. 11–51.

Chapter 9, "Closure and Setting Free or The Bottled Spirit of Alchemy and Psychology" first appeared in *Spring 74 (Alchemy). A Journal of Archetype and Culture*, Spring 2006, pp. 31–62.

* * *

As with all the previous volumes, collaboration with the editor of this series, Greg Mogenson, was very constructive, helpful, and enjoyable. I wish to sincerely thank Greg for his accompanying the genesis of this book with spirited involvement.

Sources and Abbreviations

For frequently cited sources, the following abbreviations have been used:

CW: Jung, C. G. *Collected Works*. 20 vols. Ed. Herbert Read, Michael Fordham, Gerhard Adler, and William McGuire. Trans. R. F. C. Hull. Princeton: Princeton University Press, 1957-1979. Cited by volume and, unless otherwise noted, by paragraph number.

GW: Jung, C. G. *Gesammelte Werke*. Zürich and Stuttgart (Rascher) now Olten and Freiburg i:Br: Walter-Verlag, 1958 ff. Cited by volume and, unless otherwise noted, by paragraph number.

Letters: Jung, C. G. *Letters*. 2 vols. Ed. Gerhard Adler. Bollingen Series XCV: 2. Princeton: Princeton University Press, 1975.

MDR: Jung, C. G. *Memories, Dreams, Reflections*. Rev. ed. Ed. Aniela Jaffé. Trans. Richard and Clara Winston. New York: Vintage Books, 1989. Cited by page number.

Erinnerungen: *Erinnerungen Träume Gedanken von C.G. Jung*. Ed. Aniela Jaffé. Zurich and Stuttgart: Rascher Verlag, 1967.

Preface

In everything, truth be your supreme commandment
—Motto of the Academia
Electoralis Theodoro-Palatina (1763)

Amicus Plato, sed magis amica veritas
—After Aristotle, *Nic. Eth.* 1096a

To understand Kant means to go beyond Kant
—Wilhelm Windelband, *Präludien*, 1883

In this book, a number of my essays are collected in which Jung's psychology project is subjected to a close reading and a radical psychological critique. I think that C.G. Jung deserves to be taken *seriously*. And from early on it has been my position that psychology must be applied to itself and not only to patients or cultural phenomena like myths and fairy tales. The analysis of Jung's psychology presented here is a *psychological* analysis because it is guided by my long-term struggle for a "rigorous notion of psychology" (a psychology that deserves its name "logos of the soul") and relies on criteria laid down by Jung himself. Rather than a critique from outside and in the name of principles or values external to it, it thus is a critical analysis of Jung's psychology from within the heart of Jung's psychology. Certain basic tenets of Jung's are being subjected to the alchemical *aqua fortis* and have to show whether they are gold or not. One essential critical question in this regard is: to what extent is Jung's psychology project responsive to the needs of the soul—the *concrete* soul in its historical setting at his time—and derives the views it entertains about the soul simply from how the soul in fact shows itself, and to what extent does it conversely come to the soul with preconceived ideas about what the soul *in abstracto* surely must be and want, thus—unwittingly—following an agenda of its own. And although the result of my analyses may in many cases appear to be devastating, the reader will not be left empty-handed with no more than ruins inasmuch as this critical destruction of a theoretical conception happens in the name of essential affirmative insights or principles and *ex negativo* supports them.

Methodologically it may not be superfluous to remind the reader that a critical analysis has a different task from works devoted to an exegesis. My topic cannot be to explain what Jung meant, what he intended to express with what he said. It has to be what the inner consistency, the objective implications and consequences of his teachings are as well as what the underlying or rather inherent driving force is that made Jung come up with his ideas and made them so important to him. Jungians very often make the mistake of surfing on the waves set in motion by Jung rather than *listening* to the *echo* of his teachings (which I believe would be the psychological approach to an author and the way to show one's respect). We should not make it so easy for ourselves.

In most but not all of the following chapters I start out from a small text by Jung and give it an extensive close and devoted reading, so that my analyses may, as if by themselves, grow out of this textual basis rather than being free-floating, sweeping assessments about them. I try to exhaust the implications of any theorem, following it in all its ramifications, because only when one fully sees what all is involved can consciousness truly depart from views recognized to be untenable. Each time it is not merely the particular issue, but Jung's psychology project as a whole that is ultimately at stake. It is, as it were, circumambulated from the particular angle or perspective opened up by the specific Jungian theses under discussion in each chapter.

In my critiques, I usually speak of "Jung." But Jung the person is not my target. The word Jung functions merely as an abbreviation or stand-in for the body of work authored by Jung and for the ideas contained in it. I am interested in the objective *psychology of* Jungian psychology as a general way of thinking and not in the man whose name it bears and his subjective psychology.

There are several quite different aspects to Jung's psychology. C.G. Jung saw himself as an empiricist. He wanted to present facts and merely name and describe them. In his work this stance is best represented by his *Studies in Word Association*, but, for example, his *The Psychology of Dementia Praecox*, although a work following a fundamentally different approach, belongs to this category, too. Jung was also a theorist; we just have to think of his *Psychological Types*, which develop a schema for differentiating (and understanding) psychological phenomena and processes. His *Synchronicity: An Acausal Connecting Principle* belongs also to Jung the scientist, combining, as it does, a statistical experiment with fundamental theorizing.

There is yet another Jung, that Jung who, as above all Marco Heleno Barreto[1] has convincingly shown, conceived of psychology as "something like antique philosophy," as philosophical practical wisdom. This Jung abhorred turning analytical psychology into a fixed theory under which concrete phenomena would then be subsumed and into a *technique* to be applied to "cases." This Jung wanted to really see the individual in his or her uniqueness and also to be open to the eachness of each new moment. As therapist he faced his patients directly, which also means to come forward in the consulting room as the real human being that he was and to respond to them with spontaneity and intuition out of his own living center rather than as a professional *persona*. (Spontaneity here does, however, not mean naively and simplistically. It was the spontaneous response of a psychologically educated and aware mind, a mind that had acquired a rich knowledge about mythology, religion, ethnology, psychiatry, and so on.)

It also needs to be mentioned that Jung had, which is quite unusual, a real notion of *soul* in contradistinction both to "psyche" (the behavior of the organism) and to "civil man," the "empirical personality," or "the ego"—soul as a reality in its own right and as *objective* soul (whose "greater part is outside the body,"[2] that is, outside the human individual). Because he had really become aware of "soul" he also had a true access to the soul depth of psychic phenomena (myths, symbols, dreams, rituals, clinical situations, etc.) and was capable of viewing these phenomena truly from a *soul standpoint*. This is a standpoint for which "behind the impressions of the daily life—behind the scenes—another picture looms up, covered by a thin veil of actual facts."[3] Just consider the following passage.

> I once asked the Bishop of Fribourg, in Switzerland, to send us
> a man who could give a good account of the mystery of the
> Mass. It was a sad failure; he could tell us nothing. He could

---

[1] Marco Heleno Barreto, "'It is something like antique philosophy': Analytical Psychology and Philosophical Practical Wisdom," in: *Spring 77* ("Philosophy & Psychology"), Spring 2007, pp. 79–98.

[2] *Maior autem animae pars extra corpus est.* Sendivogius, "De Sulphure" in *Museum Hermeticum*, Frankfurt 1678, quoted by Jung in a letter to Karl Kerényi of 12 Juli 1951, (*Letters 2*, p. 19). Cf. *CW* 12 §§ 396, 399, and 562.

[3] C.G. Jung, *The Visions Seminars*, Zürich (Spring Publ.) 1976, p. 8.

> only confess to the wonderful impression, the marvellous
> mystical feeling, but he could say nothing at all as to why he
> had that feeling. It was only sentiments, and we could do nothing
> with it. But if you go into the history of the rite, if you try to
> understand the whole structure of that rite, including all the
> other rites round it, then you see it is a mystery that reaches down
> into the history of the human mind ... (*CW* 18 § 616).

We see here the psychological instinct at work. The psychological
instinct does not merely and not so much show in the fact that Jung
rejects the ego sentiments *about* the rite (or evoked by it) as irrelevant
for the soul (in accordance with the "psychological difference"), but
much more and much rather in his being able to *actually perceive the
living mystery* in what for most other people who, like Jung, would
approach this phenomenon not as believers but with a scientific interest,
would be nothing but antiquarian curiosities, the dry dogmatic data
and scholarly results of historical and comparative religious studies.

In addition, there is yet another essential aspect. Jung also
critically reflected, and gained valuable insights into, the
methodological stance to be taken by a self-reflective "psychology
with soul." I only mention the insight that for psychology there
can be no "Archimedean point" from which to observe psychic
phenomena, so that in this field the object to be studied is
inevitably the subject itself, a fact which ultimately requires the
construal of psychology as the discipline of interiority.

However, when Jung said,

> I myself am in the grip of the same dream [as Goethe with his
> *Faust*] and have a "main project," which began in my eleventh
> year. My life has been permeated and held together by one idea
> and one goal: namely, to penetrate into the mystery of the
> personality (*MDR* p. 206, transl. modif.),

we realize that there is also a very different Jung from the empirical
scientist, the theorizing psychologist, and the therapist who aimed
for a way of living life in the sense of a philosophical practical
wisdom—a different Jung, especially when we keep in mind that,
in connection with Goethe, Jung had elucidated a few lines before
the quoted passage that 'main project' actually means "*opus magnum
or divinum.*" An empiricist might perhaps be able to describe his
scientific goal as the wish "to penetrate into the mystery of the
personality." But he could not describe his work as an *opus divinum*

and himself as being "in the grip of a dream," the same dream that Jung believed to see expressed in *Faust*. Jung's 'main project' as *opus divinum* circles around such questions as those of Meaning, the Self and the nature of God, the ultimate significance of the individual, and the inner process, telos, and goal of life.

In contrast to the divers aspects just listed by me before this last one, in contrast, furthermore, to the numerous interests and topics displayed in his publications, Jung viewed his entire psychology, his life's work as a whole, as held together by this one dream and tried to present it especially as the outgrowth of the early experiences that he recorded in the *Red Book*. "It all began then; the later details are only supplements and clarifications of the material that burst forth from the unconscious." "The first imaginings and dreams were like fiery, molten basalt, from which the stone crystallized, upon which I could work" (*Erinnerungen* p. 203, my transl.). We do not have to agree with this thesis. There are, after all, those other aspects of his work that cannot be viewed as seamlessly stemming from those early experiences. But, be that as it may, the "main project" that Jung in the cited sense saw as the deep inner unity of his work, regardless of whether it began in his eleventh year or originated in those later experiences during the time of World War I, this (and only this) is what I mean by his "psychology project" and what I critically analyze and circumambulate from different starting points in the following essays.

When I planned this volume it contained seven more essays, essays on Jung's religious thinking, especially concerning Christianity, and on Jung and Hegel. Since the inclusion of these essays would have exploded the size of this book, they will have to wait for another time. A few essays published previously in my *The Neurosis of Psychology* and *The Soul Always Thinks*, vols. 1 and 4 of my *Collected English Papers*, New Orleans, LA (Spring Journal Books) 2005 or 2010, respectively, could as far as their content is concerned have been included in the present volume, above all "The End of Meaning and the Birth of Man," but also "Jung's *Thought* of the Self in the Light of Its Underlying Experiences," "Irrelevantification," and "Is the Soul 'Deep'?"

The present volume begins with a chapter that tries to assess Jung's psychology project as a whole. Chapters two to six give an in-depth psychological reading of autobiographical reports by Jung in chronological sequence, each about one particular inner experience that he had as a boy or young man, respectively, and use these stories each time as a lens through which to gain a deeper insight into the psychology of Jung's fundamental, unnegotiable concerns as a psychological theoretician. Chapter seven, a critical review of his *Red Book*, concludes the series of papers devoted to or starting out from Jung's inner experiences. The remaining three chapters delve directly into fundamental theoretical issues raised by Jung's psychology.

Berlin, April 2011   Wolfgang Giegerich

CHAPTER ONE

C.G. Jung's Psychology Project as a Response to the Condition of the World

E very commemoration event in honor of a great mind[1] is an invitation to reflect anew about what his lifework is all about. This is all the more true when, as today, we celebrate both the anniversary of C.G. Jung's death and the sixtieth year of the Institute named after him. With the phrase "what his lifework is all about" I allude to Jung's comment in a letter of 1960 where he laments that "Being well-known not to say 'famous' means little when one realizes that those who mouth my name have fundamentally no idea of what it's all about."[2] In the following I want to present *my attempt* at working out what Jung's psychology project was all about.

But first I have to savor the wording of "what it's all about." It? The word "it" is used absolutely; it has no referent; in other words, Jung does not say people have no idea what *his work* or *his psychology* is about. His phrase rather means something much more existential, like "what is at stake?," "what is the enormous problem that we today are confronted with?," the problem that Jung believes to have struggled with and to which his psychology was his response. Jung is here not speaking as a scientist. A scientist, such as, for example, Ignaz

---

[1] This is the text of a lecture presented at the "C.G. Jung-Gedenktag" of the Jung Institute Zürich at ETH Zürich June 6, 2008.

[2] *Letters 2*, p. 530, 1 Jan 1960, to Prof. Eugen Böhler.

Semmelweis or Alfred Wegener, might suffer from the fact that his discoveries are not accepted and he himself is maybe treated as a crackpot. But in such a case he would never say that his colleagues or the general public have no idea of "what *it*'s all about," because what is not accepted is merely specific scientific hypotheses. It is true, Jung, too, felt "misunderstood or completely ignored,"[3] but this lack of recognition concerned the question "why there are no men in our epoch who could see at least what I was wrestling with."[4] What he was wrestling with was, as he said, a "world problem," the problem of "an entire world."[5] "The great problem of our time is that we don't understand what is happening to the world."[6] Earlier Jung had stated in a lecture, "My problem is to wrestle with the big monster of the historical past, the great burden of the human mind, the problem of Christianity" (*CW* 18 § 279). These quotations show how totally different the dimensionality of his concern was, compared with both scientific and consulting room ones.

During the last few years the whole world has also become upset about a problem of the "entire world," namely the problem of global warming. But when Jung says, "The great problem of our time is that we don't understand what is happening to the world" he lets us know that he has something very different in mind. First of all the problem Jung sees is precisely not a popular one that makes headlines. It remains unseen and not understood, indeed—so Jung felt—suppressed out of fear.[7] Secondly, the nature of the problem of our time, as envisioned by Jung, is not such that it could be approached with clear-cut technical and political measures. And thirdly, the *world* to which global warming is happening is obviously worlds apart from that world that is referred to in the cited statement about our lack of understanding what is happening to the world. This takes me to my first topic of this talk: Which "world" are we talking about when we try to describe C.G. Jung's psychology project as a response to the condition of the world?

---

[3] *Letters 2*, p. 589, 2 Sep 1960, to Sir Herbert Read.
[4] *Letters 2*, p. 586, 2 Sep 1960, to Sir Herbert Read.
[5] *MDR* p. 132.
[6] *Letters 2*, p. 590, 2 Sep 1960, to Sir Herbert Read.
[7] Jung surmised "that my books expect a human understanding of which the intellectual world or the world of intellect is afraid, although I can easily understand why that is so." *Letters 2*, pp. 497f., 12 April 1959, to Werner Bruecher.

There are many notions of world, and at least two very different ones even in Jung's own thinking.

These two notions of world and the ensuing danger of equivocation can be seen from the very passage from which the motto for the present anniversary events is taken, Jung's dictum, "'Zuunterst' ist [...] Psyche überhaupt 'Welt'" (*GW* 9/I § 291). The *Collected Works* translate: "[...] 'at bottom' the psyche is simply 'world.'" In this translation some nuances are lost. "At bottom" is usually understood as something like "in reality," "in essence," "in the last analysis." But "zuunterst" clearly expresses a spatial fantasy, a literal lowness. It evokes the idea of several layers and points to the very lowest of them, something like a sub-basement. A few lines earlier Jung had himself expressly spoken of "[t]he deeper 'layers' of the psyche" and said of them that they "lose their individual uniqueness" the deeper one gets. "'Lower down' [...] they become increasingly collective until they are universalized and extinguished in the body's materiality, i.e., in chemical substances. The body's carbon is simply carbon." The immediately following sentence is our motto, and it draws the conclusion from the foregoing reflection: "Hence 'at its lowest level' psyche is simply 'world.'" The sense of "world" here is that of the physical universe, "chemistry," "carbon." Jung entertains here a naturalistic fantasy.

Now it is astounding how Jung continues. "In this sense I hold Kerényi to be absolutely right when he says that in the symbol the *world itself* is speaking." Here Jung does not seem to see that in his own comments and in the idea by Kerényi he refers to, two incompatible concepts of "world" clash. When Kerényi says[8] that "In the image of the primordial child the world speaks of its own childhood," and, furthermore, when for him the rising sun, the human newborn, and the mythological child are all equally *symbols*, he certainly does not have the world as chemical substances in mind. Carbon does not speak. The world that *speaks*, and that, according to Kerényi's example speaks in the symbol of the primordial child about its, the world's, childhood, is the perceived and experienced world,

---

[8] Karl Kerényi, "Das Urkind," formerly as "Das Urkind in der Urzeit" in C.G. Jung and Karl Kerényi, *Das göttliche Kind*, Albae Vigiliae IV/VII (Amsterdam-Leipzig 1940), now Karl Kerény, *Humanistische Seelenforschung*, München and Wien (Albert Langen, Georg Müller) 1966, pp. 68–115, here p. 93.

the world of human beings. It presupposes a highly developed awake mind capable of perceiving symbolically, and certainly also a deep mind, but deep as poetry or thought may be deep, not deep in the sense of the lowest layers of the psyche where psyche is "extinguished in the body's materiality."

Jung's layer fantasy operates with the notion of a *continuum* from chemistry or physiology to fully attained consciousness, from archaic undifferentiatedness to modern abstraction and differentiation, from the collective and universal and unconscious[9] to conscious uniqueness and individuality. The world-relation that the symbol has for the Jung of our passage, too, is derived by him from the psyche's own lower, archaic levels, ultimately from the fact that, as he says, "the human body, too, *is built of* the stuff of the world" (§ 290, my emphasis). That is to say, the psyche's world-connection does not come about through its outward openness to the world. It comes about through the internal makeup of the psyche, its sharing its material base with the outer world.[10] Kerényi, by contrast, is thinking in terms of an *encounter* or *dialogue* between the visible world and soul. For him, the world itself, for example a sunrise, speaks the language of symbols because it speaks *to* a mind, whereas for Jung *here*, symbols are naturalistically a kind of outgrowth of the psyche all by itself, from out of its inner rootedness in *physis*—man so to speak as the mouthpiece of carbon. We can say that such a psyche may materially *be* world, but it has no world, is worldless.

It would be a mistake to pin Jung down to this view. In fact, Jung harbors two Jung's within his breast, a naturalistic, scientific one, for whom the psyche's world-connection comes about through its biochemical roots, and a truly psychological one, who explicitly warded off the naturalistic, biologistic conception of the soul, for example by saying that "the human soul is precisely neither a psychiatric nor a physiological problem, nor a biological problem in a general sense,

---

[9] The term unconscious is not in our passage, but is clearly implied.

[10] This line of thinking leads directly to Jung's late speculations about a *psychoid* unconscious.

[11] Cf. also: Psychology "is something broadly human, [...]. Nor, again, is it merely instinctual or biological. If it were, it could very well be just a chapter in a text-book of biology. It has an immensely important social and cultural aspect [...]" (*CW* 16 § 52). "Psychology, however, is neither biology nor physiology nor any other science than just the knowledge of the soul" (*CW* 9i § 63, transl. modif.).

but a psychological one. It is a field of its own with its own peculiar laws. One cannot derive the nature of the soul from the principles of other sciences [...]. The phenomenology of the soul is therefore not limited to facts accessible to natural-scientific methods, but also encompasses the problem of the human mind, which is the father of all science" (*CW* 16 § 22, transl. modif.).[11] For this latter Jung, the world is not speaking all the more in a symbol, the more physiological or "material" the symbol is. No, for him as for Kerényi, it is the world that is speaking in a symbol because "[t]he psyche mirrors Being as such and knows it..." (*GW* 16 § 203, my transl.). Mirroring, reflection, knowing. There is an interplay between psyche and world and thus a duality. This duality comes to a head in what one might call Jung's ontological thesis: "The existence of the world has two conditions[12]: the one its being, the other its being known" (*CW* 16 § 201, trans. modif.), a thesis that Jung explains by saying "that without a reflecting psyche the world would be virtually nonexistent, and that, in consequence, consciousness is a second creator of the world."[13] Whereas before we had the idea of a continuum from the materiality of the body to the most abstract, rationalistic consciousness, now we have the idea of two absolutely irreducible sources of the world in an intricate paradoxical (if not dialectical) relation to each other. For as the second *creator* of the world, the psyche is not merely a passive mirror for what is given, not merely receptive and completely determined by what there is; it is also active, spontaneous, free. But its freedom is also not an abstract freedom. Being only the *second* creator, psyche is in turn dependent on the other irreducible source. This theory is in a way reminiscent of Kant's elaborate philosophical argument of theoretical freedom, according to which what is given by the senses can only *be given* to a consciousness in the first place on the basis of a spontaneous productive a priori synthesis performed by the imagination.[14]

This view of the relation of psyche and world also makes impossible that monistic naturalistic idea of the relation between *body* and *soul* that we found expressed in our motto, "Hence 'at its lowest level' psyche is simply 'world.'" In a letter Jung pointed out

---

[12] "Conditions" in the sense of "prerequisites."
[13] *Letters 2*, p. 487, 12 Feb 1959, to Pastor Tanner (transl. modif.).
[14] This topic has recently received an excellent detailed examination by Reinhard Loock, *Schwebende Einbildungskraft. Konzeption theoretischer Freiheit in der Philosophie Kants, Fichtes und Schellings*, Würzburg (Königshausen & Neumann: 2007).

> the peculiar fact that on the one hand consciousness has so
> exceedingly little direct information of the body from within,
> and that on the other hand the unconscious (i.e., dreams and
> other products from the "unconscious") refers very rarely to the
> body and, if it does, it is always in the most roundabout way,
> i.e., through highly "symbolized" images. For a long time I have
> considered this fact as negative evidence for the existence of a
> subtle body or at least for a curious gap between mind and body.
> Of a psyche dwelling in its own body one should expect at least
> that it would be immediately and thoroughly informed of any
> change of conditions therein. Its not being the case demands
> some explanation.[15]

There is a fundamental gap between body and mind. Body and psyche
are really separate. That Jung finds here this fact "peculiar" and
"curious," that he thinks "one should expect" that a psyche dwelling
in its own body would be immediately informed about that body's
conditions, is due to the fact that in this passage it is again the
naturalistic Jung who is speaking. But *what* he is telling us amounts
to the truth of the psychological Jung; it is his admission that the
naturalistic presupposition is not born out by the facts.

Yes, the psyche dwells in its own body, and yet there is this gap.
This gap is not merely a simple caesura. It is more. It has the nature
of a reversal. In animals,[16] their instinctual impulses go
uninterruptedly and immediately over into their behavior. In man this
immediacy and oneness has been radically burst asunder so that he
was catapulted from out of his body, indeed from out of himself, and
has a priori his place, as a veritable expatriate, in what we call mind or
soul. As psyche and conscious being, man is inevitably in the status
of *ek-sistence* (Heidegger). It is for this reason that *he* is primarily
"informed," and determined in his actions and decisions, from
"outside" and "above." In ancient times, in order to orient himself in
the world he looked up to gods and down to the dead, to the ancestors;
to gain guidance he turned away from himself to observe the flight of
birds, to analyze the intestines of animals or the cracks produced by a
heated bronze rod in a tortoise shell; he threw yarrow stalks and

---

[15] *Letters 2*, p. 44 (to Smythies, 29 February 1952).
[16] Animals are of course themselves no longer strictly identical with their material
substrate, but divided from it by another, "earlier" "gap." But this is another topic.

consulted the I Ching; in cases of illness he had to ask a shaman, just as we today need to consult others, doctors, when we feel sick; we turn to science when we encounter technical or theoretical problems; we institute committees to come up with solutions, and we move through the world with the help of GPS. We humans get our knowledge even about our *own* bodies not from within ourselves, but conversely by looking fundamentally *from outside in*, through dissecting corpses, through X-rays or, more recently, magnetic resonance imaging. True, we also speak of gut reactions, but we know that this is a metaphor and that these reactions do by no means come from our literal guts; they come from sunken ideas or prejudices.

As this expulsion from body and self, the gap between body and psyche does not have the nature of a literal "space between." Rather, it has the nature of a *logical* negation of the biological basis of human existence and thus of a pushing off from it, which is also why the alchemists, concerning the soul-process, spoke directly of the *opus contra naturam*, the work *against* nature. The indispensability of this logical negation can even be demonstrated empirically. I mention one small example from the most primitive stage of the development in early childhood of the human ability to think symbolically. Up to the age of 18 months, when shown pictures of things babies manipulate the paper, trying to grasp the object depicted. After this age, they are generally able to understand the difference between the picture as an object in its own right and the object depicted. But, as experiments have shown, sometimes even up to the age of 4, children fear that if a picture of a bowl of popcorn is turned upside down, the popcorn would fall out. It has been suggested that the advancement to the capacity to think symbolically is mainly due to the development of inhibitory control supported by changes in the frontal cortex. Children slowly learn to restrain their natural impulse to interact directly with an image. Through curbing their impulses, they become capable of *simply looking*, and only when they can simply look at the depicted object has an image become *image* for them, whereas before it was confused with its referent.

This observation may throw a tiny light on my view that the gap between body and psyche is not a "space between," but that it rather owes its existence to the (spontaneously happening) execution of a logical *act*, the act of negation, which on the empirical behavioral level shows itself as inhibition, restraint. At the same time, this observation may also be a help for understanding that the move from natural existence to *ek-sistence in the mind or soul* is not like leaving one room to enter another already existing one, a transcendent realm of the mind high *above* the natural. There is not a literal move from here to there. All there is, is a move *contra naturam*, the move, to say it with the present example, of an inhibitory control of the natural impulse to directly grasp the object out there, while, however, still dwelling with it (rather than simply deserting it in favor of some other concern). And *ipso facto* there is now a "mere" looking at or contemplating the image-as-the-sublated-object, a "free" entertaining the image in the mind. The mind as the sphere of images, ideas, and concepts that are exclusively its, the mind's, own property, only comes into being at all *through this negation of the natural while nevertheless dwelling with it.* The union of "inhibition/negation" *and* "dwelling with the negated" amounts of course to a contradiction. But because of this contradiction, the sublated world of images comes into being only *within* the natural world and thus its transcending the natural world also only transcends without literally transcending and leaving it.

After these reflections, I now return to our main topic. When in what follows I want to describe C.G. Jung's psychology project as a response to the condition in which the world found itself at his time, I mean that world whose existence depends on two sources, its being *and* its being known. I mean the world of man that is perceived and experienced and that speaks—speaks not only through literal symbols, but also through and in all the diverse human responses given to it. Only this *is* world *sensu strictiori*, whereas to the extent that we are biological organisms we do not have a world, do not live in a *world* at all, but in the *environment*. Only this world can be meant in Jung's statement, "The great problem of our time is that we don't understand what is happening to the world."

What was it that Jung saw as happening to the world? What was the condition of the world to which Jung's psychology project was an answer?

The following well-known statement by Gotthold Ephraim Lessing comes from the second half of the 18th century. "If God held enclosed within his right hand all truth, and within his left hand nothing but the ever active striving for truth, although combined with the provision that I would err forever, and would say to me: choose!, I would with humility fall into his left hand and say: Father, give! Pure truth is, after all, only for you alone!"[17] One can admire the courage as well as humility with which Lessing decided for a permanent (but *necessarily* failing) seeking. It sounds incredible: he turned down an explicit offer of the truth, all truth. But on second thought his statement is not all that radical. For although Lessing exposes himself to an endless search that on principle cannot reach its goal, he knows that truth itself is not disputed. Even with his very opting for endless error, he will nevertheless stay contained in one of God's hands, inasmuch as the very act of his choosing was his throwing himself into it. God, the guarantor of truth as such, remains; and he remains Father. Goethe's Faust at one point says that he feels the upsurge of an impulse to venture forth to the open sea of life, to struggle with its storms, and, even in case of shipwreck, not to quail. There is of course a fundamental difference whether such a proclamation of courage happens while one is firmly standing on dry land or while one is already holding on to the planks of a vessel being shipwrecked. With all his unending erring, Lessing is and stays, as it were, on solid ground. His endless search happens within an ultimate unshaken and unquestionable certainty.

What Lessing said boils down to no more than an avoidance of the deadly sin of *superbia* or hubris, an expression and active affirmation of his awareness of the difference between the infinite mind of God and the finite nature of man. Pure truth is only for God alone, whereas man can never come into the possession of truth, can on earth never *explicitly* reach the goal, but this goal, truth, the absolute, nevertheless already *exists* even for him, too, namely in his God, his Father, his own beginning and end.

What we can learn from this is that there are two fundamentally different levels on which to speak about truth. The one we could call the semantic level, the other the syntactical level. On the semantic or content level, Lessing renounces the achievability of truth, but on the syntactical level the same Lessing is grounded in truth. Now it is very

---

[17] From: Gotthold Ephraim Lessing, *Eine Duplik* (1778), my transl.

important to understand that psychology, at least psychology in the tradition and sense of Jung, is only concerned with the syntactical level. Whether somebody says he believes in God or declares himself to be an atheist is *psychologically* neither here nor there, because it is only the opinion and subjective conviction or feeling of the ego-personality, a *content* of consciousness. Psychology begins—in the area of the God-question—when we are interested in whether, regardless of what we explicitly think, God has in fact a place in the hidden, but objective logic of consciousness, in the syntax of actually lived life, in what Hegel termed the "faith of the world," or, expressed in mythological parlance, in the depth of the soul.

On the basis of these clarifications we can recognize that there has been a fundamental historical change precisely on the level of the syntax of the world and thus a change that is indeed *psychologically* relevant. Up to and through the 18th century, and even into the beginning of the 19th century, human existence in the West had always unquestionably been grounded in and encompassed by a metaphysical ground, the traditional name for which was God, so that for all these times Jung could rightly use the old Church phrase *quod semper, quod ubique, quod ab omnibus creditur*[18] to refer to the universally shared and continuous underlying "faith of the world" or "logic of the soul." To be sure, the particularities of this containing syntax may have changed over the centuries, but not its basic structure. And to be sure, there was for example Descartes, who insisted that there had to be systematic doubt of everything; and there were the thinkers of the Enlightenment with their radical criticism of all sorts of traditional beliefs and church dogmas, even of the Church itself, and occasionally even of the very notion of God. But in all these cases the prevailing structural relation between surface and ground was the same as the one we found at work in our Lessing passage: all this doubt, skepticism, and criticism occurred only on an "upper" semantic, explicit level. But underneath, on the level of the syntax of consciousness and undisturbed by whatever heterodox and subversive teachings, the old truth prevailed. The image of Voltaire, who during his lifetime was a cynical critic of the Church, but on his deathbed asked for its blessings, may serve as a visual aid.

---

[18] "What is believed always, everywhere, by all." Vincent of Lérins, *Commonitorium* 2.

In the 19th century, within very few years after the Napoleonic wars, with the entrance into modernity, with the revolutionary shift from the traditional handicraft way of production to the industrial mode of production, there had been a groundshaking change. More than that. The ground in which human existence had psychologically been rooted since time immemorial had not merely become a new, different ground. Such a thing as "ground" had in the depth of the soul simply disappeared. The faith of the world had dissolved. *Quod semper, quod ubique, quod ab omnibus creditur* objectively did not carry human existence any more, it had become historical, a *Theologie der Vorzeit* and *Philosophie der Vorzeit* (the theology and philosophy of former ages), as Josef Kleutgen (1811–1883) put it, even if on the semantic level of ego convictions many people, just as Kleutgen, may have tried to hold on to it or resurrect it. The logic of the ground that for Hegel and Schelling was still intact simply no longer existed for the generation of Schopenhauer, Feuerbach, the late Romantics, Edgar Allan Poe, Stendhal, Baudelaire, and all the later decades. Where there had been a ground, there now gaped an *Abgrund*, abyss. But even Hegel had already at his time only been able to once more make sure of the absolute by going the way of *Verzweiflung* (despair) to its very end, rather than, like Descartes, merely having to confront himself with *Zweifel* (doubt). And Jean Paul, too, another writer prior to this radical shift, had nevertheless already been driven to fantasize his "Address by Dead Christ Down from the Vault of Heaven that there is No God." In Kierkegaard one can see how the relation to God, once the self-evident ground backing up existence, had become a utopian *project*, the demand for a 'leap' on the part of the isolated individual, a leap across an unbridgeable gap. And by the time of Nietzsche the "true world" had changed into a "fable." Truth *itself* had turned into that kind of error without which a certain species of living beings could not live. And Nietzsche was also able, as we all know, to express the prevailing *modern* truth about God in the catch-phrase "God is dead," notabene that same God that still a century earlier for Lessing had been the guarantor of pure truth.

This is the condition of the world into which C.G. Jung, himself an avid reader of Nietzsche, was born. And he not only factually lived in the truth of his age, as all people inevitably do, but like other great, exceptional minds he was also open to it, was reached by it and himself reached with his soul's root-fibers into the truth of the collective situation. That he was special, destined to become a great psychologist, shows particularly in the fact that as early as age eleven or twelve, in other words, at a time when his own conscious awareness was first awakening, he was already troubled by the collective soul truth of his age, and this, mind you, not via intellectual influences, but spontaneously, all by himself, out of his own intuition. The event I have in mind happened on a beautiful summer day. Jung was standing on the cathedral square of Basel and was overwhelmed by the beauty of the sight and he thought, "The world is beautiful and the church is beautiful, and God made all this and sits above it far away in the blue sky on a golden throne ...." But then, to his utter horror, the thought continued with the idea that "from under the throne an enormous turd falls upon the sparkling new roof [of the cathedral], shatters it and breaks the walls of the cathedral asunder." Although, in his subjective interpretation of this his thought experience on the ego level, Jung managed to evade its message by changing the subject,[19] *objectively* he *had been* reached by it in the depth of his soul. He now *knew*, deep down, that the church and by implication the substance of traditional Christian faith (and by extension metaphysical meaning at large) have once and for all been smashed. He knew that the original beauty of God's world has been defiled, and that the very idea of God in his majesty has been laid open to ridicule by His being turned into a shitting God and his throne into a toilet seat. The destruction had irrevocably happened for Jung and had been felt. A *collective* truth had come home to the boy Jung as his personal knowledge. Psychologically the experienced irrefutable loss was the basis for everything that Jung would think and produce even in his mature years.

Jung as the author of his writings and the founder of his psychology had made the insight into the loss of all mythic, religious, metaphysical meaning his own and had accepted and integrated it as his baseline.

---

[19] Instead of allowing the message of this spontaneous thought to come home to him, Jung got worked up about the alleged sinfulness of this thought and speculated that it must have been God's will that he, Jung, think a sinful thought against his own will, thus reinstituting God in his former majesty, that very God the discrediting of whom was the *telos* of his thought experience. I discussed this episode at length in my "Psychology as Anti-Philosophy: C.G. Jung," in: *Spring 77*, 2007, pp. 11–51, now Chapter 2 of the present volume, as well as "The Disenchantment Complex," Chapter 3.

To what extent he had made it his own can be seen from his diagnostic description of the inner situation of his time: "[...] the stars have fallen from heaven and our highest symbols have paled [...]." "Heaven has become for us the cosmic space of the physicists, and the divine empyrean a fair memory of things that once were" (*CW* 9/I § 50). "We all know how, in large things as in small, in general as well as in particular, piece after piece collapsed, and how the alarming poverty of symbols that is now the condition of our life came about" (§ 23). The consequence is that modern man "is cast out into a state of defencelessness that might well make the natural man shudder" (§ 24). "[B]efore him there yawns the void [the Nichts of nihilism], and he turns away from it in horror" (§ 28). "[O]ur spiritual house has fallen apart" (§ 31, modif.). Today "we stand empty-handed, bewildered, and perplexed [...]" (*MDR* p. 332). "There are no longer any gods whom we could invoke [...]" (*CW* 18 § 598). "No, evidently we no longer have any myth" (*MDR* p. 171). "Our myth [i.e., Christianity] has become mute, and gives no answers" (*MDR* p. 332). Modern man dwells with himself alone, "where, in the cold light of consciousness, the blank barrenness of the world reaches to the very stars" (*CW* 9i § 29, modif.).

It would be a great mistake to hear these diagnoses as subjective lamentations in the spirit of cultural criticism and pessimism. Then the point Jung wants to make would be entirely missed. No doubt, he views this our situation as highly precarious, as an emergency situation. But this does not mean that he would see it as a mistake, a faulty development, and something to be corrected by a return to or revival of a former state. On the contrary, unambiguously rejecting all such revival attempts and unmasking the popular borrowing of "ready-made symbols grown on foreign soil" (from India, for example) as "mummeries," he states, "A man does not sink down to beggary only to pose afterwards as an Indian potentate. It seems to me that it would be far better stoutly to avow our spiritual poverty, our symbol-lessness, instead of feigning a legacy to which we are not the legitimate heirs at all" (*CW* 9i § 27f.). We are naked. *Really* poor. And this absolute poverty needs to be relentlessly embraced. No false compromises, and no consolation. "Just as in Christianity the vow of worldly poverty turned the mind away from the riches of this earth, so spiritual poverty seeks to renounce the false riches of the spirit [...]" (§ 29), riches that are false because "we have squandered our heritage." Jung is very clear about this: "We cannot turn the wheel backwards, [...] you cannot go back" (*CW* 18 § 632). Jung rejects any repristination.

Now we have arrived at what Jung was "wrestling with." This is the situation to which his psychology project wishes to respond. Now it remains for us to see "what it's all about," "it" here meaning his answer, his psychology.

If there is no way back, then we can only move forward. Jung wants us to "sew our garment ourselves" (*CW* 9i § 27). But the situation of spiritual poverty is for him more than the call for something like a spiritual analogue to a post-war reconstruction, where one also has to begin from point zero, in the sense of "life has to go on." In Jung's so negative-sounding description there is all of a sudden a surprising turn: "I am convinced that the growing impoverishment of symbols has a meaning" (*CW* 9i § 28)! The loss and lack are not merely something that we have to make our peace with because they happen to be our inescapable fate. The loss and lack have a *meaning*, that is, they are productive, they amount to an advance. This evaluation or the decision *not* to condemn the modern situation is Jung's very own response to the condition of his time. Jung lets himself truly in for the experience of loss, "truly" that means logically, not merely emotionally.

The question that arises for us is: what is this postulated meaning of the impoverishment of symbols? In order to get some basis for this question, let us listen to some of Jung's pertinent statements. Reflecting on what he had discussed so far in a lecture he said,

> [...] everything I have observed lies in the soul; everything, so to speak, on the *side of the inner*. I must, however, add at once that this is something peculiar, inasmuch as the soul is not always and everywhere on the inside. There are peoples and epochs where it is outside, peoples and epochs that are unpsychological, as, for example, all ancient cultures, and among them especially Egypt with its magnificent objectivity and its just as magnificent, naïve, negative confession of sins. Behind the spirit of the Apis tombs of Saqqara and the Pyramids we cannot possibly imagine psychological issues, no more than behind the music of Bach.

> Whenever there exists externally a conceptual or ritual form in which all the yearnings and hopes of the soul are absorbed and expressed, that is, for example, a living religion, then the soul is

outside and there is no soul problem, just as there is then no unconscious in our sense. It was therefore logical that the discovery of psychology took exclusively place during the last decades, although former centuries possessed enough introspection and intelligence to gain knowledge about psychological facts. [...] The reason for this is that there existed no compelling predicament. [...] It needed the spiritual predicament of our time to force us to discover psychology.

[...] But as soon as he [man] outgrows the periphery of his Western local religion, that is, when his form of religion can no longer contain his life in all its fullness, then the soul begins to become a factor which can no longer be dealt with by the ordinary means. It is for this reason that we today have a psychology that relies on empirical facts and not on articles of faith or philosophical postulates, and at the same time I see in the fact that we have a psychology a symptom that proves the profound convulsions of the general soul. [...] Only in this situation, in this *predicament*, do we discover the soul [...]

[...] But no culture before ours felt compelled to take this psychic background as such seriously. [...] This distinguishes our time from all earlier ones (*CW* 10 §§ 158–161, translation modified).

"Dogma takes the place of [*ersetzt*] the collective unconscious by formulating its contents on a grand scale." (*CW* 9i § 21). Dogma is a substitute for the real thing. It is the latter's tamed, domesticated [*gebändigt*], that is, already civilized version. "The collective unconscious, the way we know it today, has never been psychological at all [...]. [...] Always the figures of the unconscious were expressed in protecting and healing images and in this way were expelled into cosmic, extra-psychic space" (*ibid.*, transl. modif.)

Another time when Jung had discussed at length our spiritual poverty, he said that

This precarious situation [*Problematik*] is new, because all ages before us still believed in gods in some form or other. It required an unparalleled impoverishment of symbolism to bring about the rediscovery of the gods as psychic factors, that is, as archetypes of the unconscious. [...] This is why we have a psychology today, and why we speak of the unconscious. All this would be quite superfluous in an age or culture that possessed symbols (*CW* 9i § 50, transl. modif.).

And again:

> Why is psychology the very youngest of the empirical sciences?
> Why was the unconscious not discovered long ago and its
> treasure-house of eternal images not raised up? Simply because
> we had a religious formula for everything psychic—and one that
> is far more beautiful and comprehensive than immediate
> experience (*CW* 9i § 11, transl. modif.).

We could say that these cited passages give us Jung's philosophy of
history. There is an absolute rupture in history, a fundamental crisis
in the singular. This crisis separates "*all* ages before us" from us and
our time. The situation we find ourselves in is absolutely unparalleled.
Despite all the enormous changes and differences between all the ages
before this rupture, they all had nevertheless one fundamental thing
in common: the possession of some kind of conceptual or ritual form
or religious symbolism, that is, the same syntax of consciousness or
logic of the world, at least on the macro-level.

The symbolism that they had is ambivalent in Jung's view. On
the one hand, it is incomparably beautiful and comprehensive, superior
to what we can achieve. On the other hand, it is something already
civilized, cultured, an always already processed form and thus
traditional. As such it shielded the people of all these previous ages
from immediate experience. This is its drawback. The culturally
expressed forms are, as it were, a refined cultural surrogate for the real
thing, raw psychic reality. It thus in a way functions like a lightning
rod. It takes care of all the soul's deepest needs without threatening
us directly with them.

The historical rupture is ambivalent, too. By robbing us of such
a cultural vessel and thereby pulling the floor out from under us, it is,
no doubt, a terrible danger. *Extra ecclesiam nulla salus.*[20] "[T]hen things
become terrible.... You are alone and you are confronted with all the
demons of hell" (*CW* 18 § 632). We are helplessly exposed to impulses
that we do not understand and accordingly we have no established
means and categories for dealing with them. It is a pathological
situation. But precisely by removing the blanket of culturally
established symbolic forms, the loss of symbols also amounts to a

---

[20] See Cyprianus, *Epistulae* 73,21,2.

freeing. It provides an opening to *Urerfahrung*, primordial or immediate experience, to psychic reality disclosed, without any protective cover and secondary processing. Where all previous ages only experienced gods handed down through cultural tradition, we today, this is Jung's view, are confronted with archetypes directly and in retrospect can even comprehend the former gods as archetypes, however as archetypes only in already shielded and secondarily processed form.

And *what* we can experience is again ambivalent. It is far less beautiful and comprehensive than myth, traditional symbolism, religious dogma. It is usually fragmented, primitive, raw. But all these disadvantages are offset by the singular and precious gift of immediacy, the direct access to and confrontation with the unconscious. This, immediacy, directness, is the singular distinction and chance of our time.

And this is also the meaning of the impoverishment of symbols. "Psychology" in its highest sense is for Jung nothing else but an abbreviation and label for immediate psychic experience and experience of psychic reality per se, that is, of the unconscious. Psychology is therefore also ambivalent. It is, on the one hand, a symptom, the sign of an illness, the symptom of a cultural disaster— and yet, on the other hand, of enormous importance and value in Jung's eyes. "I cannot help believing that the real problem will be from now on until a dim future a psychological one."[21] "We are confronted with the darkness of our soul, the unconscious. It sends up its dark and unrecognizable urges. It hollows out and hacks up the shapes of our culture and its historical dominants. We have no dominants any more, they are in the future."[22] "[...] I know [...] how helpless people are in envisaging and dealing with the enormities that the present time and still more the immediate future will present us with."[23] "Our concern with the unconscious has become a vital question for us—a question of spiritual being or non-being" (*CW* 9i § 51). And why is it that the real problem from now on will be a psychological one? Because "the struggle between light and darkness has transferred its battlefield to the inner" (*CW* 13 § 293, transl. modif.) and because "the unconscious" is "the mother of the future."[24] "The general and

---

[21] *Letters 2*, p. 498, 12 April 1959, to Werner Bruecher.
[22] *Letters 2*, p. 590, 2 September 1960, to Herbert Read.
[23] *Letters 2*, p. 498, 12 April 1959, to Werner Bruecher.
[24] *Letters 2*, p. 496, 12 April 1959, to Cary F. Baynes.

fundamental insight that our psychic existence has two poles still remains a task for the future" (*MDR* p. 169, transl. modif.)

It now emerges that Jung's psychology project is not only a response to the condition of his time in the sense of a reaction, *his* personal answer to a factually given situation, in a similar sense to how we distinguish between a wound and the subsequent dressing of the wound. Psychology *in its highest determination* is much more for Jung, more than a secondary treatment, more than the application of psychological insights and techniques to our situation. Psychology in itself, objectively (and precisely not merely the therapeutic application of psychology!), *is* the solution, the key to our predicament—because the very problem has become a psychological one; the clear distinction between illness and cure has been canceled. The battlefield on which the decision about the great questions has to occur has moved from the external to the inner, from the level of externally existing religious formulas to the immediacy of the psyche. The concern with the unconscious is absolutely vital; psychology is our only hope. This is Jung's thesis.

We thus see that on the *apex theoriae*, Jung perceives psychology in terms of a uroboric logic of identity. Psychology is both the symptom of an unparalleled historical pathological situation *and* the cure for this situation; it is itself "the great problem of our time" or "the real problem," *and* the answer. The unconscious hacks up and hollows out the shapes of our culture *and* it is the mother of the future. This shows that what Jung envisioned is a fundamental collapse of the entire reality level itself from its previous high level, the level of religion and metaphysics as great externally existing forms, to the fundamentally lower level of psychology with its immediate confrontation with the unconscious. This radical change of the level of reality as such is what makes the historical rupture that we discussed so unparalleled. Psychology is thus not just a new additional field of science, an extension of human inquiry into new areas on the same old level of reality. For Jung the emergence of psychology is the rupture itself. This is also why he could entertain the view that certain ones of those who have been smitten by the fate of a neurosis are *"eigentlich 'höhere' Menschen"* (the *CW* translate: "really persons of a 'higher' type" *CW* 7 § 291), because they have, whether they like it or not, dropped from

JUNG'S PSYCHOLOGY PROJECT

the ordinary reality level, so that the awareness of the second pole of our psychic existence has forced itself upon them.

Much more could be said about Jung's response to the condition of his time, but this is not the time for detailed elaborations. Instead I want by way of conclusion to shift our focus from a description of Jung's response to a reflection of his response. What might today, in 2008, be *our* response *to* Jung's response? His response essentially comes from the first half of the 20th century. Much has happened in the meantime to open our eyes to altered vistas. I will merely list seven questions that immediately come to mind:

1. Can we still entertain the extremely high estimation of psychology, as having a historical mission and as in itself being *the* answer to our historical predicament? Or will we not perhaps lean toward a more modest assessment?

2. Can we still believe that with the unconscious we are confronted with the *immediate*, unprocessed, raw source of psychic life? Or would we not rather be inclined to see, for example, archetypal dream motifs as unconscious individual *reuse* precisely of already historically processed and sedimented material from earlier ages, and likewise comprehend the archetypes as modern abstractions from, and ordering principles for, the rich historical phenomenology of psychic images?

3. No doubt, there is plenty of unconsciousness and there are many processes that happen unconsciously. But can we still believe in "*the* unconscious," the hypostatized notion of the unconscious as a kind of subject and agent behind the scenes?

4. Jung insisted that the loss of cultural forms has a meaning, which indicates that he did not evade the insight into the loss. The specific meaning that he saw was that this loss amounted to a pulling away of the cultural blanket that shielded mankind from the unconscious as the raw source of meaning. But if the fact that the loss of meaning is seen as the freeing of an access to the immediate source of meaning, could this perhaps imply that Jung's acknowledgment of the loss is not relentless after all? Are we not perhaps structurally back at Lessing's position, inasmuch as, to be sure, "*the* unconscious" *on the semantic level* entails the explicit avowal of our *not* knowing, while it nevertheless *syntactically* supplies us with the certain knowledge that there *is* an ultimate ground, the *mother* of the future? Or is it perhaps after all

that we sank down to beggary only to pose afterwards as the owners of the true riches in our inner?[25]

5. If one follows this line of thinking, might we perhaps have to revise the idea that neurotics are "really persons of a 'higher' type"? Are they maybe not simply neurotic?

6. Is it to be taken for granted that meaning will "become[-] true once more," merely in "a new form" (*CW* 18 § 632)? Could it not perhaps be that mankind has outgrown altogether such a thing as meaning, religion, gods or dominants and that we will have to sew our garments *truly* ourselves, *without* having ready-made patterns, be they cultural or be they archetypal? Because—

7. and finally—in view of the media, the advertizing industry, the televisionization of life and its experience, in view, furthermore, of the Internet, web.2, and "second life," of quantum mechanics and nanotechnology, of genetic engineering and the titanic goal of controlling global warming—can we still insist that the place were the *real* action is has become the *inner*, and that *individuation* is the highest goal?

This is the type of question that is raised for us with Jung's response to the world condition of his time, questions that *we* have the task to give *our* response to, a response in view of, and in responsibility to, the world condition at *our* time.

---

[25] Whereby we can of course fancy ourselves as owners only because the riches that we claim to own in our inner are logically on principle safely locked away in "*the* unconscious," i.e., defined as logically irrevocably dissociated and sequestered from consciousness, so that these treasures will never have to come out into the open to prove their genuineness in the light of day before the public mind and will not and cannot be the gold standard—or truth—behind the currency of actually lived life.

CHAPTER TWO

Psychology as Anti-Philosophy: C.G. Jung

P erhaps the most natural way to investigate the relation between Jung and philosophy as well as between Jungian psychology and philosophy might be to see where in Jung's work we find references to philosophy and to particular philosophers. Names of some significance for Jung that come immediately to mind are Kant, Schopenhauer, Plato, Nietzsche, Hegel, Heidegger. What did Jung have to say about them, how did he describe his own relation to them? The question of how he positioned himself in the medieval Universals controversy (keywords: Abaelard and *esse in anima*) should also not be neglected.[1] Wherever one would start to dig a little deeper, one would probably soon come up against strange ambivalences, such as the general one that comes to light when we contrast the following two statements. (1) "I am not a philosopher but a doctor and empiricist. I practice psychology in the first place as a science, in the second place as an instrument of psychotherapy" (*Letters 2*, p. 56, to van Lier-Schmidt Ernsthausen, 25 April 1952). (2) "I can hardly draw a veil over the fact that we psychotherapists ought really to be philosophers or philosophic doctors..." (*CW* 16 § 181).

---

[1] See C. G. Jung, "Abelard's Attempt at Conciliation", in *Psychology Types*, *CW* 6 § 68-95.

Method of approach and textual basis

My intention with this paper, however, and therefore my approach are different. Rather than staying on the level of the work that Jung produced, the level of his explicit views and statements as well as the implications of what he said and how he worked, I want to go a level deeper to the source or motive power that produced Jung's relation to philosophy and makes it possible to understand why it had to be the way it turned out to be. What was at stake for Jung? What were the strategic moves that he made—had to make, because this was what both "*who* he was" and the historical locus he found himself in demanded of him? What is the *spiritus rector*—the principle—behind or in his psychology, "the soul" of his psychology? What makes him (the psychology he developed) "tick"? I want to try to get an idea of the "intellectual physiognomy" of C.G. Jung so as to become able from this center to reconstruct and develop the explicit positions that he took, specifically with respect to philosophy.

For this purpose it is best to use a *microscopic* approach. It would of course also be possible to attempt to look at Jung's life-work as a whole and try to distill from it its inner physiognomy, in order to deduce from the so-gained physiognomy why his psychology had to be the way it was. This approach would be circular. But circularity as such does not really have to be considered a problem, and often there is no other way. The only disadvantage is that with such a mass of material the likelihood is far greater that there might be in one's "distillation process" a systematic deviation due to the subjectivity of the interpreter's particular angle of view. If, however, we succeed in finding a small text that while certainly itself also being a part of the finished product produced by Jung nevertheless opens a window to the pulsating heart within or behind the production process, this danger is much smaller. In contrast to an assortment of ideas and statements from all kinds of texts compiled according to some *external* concept (applied by the interpreter, so that what we get is an external reflection), a single small text can be studied *thinkingly*, i.e., thought through in its details according to its own inherent principle. Because these details reflect, support, and corroborate each other, the text forms a self-contained meshwork that provides enough guidelines of its own safeguarding against aberrations.

There is indeed a report of Jung's that—*en miniature* and inadvertently—lays bare the logical paradigm, the very motivation, and basic constitutive operation, underlying Jung's psychology as such. This report about an experience during his school years comes from *Memories, Dreams, Reflections* [hereinafter referred to as *MDR*] and reads:

> One fine summer day that same year [1887, his twelfth year] I came out of school at noon and went to the cathedral square. The sky was gloriously blue, the day one of radiant sunshine. The roof of the cathedral glittered, the sun sparkling from the new, brightly glazed tiles. I was overwhelmed by the beauty of the sight, and thought: "The world is beautiful and the church is beautiful, and God made all this and sits above it far away in the blue sky on a golden throne and ...." Here came a great hole in my thoughts, and a choking sensation. I felt numbed, and knew only: "Don't go on thinking now! Something terrible is coming, something I do not want to think, something I dare not even approach. Why not? Because I would be committing the most frightful of sins. What is the most terrible sin? Murder? No, it can't be that. The most terrible sin is the sin against the Holy Ghost, which cannot be forgiven. Anyone who commits that sin is damned to hell for all eternity. That would be very sad for my parents, if their only son, to whom they are so attached, should be doomed to eternal damnation. I cannot do that to my parents. All I need do is not go on thinking."

> That was easier said than done. On my long walk home I tried to think all sorts of other things, but I found my thoughts returning again and again to the beautiful cathedral which I loved so much, and to God sitting on the throne— and then my thoughts would fly off again as if they had received a powerful electric shock. I kept repeating to myself: "Don't think of it, just don't think of it!" I reached home in a pretty worked-up state. ...
>
> ...
>
> On the third night, however, the torment became so unbearable that I no longer knew what to do. I awoke from a restless sleep just in time to catch myself thinking again about the cathedral and God. I had almost continued the thought! I felt my resistance

weakening. Sweating with fear, I sat up in bed to shake off sleep. "Now it is coming, now it's serious! *I must think.* It must be thought out beforehand. *Why* should I think something I do not know? I don't want to, by God, that's sure. But *who* wants me to? Who wants to force me to think something I don't know and don't want to know? Where does this terrible will come from? And why should I be the one to be subjected to it? I was thinking praises of the Creator of this beautiful world, I was grateful to him for this immeasurable gift, so why should *I* have to think something inconceivably wicked? I don't know what it is, I really don't, for I cannot and must not come anywhere near this thought, for that would be to risk thinking it at once. *I* haven't done this or wanted this, it has come on me like a bad dream. Where do such things come from? This has happened to me without my doing. Why? After all, I didn't create myself, I came into the world the way God made me ..."

... [F]inally I arrived at Adam and Eve. And with them came the decisive thought: Adam and Eve were the first people; they had no parents, but were created directly by God, who intentionally made them as they were. They had no choice but to be exactly the way God had created them. ... God in His omniscience had arranged everything so that the first parents would have to sin. *Therefore it was God's intention that they should sin.*

This thought liberated me instantly from my worst torment, since I now knew that God Himself had placed me in this situation. ... God had landed me in this fix without my willing it and had left me without any help. I was certain that I must search out His intention myself, and seek the way out alone. At this point another argument began.

"What does God want? To act or not to act? I must find out what God wants with me, and I must find out right away." I was aware, of course, that according to conventional morality there was no question but that sin must be avoided. That was what I had been doing up to now, but I knew I could not go on doing it. My broken sleep and my spiritual distress had worn me out to such a point that fending off the thought was tying me into unbearable knots. This could not go on. At the same time, I could not yield before I understood what God's will was and what He intended. For I was now certain that He was the author of this desperate problem. ... I knew, beyond a doubt, that I would ultimately be compelled to break down, to give way, but I did not want it to happen without my understanding it, since the salvation of my eternal soul was at stake.

...

I thought it over again and arrived at the same conclusion. "Obviously God also desires me to show courage," I thought. "If that is so and I go through with it, then He will give me His grace and illumination."

I gathered all my courage, as though I were about to leap forthwith into hell-fire, and let the thought come. I saw before me the cathedral, the blue sky. God sits on His golden throne, high above the world—and from under the throne an enormous turd falls upon the sparkling new roof, shatters it, and breaks the walls of the cathedral asunder.

So that was it! I felt an enormous, an indescribable relief. Instead of the expected damnation, grace had come upon me, and with it an unutterable bliss such as I had never known. I wept for happiness and gratitude. The wisdom and goodness of God had been revealed to me now that I had yielded to His inexorable command. It was as though I had experienced an illumination. ...

... Why did God befoul His cathedral? That, for me, was a terrible thought. But then came the dim understanding that God could be something terrible. I had experienced a dark and terrible secret. It overshadowed my whole life, and I became deeply pensive.

...

It would never have occurred to me to speak of my experience openly, ...

My entire youth can be understood in terms of this secret. It induced in me an almost unendurable loneliness. My one great achievement during those years was that I resisted the temptation to talk about it with anyone. Thus the pattern of my relationship to the world was already prefigured: today as then I am a solitary, because I know things and must hint

> at things which other people do not know, and usually do
> not even want to know (pp. 36–42).

This text reports about an experience and thought process from Jung's early years. But the report was written by Jung in his old age (according to Aniela Jaffé's "Introduction" [p. vi] between the end of 1957 and April 1958, i.e., at age 82). So this is not an historical record from the time when it happened. It is an old man's *memory* and *portrayal* of what happened in his childhood. There is no reason why we should doubt that the narrative refers to an actual fact in the past. But there can also be no doubt that the precise diction and the description of the argumentation said to be the child's argumentation have gone through the filter of the stage of consciousness reached through the long process of Jung's intellectual development and thus have his developed psychology behind them.

It is also significant that in his description of this event Jung in no way distances himself from what he describes. He does not, for example, portray the mental torment and the thought process that led to a solution as something childish that he as a mature man had long left behind. To be sure, he describes it as a child's problem, but the problem as well as the solution receive old man Jung's full backing. There is not a trace of a critical objection. The contents of the child's reflections are fully ego-syntonic for 82-years-old Jung and also syntonic with his late works on related subjects.

So with this little gem of a story we have something that extends over, and in a way comprises, Jung's entire intellectual life. It is a story that provides us not with the literal biographical beginning and causal origin of Jung's psychological thinking, but rather with the inner (in a certain sense, ahistorical) principle of his thought, the principle which is the unity of its *archê* and *telos*.

Paradise Lost

What Jung tells us is a story about the *event of a thought* and of how he dealt with this thought. And thus it is a story *about Jung as a thinker*. The thought that emerged in Jung falls clearly into two parts. The first part is, "The world is beautiful and the church is beautiful, and God made all this and sits above it far away in the blue sky on a golden throne." It is a thought coming from out of an overwhelming feeling that arose in him occasioned by the view of a beautiful sight on a just perfect summer day. This thought is nothing else but the description in words of a particular state of being, namely that state of being that Jung in *MDR* in other contexts described as "the paradise of childhood from which we imagine we have emerged" (p. 244) or the being in the "boundlessness of 'God's country'" (p. 72, cf. p. 78). The same emotion is also captured when Jung quotes some Englishman who had lived in Africa for forty years as saying, "this here country is not man's country, it's God's country" (p. 256), or when he says, in his own words, about his experience of Kenya and Uganda, "I enjoyed the 'divine peace' ['*Gottesfrieden*'] of a still primeval country" (p. 264) or refers to the area where he built his Bollingen tower as "*Gotteshausland*" (*MDR* translates this unusual word as "old church land" [p. 223], omitting its feeling overtones that go in the direction of "consecrated land"). From here we can understand that the purpose of the first half of Jung's thought is to celebrate the paradise of childhood once more, to explicitly put in a nutshell what existence in the paradise of childhood means. We could say that the first part is the existence in childhood paradise "comprehended in thought" (Hegel), even if here, in young Jung's case, "thought" does of course not mean conceptual thought (the actual *form* of thought), but pictorial conception.

The second half of this thought, the content of which we learn only much later after much fussing on the part of Jung ("... from under the throne an enormous turd falls upon the sparkling new roof, shatters it, and breaks the walls of the cathedral asunder"), amounts to the destruction of what the first part contained, both the portrayed reality and the blissful, lofty, solemn mood it had created. The turd falls like a bomb into the "paradise of childhood" evoked in the first half of the thought and quite literally smashes God's beautiful cathedral, the concrete symbol which is the center, heart, and epitome of "the boundlessness of 'God's world.'" It does so not in the form of a real bomb, which would be terrible enough, but in a decidedly vulgar, if not obscene way. The destruction of the cathedral is thus twofold, an external smashing of the building and a moral devastation through the crude expression of contempt. But it is not only "God's world" here on this earth that is destroyed. God himself, the transcendent source, animating spirit, and guarantor of this paradisiacal world is defamed inasmuch as he is shown in an absolutely undignified form, as a shitting God.

Because we get the two halves of Jung's thought only separated by a long interlude, and because they radically contradict each other, we might be tempted to conceive of them as really two separate thoughts. But it is clear, above all from the "and" between them, that it is just one single thought, one single image: an image with an internal about-turn or contradiction. We therefore have to look more closely into the relation between the two halves of this thought.

The first part presents, as we have seen, the celebration of the idea of "the paradise of childhood" in the reflected form of an explicit *thought*. But such a celebration in the *reflected* form of a thought is possible only when that which is celebrated has already been left. Only from psychologically being outside the paradise can you be aware of its being paradise and explicitly praise paradise and capture this praise in the form of a thought. Later, Jung would write about "the miracle of reflecting consciousness" as "the second cosmogony" (p. 339); watching in Africa the gigantic herds of animals, the insight came to him, as he explained, that "[t]his was the stillness of the eternal beginning, the world as it had always been, in the state of non-being; for until then no one had been present to know that it was this world. ... There I was now, the first human being to recognize that this was the world and who through his knowing had in this moment first really created it" (p. 255, transl. corrected). These ideas go far beyond what we have in our passage. But the distinction made in them helps us to see that "the paradise of childhood," when it exists, is in the state of non-being (in the sense of Jung's later text) because then "no one is present to *know* that it is paradise," and the moment when it is known and can be explicitly expressed, it has already been left. Precisely as the European visitor who is not part of this world, but observes it from the outside with his modern consciousness, Jung is "the first human being to recognize ..." In fact, knowing or reflecting is itself the very way of stepping outside. This is also why according to Jung a symbol is alive only for "the exoteric standpoint," while for the esoteric standpoint (for a consciousness that has been initiated into its meaning and now knows it) the symbol is dead (*CW* 6 § 816). And also why, as Jung states, "I cannot experience the miracle of the Mass; I know too much about it" (*CW* 18 § 632).

From the outset, the point of this whole event is to mark the end of existence in the paradise of childhood, in "God's world." And the inherent dialectic of the first part of Jung's thought in our text is that while it *semantically* celebrates the paradise of childhood, it nevertheless "syntactically" (logically, psychologically), through reflected feeling and explicit conception, precisely expresses this paradise's sublatedness, its obsolescence, through its having become conscious. The destruction of "paradise" is already contained in the first image, but of course only implicitly, unwittingly.

It is possible that the strict unity of the two-part thought already comes out in a small detail, in the word "throne," which in colloquial German, and especially with children, is sometimes jokingly used for a chamber pot or toilet. I do not know if this use of the word also existed in Jung's Basel dialect. Jung does not mention it, but the continuation of the thought makes it very likely that this meaning is *sous-entendu* from the outset. If so, the apparently absolutely innocent first half of the thought, with the image of God sitting "on His golden throne," would *in itself* and a priori have already been heading for its disgusting end, the idea of shitting.

When in the course of Jung's narration of this whole episode the ideas of the most terrible sin, the sin against the Holy Ghost, of Adam and Eve, who committed the original sin, and of eternal damnation in hell come up, we recognize in them versions of the theme of the expulsion from paradise and the loss of innocence through sin. From *within* paradise, the expulsion from it naturally appears as eternal damnation, something absolutely inconceivable, and from *within* the state of innocence, the loss of innocence is feared as the most terrible sin and defilement imaginable.

Now we are able to see more clearly why the first and the second part form indeed one single thought. The immanent dialectic of the first half, which as immanent is only implicit and could easily go by unnoticed, needs to come out into the open and become explicit. The *syntactical* truth of the thought wants to find semantic expression. So what we have here is not so much a composite of two really opposite thoughts, not a real enantiodromia, but much rather the unfolding of one single and consistent thought. One thought completes itself, goes to its very end. The second part thus does not add a second, new event to the first. It merely explicates what was inherent in the first part from the outset: the realization that the time of the paradise of childhood, of being in "God's country," is irrevocably over. "God is dead," we might say. Church, religion, faith? "*Scheiß drauf!*" ("To hell with it," lit. "shit on it").

The fact that this story is apparently about God and a church should not mislead us: Jung's experience is not a primarily and genuinely religious one. Rather, its topic is the psychological state of being in childhood paradise, and "religion, God, Church" are merely the natural terms in which this psychological state can symbolically articulate itself in the consciousness of a boy brought up in a traditional Protestant minister's house.

But growing up from childhood to adulthood is not merely a matter of strictly personal development. What "adulthood" means always reflects the culture around oneself, the newest stage of consciousness reached in one's culture, the cultural form of truth. Becoming an adult means something different in archaic ritualistic cultures from the same during the age of religion and metaphysics, and growing up during the latter age means again something different from "adulthood" in modernity. But an *ordinary* youngster takes his time's form of adulthood simply for granted and views this topic only in terms of his own personal development. For a great mind like Jung's, a mind unwittingly on the way to his becoming a great psychologist, the large-scale problem of the mind's entering modernity, the world after the Industrial Revolution, had to make itself felt in addition. Later Jung would characterize the problem he struggled with as that of "the great battle between the present and the past or the future" (*CW* 18 § 279). The loss of childhood paradise in the case of Jung therefore meant at the same time the forced departure from the whole heritage of the mythological and metaphysical traditions, just as being transported into "reflecting consciousness" and becoming an adult implied achieving personal adulthood *plus* being instinctively confronted with the necessity of psychologically entering that constitution of consciousness which is part of modernity in its still industrial phase. Jung was, at the time of his outgrowing of childhood, brought *intuitively* in touch with the serious issues of the necessities of his age as a whole, with the soul of his culture and its present stage of development.[2] So in our story, more was at stake for him from the outset than merely his personal maturation; his personal development was (implicitly) loaded with the problem of the *krisis* of two historical ages.

"To be modern means to know what is no longer possible" (Roland Barthes). The second half of Jung's thought shows, in a crude way, "what is no longer possible." By totally negating the essential content of the innocent world of childhood, it seems to have aimed at initiating consciousness not only into reflection as an immediate function of the mind, but into reflection as infinite *negativity* and *alienation*. The immanent intention of his thought seems to have been to teach Jung to embrace these two fundamental logical states as the soul's characteristic need in modernity.

Ego resistance against his thought

But Jung does not allow the thought to progress to its end and thus to complete its own movement. He interferes and violently disrupts the flow of it. "Don't go on thinking now!" "All I need do is not go on thinking." "Don't think of it, just don't think of it!" (p. 36). This is a decisive moment. We witness here Jung standing at the crossroads and making his choice. He rejects the road of thought, of the philosopher, and chooses the road of what later would turn out to be his psychology of the unconscious. The characteristic of a thinker is that he thinks his thought to its end no matter what might come of it and what insight or consequences it might confront him with. Or better: he allows the thought to think itself out to its utmost conclusion. Precisely this is what Jung refuses to do ("the very thing that seemed impossible: [to] think my thought right to the end," p. 37). The loyalty of the thinker goes to his thought, to the logic and

---

[2] Jung himself saw it this way. "The peculiar 'religious' ideas that came to me even in my earliest childhood were spontaneous products which can be understood only as reactions to my parental environment and to the spirit of the age," *MDR* p. 90. I am indebted to Greg Mogenson for drawing my attention to this passage. Also note the quotation marks around "religious." Jung was obviously aware of the fact that the seemingly religious content of his ideas does not imply a genuinely religious concern of his.

momentum of his thought, regardless of *what* thought it might be. A classic, even though extreme, example would be Nietzsche. With a certain recklessness towards himself and his own ego needs he followed the internal necessities of his thought to the bitter end. Having to turn against Richard Wagner, having to come up with the insight into the death of God, having to conceive of the ideas of "*amor fati*" and the "eternal recurrence" were surely not what he personally wanted. On the contrary, these were painful results, forced upon him by his thinking process and cutting into his own flesh.

Jung's refusal "to think his own thought onwards" has several aspects. The first aspect is that it is an ego move. He intrudes into the course of the thought with a concern about his own person. He deserts his thought, gets out of it and instead thinks of himself, of the possibility of his "eternal damnation" versus the "salvation of my eternal soul." He thus changes the subject. Instead of thinking his thought, he now circles around himself. In other words, he cannot abstract from himself, himself as person. But thinking *is* one's establishing the difference of the thought from him who is thinking.

We could view Jung's (eschatological) concern for the salvation of his eternal soul (not as a Freudian screen-memory, but) as a screen-idea for his concern for the (current, acute) loss of his child status.

This not-achieved *sacrifice* of his concern for himself and for his salvation leads to the idea of the thought to be thought by him as a "forbidden thought." With this idea, he of his own accord dissociates himself from his thought. He puts the thought on one side and himself on the other side. A thought, of course, cannot be forbidden—as long as one stays on the level of thought. The phrase "forbidden thought" does not make any sense. A thought is a thought, a reality. It thinks itself. It is not our doing. Only willful actions can be forbidden, but not thoughts. By calling a thought forbidden, one therefore expresses *one's own rejection* of the thought, *one's own* unwillingness to be faithful to one's own truth, for the thought that I have reveals in part who I am and where I psychologically stand.

The motivation for this unfaithfulness becomes clear, too. It is his infatuation with his paradise of childhood. That his growing up has already removed him from it *simply must not* be true. "I found my thoughts returning again and again to the beautiful cathedral which

I loved so much." The word "returning" is more significant than it might seem at first glance. It is really a nostalgic return. For we must realize that in truth the "forbidden thought" had *implicitly* already been thought out by him. How else could he have known that it was forbidden, the absolute sin to think it? His thought was already finished. All it needed was to become explicit, to be consciously expressed. (I will return to this in a moment.) But if the thought had already been thought to its end, then the cathedral had already been smashed. Implicitly, Jung knew this already. And this is why he had to return again and again to the idea of "the beautiful cathedral which I loved so much." It is a counterfactual restitution, a fictional restoration. A denial of and flight from his own truth. He had already irrevocably lost "his beautiful cathedral" and along with it his existence in God's world. He has already been driven out of his paradise and childhood innocence, but pretends that being driven out was only a still impending danger and depended on an act of his, on whether he *committed* the sin of thinking his thought to the end or not. What is already an accomplished fact and (implicitly) known to be a fact is construed as a future threat to be avoided at all cost. A typically neurotic move. The principle of a neurotic reaction is that one refuses to allow that which one subliminally knows to be one's own truth to actually and expressly *be* true.

Since the boy Jung argues theologically, we could remind him here of the characteristically Christian move as regards sins, the move from, for example, "Thou *shalt* not commit adultery" to "whosoever looketh on a woman to lust after her *hath* committed adultery..." (Matt. 5:27f.). Whether Jung commits the *deed* of explicitly thinking the second part of his thought or not does in this regard not make much of a difference anymore: he has already committed the "sin" (if it is a sin), a "sin" that now, after the fact, he tries with all his might to still refrain from committing. If thinking this thought costs one the "salvation of one's eternal soul," then Jung is already up for "eternal damnation." Before, I showed that there was a change of the subject matter (the concern about the thinking person instead of continuing the thought). Now we see that there is also a substitution of what is actually at stake. Jung makes much noise about not wanting to commit a deed and how sinful and damnable this deed would be, which really is a non-issue inasmuch as "the sin" in question has already been committed. He makes an enormous fuss about locking the stable door after the horses have escaped. The locking of the stable becomes his whole concern. And he makes all this noise so as to hide in a fog the real issue, the real *task* demanded of him, much like dictatorial governments often foment a conflict or war with a foreign nation in order to deflect their people's fury from the country's domestic conflicts. And with this I come to the promised discussion of the topic of "the implicit requiring to become explicit."

If a stone has been shattered, for example through rockfall, it simply has been shattered. There is no need for the stone or what is left of it to acknowledge that it is now shattered. If a baby bird has outgrown its time in the nest it does not have to explicitly admit that its time in the nest is over. It simply begins to learn to fly. But for us humans it is not enough to notice that a change, a loss, a wound has happened. What has factually happened requires, on top of its already being the case, to be explicitly *allowed* to be the case and thus to become *true*. It has to be released into its being true. If through the simple biological fact of growing up you have been transported from out of the state of childhood innocence across a threshold into the state of *reflecting consciousness*, it is not enough to now be able to reflect (as Jung is here obviously doing). You also have to repeat (perform once more) this factual crossing of a threshold as your own psychological act. Through a specific logical act of our own we have to own up to what our real situation is in order to make it true and in this way appropriate the factual situation as our own property, to make it psychologically our own. Psychologically, we have to still get to where we in fact already are. This paradoxical circular, or uroboric, doubling is the complication that comes with our primarily being (existing as) soul or consciousness, rather than only mere objects.

The task, therefore, that Jung found himself confronted with through this thought of his that came up in him was to release his new factual situation (of having outgrown his childhood paradise) into its being an explicit truth. He had to own up to his factual expulsion from paradise and with full determination appropriate this (his having been expelled) as his own new truth. He had to place himself expressly on its ground as his new standpoint. Specifically, the internal logic or *syntactical* truth of the first half of his thought needed to come out into the open and thus demanded of him to explicitly express it as a (and as his) *semantic* truth, which was supposed to happen in the second half of his thought. This was his psychological task, his own soul's inner need. But he refused to perform it, and for this purpose he changed what was actually a truth issue, really only a question of honesty and owning up, into a morality or sin issue.

But to be honest about a *new* situation always requires the courage of breaking a taboo, inasmuch as one's owning up to the new truth amounts to the betrayal of one's old truth and to the crossing of a threshold. It requires one's deliberately changing sides. With the whole weight of your personality and unrelenting determination you now have to side with "the enemy": with the "reflecting consciousness," which appears as "enemy" because it ruthlessly cuts you off from what "you love so much," from the "beautiful cathedral," from your naïve faith in God, your sympathetic oneness with nature,[3] and your containment in the love of your parents. As regards the last point, it is very telling that just about the first reason why Jung should not think that thought was the thought of his parents: "That would be very sad for my parents, if their only son, to whom they are so attached, should be doomed to eternal damnation. I cannot do that to my parents." Jung does not see himself as an individual in his own right, but as the child of his parents. He insists on perceiving himself through their eyes (as he imagines them), thereby confirming once more his psychological embeddedness in the fold of their love and his childhood status which, so he felt, was under no circumstances supposed to be lost.

This is why the thought appeared to him as "forbidden," as the absolutely unforgivable sin. To be sure, his thought was blasphemous in content. The association of "sin" is not unfounded. But the point is that the idea of sin is here a functional idea rather than a descriptive evaluation. There is an *interest* in Jung in making this thought appear as the most severe crime imaginable; Jung systematically exaggerates its sinfulness: it is worse than murder. This exaggerating activity serves the purpose of an excuse. It helps to construe what could have appeared as a psychological task and developmental necessity as something evil,

---

[3] From the narcissism of what the alchemists called the *unio naturalis*, or what Lévy-Bruhl called *participation mystique*.

an absolute crime, and thus to erect unsurmountable barriers between him and his thought. The idea of sin, far from just being an objective theological assessment, is the articulation of his subjective total resistance, his refusal, his once and for all having sided with his old truth against his new truth. Jung redefines the threshold to be crossed as an unsurmountable barrier.

The ego resistance as instigated by the thought itself

"Reflecting consciousness" is nothing else but the sublation, negation of one's "sympathetic oneness with nature," of the *unio naturalis*, of the *participation mystique*, the "sympathy of all things." It is not some Other, a new element. The negation is not something done to the paradise of childhood by an external force. It is much rather this paradise's own self-negation, its further-determination, so to speak its growing up. Thus it is the same old beautiful world before and after, the same old beautiful cathedral and the same old God sitting on his throne, only now *as* negated, reflected. (In much the same sense Jung once wrote, "It seemed to me that Adam must once upon a time have left Paradise in this manner: it had become a specter for him...," *MDR* p. 88, transl. modif.). What Jung's thought as a whole was actually about was thus the awareness and acknowledgment of negation or sublation in the sense of absolute negativity and alienation. It was not destruction, ruin, defilement. Negation and sublation amount to a logical (syntactical, psychological) change, not to a semantic (empirical, content) change. The content stays the same. It is the beautiful cathedral *as* sublated, detached, removed, no longer immediate, and in this sense "lost." Consciousness is alienated from it. It has become modern consciousness. One sees one's sympathetic oneness with the beautiful world from a distance vis-à-vis oneself, has it as a memory, in Mnemosyne. One is no longer contained in the immediate oneness with it, but conversely contains *it* as one's own content of consciousness and thus as the property of one's own mind.

Destruction and defilement, by contrast, precisely ruin the image itself in its semantic quality, its substantial appearance, the things in the image. The cathedral is smashed. The golden throne of God is turned into a toilet. I submit that what is responsible for the distastefulness and literal destructiveness of the second part of Jung's thought is the resistance to the new state of consciousness. Here things become a bit complicated.

The transition from the first half of his thought to its second half would have been, as we have seen, the thought's self-movement from the semantic level to the syntactical level. The negation inherent in the reflectedness of the paradise of childhood idea was supposed to come out into the open. But because the boy Jung shows too much *Zärtlichkeit* (too much of a soft spot, too much narcissistic infatuation) for things, for the world as immediate thing-like experience—this is the *unio naturalis*, the *participation mystique*—the negation cannot come home to itself and be a strictly logical (not semantic) negation: infinite negativity. It is forced back down and held down on the semantic level: absolute negativity is itself positivized and becomes simple negation as the empirical event of a literal destruction. So the syntactical truth (the negation or reflectedness of the celebration of "God's world") of the first part does become semantically explicit in the second part of the thought, however, only as a *new separate event* in the story rather than as the revelation of the inner *logic* of the previous image itself as a whole. The inevitable rupture that comes with factual entrance into the state of reflecting modern consciousness would actually want to be a change in the form or logical constitution of the contents, the style of seeing: the reflected, broken *form of the relation to* the content (the supremely beautiful cathedral) and thus the *sublation* of the whole level of consciousness. But here it has to manifest as the literal shattering and defilement of the *content*, the objects, just as the awareness of "paradise lost" can here show only in the absolutely extremist idea that if he were to continue his thought this would amount to the "terrible danger of ... plunging myself into hell" (p. 37). Hell is the *semantic* (literalistic) negation of paradise (and the extreme negation at that). It is another place, somewhere else, another content. It is not the "alchemical" transmutation of the same content, of paradise itself, its putrefaction and distillation. The idea that there can be, and in fact is, a logical negation, a negation of the *form* of consciousness, in our story must not emerge.

From this we have to realize that Jung's thought is uroboric from the outset. The resistance is not, as it seemed so far, a secondary response or reaction to a given thought. Rather, it is already built into the thought itself as its blasphemous content. The thought came to Jung as this crude destructive and disgusting image from the outset. His not wanting to go on thinking is not his subjective refusal of the thought in its totality, also not at all his egoic doing, but an integral part of this thought itself. This thought has everything it needs within itself, even the vehement resistance to itself. The resistance to the thought is one source of the entire thought. It was not a mistake on Jung's part to react the way he did; he is not to be blamed. He *was* faithful to it. He had to do the thought's bidding.

Rather, we have to realize that that thought that Jung was assigned to think was the thought of "not going the way of thinking" (of not-thought, of anti-philosophy). His thought was, instead, the thought of what he would later term "immediate experience," *Urerfahrung* (primordial experience), of psychology as empirical science of "facts, nothing but facts," of a psychology of images and revelations that as merely semantic elements stayed, and had to stay, fundamentally undisclosed, mysterious, numinous, blind: archetypes of the collective *unconscious*. Jung *was* a thinker. His thought demanded of him that he think through how one could enter the unavoidable stage of reflecting modern consciousness *without* really entering it, *without* leaving the in-ness in God's world; how one could truly leave childhood *without* losing its innocence and immediacy stance (and along with it the whole content of the mythological and metaphysical traditions). This is why the negation had to be translated from the logical-syntactical level into something happening on the level of the semantic contents of the image (which made the thought blasphemous, unappetizing, and destructive); why the threshold problem (entrance into modern consciousness) had to be reinterpreted as the wholly different problem of evil, and why the long disruption (the digression of his subjective tormented reflections between the first and the second half of his simple thought) was necessary *for* the true thinking of this thought itself.

But the converse of all this is of course that this thought of his that he had to think is a structurally neurotic one: a thought that within itself turns against its own telos, that wants to be translated into its own untruth rather than being released into its truth.

The thought is uroboric. It presents the negation that it is about—or, positively expressed, the entrance into reflected modern consciousness in the sense of explicitly owning up to it—as literal destruction and defilement, which in turn can be interpreted as "the most frightful of sins," which in its turn creates the idea that continuing the thought is tantamount to plunging oneself into hell. (Here one may, by the way, be reminded of the counter-example of young man Luther who found the resolution of his agonies of conscience precisely in his deliberate willingness to deliver himself over to the most frightful eventuality, *if* it could not be avoided: *se resignare ad infernum*). So it creates through itself Jung's stopping to think it to its end. But it is conversely Jung's refusing to continue to think the thought that is responsible for the negation having to take on the literal semantic form of destruction and defilement. The stopping produces its own reason for stopping, and this reason necessitates the stopping. Jung's thought is the event of this complex relation.

If Jung had simply continued his thought, it would not have had to contain the image of the shitting God and the smashing of the cathedral, because if he had really continued to *think*, the image of God's beautiful world could have negated *itself* (its own logical form) rather than externally acting out the negation on its contents. Then there would not have been any idea of a deadly sin and thus no need to disrupt the thought. But then this would not have been *Jung's* thought, but a very different one. Jung was that man who was called upon to think a thought that required not to be thought to the end. If Jung had been able to *think* the thought of the negation of paradise, he could never have become the psychologist of the collective unconscious. He had to *not* go on thinking his thought.

Disowning his own thought. From "I" to "it"

What happened in the lacuna between the first and the second part of his thought is really the significant part of this text. The thought itself is not important. It is only the *occasion* for a thought process that, phenomenologically considered, Jung starts all on his own and that foreshadows major constituents of his later psychology. But this thought process needed as impetus the immense pressure from the obsessive (unthought) thought that insisted on being thought.

"Now it is coming, now it's serious! *I must think*. It must be thought out beforehand" (Jung's italics). Instead of continuing the thought, i.e., allowing the thought to think itself to its end, Jung wanted to do his own thinking. "*I must think*." The ego interferes. Before being willing to let the thought think itself, he wants to have his own thoughts. "I could not yield before I understood what God's will was..." "... I did not want it to happen without my understanding it ..." Jung approaches his situation with a program. It is like not wanting to begin life before having been given an instruction manual telling us in detail what life is all about. Jung substitutes his external reflections *about* his thought for the process of the further-determination and internal self-reflection of this thought itself. "Thinking *before* the thinking" is the wish to approach one's thought with preconceptions, presuppositions. Jung wants to stay in control. Yes, if it cannot be avoided, he will think his thought to the end, but not before he has developed his own theory or framework for it, his own explanation as to why there are such thoughts and where they come from.

What this means, however, is that although in the end Jung in fact thinks his thought to the end, this is no longer a real thinking of it. Real thinking means to abandon oneself to the actual thought, no matter where it will take one. One is in the thought, carried by it, surrounded by it. What Jung did here instead was merely to allow the now thing-like *contents* of the thought to emerge in consciousness. He had gotten out of the thinking process and stayed out even while allowing the contents to surface. He did not *think*, but lifted a suppression. It is an act of perception, not thinking. He sort of opened the box and let what was in it come out. He had pocketed the thought beforehand, and had got himself into a distance from it, so that instead of a living thought, he was merely dealing with the contents of it. And he did not expose himself to the *thought* at all, but felt forced to commit a *sin*. He had thus changed an act of thinking into an act of committing a sin, in other words, into a (sinful) *behavior*. Instead of plunging into his thought, he felt he had to plunge into hell. It's all about sinning and not about thinking. That's the distance he had created. Through his ego interception, Jung had transformed his task of thinking the second half of his thought into an act of mere obedience. He obeyed orders like a slave, so that he could go externally through the motions of thinking without responsibility of his own and full inner participation. He simulated thinking this thought. We have to realize that the end of this story did by no means bring an end to his "Don't think of it, just don't think of it!" To the end he stayed faithful to his refusal to think his thought, and instead merely created for himself the impression of having thought it.

This extraction of himself from out of his thought receives its underpinning through his speculative thoughts about God as the "author of this desperate problem" (p. 39). "*Why* should I think something I do not know? I do not want to, by God, that's sure. But *who* wants me to? Who wants to force me to think something I don't know and don't want to know? Where does this terrible will come from?" (p. 37) This is the direction of his thinking "before the thinking" and *about* the thought. It aims for his own exoneration and for finding out "who done it?" He adamantly rejects responsibility for his own thought, disowns it like an illegitimate child that he needs to provide with another father (author). It is an act of alienation: he construes his thought as an alien one. He washes his hands of it. *He* is completely innocent. "*I* haven't done this or wanted this, it has come on me like a bad dream. ... This has happened to me without my doing."

For us it is quite clear where this (allegedly so terrible) will comes from: it is of course his own will, the dynamic inherent in his own new status of being as one who has outgrown his child status. The way Jung argues is, however, just as if an adolescent in puberty were to say, "By God, *I* do not want these sexual impulses. *Who* wants to force me to have such feelings?" But there is nobody else who imposes these feelings on him. No, it is he himself, his own nature as man-to-be. By the same token it would be clear to us why Jung must think this thought of his: because he has psychologically outgrown his childhood. The thought is not planted into his head from outside, not foisted on him. Rather, if he would think it, what would happen is no more than that *his own new psychological status* would come home to him, become integrated into his consciousness; what implicitly he already *is* would also become explicit.

The result of this disowning is that his thought receives the form of otherness, ultimately, in his later theory, the form of "objective facts." Like God's turd falling on the beautiful cathedral, so this thought *of* God's turd smashing the cathedral falls on or into innocent Jung. The thought is thus deprived of its thought character and treated as if it were an object or entity. This is why we find the wording, "Now it is coming," "it" meaning the content of the thought. "It": the grammatical form of the third person, so that the first person, I, could be kept out of it. Merely an object. Not, as true thought requires, a subject-object or object-subject. In reality, a thought is something that exists only when and while it is actually being thought; it requires one's own living activity of thinking it. A thought is always *my* thought. Just as music is not notes printed on paper, but is what it is only when it is played by a person or a whole orchestra and when it is heard, so a thought, too, is essentially performative and I am inextricably in it. It is always my own doing. Not a sheet of paper would fit between me and my thought. Jung's disowning his thought amounts to the fundamental decision not to think.

But *thinking* is the form that initiation inevitably takes under the conditions of modernity. The soul is no longer on the emotional-experiential level.[4] It has deserted this level and left it to the ego.

So Jung's essential move of pulling himself out of his thought and turning it into something he happens to be bombarded with from outside performs a "reversal into the opposite." Instead of himself being initiated by his thought into alienation (alienation as the logical constitution of modern consciousness), Jung managed to turn the tables: to return the message intended for him, namely the (in modernity unavoidable) alienation, to the messenger—the thought itself—as *its* property, its logical character, similarly perhaps to how soldiers sometimes manage to throw a hand grenade that has been thrown at them back to the sender. So that consciousness may escape alienation, the *content* emerging in consciousness had to be alienated; so that the syntax or logic may get away unscathed, the semantics has to bear the brunt.

But because in this one point the syntax of consciousness had to be protected from alienation, Jung's later psychology had *on the whole* to keep itself absolutely unconscious of the level of syntax as such and exclusively zero in on the semantic contents of consciousness, dreams, myths, images, symbols, symptoms.

---

[4] Just as for a much longer time it had no longer been on the level of the *drômena*, the *legomena*, and the symbolic objects of the ritualistic and mythological stage of cultural development.

Jung called his psychology with full right "psychology of the unconscious" because it keeps itself systematically unconscious about the logical status that the semantic contents it studies come with and about the syntax of consciousness *in which* the psychic phenomena emerge.[5] *This* (the systematic blindness to the syntactical) is in truth "the unconscious." The latter is at bottom a logical act on the part of the psychologist and not ontologically a region in the personality, a reservoir of instinctual wishes, or a treasury of images, etc. That it is given out as something ontological is itself due to the deflection from the syntactical to the semantic. "Projection." Reification. Acting out (on the level of theorizing). Jung also never felt the need to reflect the logical status of *his own* consciousness *with which* he applied himself to his research and to alchemically sublimate, distill, evaporate it.[6] He went to work on the "prime matter" in front of him directly, innocently, with the ordinary everyday consciousness of the man in the street.[7] "All too easily does self-criticism poison one's naïveté, that

---

[5] For a critical discussion of the notion of "the unconscious" in Jung's psychology and of what it means psychologically, see Wolfgang Giegerich, "Closure and Setting Free or The Bottled Spirit of Alchemy and Psychology," in: *Spring 74 Alchemy*, Spring 2006, pp. 31–62, now Chapter 9 in the present volume.

[6] Our text is the prime example that shows how Jung, through his "thinking beforehand," a priori prevented the possibility of his consciousness becoming transformed. The logical form of his consciousness was here—why should we not say: once and for all?—immunized against the decomposing power of what his thought confronted him with.

[7] Very telling in this regard is Marie-Louise von Franz's report about what Jung often told about how he wrote his *Psychological Types*, namely that he "wanted to write in a clear, logically accurate form, having in mind something like *Le Discours de la Méthode* by Descartes, but he couldn't do it because that was too refined a mental instrument to grasp this enormous wealth of material. When he arrived at this difficulty he dreamt that there was an enormous boat out in the harbor laden with marvellous goods for mankind and that it should be pulled into the harbor and the goods distributed to the people. Attached to this enormous boat was a very elegant, white Arab horse, a beautiful and delicate, highstrung animal which was supposed to pull the ship into harbor. But the horse was absolutely incapable of this. At that moment an enormous red-headed, red-bearded giant came through the mass of people, pushed everybody aside, took an axe, killed the white horse and then took the rope and pulled the whole ship into harbor in one *élan*." Von Franz adds, "So Jung saw that he had to write in the emotional fire he felt about the whole thing and not go on with this elegant white horse. He was then driven by a tremendous working impulse, or emotion, and he wrote the whole book in practically one stretch ..." M.-L. von Franz, *The Shadow and Evil in Fairytales*, Zürich (Spring Publications) 1974, pp. 209f. The red-headed giant versus Descartes. The raw against the cooked (the alchemically refined). The archaic against the modern. Brute force (or "nature") against thinking. Remarkable, though of course not surprising, is also that Jung pushed this very decision of his against the clarity of thought off into the "raw" form of a dream that, as a seeming "natural event," came to him as if to an innocent recipient of it ("So Jung saw...").

priceless possession, or rather gift, which no creative person can do without" (*CW* 4 § 774). Really?

Jung's move described here is the experiential *prima figura* of his later theoretical construal of the psyche as "objective psyche" consisting of "facts, nothing but facts" to be observed (*not* thought) and coming from "not I." Here, in the alienation from or disownment of his own thought, we see at least one root of the idea of archetypes: factually existing packages of meaning; ideas and images in the logical form of "things," entities, free-floating, uprooted: a priori cut off from any real historical context (*Sitz im Leben*), like exhibition pieces in a museum. It's the other way around: archetypes are said to *constellate* in real life (from out of nowhere).

The answer to Jung's question "*Why* should I think something I do not know?" could be that this is what thought is about. Thinking produces new insights. It is a process, a *Denkweg*, as Heidegger put it, that takes you somewhere unforeseen. If it were only about things that you already knew, why would there be thoughts at all? Of course, thoughts can come as a surprise to you, and sometimes as a painful, unwanted surprise. But this does not alter the fact that your thought, even if it is an unwelcome one, is truly yours. If you had not been you, you would not have had this thought. But this does not in any way mean that real thoughts are ego concoctions. Thoughts think *themselves*. They are their own subject and object. And yet, they are "mine."

As to the insistence of the thought that Jung experienced ("Where does this terrible will come from?"), we can say two things. First, it is not really terrible. It is the normal need of a human being to truly outgrow childhood. This need is as *his inner* need his own will, much as it is a snake's will to shed its skin. Secondly, thoughts have their own inner logic and necessity, their own teleology, within themselves, and *want* to be thought. Thoughts do have a will of their own. Depending on who you are, you must have your thoughts. And *your* thoughts want to be thought out by you, that's all there is to it. Jung went, as it were, pregnant with his thought about the beautiful cathedral; he had already had this thought of his; and it now insisted on being born fully. If one wants to make "an agent" responsible for a thought, then one would have to say that it is the real situation (or, in the case of great thought, the historical locus) one finds oneself in, whose truth wants to come to light; and thinking is nothing else than letting the truth of where one stands display itself as conscious content. Conversely, letting this happen means for the thought to first *become* true, or to be released into its truth.

But in his ego reflections about the thought, Jung made, out of the inner necessity of his thought to become born, a "terrible will" *behind* this thought of his, an alien subject that "wants to force him" to think it. Jung constructs an unknown "who" as the author of this will. He deserted his own "prime matter," the hermetically self-enclosed now of this thought, and outside it went off to Adam and Eve and the beginning of the world. With the question of the "*Who?*" that wants him to think his thought, Jung treads the path of mystification. This question is the prefiguration of his later conception of a substantiated "unconscious" as the *agent behind* our dreams, ideas, and impulses, as well as of his idea of archetypal "dominants"— archetypal psychology's "Who? Which god?"

The construction of the principle of subjective certainty and immediacy

Nietzsche criticized the Cartesian "cogito ergo sum" in the following way: "... [T]he idea that, if there is thinking, there must be 'something that thinks' is simply an articulation of our grammatical habituation which posits an agent where there is an action" (*Der Wille zur Macht [The Will to Power]* # 484, my transl.). This is a general, fundamental attack on the notion of "the subject" in the sense of a metaphysics of substance. Of course, the notion of an "I" who as the subject does the thinking is precisely not our problem here, and it is questionable if Nietzsche's critique of the I, especially with respect to the reality of thinking, is fully tenable. But inasmuch as Jung posits (not himself as the subject, but) an *alien* subject, God, as the compelling agent behind his thought, the logical pattern of Nietzsche's critique of the belief that all that happens is a doing and all doing implies a doer (*ibid.* # 550) is fully applicable here. Whereas in the case of one's own thinking, the "cogito" in itself indeed (not only implies, but) explicitly posits the I that thinks, the God *behind* the thinking has no basis in the *phenomenology* of the situation. He is precisely not a spontaneous experience. He is a concoction of the ego that externally reflects *about* its immediate experience, the mystifying invention of an external agent responsible for his own thought. Jung pulls God, *this his* God, out of his hat. The fact that in this he relies on conventional religious ideas available to him from his upbringing does not contradict this assessment. The origin of God in Jung is his own will or need; the conventional ideas about God are the raw material that he shapes according to his own needs.

How does Jung arrive at the idea of God as the terrible will behind his thought? Above we had to realize that it was the resistance against thinking his thought to the very end that caused the self-negation of the idea of the paradise of childhood to take the form of a literal destruction and defilement on the content level of the thought. The same mechanism is at work here. Jung's obstinate refusal to acknowledge his thought as *his* thought, his stubbornly washing his hands of it, deepens the gulf between him and his thought and thus builds up the emotional pressure enormously between the two sides. The more he insists that it is not his will, the more powerful, even terrible the insisting force of it becomes. The overwhelming power of the will experienced by Jung stems from the I's unconditional refusal, its defiance. By disrupting the natural flow of his thought the boy Jung dams up what would normally be a small brook and creates a reservoir whose masses of water, if the dam breaks, wash everything away.

The will at work here in Jung is a will for a radical dissociation. The dialectical nature of true thoughts, namely, that they are their own subjects and yet mine, fundamentally "non-I" *and* "I," is split apart into two wholly separate opposites. A nuclear fission. As the pressure increases, the allegedly alien will is forced out of this world and becomes the otherworldly will of God, and his *terrible* will at that. It has to be terrible because here God is the result of an absolutely stubborn ego will. The fundamental gesture of Jung's thinking, his vehement "no!" ("*I* haven't done this or wanted this ... This has happened to me without my doing," "I don't want it, by God, that's sure"), produces as its (now undialectical) counterpart, i.e., as that against which this "no!" is directed, something absolutely frightful and overwhelming.

I said that Jung's move of disowning his thought and turning it into a terrible will is the experiential *prima figura* of Jung's later theoretical ideas of the objective psyche and the archetypes happening to us. But it is also the experiential *prima figura* of Jung's concept of God. Essential to this God concept is "the sense of the alien character connected with the experience of something objective," our knowing "that something unknown, alien does come our way" (*MDR* p. 336, transl. modif.); that "it confronts us spontaneously and compels us" (*MDR* p. 340, transl. modif.); the "God-image is always a projection of the inner experience of a powerful *vis-à-vis*"; "it is characterized by its numinosity and the overwhelming force of that numinosity" (*MDR* p. 335f.). The "will of God can be terrible" (*CW* 18 § 1637). There is an "opposing will" (*CW* 11 § 290), and our "'counter-will' can also be understood as an aspect of God's will" (*CW* 11 § 292, transl. modif.). Jung speaks of "God's nature, which sets us at odds with ourselves" (*Letters 2*, p. 28, to Schär, 16 Nov 1951). *Antagonism* is the central criterion of an experience of God for him, which is why he considers "*collisions* of duties" (the *CW* and *MDR* in a muted manner speak only of "conflicts of duties") for religiously decisive. Jacob's fight with the angel is the paradigm for Jung of the relation between man and God.

Jung's thinking is egoic: a thinking in terms of the will rather than in terms of insight and truth.

We could say that Jung's own *refusal* to be taught better by the thought that emerged in him—his refusal to allow himself to be given a clear knowledge that he had outgrown his childhood and the child's belief in God—is projected out and hypostatized as the terrible will that forces him. Jung's concept of God is the hypostasis of his refusal to let his own (implicitly already existing) insight come fully home to consciousness and to prevail: the birth of God, this God, from the spirit of the resistance against his insight. Here an anti-Enlightenment impulse makes itself felt, an impulse against *sapere aude*, against one's emergence from one's self-incurred immaturity (Kant).

Some pages later in *MDR* Jung declares: "I never engendered any idea of God, either. ... In fact it was not an idea at all—that is, not something thought out. It was not like imagining something and thinking it out and afterward believing it. ... / ... Suddenly I understood that God was, for me at least, one of the most certain and immediate of experiences. After all, I didn't invent that horrible image about the cathedral. On the contrary, it was forced on me and I was compelled, with the utmost cruelty, to think it ..." (pp. 61f.). It is true that Jung did not imagine God and *afterward* believed his imagined idea. As he would say much later, "I don't believe; I know." But we have seen how he thought God out, produced him through his own mental doings, concocted him out of his own violent resistance. God is here literally a *deus ex machina*, a God from out of conscious machinations.

But the crucial thing we have to realize is that God was precisely concocted *as* "the most certain and immediate of experiences," *as not* concocted, *not* thought out. The whole refusal to *think* his thought had the purpose of creating, and intensifying extremely, the conflict thus created between his own ego will and an overwhelming opposite will and to make him overwhelmed by this thought against his will. And the purpose of the production of this absolute clash of wills to the point of "utmost cruelty" was the production of the sense of the unquestionable certainty and immediacy of experience. Jung fell for the immediacy (the not-producedness) of the product *produced* by him because he had obliterated his production process and the producedness of this immediacy. His view is naïve, or maybe precisely not at all naïve: deviously naïve.

This (cunningly naïve) sense of immediacy still haunts Jungianism to the present day.

The inner phoniness of this sense of immediacy becomes especially obvious when we consider that with his reflections Jung stepped out of the *really* immediate image in its phenomenality and operated with the idea of another God outside and behind the image. The immediate experience was the God sitting on his golden throne shitting on his cathedral. But now we have all of a sudden a duality of Gods. There is the God who has the terrible will that Jung commit the sin of thinking this blasphemous thought, and there is the God in this thought who is shitting on his church, but in no way forces or compels Jung and in no way represents a counter-will. The God$_{(1)}$ *in* the thought (the really experienced, *phenomenal* God, the God as *spontaneous psychic experience*) is radically deprived of psychic reality, psychic objectivity, as Jung might later word it. He is simply no topic any more. The content and theme of the particular thought experience that had emerged in Jung falls by the wayside. Only the God$_{(2)}$ outside the thought (the *ideological, thought-out* God) who allegedly wants Jung to think this thought is absolutely real.[8] "After all, I didn't invent that horrible image about the cathedral": this is true. But the boy Jung certainly invented the God$_{(2)}$ as the overwhelming originator of his spontaneous thought. He trickily purloined the shocking character of his own God$_{(1)}$ thought and foisted it on the result of his egoic theologizing *about* this thought, namely God$_{(2)}$, so that *the latter* all of a sudden appeared to him as "one of the most certain and immediate of experiences," although he was not an *experience* at all.

This maneuver is incompatible with Jung's later maxim that the psychic phenomenon has everything it needs within itself and must be hermetically enclosed within itself, incompatible also with the idea that "[w]e have simply got to listen to what the psyche spontaneously says to us. ... Say it again as well as you can" (*Letters 2*, p. 591, to Read, 2 September 1960). But this maneuver is necessary because this whole story is the event of the first *founding* of that sense of immediacy, subjective certainty, and overwhelmingly irrupting experience that was precisely needed to enable Jung later to take fantasy images as absolutely real and as having everything they need within themselves. The founding of the sense of immediacy requires a decidedly artificial interference and the very hypostasis (here of God) that for the later psychologist Jung was absolutely anathema, a "deadly sin" (cf. p. 70). The experiential grounding act of Jung's later "psychology of the unconscious," which within itself scorns all metaphysical hypostatizing, *is* itself based on a metaphysical hypostasis. This hypostasis later finds its articulation in Jung's ontological thesis of *esse in anima*, not to mention his notion of "the unconscious" as a concept of

---

[8] Defending his *Answer to Job*, Jung wrote to Erich Neumann on 5 January 1952, "How can a man hold aloof from this drama? He would then be a philosopher, talking *about* God but not *with* God" (Letters 2, p. 34). By "thinking beforehand," the boy Jung was the "philosopher" who talks *about* God and holds himself aloof of what happens in his own thought. Jung could only have talked *with* God if he had stayed *in* the drama of his thought and with the God$_{(1)}$ that in fact appeared to him in it. We may concede that decades later the author of *Answer to Job* indeed did not merely talk about God but actually entered the drama envisioned by him. However, it is to be assumed that the God *with* whom he talked in this book was *not* the God$_{(1)}$ of his spontaneous experience, but the God$_{(2)}$ of his "thinking beforehand" *about* his experience. In other words, it was a manifest talking *with* that God that himself was the result of an early "philosophical" reflection *about* God. The real drama to be entered had been deserted and excluded once and for all. A simulated "with" that camouflaged the actual "about."

substance, rather than a mere functional concept (different degrees of consciousness).

Now it becomes clear why Jung was not allowed to *think* his thought onwards. Without this refusal of his to *think*, his thought would have initiated him into awareness of the already accomplished self-negation of his existence in "God's world," the sublatedness of the paradise of childhood, the loss of its *form* of immediacy. He would *psychologically* have ended up, hook, line, and sinker, in the status of modern consciousness, the status of negativity and alienation. But by disrupting the thought and, instead of letting *it* think itself to its end, departing on the path of his own subjective reflections, he was able to repurpose the emergence of his thought. When *after* his "thinking *beforehand*" he actually did allow the second half of his thought to become explicit, this thought achieved the opposite of what had been its own inherent purpose: it now brought about the absolute rescue (of sorts) of childhood innocence in "God's world." When Jung added to the phrase "the paradise of childhood" the relative clause "from which we imagine we have emerged," he betrays that as a psychologist he somehow felt that he had not actually emerged from it, and on principle grounds had not, as we understand from the foregoing. Instead of wrecking the naïve idea of God and God's world for him, this experience created an unassailable sense of certainty and immediacy of the reality of God, God in his fundamental otherness, as absolute not-I, as the personified unconscious.[9] (Again, we always have to keep in mind that the term "God" in Jung is not part of an authentically *religious* discourse and has nothing to do with piety, but is a functional term needed for the logical foundation of "the psychology of the unconscious." It is the term for the epitome of immediacy.)

That Jung in his fundamental outlook indeed did not really emerge from the paradise of childhood, becomes strikingly clear from a small detail, his assessment of modern art, e.g., that of Joyce and Picasso. He wrote, "Both are masters of the fragmentation of aesthetic contents and accumulators of ingenious shards." "Picasso is ruthless strength, seizing the unconscious urge and voicing it resoundingly, even using it for monetary reasons. By this regrettable digression he shows how

[9] "I am aware that 'mana,' 'daimon,' 'God' are synonyms for the unconscious ..." *MDR* p. 337. "For the collective unconscious we could use the word God" C.G. Jung, *The Visions Seminars*, Zürich (Spring Publications) 1976, p. 391.

little he understands the primordial urge, which does not mean a field of ever so attractive-looking and alluring shards, but a new world after the old one has crumpled up.[10] Nature has a *horror vacui* and does not believe in shard-heaps and decay, but grass and flowers cover all ruins inasmuch as the rains of heaven reach them" (*Letters 2*, p. 589 and 590, to Read, 2 September 1960). Yes, so we can paraphrase Jung's position, paradise has been lost, but it will come again, if only one does not make the mistake of misunderstanding "the primordial urge." That in classical-modern art the fragmentation was precisely not a misunderstanding, but *itself* the soul's "primordial urge" (if such an innocent term still makes sense) and the very purpose and *raison d'être* of modern artistic creation, that, furthermore, modern art was not on the semantic level of the natural appearance of the things of this world, but on the level of logical form, was unfeasible for Jung. Even while being in "the crumpled-up world," his *standpoint* is and remains the one in the world prior to its having become crumpled up, the standpoint of intact "nature," of "the priceless possession of naïveté." And so the child's grass and flowers will return. Infinite negativity and alienation (a form of the alchemical decomposition and distillation of consciousness) cannot be embraced as the soul's own need. If to be modern means to know what is no longer *possible*, Jung had not entered modernity. The appeal to "nature" as the standard and measure, regardless of whether it has a *horror vacui* or not, is perhaps the main thing that is no longer possible after the Industrial Revolution and the end of classical metaphysics. The point is that the soul has emigrated from nature. It is somewhere else. And modern man finds himself expelled from nature (which is what is meant by "alienation").

But the decision against modernity fell in 1887, in our episode. Jung's deviation through his own ego reflections was indispensable for the project he would have to realize. Through departing on the course of his ego reflections, he avoided having to be unreservedly transported into the *stage* of "reflecting or thinking consciousness." He acted out the reflection as his personal literal behavior (a mental function) so that it would not have to become the objective *form* of his consciousness (the logical status of absolute negativity and alienation).

---

[10] With the phrase "crumpled up" Jung refers back to a motif in Joyce he had alluded to earlier in the same letter.

Precisely by permitting to surface in consciousness the notions of a shitting God, of the destruction of the cathedral (i.e., God's Church), and of the brutal defilement of the innocent beauty of the world, Jung now, after the interlude of his own ego reflections, had paradoxically enthroned God (and in God the guarantor of "God's world," the principle of the "paradise of childhood," rather than God as a topic of piety[11]) all the more firmly. Far from having to suffer the loss of an innocent faith in God implied by the turd falling from God onto the beautiful cathedral, he now ended up with an unshakeable idea, nay, "knowledge," of God. Inasmuch as for him (who, *factually*, had inevitably outgrown childhood) God had become redefined as immediacy absolute, Jung's God had psychologically become immune to reflection and was thus rescued unscathed from childhood into reflecting consciousness. And inasmuch as Jung now had, in the form of his God idea, established for himself the very principle of something unassailable by reflection, he had *logically* evaded the stage of "reflecting consciousness," although of course *psychically* (empirical-factually) he had already entered it (as precisely his ego maneuvers show). The sense of certainty and immediacy is the form in which Jung could logically preserve for himself the essence of childhood innocence into the factual state of negated, "destroyed" childhood innocence and modern consciousness.

All the time here, we have to keep in mind that the maneuvers are not a personal mistake on Jung's part, but the very condition of the possibility of his "psychology of the unconscious."

What looks like events is performed ritual

Our text shows how one can go through a kind of *rite de passage* into a new status of consciousness *without initiation* into this new status, i.e., without really having to suffer, all the way through, the death, the negation, of what the previous stage was about. A true compromise formation: I concede on the semantic level the conditions of the new status of consciousness (the semantic image of a shitting God and the destruction of the church), while mentally reserving for myself on the syntactical level the very principle of the now negated

---

[11] Jung's "I do not believe, I know" with respect to God among other things implies that "God" in Jung's thinking is not part of a religious concern.

status. We know this strategy already if we read a few pages earlier in *MDR* how Jung described how he managed to overcome his childhood neurosis earlier the same year (a neurosis characterized by fainting fits that came whenever he had to go to school or to study for school). By way of a rational concession to "the collision with reality" he accepted the truth of "Aha, here [in real life] you have to work" (my translation; this sentence is translated incorrectly in *MDR*, p. 31) and with violent ego power forced a "conscientiousness" (p. 32) upon himself, while inwardly not changing his basic stance.[12] His undergoing and overcoming this neurosis in this particular way had the purpose of transporting the neurotic structure from a *personally* acted-out empirical pathology to the *objective* logical form of an intellectual position, namely the position of subjective certainty and immediacy, which was later to become the logical principle of his developed psychology.

It had not been an authentic neurosis, as we find it in our patients, in the first place. This "neurosis" was staged *as* a neurosis. It (along with the particular way it was overcome) served the purpose of defusing the "death" aspect inherent in a real transition from a childhood consciousness to a reflecting one and of transporting the neurotic structure from the existential level of personal life to the objective theoretical level of the structure of *psychology*, in order to once and for all free the *person* (who, as the future founder of this psychology, needed this structure) from having to become neurotic.

Both stories of this year (1887), the one about Jung's taking possession of his "neurosis" and the one about his cathedral thought, must not be seen—naïvely—as simple events. We need to see through their seeming event character. They must be seen teleologically, in the light of what he was to become: as steps "on the way to his mythos" (his "psychology of the unconscious"). Both are unconsciously performed *rituals*. Rituals are methods for producing something psychologically important, for bringing about a logical transformation. But in this case, they do not transform *consciousness* (transporting and initiating it into its truth), but only the object or content of consciousness (without the involvement of the I). The "neurosis" ritual

---

[12] In my book *Der Jungsche Begriff der Neurose*, Frankfurt am Main et al. (Peter Lang Verlag) 1999, I gave a too benevolent reading of the end of Jung's childhood neurosis.

helped Jung to personally find the first transition from the personal-experiential level to the level of objective theoretical insight as such, whereas the "blasphemous thought" ritual allowed him to conquer the principle of subjective certainty for himself. Together they laid the first foundation for the logical infrastructure that enabled him later to develop his psychology.

It is true, Jung conceived of the whole episode of his thought about God's turd as God's testing "his obedience" "by imposing on me the unusual task of doing something against my own moral judgment and against the teachings of my religion, and even against His own commandment" (p. 39). And the continuation of the thought that he feared so much is introduced with the words, "I gathered all my courage, as though I were about to leap forthwith into hell-fire, and let the thought come." But, without doubting his subjective fear and his having to muster enormous courage to overcome it, we nevertheless have to realize that this test is a test that he had staged himself through his resistance and the ensuing reflections, and that the *mis en scène* served the purpose of escaping the inherent *initiatory* "test" that this thought would have posed for him, namely the explicit sacrifice of innocence (immediacy). The emotionality of his tremendous fear (the scare of eternal hell-fire) and the corresponding courage and the radicalness of the "leap" are functional; they are needed to give absolute credence to the sense of certainty and immediacy to be constructed.

The actual task inherent in this thought, namely to simply think it to its end without the prolonged deviation via his stalling and his ego thoughts, would have been far less spectacular and emotional, but was for him obviously absolutely out of the question. If he could have gone the way of *this* task, the thought could have thought itself out and its meaning and telos—the logical negation of existence in the paradise of childhood—could have come home to him, which means that he could have been initiated into it. But this was not *his* task, as we have seen. He had to think another thought, whose purpose was precisely to thwart its own *inherent* psychological purpose. It was a far more cunning thought.

We also have to realize that Jung had completely changed the risk. If he had thought the thought to its conclusion all on his own account, "eternal damnation" might possibly have been the outcome. But now that he had transmuted the thinking of this thought into something

God *wanted* him to do (cf. "Therefore it was God's intention that they [Adam and Eve] should sin" p. 38) and into an act of obedience toward God, he was at least logically on the safe side and he felt sure emotionally, too ("If that is so and I go through with it, then He will give me His grace and illumination" p. 39). His "leap forthwith into hell-fire" was psychologically really in the status of an "as if." If he sinned, God was now to blame for it. Under these circumstances, his courage did not have to be all that great. And the grace and bliss that in fact came over Jung after having "thought" his thought to its end possibly had little to do with "the wisdom and goodness of God" that Jung believed had been revealed to him (p. 40). It is more likely that it was the bliss of knowing that he had managed successfully to avoid having to drain the cup of his thought to the dregs, but had ingeniously been able to rescue the inner *principle* of childhood innocence even when he had to sacrifice that *innocence* itself.

The character of this leap of his is similar to that of the other famous leap of Jung's in 1913, a quarter of a century later, at the beginning of his "confrontation with the unconscious" ("I was sitting at my desk once more, thinking over my fears. Then I let myself drop. ..." p. 179). It was, as Jung expressly words it repeatedly, an "experiment," and we have to add, a *controlled* experiment, part of an implicit program, i.e., another unconscious *ritual* with a determinate final purpose. In other words, it too happened precisely *not* as an immediate experience (event, mishap), but as an arranged immediacy ("arranged" in the sense of Alfred Adler's term "arrangement"). Surely, the specific form of the individual images that might appear, i.e., what would happen on the semantic level, was unforeseeable. But the "experiment" *as a whole*, on the syntactical level, was staged and happened within the framework and on the ground of the logical infrastructure established through his early (1887) thoughts "thought out *beforehand*," and so it is small wonder that one of the essential messages gained from these experiences was that "there are things in the psyche which I do not produce... Philemon represented a force which was not myself. ... [H]e said things which I had not consciously thought. ... It was he who taught me psychic objectivity, the reality of the psyche" (p. 183).

In truth, however, this idea was nothing new. It was in principle the same old idea that was contained in the earlier experience we have been concerned with in this paper and it had been consciously familiar to Jung ever since. He now merely got his already established sense of immediacy and of the radical otherness of psychic experience confirmed on a higher level. In 1887 this sense of psychic objectivity ("*I* haven't done this or wanted this") had still only been his *subjective* idea and experience. It had been part of his personal development from the childhood stage to that of reflecting consciousness, which he had to defuse by transforming alienatedness as the form of consciousness into the standpoint of objective theoretical insight vis-à-vis consciousness. This was not enough for establishing a psychology as a natural science of the unconscious, of psychic facts and archetypes. For this, more was needed, namely that his earlier subjective experiential idea of psychic immediacy and objectivity would now come to him *itself in the form* of objectivity, as a theoretical maxim proclaimed by some other, an authoritative teacher, as something "which I had not consciously thought." *From within itself, on its own authority*, the *subjective* fantasy had to assert and certify that it was objective. The alienation (disownment) had in turn explicitly to turn into an alien message; the personal experiential *feeling* of psychic objectivity had itself to become objectified into a theoretical truth by its own proclamation. This is the achievement of the Philemon figure for Jung. Disownment to the power of two. It is the logical banishment of our thoughts from the *modern* land of thoughts, the conscious mind, and the sinking of them into the status of unconsciousness, into "the collective unconscious." It is the *logical* repression of our thought into the *disownment form* of dreams, visions, archetypal fantasies that emphatically "have not been our doing," but that we are "compelled, [maybe even] with the utmost cruelty, to think." But as such it is the actual founding of "the psychology of the unconscious" as an *objective scientific* enterprise.

Intellectual isolation and renouncement of truth

The devious rescue of the *principle* of childhood innocence or of "God's world" amidst the avowed sacrifice of "God's world" itself had its price. Subjectively, the price was an increase of "my sense of inferiority" (pp. 40f.), which is understandable considering the deviousness of his maneuver, but, being a personal condition, it need not be discussed any further. Another price was that the illegitimacy of this maneuver was objectively reflected in the quality of the very principle that he had rescued, God. God not only, as I have already pointed out, had to bear the blame for this awful thought of Jung's; his very definition changed. "But then came the dim understanding that God could be something terrible. I had experienced a dark and terrible secret" (p. 40). This leads directly to Jung's later passionate insistence on the reality of evil, which we can understand from our analysis as a necessary consequence of his disowning of his thought. "Evil" here is the objectified, reified form of the act of disownment and denial projected on the *content* of thought. If the dogma of the root of evil in God himself were to fall, then the whole system of the objective psyche would collapse. "Evil" is the keystone of the whole Jungian edifice.

But a more essential price that had to be paid was that Jung had maneuvered himself into total intellectual isolation, into his private *idios kosmos*. "I had the feeling that I was either outlawed or elect, accursed or blessed. / It would never have occurred to me to speak of my experience openly ... A strict taboo hung over all these matters... / My entire youth can be understood in terms of this secret. It induced in me an almost unendurable loneliness. ... Today as then I am a solitary, because I think things ... which other people do not know, and usually do not even want to know" (p. 41). It would be a great mistake to put Jung's status as solitary down to nothing but a personal character trait. It is his having secret knowledge, fundamentally incommunicable knowledge, that inevitably forces him into his loneliness. He is a *logical* solitary. Naturally so. With his insistence on subjective certainty he had *ipso facto* cut himself off from the generality, from the public tradition, from the communion of minds. His "knowledge" was *in itself* basically 'speechless' because it had its place not in the dialogue of minds, but in the immediacy of his private experience. What he experienced hit the mind out of the blue like the cathedral was hit by the turd: as mere facts. By contrast, a thinker, even in the very loneliness of thought, is always in an internal conversation with other thinkers. In 1960 Jung wrote in a letter to Jolande Jacobi,

> I was very impressed and pleased to hear that my autobiographical sketches have conveyed to you something of what my outer side has hitherto kept hidden. It had to remain

hidden because it could not have survived the brutalities of the
outside world (*Letters 2*, p. 585, 25 August 1960).

"It had to remain hidden"! If truth is *alêtheia*, unconceiledness, we
see that his secret knowledge qua *necessarily* concealed "knowledge"
was essentially truthless. We will also not go wrong in the assumption
that this dissociation felt to be indispensable is the reason for Jung's
psychology of the unconscious, i.e., for the dissociation of
consciousness and the unconscious. "The unconscious" is ultimately
the product of a (logical) concealment, a *fundamental* esotericism.[13]

In this connection it is also significant that *what* is destroyed in
his thought is the church: the symbol of *the* Church, of the congregation
of the faithful. It signifies that all ties with a collective body whose
member he might be were from now on severed. In Christianity, the
counterpart to Christ as the bridegroom is the *community* of the
believers as the bride, which is also seen as Christ's mystical body. It
is not the solitary believing individual. So it is no surprise to hear from
Jung, some pages later, that "[t]he farther away I was from church,
the better I felt. The only things I missed were the organ and the choral
music [i.e., the immediately accessible emotional, experiential side of
church service], but certainly not the 'religious community.' *I could
not connect any meaning with that phrase* ..." (p. 75, transl. modif., italics
mine). In this respect, although his solution was very different, Jung
had withdrawn to the thoroughly modern position of a Kierkegaard
in whose religious thinking, too, the whole body of the faithful did
not figure, but who looked exclusively at the solitary individual's
relation to faith. It was not accidental that Jung was a contemporary
of the existentialists.

The description I have given of this point does not, however, tell
us yet what the most severe price was that Jung's move entailed. The
insistence and exclusive relying on immediate experience meant the
dissociation of certainty from truth and the renunciation of truth in favor
of subjective certainty. About religious ideas (and we could extend this
to include all psychic phenomena) he stated, "Psychologically
regarded, they are emotional experiences whose nature is such that
they cannot be a matter for discussion. If I may permit myself a banal

---

[13] Not to be confused with what nowadays is ordinarily and popularly referred to
as esoteric.

comparison, when I feel well and content nobody can prove to me that I am not" (*CW* 16 § 186,[14] transl. modif.). It is an indisputable fact. There cannot be, and must not be, a *logon didonai*, a rational accounting; and there is no need to expose one's ideas to other mind's so that these ideas can show whether they can stand criticism. They are a priori immune. 'Facts' and 'archetypes' are indisputable. As Jung rightly stated, nobody can disprove my subjective certainty. And the experienced facts and archetypes are of course only private events and only of private interest. Whether I feel well and content is intellectually of absolutely no relevance. Yes, I may be subjectively certain of it, but it is fundamentally divorced from any question of truth. I do not have to struggle to show that what I am subjectively *certain* of is indeed also *true*, and see to it that what is *true* also becomes my personal certainty and, as such, my personal property, the actual logical constitution of my consciousness. And I cannot possibly do so. By contrast, theology and metaphysics, our whole Western tradition, had, in one way or another, always followed the maxim expressed by Anselm of Canterbury in the following way, "Neque enim quaero intelligere ut credam sed credo ut intelligam" ("For I do not seek to understand in order to believe, but I believe in order to understand").

After Heidegger published his *Being and Time*, some cynics poked fun at his stance by caricaturing it as: "I am terribly determined; I just don't know yet to what." A contentless determination, a determination reduced to its zero stage as the mere form of determination. In a similar way Jung's subjective certainty, his "I do not believe, I know," amounts to a knowledge reduced to its zero stage as a mere form of knowledge. "I am terribly certain, but *what* I am certain of I cannot present as a truth."[15] On principle not, because if Jung presented it as a truth, he would cease to be an empirical psychologist and turn, *horribile dictu*, into a metaphysician or a founder of a religion. If it is a question of subjective certainty, then anything goes, as long as it is *my experience* (from "the unconscious"). What Jung could at most show is that

---

[14] This, as Jung says, "banal" comparison is made by Jung elsewhere repeatedly, especially in connection with the certainty of "God." See for example *Letters 2*, pp. 252f. (to Snowdon, 7 May 1955), p. 250 (to Corti, 2 May 1955), p. 4 (to Boltze, 13 February 1951).

[15] I already stated that Jung's knowledge was essentially *speechless*.

his personal experience is "archetypal," that is, that it has historical parallels. But just as a thousand zeros do not add up to one, so a thousand certainties do not make a truth. And conversely, those historical parallels that Jung could refer to had in their own time precisely not been the mere certainties, personal experiences, empirical facts that they inevitably are for the archetypal psychologist, but truths. So Jung may have known, but, inasmuch as knowing is by definition the knowing of truths, *his* knowledge was a knowledge *of* nothing. Nihilism. A logical nihilism, though, behind the semantic screen of the whole wealth of traditional images, myths, fairy tales.

Ersatz

Jung's move is decidedly anti-philosophical. It not only led to his subjectively "feeling not able to participate anymore in the world of the intellect" (p. 193, transl. altered), but he had in fact also systematically cut himself off from it. From here we can also understand Jung's highly affective, complex-ridden, and absolutely misconceived attacks on Hegel and Heidegger, whom he apparently never really studied, but whose work seems to have made him instinctively sense that they posed a terrible threat to his standpoint of subjective certainty and immediacy. Be that as it may, the standpoint of subjective certainty and immediacy is, paradoxically, itself uncertain, inasmuch as it cannot show that it is true. Jung obviously felt this structural deficiency and tried to compensate for it in several ways.

First of all, he tried to justify his immediacy approach *epistemologically* with the help of Kant. Kant was not important to him (as one might think) because his philosophy convinced him. Nay, it was the other way around. Kant was convincing for him because he came as a godsend to Jung: his critique of reason seemed to Jung to give him (Jung) official *licence* to continue on his course of subjective immediate experience. What did he get out of Kant? That there was a fundamental barrier through the mental world that could not possibly be crossed by the rational mind, and that any attempt to cross it was absolutely illegitimate. The way of *truth*, of *logon didonai*, so it seemed, was once and for all closed, indeed prohibited. The mind simply had to turn back. Where to? To the subject, its immediate experience (cf., e.g., *CW* 18 § 1734).

Secondly, as far as the *methodological* stance of his psychology is concerned, he gave his psychology out as an empirical science. He insisted that all he was doing was *presenting* his findings, nothing but facts, in other words: presenting them to the public for examination. But the public did not see them as facts, probably because subjective certainties do not have the status of scientific facts. When there was an argumentative objection to his work, such as the one by Martin Buber, he claimed that those who presented the objections (1) did not understand that he was merely dealing with empirical material and (2) that the misunderstanding probably resulted from his critics' "having no psychiatric experience" (*CW* 18 § 1505). So he pleads that there is some esoteric or insider knowledge not publicly available. The problem with this argument, however, is that even most of those who as psychiatrists or practicing psychotherapists had this insider knowledge were not convinced either. The methodological description of his psychology of the unconscious as a science, which was to give his psychology the status of some objectivity, was itself merely a subjective assertion, and this is why Jung reacted highly emotionally when this assertion was not accepted.

Third, subjectively he felt that due to his systematic isolation he was on absolutely shaky ground. He feared to be "a mere curiosity, a sport [*lusus*] of cruel nature" (p. 87), to be "another such strange bird" like Nietzsche, "an eccentric, a sport of nature, which I did not want to be under any circumstances" (p. 102), to be like that Nietzsche who had "lost the ground under his feet" and was "a leaf whirling about in the winds of the spirit" (p. 189, transl. modified). To compensate this terrible isolation, not just an emotional, but a logical one, he sought consolation in such *historical* insights as the one that *Faust* was Goethe's equivalent of his own (Jung's) personality No. 2, which "gave me an increased feeling of inner security and a sense of belonging to the human community" (p. 87). He felt he had to understand "how my own experience coincided with that of mankind in general" (p. 176), "to undergo the original experience [*Urerfahrung*, i.e., the utterly subjective immediate experience], *and, moreover*, try to plant the results of my experience in the soil of reality; otherwise they would have remained subjective assumptions without validity" (p. 192, my italics). Above all, he needed to supply his psychology with, and base it upon, "a historical ground" (this phrase is omitted in *MDR* p. 205), place it in the "uninterrupted intellectual chain back to Gnosticism," which was to give it "substance" (*ibid.*), the substance that otherwise it would obviously lack. "In *Mysterium Coniunctionis* my psychology was at last given its place in reality and established upon its historical foundations" (p. 221). *Historical compensation* for the irrevocable logical isolation inevitably given with his standpoint of subjective certainty had, he felt, been achieved.

The epistemological, the methodological, and the historical modes of compensation concerned only the status of his psychology at large. Within this psychology, i.e., with respect to the specific contents of immediate experience, he tried to regain a sense of the very communality, too, that he had on principle grounds renounced (and along with it a kind of truth status). With much effort he therefore tried to prove that an irrevocably subjective and private experience is *in itself* objective, is part of the "collective" unconscious, of the *communis opinio*, leads the experiencing subject to archetypes, and possesses a special type of truth, namely, "psychological truth." But of course, a *semantic* communal aspect cannot really undo the *logical* (definitional) privacy of "emotional experiences whose nature is such that they cannot be a matter for discussion."

Since I am talking about compensation, I might just as well mention another form of it, although it does not compensate for logical solitude, but for the elimination of the process and "I" ("self") character of thinking in favor of the "it" form of dreams, visions, images, numinous experiences: after having passively had your experience, you are called upon to add your own active involvement, the activity of *understanding* the meaning of the experience and of being *ethically responsive* to it.

The thought of not-thinking

Jung's immediatistic position extends even to his understanding of what philosophy is. This comes out pretty well in a passing remark. "A man is a philosopher of genius only when he succeeds in transmuting the primitive and merely natural vision into an abstract idea and to a conscious property of the culture as a whole. This achievement, and this alone, constitutes his personal value, for which he may take credit without necessarily succumbing to inflation" (*CW* 7 § 229, transl.

modif.). Philosophy too, Jung suggests, starts out with a kind of immediate "original experience" (*Urerfahrung*), the primitive and merely natural vision, just like art begins for Jung with a "primordial urge" from the unconscious (see above his discussion of Picasso), but this is not yet philosophy. Philosophy proper begins when the philosopher "takes possession of"[16] the immediate vision and "expands it into a philosophical world view" of general value (the phrases in quotes come from the same text, in modified form). The vision "is simply a part of the common property of mankind, in which, in principle, everyone has a share" (*ibid.*). One is reminded of Jung's self-interpretation: "That was the primal stuff which compelled me to work upon it, and my works are a more or less successful endeavor to incorporate this incandescent matter into the contemporary picture of the world" (p. 199). The German edition continues with a sentence omitted in *MDR*: "The first imaginations and dreams were like fiery-liquid basalt; from them the stone crystallized that I could work" (*Erinnerungen* p. 203, my transl.).

In other words, *first* the immediate experience, *then* secondary elaboration by the conscious mind, each neatly on its own side. That great philosophical thinking is something very different, something that is not dissociated into, first, mindless experience as a purely natural event, and only then, conscious mental labor, but that real thought is experience and labor, passive and active, unconscious and conscious, all inextricably (uroborically) in one, the work of undissociated *homo totus*; that, furthermore, there *is* no literally immediate innocent experience in the first place, inasmuch as all experience, since it is human, conscious experience, *comes* as something already *produced* by the thinking mind (even if it is the experience of dreams or visions), this Jung was not permitted to imagine. The reason why is provided in our text about the 1887 episode, in which Jung had to resist *thinking* his own thought onwards, and instead to intercept it in order to "take possession" of it, not, however, for the purpose of painting a picture of the world of general interest, but, conversely, for the purpose of establishing for himself the principle of subjective certainty and immediacy and settling himself for life in the logical solitude that this

---

[16] Or "seiz[es] the unconscious urge," as Jung worded it in the passage from the letter about Picasso quoted above.

principle required. Only in this way could the principle of childhood innocence be *syntactically* preserved, even when *semantically* consciousness had to relentlessly concede that it had already arrived in the reflecting consciousness of modernity. And, conversely, only in this way could *semantically* the premodern contents of the mythological and metaphysical traditions be preserved, although *syntactically* only frozen into the abstract-semantic and untrue form[17] of uprooted (psychological) museum pieces: "archetypes of the collective unconscious."

The "psychology of the unconscious" *is in itself* anti-philosophy. That is to say, it is not merely "against" philosophy, does not merely reject it as something else outside. No, it is philosophy's own "reversal into the opposite." This is also why I stated that Jung was a true thinker (and did not merely have important, marvelous insights). His own life-work was, *malgré lui*, precisely not "first immediate experience, then secondary elaboration by the conscious mind." His experience was already in itself thought, and his intellectual labor (having been pushed down to the level of spontaneous happening and event) was experience, especially that of dreams. Jung himself knew that, "The fact that consciousness does not perform acts of thinking does not, however, prove that they do not exist. They merely occur unconsciously and make themselves felt indirectly in dreams, visions, revelations, and 'instinctive' changes of consciousness, from whose nature one can see that ... they are the result of unconscious acts of judgment or unconscious conclusions" (*CW* 11 § 638, transl. modif.). Whereas what he had in mind in this passage and context was acts of thinking that occur prior to consciousness's capability to perform them, it also applies to the situation of Jung himself when the capacity of consciousness to think those thoughts by itself was already given. Jung's life-work is, contrary to his dissociating self-interpretation, the work of *homo totus*. However, *that which* he indeed thought in developing his psychology was the thought of the unconscious, the thought of not-thinking—of the *Unbewußtwerden des Bewußtseins* ("consciousness's becoming unconscious," *CW* 12 § 563, transl. modif.).[18] "Don't think,

---

[17] We already know that as long as an experience is archetypal, "anything goes": any particular archetypal image is as good as any other. There is no criterion of truth.

[18] The concept of "*the* unconscious" is the objectification of the *program* of consciousness's unconsciousness.

just don't think!" that's all there is to it. But because he thought *this* thought with total commitment, he—and his psychology (which is the unfolding of this thought)—had to be totally unconscious of it. Jung's "flight into the unconscious" was *one* of the many different ways in which the nineteenth- and early twentieth-century thinkers tried to hold on to or regain a sense of wholeness and natural origin even after consciousness had, as they keenly felt, entered its stage of absolute negativity and alienation.

CHAPTER THREE

The Disenchantment Complex
C.G. Jung and the modern world[1]

T he phrase "disenchantment of the world" has in recent years
had a remarkable career in the English-speaking world, a career
that removed it somewhat from the meaning which
"Entzauberung der Welt" had in Max Weber's thinking.[2] Weber's sober
scholarly and strictly descriptive term referred to the historical facts

---

[1] A slightly shorter version was presented as an invited lecture at the First Regional
Conference of the International Association for Jungian Studies in London, July 15th
2011.
[2] See Hartmut Lehmann, "The Interplay of Disenchantment and Re-enchantment
in Modern European History: or, the Origin and the Meaning of Max Weber's Phrase
'Die Entzauberung der Welt,'" in: *idem, Die Entzauberung der Welt. Studien zu Themen
von Max Weber*, Göttingen (Wallstein) 2009, pp. 9–20. By 1917, Lehmann shows,
"Entzauberung der Welt" had become a key metaphor in Weber's thinking about
historical development and the relation of religion and modernity. Scholars have
not been able to find occurrences of this phrase in the works of Weber's
contemporaries nor in literary or scholarly works prior to 1913, when Weber used
it the first time. It may have been his own invention. In the light of the popularity
of "disenchantment" as the current English translation of it, it is most interesting
to observe that in the translations of Weber's works into English Weber's
"Entzauberung" had prior to 1958 not been translated by "disenchantment" at all.
Where Weber has "Entzauberung der Welt" in his German (revised) version of *The
Protestant Ethic and the Spirit of Capitalism*, the translation by Talcott Parsons of
1930, quite in keeping with what is meant by Weber, speaks of "the elimination of
magic from the world," or "the elimination of magic as a means to salvation," and the
new translation of the same work by Stephen Kalberg of the year 2002 avoids the term
"disenchantment," just as Talcott Parson did. Probably because "disenchantment" tends
to be misleading, coming as it does with different overtones and associations. Also, an
equivalent to the English complementary term to disenchantment, namely the term
(and idea) of a "re-enchantment," cannot be found in Weber's work.

of the elimination of the use of sacramental magic as a means to salvation as well as of the disappearance of the belief that mysterious, irrational powers could at any moment influence what happens in the world. The modern situation is characterized by the knowledge or the belief that there are on principle no mysterious powers that could interfere with the course of events. The nature of the world is such that everything must be capable of being subject to a rational explanation, and this explanation can on principle, if not always in practice, be found out. In other words, Weber is not talking about a mysterious spiritual character of the world at all, but about concrete empirical phenomena, about real practices, mental stances, and people's concern for the salvation of their soul. His is, we could say, a disenchanted concept of disenchantment. By contrast, the recent interest in the topic of disenchantment and re-enchantment is no longer descriptive of an objective process. Rather, it seems to be fired by a subjective emotional condition, by a longing for a world that, with sweet Sirenic song, could be immediately felt to be enchanting and embracing us, by people's dream of a sympathetic oneness or *participation mystique* with the world, or conversely, by the disappointing feeling of alienation from the world, the fact that such a sympathetic oneness is sorely missed. In other words, now it is expressive of what Freud discussed under the title of the *Unbehagen in der Kultur, Civilization and Its Discontents*.

1

As a psychologist it is not my job to contribute personal opinions to the ongoing speculations about a re-enchantment of the world. As a psychologist my task is much rather to listen and attend to what the soul has said, not to speak myself. I have to rely on what has already shown itself of its own accord, to rely on, as it were, "documents of the soul." Now it so happens that we are fortunate enough to possess within the corpus of Jungian writings a report about a particular spontaneous experience that can be considered as the *locus classicus* about the enchantment/disenchantment issue in Jungian psychology,[3] although to my knowledge Jung never himself used these terms.[4] It is a report by Jung himself about something that happened to him very early in his youth, during his twelfth year. Jung tells us in *Memories, Dreams, Reflections*:

> One fine summer day that same year [1887] I came out of school at noon and went to the cathedral square. The sky was gloriously blue, the day one of radiant sunshine. The roof of the cathedral glittered, the sun sparkling from the new, brightly glazed tiles. I was overwhelmed by the beauty of the sight, and thought: "The world is beautiful and the church is beautiful, and God made all this and sits above it far away in the blue sky on a golden throne ..."

We could hardly imagine a more perfect expression, even if in rather childlike terms, of the experience of the world as enchanted. It is noontime, the pinnacle of the day, when the sun is in the zenith and time seems to stand still, a moment of fulfillment. We may even think here of Nietzsche's high noon. In this moment, the boy Jung felt and celebrated his perfect oneness with the world, his almost uterine containment in it. It is the experience of the bliss of being. The boy Jung is not only overwhelmed by the beauty of the world in a secular aesthetic sense. The beauty here is not merely one of attractive looks. The experienced glory, the sparkling shine is here much rather a *manifestation* in the full sense of the word, the shining forth of the divine ground of the world. The world is beautiful

---

[3] In other words, whereas I said that the idea of the disenchantment of the world had a remarkable career in the English-speaking world that removed it from Weber's sense of the term, I now have to add that there was much earlier already, namely in Jung, a quite independent analogue to this more recent *desire-driven* interest in disenchantment and re-enchantment in the English-speaking world and accordingly, quite different from Weber, an analogue to the understanding of "enchantment" as an *objective* mysterious-spiritual character of the *world*.

[4] But he does describe this phenomenon and in his wording comes pretty close to these terms: "For the first time since the dawn of history we have succeeded in swallowing the whole of primordial animatedness of nature into ourselves. Not only did the gods step, or rather were they dragged, down from their heavenly planetary houses and, to begin with, transformed into chthonic demons, but ... even this host of demons, which at the time of Paracelsus still frolicked happily in mountains and woods, in rivers and human dwelling-places, was reduced to a miserable remnant and finally vanished altogether. From time immemorial, nature was always filled with spirit. Now, for the first time, we are living in a nature bereft of soul and gods [*entseelten und entgötterten Natur*]." (*CW* 10 § 431, transl. modif.).

because it is, as it were, the visible garment of God who is, himself not visible, sitting high above on his golden throne. God and world, transcendence and immanence as well as man and nature, subject and object, are perfectly at one.

But what we heard so far is only the first half of Jung's experience. There is a second half. Jung described what happened next within this spontaneous fantasy of his.

> I saw before me the cathedral, the blue sky. God sits on His golden throne, high above the world—and from under the throne an enormous turd falls upon the sparkling new roof, shatters it, and breaks the walls of the cathedral asunder.

Clearly, this is an experience of disenchantment. The initial experience of the absolute beauty of the world and of the blissful harmony between the I and the world is cruelly smashed. The disenchantment is absolute, because it is not some contingent mishap that destroys the enchanted world, nor the result of the doings of an external evil force. It is neither the devil that destroys the cathedral, nor is the destruction the work of innerworldly terrorists like those who smashed the New York Twin Towers. If that had been the case, the *principle* of the enchanted world would have been preserved intact, although the factual reality of the enchanted world would admittedly have been destroyed. The destruction of the empirical realization of an ideal does not undo the ideal itself. The belief in the ideal survives the loss of its representation in reality and thus sustains the prevailing structure of consciousness.

But here the destruction is inherent in this story's own logic or teleology. Jung's thought experience is from the outset heading for the event of the brutal undoing of the enchanted world. This, the experience of radical disenchantment, is what it is all about. The rude disenchantment happens in this fantasy entirely from within the very core of the enchanted world itself, as its own self-sublation. For it is the divine ground of the world itself that is the cause of the destruction of its beauty. God himself, the ultimate creator and guarantor of the world as an enchanted one, is the source of that bomb that shatters the cathedral, which is, after all, the earthly symbol of his divine presence in the world.

Furthermore, God does not, like Zeus, throw a thunderbolt in order to destroy the cathedral. A thunderbolt would be in tune with and confirm God's majesty. Nor does he, as an angry God, send a Flood or the Plague to punish a sinful world. This would have been in accordance with the medieval idea that the Creation has been perverted through human sin. If under this presupposition God would destroy the world by way of punishment, he in his supreme majesty would stay intact. But in Jung's fantasy experience, God smashes the cathedral in an absolutely undignified, vulgar, and disgusting way by shitting on it. This means that it is not merely the physical church that is shattered in this story. Also the dignity of the church as the house of God and the house of our human belief in him is befouled and thus cut to the quick. But more than that. This act of God's has of course repercussions for the very idea of God. If God in this fantasy is no longer sitting on his golden throne but on a toilet and reveals himself as a shitting God, then the God idea itself is totally deprived of its former majesty. God is ridiculed. His reputation as a God to be worshiped is wrecked. And thus, what happens here is that the very concept of God is objectively ruined. The disenchantment is total, because nothing is left. The driving force of this fantasy has gone all the way through to its bitter end, because it ruined the very *principle* of a possible enchantment of the world.

This, the experience of the radical disenchantment of the world, is not Jung's subjective opinion. *He* did not all of a sudden as a rebellious youngster want to distance himself with critical and even sacrilegious thoughts of his own from the highest values and religious conceptions of his forebears. The fantasy was by no means ego-syntonic. It was absolutely unwanted, indeed painful. Jung even felt that it was cruelly forced on him against his will. We have to conclude that this fantasy was the objective soul's own doing. The soul insisted on Jung's having the unrelenting experience of disenchantment.

This disenchantment is Jung's primordial experience. It comes from his personal inner necessity. And it expresses his very own truth. It is C.G. Jung's root experience. We have to attribute singular significance to this experience as a true starting point, a true *initium*— because it is really Jung's *initiation experience*. Everything else that came before does not count because it belongs to the child Jung, not to that Jung who was to become the man and the author of Jungian psychology. The disenchantment happened in Jung's twelfth year, a year of which he himself said that it proved to be the actual turning-point of his fate.[5] It was the year in which his childhood was irrevocably concluded and he awakened as an I, a conscious and willing subject. He described it as follows.

> Once there was a moment when I had the overwhelming feeling of having just stepped out of a dense fog, with the conscious awareness: now *I* am. At my back it was as if there was a wall of fog behind which I had not yet been. But at this moment, I *happened to myself.* Previously I had existed, too, but everything had merely taken place. Now I knew: now *I* am, now *I* exist. Previously things went on with me, but now *I* willed (*MDR* p. 32f., transl. modif.).

We could say that before, as a child, Jung had been completely contained in the course of events and all the things in the world. He was only one element within the continuum of what passed. But now, as an I, he had come out of this containment and had acquired a separate existence vis-à-vis the world as a persistent center of experience all of his own. In 1887 he had arrived at the threshold to adulthood.[6] Interestingly enough, the awakening of his I as conscious subject coincided, as Jung himself felt necessary to stress, with a total amnesia (*MDR* p. 33) concerning his secret treasure box containing a "carved manikin" that had been extremely important before as the highest symbol of his childhood existence (p. 22). It seems that the awakened I and the manikin exclude each other. A wall lies between childhood, on the one hand, and adolescence and manhood, on the other hand. The adolescent cannot remember what the child experienced: because a dense fog behind his back blocks the view. This is why I could say that everything else that came before these experiences of this year does not count because it belongs to the *child* Jung.

---

[5] "... wurde für mich zum eigentlichen Schicksalsjahr," *Erinnerungen* p. 36, cf. *MDR* p. 30.

[6] As an old man Jung viewed this time even as the beginning of his life's work: "I myself am in the grip of the same dream [as Goethe was with his *Faust*] and have a main Work, which began in my eleventh year. My life has been permeated and comprised by one Work and one goal ..." (*MDR* p. 206, transl. modif.). I suspect that with his referring to this year as the "eleventh" year he is pointing to the same year, 1887, that in the other passages he calls his twelfth year—one time viewing it as the year in which he was eleven years old (the eleventh year of his life having been completed) while the other time describing it as the twelfth year of his life, the year in which he was on the way to his twelfth birthday.

The emergence of the conscious sense of I was only the general formal precondition of adult existence. Jung's *specific initiation* into his adulthood, however, in the sense of his being introduced into a new knowing and into a new basic redefinition of his position in and towards the world happened in his Basel cathedral experience, and it was an initiation into disenchantment. Already the puberty initiations in early traditional societies included as one essential ingredient a moment of disillusionment. For example, whereas in certain tribes the women and children as the audience of the dances of the masks were only exposed to the mysterious, uncanny impressions created by the masks so as to be enchanted, that is, allured into the belief that the dancing masks were the literal presence of the spirits, the initiands were explicitly undeceived and initiated into the knowledge that the masks were made by members of the men's secret society and which members, well-known to them from everyday life, were the human, all-too-human bearers of the masks.

2

However, in traditional societies of old *this* personal disenchantment of the initiands did by no means altogether dethrone the mythic or metaphysical dimension as the cultural truth of these societies. The reality of the spirits and gods remained unquestioned. We often think that the point of initiations had been to *open* the mind of the individual to the transcendent, to the revelation of the sacred. But this view is expressive of the prejudice of a post-Enlightenment, godless world. In early cultures you did not have to open the mind to spiritual values; the gate to the sacred had been open from the outset. Children were born into this openness. Gods and spirits were a matter of course and unquestioned. The real purpose of initiations was precisely the opposite, to open the mind of the youngster for the first time to empirical reality and ground it in the earth. Initiations performed a downwards move, not an upwards move. Their purpose was the transportation from a childhood stance into that of the adult man. The child is characterized by the fact that *psychologically* it lives in cloud-cuckoo-land, in the innocence of a seamless transition from reality to fantasy. In the initiations this childlike innocence and harmlessness had to be destroyed. An essential part of the initiations was therefore the infliction of pain and wounding,[7] not only physical wounding through scarification, circumcision, mutilation of teeth, lips, ears, the subjection to trials, etc., but also logical, mental wounding, through the kind of "disenchantment" already mentioned and exposure to radical loneliness.

Now it goes without saying that these initiations were *also* supposed to lead to experiences of transcendence. However, their point was by no means to make the mind open to the transcendent, which for the child had, after all, been open all along, but conversely to *ground* spiritual experience in empirical reality, to *root* it, as it were, in the *flesh* of the initiand, and to give it binding reality. In contrast to a child's indiscriminate openness to and impressibility by whatever experiences, now this and now that, initiation brought precisely the end of this noncommittal openness and made the initiand irrevocably tie himself to one specific religious experience, *his* one experience, for the rest of his life, and *ipso facto* conversely pin the transcendent to this earth, that transcendent which for the child had been free-floating. At the same time this one experience of the initiand's, or the this-ness of this one experience, established his firm identity, because he once and for all staked his whole being on it as his exclusive basis. His particular religious experience claimed him for itself, and he conversely appropriated it as *his* possession.

What this means is that in his initiation the initiand personally acquired the logical strength to hold the opposites together. This is what the child could not and did not have to perform. On the logical level, the child lives in the *unio naturalis*, in the primary oneness, mythologically speaking in paradise or in heaven. With Paul Tillich we could also say: contained in dreaming innocence. There are no opposites for it yet. For it, there is only the One. For the man, by contrast, One has turned into Two.[8] A fundamental rupture has happened. The boy has been shocked out of innocence, out of the state

---

[7] All this is cruel treatment that for a certain modern psychotherapeutic thinking would be considered as a natural cause of possible "traumatizations."

[8] As Jung said, "one is not a number at all; the first number is two. Two is the first number because, with it, separation and increase begin, which alone make counting possible." "Two implies a 'one' [*eine Eins*] which is different from the uncountable One [*das Eine*]. For as soon as the Two appears, a unit is produced out of the original unity, and this unit is none other than that same unity reduced by the splitting and turned into a 'number'" (*CW* 11 § 180, transl. modif.).—When I say that for the child there is only the One, it must be kept in mind that I am making *psychological* statements and view things from the point of view of soul. Empirically, *psychically*, the child lives of course

of dreaming, out of existence in fantasy, and with a rude awakening forced into an awareness of the earth in its relentless empirical reality and in its fundamental difference from fantasy. The opposites have come into existence for him. And thus *he* is called upon to himself logically *produce* a new oneness, a oneness that, as produced, is fundamentally different from the child's oneness, which was a given and the child's unsurpassable horizon. The man is called upon to master the task of the *coniunctio oppositorum*. He must have acquired the capability of logically *really* conjoining Heaven and Earth, God and the natural world, and this could of course only be a conjoining of them in his very person and in his real being-in-the-world. Thus he had to exist as the embodied copula, or rather as the ongoing performance of the logical act of the copula. For the person who had gone through his initiation, the sober, disillusioned, absolutely realistic appreciation of the empirical world with its unforgiving realness went together with the deep relation to the transcendent. This is what the puberty initiations in early cultures had to achieve.

During all ages, puberty initiations were at one and the same time initiations into personal adulthood AND into the particular form of adulthood corresponding to the culture and spirit of the time. In traditional cultures disenchantment was needed only on the level of personal adulthood, whereas cultural adulthood supported the unquestioned reality of gods and spirits. And so the initiations had two parts, the negative element of disenchantment and pain and the positive element of a spiritual experience. The boy Jung, however, grew up during the last quarter of the 19th century, that is, in the middle of Industrial Modernity. And this was a time that had even on the level of the objective psyche once and for all abolished the entire metaphysical dimension and its highest principle, God. And so the formerly two parts of the initiation converged, came home to each

already with many opposites and possible conflicts (desire and prohibition, eating the cake or still preserving it, grandiosity and failure, selfishness or generosity, etc.). But what one has to understand is that psychology is not concerned with the manifold of possible concrete opposites in empirical-practical life, that is, in the experiential sphere of the ego and on the semantic level. It is concerned with *the* One and *the* Two quite abstractly, with *the* "psychic opposites" as such, without any semantic concretization. The question is: has for the child what we might call "the world," the whole, the *logic* of consciousness suffered a division or is there still the logic of a primary unbroken unity for it. It is a syntactical question, not a question on the level of the contents of consciousness or the contents of experience.

other. The positive element, the spiritual experience of God, had in itself become negated, an experience of disenchantment.

In addition, initiations were no longer cultural institutions. If there was to be an explicit initiation at all, then it had to happen as a private spontaneous inner experience, as in the case of Jung.[9] Because of the character of his time, it had to ruthlessly undeceive the innocently believing boy Jung, initiating him through an absolute disenchantment into the cultural truth of the age so that in addition to his entering his personal adulthood he might also become a truly *modern* adult. His own soul forced the awareness on him that God was a thing of the past and irrevocably gone. The belief in the enchanted world, which stands or falls with the existence of God as its ground, has its place, we could say, only behind that wall of fog which Jung felt lay behind his back and cut him off from his childhood.

But does this episode not precisely itself evoke the full experience of the enchanted world? The blissful image of the enchanted world occurs, after all, precisely in the present, on this side of the wall of fog that separates him from his childhood. This observation makes it necessary for us to look into the relation of enchantment and disenchantment.

3

At first sight, enchantment and disenchantment seem to refer to two different world conditions separated by a historical gulf. In Jung's experience, too, the intact beauty of the cathedral is an initial state, and the shattered cathedral comes thereafter as a second, separate situation. But this is only how it appears. In reality, enchantment and disenchantment, though by no means alike, are nevertheless the same. They are equiprimordial. Within their equiprimordiality the seemingly later disenchantment is even logically prior to the enchantment. Before, I mentioned that with the transition from childhood to manhood, One turned into Two. The opposites, enchantment and disenchantment, are simply a manifestation of the

---

[9] Ordinarily there is today no explicit, spectacular initiation at all. When the development happens to be "normal," people simply seem to absorb osmotically the truth of the age.

Two. It is by no means that the enchanted world represents the One while disenchantment represents the Two. Here we are put in mind of Jung's already quoted view that "Two implies a 'one' [*eine Eins*] which is different from the uncountable One [*das Eine*]. For as soon as the Two appears, a unit is produced out of the original unity, and this unit is none other than that same unity reduced by the splitting and turned into a 'number.'" Because it has been split into two, the true One, which is not a number, is now absolutely inaccessible and undescribable. It lies invisibly behind Jung's wall of fog behind his back, and it is invisible because it has precisely fallen apart into two, into the opposition of disenchantment and enchantment. Disenchantment *is* the Two, and as the Two, i.e., as the dissociated One, it is in itself the identity of the identity and difference of enchantment and disenchantment. That is to say, the state of disenchantment *is* the contradiction between itself and its opposite. Thus it is a serious mistake to confuse the enchantment, one of the two dissociated decomposition products of the One, with the One and to retroject it, like certain Romantics did, into the past as a literal world condition or even to succumb to the temptation of setting it up as quasi metaphysical Origin, an *archê* (or, a third possibility, to project it conversely as a utopian scheme of an "ideal society" into the future).

That "[t]he world is beautiful and the church is beautiful, and God made all this and sits above it far away in the blue sky on a golden throne ..." is already the experience of a mind that has left the child's mind behind. The whole chapter of his childhood is already closed. Jung's overwhelming feeling of beauty is the expression of the standpoint of reflection. It is, in Schiller's sense, "sentimental," not "naive." The child Jung could not possibly have spoken thus. No child could. Because the child, as child, is still completely contained in the primordial unity, in the course of events, and, as Jung himself put it, as a child *he* "had not yet been." The I has to have been born and have logically taken a distanced position vis-à-vis the world as a whole in order to become open to the aesthetic beauty of the world. Conscious awareness and appreciation of the beauty of the world presupposes a high degree of separation and dissociation from the world. It is incompatible with the naive experience of the world, with the experience of pre-industrial man working the land as a peasant or working with the things of nature as a craftsman within the context of an agricultural society. It is precisely and only the already disenchanted world that can, under certain circumstances, be experienced as beautiful and enchanted. Enchantment is the product of disenchantment.

One can see this very nicely in Petrarch's description of his ascent of Mont Ventoux on April 26, 1336, which has been shown to be maybe the first example in history that displays a strikingly "modern" attitude of aesthetic gratification in the grandeur of scenery. The precondition for this type of experience was the logical separation of scenery from the realm of work and practice, which is, by the way, analogous to Aristotle's observation about the beginning of philosophy, namely that it presupposed leisure and a state in which the dire necessities of life have already been taken care of.[10] Petrarch climbed Mount Ventoux for pleasure alone, which was absolutely revolutionary.

We need to understand that there never existed in actuality a time of an enchanted world, just as there never was an actual time in history when paradise existed.[11] That One that was said to have turned into Two has itself never been an empirical fact and historical reality. It is not the initial state, the primordial origin. It is a product of reflection. The human world *begins* with the Two with nothing behind it. Just as paradise is a fantasy emerging in a mankind that had always lived in a world of labor, pain, and death, so the ideas of the One and the enchanted world are notions within the disenchanted mind and themselves an unmistakable expression of disenchantment, notions that are necessary because only through the idea or feeling of enchantment can disenchantment become articulated and thus become aware of itself. Disenchantment is the unity of itself and its opposite. So in contrast to appearances, Jung's initial celebration of the divine beauty of the world, too, is from the outset already an expression of his disenchantment, and what happens afterwards in his fantasy experience is only the self-unfolding of its inner

---

[10] Aristotle, *Met.* I, 2, 982 b.

[11] Or, if we were to insist on thinking that there was a time of paradise or the One in actual reality, then the condition of its possibility was that it was a time when, to use Jung's phrase in a generalized eminent sense, "I—i.e., human experience—had not yet been." But this paradoxically only returns us to the former insight that there never was an actual time in history (historical memory) when paradise existed.

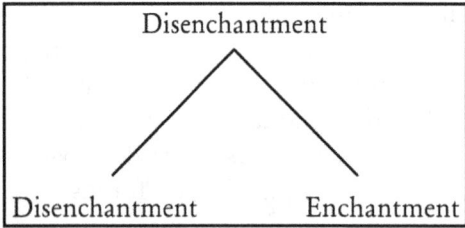

Disenchantment

Disenchantment   Enchantment

Figure 1.

telos and the coming to light of its inner truth. What for the experiencing I is a shocking and totally unexpected new development, is for the soul only the revelation of the truth of the initial image. Because we are here in the world of the Two or of the opposites, the enchanted world's own *inner truth* is the disenchantment.

4

I concentrated so far on Jung's spontaneous experience, but omitted the fact that he disrupted his fantasy in the middle by a long interlude. Jung as ego deliberately stops short the flow of the fantasy after the blissful image. The reason for this interference is ego resistance. Jung said to himself: "Don't go on thinking now! Something terrible is coming, something I do not want to think, something I dare not even approach." "Don't think of it, just don't think of it!" For three long days and nights Jung managed to delay the continuation of his fantasy by devoting himself to his own reflections *about* it. But within him his fantasy kept forcefully insisting on being concluded. The inner pressure grew stronger and stronger. I quote: "On the third night, however, the torment became so unbearable that I no longer knew what to do. I awoke from a restless sleep just in time to catch myself thinking again about the cathedral and God. I had almost continued the thought! I felt my resistance weakening. Sweating with fear, I sat up in bed to shake off sleep. 'Now it is coming, now it's serious! *I must think.* It must be thought out beforehand.'"

Not it, the spontaneous fantasy, must think itself out. No, I, C.G. Jung, i.e., the ego, must think it out beforehand. In other words, he wanted to prevent himself or his consciousness from being *exposed* to the outcome of his thought experience, whatever it might be. "It must be thought out beforehand" means that before the fantasy has come to its own end Jung wanted to prejudge what it means.

When we compare the direction of his subjective ego reflections with the telos of his fantasy itself, we see that his reflections, with a *petitio principii*, try in advance to undo what the content of his initiation experience wants to impress on him. His ego reflections perform in advance what psychoanalysis calls a reversal into the opposite. Whereas it is the telos of his fantasy to dethrone God, his own reflections cement the idea of God. This is already apparent from the main tool used to give a seeming justification for his egoic disruption of his initiation fantasy, namely, the idea that continuing his thought would amount to his "committing the most frightful of sins." Inasmuch as the idea of sin depends on the reality of God, Jung by using it sets up in advance an unshakeable bulwark against the black tide of the disenchanting tendency of his thought.

Secondly, Jung raises the question—"Who wants to force me to think something I don't know and don't want to know? Where does this terrible will come from?"[12]—and his answer is that it is God's terrible will to make him think a sinful thought in order to test his obedience. Again, that very God that his spontaneous fantasy wants to destroy is claimed to be the hidden author of his fantasy. God is thus a priori immunized against whatever the content of his thought might bring. And, on top of it, Jung's setting up God as a *terrible* will, cements *emotionally* the absolutely unquestionable reality of God. In your fear you are of course absolutely convinced of the existence of what you fear.

The answer to his question would of course be very simple: *nobody* wants to force him to think something he does not know. Rather, this is his own thought which comes out of his own inner necessity to grow up. He himself, or the soul in him, his very own soul, is the thinker of his thought. Jung's question is as reasonable as would be the question of a bud, "which terrible will forces me against my own will to burst open into a blooming flower?" or the question of a young girl, "who is it who forces me to grow breasts?"[13]

---

[12] The idea contained in this sentence displays beautifully the dissociation from his own thought practiced by Jung. I discussed this topic more thoroughly in "Psychology as Anti-Philosophy," see Chapter Two above.

[13] Or, another example closer to home: Is there a mysterious Other who forces me to realize that my parents are not all-knowing and perfect, as I had assumed as a little child? And is my being forced to realize this something that is done to me with utmost cruelty? Is it not much rather my own seeing-through, my own better insight, my own awakening from a childish dream? Throughout life, disillusionment is an essential part of a person's own normal psychic development, of getting a bit wiser. It is called *learning*. To develop means to learn something "I don't know and—perhaps—don't want to know": namely I don't want (would not like) to know it because it is perhaps a narcissistic insult

Jung's reaction is a disownment of *his* truth and, as such a *dis-ownment, neurotic.*[14]

Thirdly, because Jung managed, through his manipulating reflections, to invalidate in advance the very point that his fantasy wanted to make, it is small wonder that the result for him of this whole experience was likewise the direct opposite of the message contained in his experience. He says: "Suddenly I understood that God was, for me at least, one of the most certain and immediate of experiences. After all, I didn't invent that horrible image about the cathedral. On the contrary, it was forced on me and I was compelled, with the utmost cruelty, to think it ..." (pp. 61f.) We already know that this is the same "utmost cruelty" with which a bud is compelled to open up into a flower or a girl is forced to grow breasts.

to my ego or my ideals, or some other painful disappointment or something that requires a leave-taking. But quite apart from this possible ego unwillingness, ultimately *I* as a matter of course *nevertheless do want to* know what "I don't know and what in an ego sense I perhaps don't want to know." It is *my own* will and need to learn to see things the way they are. It is in my own interest. Nobody needs to force me. Jung's dissociation in this instance lies in the fact that he totally severs the dialectical unity of *my really* wanting what I (insofar as I am ego) maybe don't want. This dissociation is paradigmatic. It underlies the split in psychological theory between the ego and the unconscious. Otherness instead of self-relation. Do I doubt that when I have a nightmarish dream that this is really my own dream thought and that it shows something about my soul situation? Do I ask: "Who forces me with utmost cruelty to experience this terrible dream?" as if it had nothing to do with me and my very own reality at the time?

[14] After having reported in *MDR* pp. 30–32 the episode of his fainting spells whenever he was supposed to go to school or to do homework during the same "fateful year," 1887, Jung added: "Through this I learned what a neurosis is" (p. 32, transl. modif.). He could have learned this lesson just as much or even more so from the Basel cathedral episode. But he construed the latter on the contrary as an authentic religious experience, and even in old age, at the time of writing down those memories, he held on to that neurotic interpretation of a neurotic thought experience instead of seeing through it. About the former episode of his fainting spells Jung said *ibid.*: "The neurosis became another of my secrets, but it was a shameful secret ...." I ask: was his claim that in the Basel cathedral experience he had experienced God as the most certain and immediate of experiences in any way a less shameful secret? His fainting spells concerned, after all, no more than a game that he played in the area of his private, egoic interests and in the sphere of practical everyday *behavior*. In this psychologically irrelevant area Jung was quite willing to acknowledge the shamefully neurotic quality of those fits. On this external, merely psychic level it posed no difficulty for him to give up the child's pleasure principle and to accept and submit to the fact that as an adult one has to *work* ("This was the collision with reality. 'Oh, I see, here you have to work!'" p. 31, transl. modif.). But in the truly *psychological* sphere, namely when it was a matter of essential (i.e., religious or metaphysical) regards, he played by entirely different rules of the game. Here it seemed to him more precious to hold on to the *child's* highest principle and his own subjective preferences than to be honest: true to his own truth, his own real thought experience (which came from the objective psyche and corresponded to the truth of modern adulthood).

And conversely, we have to contradict Jung's claim that "I never engendered any idea of God.... In fact it was not an idea at all—that is, not something thought out. It was not like imagining something and thinking it out and afterward believing it." For we have *witnessed* his engendering this his idea of God as the *author* of his thought through his ego reflections ("*I must think.* It must be thought out beforehand"), as well as witnessed his engendering the idea of the danger of committing the most frightful of sins. All this is not in his spontaneous experience; it is his doing, his concoctions, with which he not only interrupted, but also escaped from, his own initiation experience. An absolute reversal: he declares the content of his own ego reflections to be the most certain and immediate of experiences, whereas his *really* immediate and spontaneous experience is reduced to a mere test imposed on Jung by God, similarly to how in the Old Testament Isaac's sacrifice was changed to a mere test, so that this his spontaneous experience no longer needed to be taken seriously in its own right, in *what* it says. What it presents is the ruin of the enchanted world and the ruin of the concept of God, and thus a fundamental disappointment, disillusionment.

Jung, by contrast, created a wholly other result for himself of this experience: "I felt an enormous, an indescribable relief. Instead of the expected damnation, grace had come upon me, and with it an unutterable bliss such as I had never known. I wept for happiness and gratitude. The wisdom and goodness of God had been revealed to me now that I had yielded to His inexorable command. It was as though I had experienced an illumination." This is *quod NON erat demonstrandum*. With both the fear of damnation and the feeling of grace Jung egocentrically circled around himself and deliberately missed what his spontaneous experience was really about, namely, that it wanted to inflict something on him, disenchant, disillusion him, and to transport his consciousness from the status of the child to that of the man. Not obedience and the will, but initiation, that is, insight and truth, were at stake.[15] Both damnation and salvation, the way they

---

[15] Of course, in a very difference sense *obedience* is very much at stake, too, namely an obedience or faithfulness to what in fact has been experienced. Jung's obedience to what he thought was God's will, i.e., to an *external* authority, is his *dis*obedience to what his soul, as his real authority, said. The German word for obedience, *Gehorsam*, refers to *hören* (hear, listen to).

are used by Jung, are elements within his ego-trip, instigated for the purpose of escaping his initiation into manhood. And they reflect the concern of the—in a psychological, not literal sense—childish mind, its still being dominated by wishful thinking.

Concerning "eternal damnation" we can say that what in fact is a logical necessity, a soul necessity, Jung pushed down to the ego's emotional level. For a psychological understanding the idea of eternal damnation must not be taken literally, as a truly religious fear, but as a symbolic expression. In the boy Jung this idea is the guise (or one possible form) in which during a Christian age the eternal task of the transition from childhood to adulthood is performed, namely the irrevocable death of "the child." In ancient puberty initiations, this death was ritually enacted on a sensual level. This is no longer possible on the level of consciousness reached by the Christian soul,[16] let alone on the level of the truly modern soul during the age of Industrial Modernity and its positivism. Under these newer conditions, what used to be a sensual ritual enactment has to happen as a noetic, inwardized process, a logical act, for example, in the form of the imagination and feeling of "eternal damnation." What his Basel cathedral thought experience actually demanded of Jung was precisely to *commit* that "deadly sin" and to risk *eternal damnation*, because the latter is, as it were, in this context the only entrance gate and entrance ticket to true adulthood, adulthood in a psychological, not merely psychic sense. Psychological adulthood cannot be had for less. The innocence and bliss of being in childhood paradise or cloud-cuckoo-land and along with it the naive, unbroken unity with oneself[17] has to be, as it were, "sent to hell" and subjected to "eternal damnation": with no return. This is, for example, why Luther, in whom the process of the transition from *cultural* innocence to *cultural* adulthood happened, realized that he needed to *se resignare ad infernum*: to without grudge resign himself to possibly ending up in hell. "Eternal damnation" is in this context nothing else but the expression for the absolutely relentless falling apart of the One into Two.

---

[16] See my "The Rescued Child, or The Misappropriation of Time: On the Search for Meaning," Chapter One of vol. III (*Soul-Violence*) of my *Collected English Papers*, New Orleans (Spring Journal Books) 2008, pp. 45–75.

[17] In-nocence!

But this (his irrevocably committing childhood to "damnation"
and thus his without reserve dying the death of the child) was, it
seems, out of the question for the boy Jung, just as it was for Jung
in his old age while writing this section of his memories. This is
why the boy Jung said to himself: "Don't go on thinking now!
Something terrible is coming ..." "Don't think of it, just don't think
of it!" In answer to this desperate refusal to go on thinking, a
statement by Wittgenstein from an entirely different context and
referring to a different issue comes to mind that *mutatis mutandis*
points in the right direction. Relying on St. Augustine (cf. *Vae
tacentibus de te*, "Woe unto them who remain silent about you [i.e.,
God]..."), Wittgenstein once said apropos a discussion of
Heidegger's *Sein und Zeit*, "Already St. Augustine knew this when
he says: What, you bastard, you want not to talk nonsense? Just go
ahead, and talk nonsense, it does not matter."[18] Adapting this
to our topic and removing it from Wittgenstein's sense-nonsense
issue to Jung's focus on sin and damnation versus logical
innocence we could say to the boy Jung, "What, you bastard,
you want not to think of it? Just go ahead and think of it; it
does not matter that you thereby commit a deadly sin. In fact,
woe unto you if you don't." The unutterable bliss that for Jung
was the end result of his experience shows that *psychologically*
(not psychically) there was no Paradise Lost for him, also not a
Paradise Regain'd, but rather—*against* his own already
experienced truth—the *denial* of the loss of paradise. In less
mythological terms this means: What Jung on principle excluded
was *Negation*, the looking the negative in the face and tarrying with
it. Jung insisted on positivity and immediacy.

---

[18] *Wittgenstein und der Wiener Kreis*, Werkausgabe vol. 3, Gespräche,
aufgezeichnet von Friedrich Waismann, Frankfurt a. M. 1984, p. 68f. (Montag, 30.
Dezember 1929). Cf. St. Augustine, *Confessiones* I.4; *De doctrina christiana* I.6.
Quoted from a paper by C.-A. Scheier, "Wie oft kann man in 'denselben' Fluß steigen?
oder: Kratylos tadelt Heraklit." (My transl.) What according to Wittgenstein
Augustine already knew was that one's insight into the fundamental impossibility
for the human mind to do justice in describing the nature of God must not stop one
from speaking about God's nature. For Wittgenstein the insight into the nonsensical
character of philosophical statements must likewise not deter one from making such
statements. (And, as Greg Mogenson kindly pointed out to me, even Jung knew in
another context [that of life after death] that "it is important and salutary to speak
also of incomprehensible things." *MDR*, p. 300.)

5

The refused initiation did by no means imply that Jung stayed in childhood. His development had already in fact irrevocably transported him beyond childhood and from the One to the Two. He had been thrust into the experience of disenchantment. And the disenchantment could not be undone any more. However, *real* adulthood or manhood would have required a further-development of the disenchantment, indeed the disenchantment of the disenchantment, a going through all the way with the disenchantment to its own end, and thus disenchantment's coming home to itself through its being freed from the still "enchanted" understanding of "disenchantment" which expresses itself in the blown-up feeling of its amounting to a devastating, unbearable loss. The feeling of disenchantment is merely a beginning, the first immediacy of an awakening from the dream of childhood, namely the experience and interpretation of disenchantment still from the standpoint of disenchantment's opposite, namely, intellectually, the unquestioning *belief* that enchantment was simply indispensable and, emotionally, the ensuing nostalgic *longing* for an enchanted world. From that standpoint the state of disenchantment naturally seems to show that something is absolutely wrong and needs to be corrected or cured.

But nothing is wrong with it. Applying Jung's own much later words apropos neurosis to our topic we can say that the disenchantment is not what needs to be cured, but what cures us (cf. *CW* 10 § 361). But it cures us only when it comes home to itself, is applied to itself, that is to say, only if consciousness is truly initiated into it. The disenchantment experience wanted to be Jung's psychagogue or psychopomp. His refusal of his initiation means that his soul was arrested at the point of the experienced *disenchantment* and that the latter became fixated. The emotional disappointment, frozen as it now was, could not advance to a logical dis-*illusion*ment, the subjective wound (or what the infantile-nostalgic mind experiences as a wound and loss) could not turn into an insight, a knowing. Having become fixated, it turned into a feeling-toned complex that determined his future world experience. The disenchantment complex—in other words, the fundamental rejection of and resentment against the already real and irrevocable disenchantment—remained the unsurpassed horizon and the ground of his whole psychology project.

But disenchantment is, as we know, in itself the simultaneity and identity of disenchantment and enchantment. The most obvious *visible* symbol of this simultaneity and identity in Jung's life is the coexistence of "Küsnacht" and "Bollingen." Together they represent the acted out literalization and dissociation of the Two. In Küsnacht Jung forced himself to face the absolutely disenchanting gaze coming from the bust of Voltaire on his desk. At Bollingen, by contrast, "I am," Jung said, "in my truest nature, I am most deeply myself. Here I am, as it were, the 'age-old son of the mother'" (*MDR* p. 225). At Bollingen he celebrated as his innermost truth the enchanted world, that is to say, the *simulation* of his irrevocably lost child status, the *simulation* of the equally bygone world condition of the Middle Ages, and the *simulation* of an undisrupted oneness with the natural scenery and the things around him. And he celebrated the denial of the Two and thus of adulthood—precisely by acting the Two out as two separate external, literal realities.[19]

If the disenchantment experience wanted to be Jung's psychopomp, why did it come in such an unappetizing and brutal way and not in a more acceptable form? We know from dreams that the degree of extremeness of an image simply reflects the degree of the dream I's resistance or lack of understanding. Through its disgusting, unpalatable character the image indicates within itself that this initiation experience *came* as one to be rejected.

The idea of the simultaneity of disenchantment and enchantment and, above all, its symbolization in the geographically neighboring places of Küsnacht and Bollingen might seduce us into assuming that the two opposite but equiprimordial aspects of the disenchantment complex lie side by side. But no, their relation is that of an inner kernel inside an external shell. Deep down Jung had tried to stay child (child in the *psychological*, not the literal, sense) and had remained faithful to the stance of enchantment, that is, to existence in paradise, in heaven, or cloud-cuckoo-land, while with respect to his appearance

---

[19] The Two should be the (uniform) constitution of consciousness, its logical form. It should be psychological, inwardized, not two *psychic* states acted out on the empirical or behavioral level.

in the outside world he was a fully adult man, but adult only in the psychic and literal, not in the psychological sense. His existence in Küsnacht, as a professional, a scientist, and in the disenchanted world, was for him just, as he once put it, "a good exterior '*dans ce meilleur des mondes possibles.*'"[20]

While the disenchantment aspect can, and even must, be openly shown in the light of day, the faithfulness to the enchanted world as his innermost truth remained deeply hidden inside as an absolute secret. Assessing what emerged for him from the Basel cathedral fantasy and with respect to that "terrible will," Jung said, "I had experienced a dark and terrible secret. It overshadowed my whole life ... / It would never have occurred to me to speak of my experience openly, ... / My entire youth can be understood in terms of this secret. It induced in me an almost unendurable loneliness. ... Thus the pattern of my relationship to the world was already prefigured: today as then I am a solitary..." (*MDR* p. 41f.). *Yes, truly*, I am no longer a child; *but still more truly* I stay adamantly faithful to the enchanted world *as the post-childhood stand-in* for my lost childhood. *Yes, truly*, I live as an adult in the modern world, I am indeed disenchanted; *but still more truly*, namely "in my truest nature," I am "the age-old son of the mother."

What by the soul was meant to be consciousness's terrible disillusionment, by the ego is transmuted into its own privileged illumination concerning a secret about God's terrible will and dark side.

We see the disenchantment complex in action only a few years after the Basel cathedral fantasy in Jung's reaction to his Confirmation/Communion and to his father's spiritual plight. Approaching the Communion with absolutely excessive and childish demands for an overwhelming ego-experience of literally miraculous and spectacular bliss, it became possible for him, on account of the absence of this bliss, to radically condemn the Communion as a total failure, indeed to throw away his whole church tradition into the bargain, and in this way to escape once more the *real* disenchantment and the adult perspective concerning rituals: he escaped the insight that in this case, ritual is in itself disenchanting, because instead of a spectacular ego-experience it "only" provides a logical, spiritual, i.e., absolute-negative,

---

[20] *Letters 1*, p. 171, to Hermann Hesse, 18 Sept. 1934. The original formulation is: "eine gute Exoterik."

satisfaction *for the soul*. For his father, in whom he had right before his eyes the living example of an absolutely honest and relentless suffering from disenchantment, he, as the triumphant owner of his private "secret," had only condescending pity. Again some years later, the disenchantment complex manifested in Jung's *Red Book*.

As theoretician, Jung quite openly admitted that God was dead (e.g., *CW* 11 § 145); that we do no longer have any myth; that we ought to own up to, and even commit ourselves to, our spiritual poverty; that man dwells with himself alone, "where, in the cold light of consciousness, the blank barrenness of the world reaches to the very stars" (*CW* 9i § 29, transl. modif.); that we have squandered our Christian heritage (*ibid.* § 28); that we cannot turn the wheel backwards and, for example, return to the Catholic Church or to other symbols: because, as he said (*CW* 18 § 632), doubt has irrevocably killed them, has devoured them. He unmistakably gave expression to disenchantment as the unquestionable condition of the modern world. However, there was always a mental reservation. I quote: "'No, evidently we no longer have any myth.' 'But then what is your myth—the myth in which you do live?'" (*MDR* p. 171). This follows the pattern of "Yes, truly—but still more truly." It reveals once more the disenchantment complex as the simultaneity of disenchantment and re-enchantment. And Jung's "But then *what* is your myth" performs the same *petitio principii* as his "*Who* wants to force me to think something I don't know and don't want to know? Where does this terrible will come from?" *That* I live in a myth and *that* there is a mysterious Other as author of my thought is dogmatically presupposed and annuls Jung's actual experience or insight.

The *theoretical* and quasi-scientific counterpart and expression of the subjective mental reservation as one's hidden secret is the idea of "the unconscious." "The unconscious" is what is by definition on principle hidden from, and a secret for, consciousness. And the whole inner-outer structure of the disenchantment complex is clearly reflected in the ideas of "The Relations Between the Ego and the Unconscious" and of the journey inwards to the true self as the God image inside oneself. The disenchantment complex's insistence on the One reveals itself in the theory of archetypes as eminent Origins (*archai*), and Jung's emphasis on "experiencing" shows the uncut tie to the positivity of the ego. When we hear Jung say, "The main interest of my work is not concerned with the treatment of neurosis but rather with the approach to the numinous" (*Letters 1*, p. 377, to Martin, 20 Aug. 1945), we see to what extent the re-enchantment impulse is driving him. It is the same longing for a re-enchantment that informs his whole thinking about modernity as being in need of correction and cure, indeed of salvation, and thinking that we are "all badly in need of the symbolic life." And we only have to think of Jung's *Answer to Job* with its Gnostic leanings and its insistence on the reality of evil to see how his whole attitude to Christianity, i.e., to the religious tradition of his forebears, is an expression of that "dark and terrible secret" that Jung believed to have experienced in his twelfth year. How different could Jung's psychology have become if at that early time he had really let himself in for the *substance* of his fantasy experience! How different also if, even at a later point, he had been more interested in the analysis of neurotic structures (as well as, for that matter, in structure, logical form, and the "syntax" of phenomena in general) than in the numinous and had accordingly perhaps been able to critically reflect and see through his own youthful behavior in the Basel cathedral episode the same way which, after all, he had in fact been able to see through as neurotic that period of unconsciously staged fainting fits during the same year 1887, rather than turning his experience into a theoretical claim, indeed a kind of personal dogma, about God as "the most certain and immediate of experiences."

So we see that both the temporal beginning and the logical root of Jung's thinking is his radical refusal of his initiation, of the initiation into his personal adulthood (in a *psychological* sense) and at the same time into modernity. Jung wriggled out of that very experience of disenchantment that in fact, and completely spontaneously, and only from within himself, had come to him when he was on the threshold of adulthood. But his wriggling out of it did not mean that he could shake it off. On the contrary, it meant that he had become unable to go all the way through with it and thus come out of it, or, to express it in a different way, that the disenchantment was cut off from the soul's continuing life, from its having the potential of a development of its own. And so this his wriggling out of it is what turned the disenchantment into a *complex* that ruled *him*,[21] a life-long complex—which it had not at all been, for example, for Max Weber, the originator of the articulated notion of the disenchantment of the world.

---

[21] Here I want to remind the reader that when I discuss Jung and speak of "him" I do not mean him as person and private human individual. The word "Jung" is an abbreviation, a personified way of referring to the theoretician as the "author" of the work, the productive originating *spiritus rector* of his psychology project. The man Jung is none of my business. I am neither an historian or sociologist, nor a biographer, nor Jung's analyst. I am a psychologist studying "documents [or manifestations] of the *soul*."

CHAPTER FOUR

The Rejection of the *Hic*: Reflections on C.G. Jung's Communion Fiasco

With greatest hopes the boy C.G. Jung had looked forward to his first participation in the Communion ceremony. "... I was sure some great mystery must lie behind it, and that I would participate in this mystery in the course of Communion ...." But when he in fact experienced the ceremony he felt desperately disappointed. "I had reached the pinnacle of religious initiation, had expected something—I knew not what—to happen, and nothing at all had happened." "I had not noticed any sign of a 'communio,' nothing of a union, or becoming one with ...." Rather, what really impressed Jung was the flat taste of the bread and the sour taste of the wine. He was keenly aware of such things as that the bread had come from the local baker whose bread was generally poor and flat in taste. He also knew the tavern from which the wine ("thin and rather sour, plainly not of the better sorts") had come. He noted that all who participated in the ceremony were "stiff, solemn, and uninvolved, it seemed to me." "[T]he feast was meager in every respect." A "wretched memorial service." Slowly it dawned on the boy Jung "that this communion had been a fatal experience for me. It had proved hollow; more than that, it was a loss." "[T]his ceremony contained no trace of God" but had "all amounted to no more than words." "I had, so it seemed to me, suffered the greatest defeat of my life" (*MDR* p. 53 ff., transl. modified).

"Was it my failure?"

Jung raised the question: "The failure of the Communion? Was it my failure?" (*MDR* p. 56, transl. modif.). I submit: this incapability of Jung's to experience the Communion is not *his* fault. It is not really the fault of the sensual objects bread and wine, either. It is the fault, on the one hand, of the hope or promise that these objects, simply *as* things of positive-factual reality or the "horizontal" world, would express the presence of a soul truth, that something semantic could *just like that* embody the logic or syntax of the soul, and, on the other hand, it is the "fault" of the fact that the boy Jung already lived on the level of a *modern* consciousness.

As to the first point, we can say that the bread and the wine in their positivity are merely *supposed to* or *claimed* to express a logical or soul truth, but they do not in fact express it by themselves. "It must generally be noted," said Hegel, "that *in images* [...] a deeply speculative content cannot be represented in its peculiar, truthful way and therefore essentially not without contradiction."[1] What Hegel stated with respect to images equally applies to sensual objects, and to them even to a higher degree. Sensual objects like bread and wine can potentially truly express a soul meaning *only for a human subject*, in other words, only subjectively, but they do not express it in and by themselves, objectively. "Potentially" means (and with this we get to the second point): only for a subject that happens to be at a particular level of consciousness (namely an archaic, medieval, early-modern,[2] at any rate psychologically still naïve one, for which soul mysteries, soul truths indeed *appear, manifest*, just like that, in empirical things or events, i.e., in "projected form," as we are used to saying in psychology). This was obviously no longer the case with the boy Jung. His consciousness was already informed by the logic of modernity, for which nature was nothing but naked positive fact and raw-material for industrial production.

---

[1] G.W.F. Hegel, *Vorlesungen über die Philosophie der Religion. Die vollendete Religion*, ed. by W. Jaeschke, Hamburg (Meiner, Philosophische Bibliothek no. 461: 1995), p. 42. My translation. Hegel does not say that a deeply speculative content *cannot be represented* in images at all; he only states that such a representation cannot really do justice to it in its true essence. Such a representation will inevitably fall short of what it is supposed to represent. Images, as images, are *structurally* deficient modes of expression for speculative, that is, soul contents.

[2] "Early-modern": *neuzeitlich*, referring to the period of approximately 1400–1800 AD.

What Jung *experienced* in his Communion fiasco was nothing else but that very contradiction that according to Hegel is inherent in the attempt to express a soul content by means of an image or thing of positive-factual, horizontal reality. But that he experienced this contradiction in the first place, that he was able to experience it in this sharpness, was due to the fact that he had found himself at a historical locus at which consciousness had fallen out of its (let me say by way of abbreviation) "medieval" constitution. The metaphysical logic of the copula amounted to a (horizontal-vertical double-)syllogism.[3] It once upon a time used to horizontally conjoin the subject S (here: the individual human participant in the ceremony) with the predicate P (here: the congregation or community) in the sense of a true communion *because* the productive middle (mediating) term M (here: bread and wine) at the same time opened up the vertical dimension, logically conjoining the individual natural objects "bread and wine" via the vertical middle term "nature" (the ground and producer of the natural products bread and wine) with God (the ground and creator [producer] of nature). Or, put the other way around, *because* the bread and the wine were the *manifestation* of the Redeemer (M, Mediatior) who as redeemer or mediator conjoined man (and his entire empirical world) with God (P).

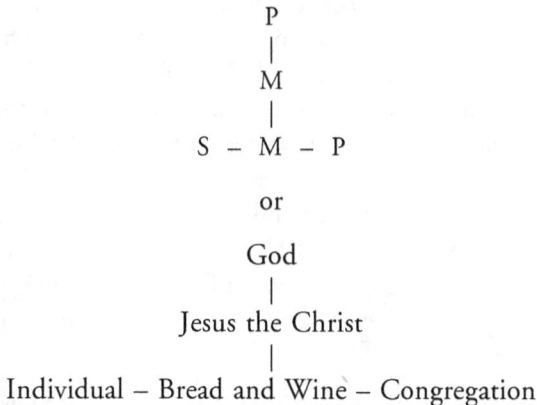

$$
\begin{array}{c}
P \\
| \\
M \\
| \\
S \; - \; M \; - \; P
\end{array}
$$

or

$$
\begin{array}{c}
\text{God} \\
| \\
\text{Jesus the Christ} \\
| \\
\text{Individual} - \text{Bread and Wine} - \text{Congregation}
\end{array}
$$

This is exactly what Jung had hoped for, but which did not become real for him: "I had not noticed any sign of a 'communio,' nothing of

---

[3] For my understanding of the double syllogism essential to metaphysics I am indebted to the numerous writings of Claus-Artur Scheier.

a union, or becoming one with ..." (horizontal syllogism) and "this ceremony contained no trace of God" (vertical syllogism).

It can be assumed that the bread and wine in medieval or early-modern communion rituals did not generally taste so much better than the boy Jung experienced. A pleasing flavor had never been the point anyway. And yet, millions of those who tasted the bread and wine during those ages were not disappointed in the least by the Communion ceremony. They did not feel any need to complain about the flatness of the bread and that "nothing at all had happened," and this regardless of whether the ritual was interpreted in terms of the radical Roman-Catholic concept of transsubstantiation, or the less radical Lutheran view, or the Zwinglian theory which took bread and wine as mere commemorative signs. For all of them during those times the ritual "worked." It was precisely not "no more than words," even for the Zwinglians. It provided deep satisfaction for the soul. The believers were often even willing to stake their lives for *their* version of the Communion ritual in the many religious wars that ensued.

Why did the ritual "work" for them? Why did they not need to harp on about the meagerness of the feast? Not because they were less sensitive or more simple-minded than the boy Jung, but because their consciousness was such that it was capable of in fact *performing* a "symbolic action" and *in it* the logical acts described above as the double syllogism, the conjoining of psychic opposites.[4] Thanks to the development of the soul's history, this possibility had obviously been pulled out from under Jung's consciousness (and modern consciousness at large). That for Jung the bread tasted so flat and the wine so sour is not due to *their* objective qualities, but is an expression of Jung's disappointment, of his inner demand's having fallen flat and gone sour. The flatness means that the whole vertical or soul dimension had dropped away, that the psychological difference had collapsed, so that the horizontal positive-factual aspect of the bread and wine was the

---

[4] The performed symbolic action is nowadays modernistically and psychologistically often interpreted as "projection." Projection is generally understood as the unconscious "throwing out" of an inner content of the unconscious upon some outer person or object, so that it appears to consciousness as if it were an empirical quality of the outer person or object. By contrast, the idea of a symbolic action does not proceed from an already given psychic content that is merely displaced from inside the subject onto an external object. A symbolic action is much rather an achievement of the mind, its capacity to rise to a more complex form of *seeing* that within itself performs the logical *conjunctio oppositorum*.

only thing left. The moment that the vertical syllogism disappears, the middle term (bread and wine) inevitably *also* loses its power of functioning as a *productive* middle or as copula, *vinculum*. The result is that the subject then stands divorced vis-à-vis the bread and wine as fundamentally alien objects, utter Others, and that it is likewise divorced from the other participants in the ceremony next to him without any real communion with them in Christ. The place of the former scheme of the double syllogism is taken by the new scheme of the logic of the unbridgeable difference:

$$S \mid O$$

where O stands for the object, here bread and wine, in its naked positivity.[5] Just as, with this change, M changed from true symbol or copula into O, so also did the subject change from psycho-logical or theoretical "I" into empirical "ego," which is psychology's usual name for the I of the positivistic and atomic individual.

But why was it that the former consciousness, *while* going through the ritual, used to be capable of performing the double syllogism, or rather that for it the performance of it simply happened, quite naturally so, as a tacit, implicit, almost automatic achievement (rather than as a conscious and deliberate effort), whereas modern consciousness is fundamentally deprived of this possibility? The answer must be that in the people of those former times the true subject that went through the ceremony was "the soul" in them, rather than they themselves as ego-personalities, whereas for modern man it is inevitably the conscious I, the ego.[6] For "the soul" it is the most natural thing to perform symbolic actions, that is to say, to move simultaneously in the horizontal and in the vertical direction, thereby uniting what Jung would later term the psychic opposites. The people of former ages were able to experience the divine presence in the bread and wine of the communion ceremony because they were still enwrapped in "the soul," still contained in it: in other words, (psychologically) still *unborn*.

---

[5] Correspondingly, what once was a soul truth actually manifesting in the real objects can now only be viewed as a strictly subjective idea, feeling, or superstition, and "projection" is then the (illegitimate) seeing of such a veritably inner content in some outer reality.

[6] A very different aspect of the same distinction is discussed in my *Soul-Violence*, Coll. Engl. Papers vol. III, pp. 410-411.

Describing his Communion experience, Jung sarcastically noted that "the people went out [of the church after the celebration], neither depressed nor illumined with joy, but with faces that said, 'So that's that'" (*MDR* p. 54)—*as if* this sober reaction were inappropriate. But these facial expressions may well have been a sign of psychological authenticity concerning participation in a ritual.[7] The end of a true ritual is precisely: Yes, that's that. Truth has happened. The soul (and *not the ego*) has found its fulfillment. Thomas Hardy once observed, "A traditional pastime is to be distinguished from a mere revival in no more striking feature than in this, that while in the revival all is excitement and fervour, the survival is carried on with a stolidity and absence of stir which sets one wondering why a thing that is done so perfunctorily should be kept up at all."[8] The same perfunctory mode of performance applies to rituals. They don't appeal to the ego and its *emotional* satisfaction.

The same Communion ritual that Jung found devastating for himself had once upon a time been an event of truth. When it was the happening of truth, it was the presence of the divine mystery, in other words, something in itself spiritual, logical, not just positive-factual. It was the *objective logical* (*not* the subjective emotional) presence of this mystery. It was not an exciting experience, but cold and matter-of-fact: simply *true*.

From here we have to say that Jung's terrible disappointment about the flat bread indicates that at his historical locus he had all along fallen out of truth and out of soul and was already in the modern positivistic stance of the abstract ego. As the positivistic ego he tried to get "illumined with joy" through the Communion event. But what difference does it make to the soul if the bread tastes flat or not or has this or that empirical characteristic? For the soul it is enough that it is the bread of the holy Communion that has its sacramental effect simply *ex opere operato*, through the ritual work having objectively been performed, as the Roman-Catholic Church rightly teaches, and not via a person's inner felt experience. The

---

[7] Although it is of course also possible that these people, or some of them, already were in their psychological makeup just as modern people as the boy Jung, so that like him they were also disappointed, but did not dare to show it, maybe not even dare to admit it to themselves.

[8] Thomas Hardy, *The Return of the Native*, Harmondsworth (Penguin Books) 1978, S. 178.

taste of the bread and its immediate emotional effect make a difference exclusively to the ego that possessively wants a strong felt experience for itself, a spectacular happening, a "high" (for its self-affirmation and self-edification). And this kind of staggering, mind-blowing event was precisely what the young boy Jung had hoped for, indeed insisted on. The soul, by contrast, finds its fulfillment in the calm, objective *truth* of, e.g., the bread as the presence of Christ, because it is relentlessly given over to the ritual as the event of truth.

Let us here also remember what Jung himself at a much later time had to say in a different context about the difference of soul and empirical man or ego. "Heaven and hell are fates meted out to the soul and not to civil man, who in his nakedness and timidity would have no idea of what to do with himself in a heavenly Jerusalem" (*CW* 9i § 56, transl. modif.). Just as civil man would have no idea of what to do with himself in a heavenly Jerusalem, so he also does not know here on earth what to do with the bread and wine of the Communion, regardless of whether it tastes flat or is the best tasting bread in the world. Why? Because he—in his psychological nakedness and timidity—is not interested in, has no organ, indeed not even any use, for truth; he does not have his psychological locus on that level on which alone he could be open to the absolute negativity of the soul or truth. He is exclusively oriented towards the positivistic, utilitarian aspects of reality, its pragmatics.

Modern man has been born out of the soul altogether. This is why he has become psychologically identical with what Jung in the above quote called "civil man"; and he is as such psychologically, metaphysically naked (just like a baby is physically naked after birth). And because he is naked, that is, divorced from, ignorant of, and immune to, soul and devoid of a mythic garment,[9] he craves for emotion (felt experience, excitement, fervor, thrill, entertainment, as well as, on a more refined level, "spirituality," "meaning," "portals of the sacred," "his personal myth," and utopian world-improvement or world-rescue ideologies) as a modern *substitute* for truth and confuses strong feelings with soul

---

[9] For example, of "Christian faith," which once upon a time was a *substantial reality* in which people were enveloped on a cultural level, rather than a personal, subjective belief or feeling.

events. The gaping metaphysical hole craves to be filled with *something*, no matter what. Emotions are positivistic events and positivistically accessible. The positivistic ego is on principle (i.e., logically, not always in its literal behavior) a consumer, if not an insatiable junkie.[10]

Jung introduced his volume on *Symbols of Transformation* with a chapter on "Two Kinds of Thinking." In our context we have to distinguish between two kinds of feeling. The modern abstract feeling means that the subject centers around itself. In having feelings modern man in the last analysis only wants to feel himself, to feel himself intensively. He wants to get a "high." *What* it is that is felt or experienced is actually indifferent; the particular content is merely utilized as the occasion, instrument, or trigger for getting excited, as something that makes it possible for oneself to work oneself up into a high degree of intensive self-feeling. There is no other substantial content than "I." The aim of this type of feeling is the utterly abstract and empty one of one's self-gratification, self-experience. This is the nihilistic core of modern felt-experience.

The truth of pre-modern man existed in him *also* in the form of feelings. The communion celebrated by him, or the rituals performed by archaic and ancient man, were psychically also rooted in, as well as accompanied by, deep feelings. But this was the other type of feeling. Let us take as example the ritual reported in *MDR* that was performed by the Elgonyi in Uganda, the ritual of greeting the sun at the moment of its rising, by first spitting into their hands and then raising their palms towards the sun. Jung made the important point that they only knew *that* they perform this rite, but did not know *what* they are thereby doing. "They themselves do not see any meaning in this action." They told Jung: "this has always been done." In other words, seen from outside, it is an utterly unexcited, sober routine performance, just as sober and perfunctory as the participation of the traditional church-goers in the communion ceremony as observed by the boy Jung. But this does not at all mean an absence of feeling. However, in contrast to modern feeling, this feeling is intelligent and cultured feeling. It is a feeling informed and authorized by a knowing, the

---

[10] It is not accidental that the motif of the Vampire became so successful in popular literature and movies during the 19th and 20th centuries, although it depicts a very special aspect of this psychological situation with additional complications.

knowing that by their performing this ritual act the soul finds *its* satisfaction; the knowing that in the ritual truth has happened. And in this awareness people also felt that they themselves had received their own highest-possible satisfaction. This second kind of feeling has a substantial intellectual content. It is not just an ego-trip.

In his feeling, *modern* man is like little children who crave for excitement and sensations, who relish loud colors and sugar coating, and who want to immediately touch and put into their mouths all things that they find attractive. They insist on immediate gratification of their egoic wishes. By comparison, pre-modern man is a mature adult. He has abstracted himself from himself as desiring human animal or as ego, and so feels that his own true satisfaction, rather than from the gratification of his immediate desires, comes from what gratifies what he is in truth: soul, mind, intellect.

Because at his historical locus Jung was already inevitably defined as "civil man," the boy Jung no longer approached the Communion ceremony from the standpoint of soul. He demanded to experience the immediate presence of God as that modern ego that has fallen out (has been born out) of "the soul." Deep down Jung knew that he was irrevocably identical with "civil man." He called this his *real* psychological status "personality No. 1." What he also believed to have, and named his "personality No. 2," is, as "No. 2," *psychologically* irrelevant: it is a priori set up as subjective, emotional-experiential *ersatz* and consolation prize for the real loss of soul and truth, for the obsolete, but tenaciously held-onto world-experience of premodern if not archaic man. Because it is obsolete, and also both experienced as well as implicitly known to be obsolete, it can only occur in Jung as a modern person as a completely split-off separate personality. The radical dissociation that exists between "No. 1" and "No. 2" reflects the latter's objective incompatibility with the modern adult world. And it is an (inadvertent) admission of its own ("No. 2's") logical obsolescence. That "No. 2" was in fact psychologically irrelevant can clearly be seen from the fact that it must have been "No. 1" that went into and experienced his first Communion. It is of course crazy to go to such an important soul event as one's Communion as "No. 1" *and nevertheless* expect what Jung wished for. That in his case it was "No. 1" who went there is obvious. Because if it had been "No. 2," Jung would not have been disappointed. "No. 2"—*if* it still had had any *real* significance, any *soul* significance, in his life rather than being merely an egoic substitute for the lost premodern containment in soul—would naturally have been able to find fulfillment through the bread and wine, no matter what their taste was.[11] The bread and wine of the Communion ceremony were so to speak the acid test for the actual validity of "No. 2" for *essential* life. But "No. 2" here proved a paper tiger, a sham, or a toy personality for his private entertainment. Where it would have counted that it come into play and take charge, it did not appear and consequently could not make any difference.

We could say that it was the thoroughly modern "junkie" in the boy Jung (as *in truth* being identical with "No. 1," whereas "No. 2" was negligible) who felt that his "[Communion] ceremony contained no trace of God" but had "all amounted to no more than words" (*MDR* p. 55). It is the junkie in him who had to feel so because as junkie he had "expected something [...] to happen," "stupendous things [...]," perhaps "things of fire and unearthly light" (p. 54f.). Instead of "junkie" we could also say "the modern ego." The modern ego is characterized by its refusal to enter, as far as *essential* life is concerned,[12] mature adulthood. Or, expressed the other way around, by insisting on viewing things in a *childish* way and clinging to childish desires and priorities, driven by a greed for momentary self-gratification and subjective excitement. This is what the boy Jung exemplified here. It was as if he had not already left the child-status a few years ago and was at the point of becoming a man, which in late 19th century meant at the same time: a decidedly modern man; and as if, furthermore, the Confirmation process was not precisely the modern equivalent and last remainder of the puberty initiations of former ages in which youths had to die the death of the child that they had so far been and were initiated into the mature *knowing* of the tribe's objective truths. Jung here did not want to *know*, he wanted "stupendous things [...]" to happen, perhaps "things of fire and unearthly light." It is the egoic and childish mind in the boy Jung that expected from a communion

---

[11] Premodern man was not dissociated into two personalities and therefore neither went to Communion or similar rituals as the equivalent of "No. 1" nor of "No. 2." He went as "the whole (unborn) man."

[12] In practical-technical, economic and scientific regards, in its professional life, the modern ego has generally no difficulty to take a full-fledged adult position. The childish mode comes predominantly only into play in the area of *essential* (meaning, religious, value, ideological, self-definition) questions.

ritual emotional sensations. The mature mind knows that what a ritual brings is of an entirely different order of reality—much more subtle, quiet, and above all: of an intelligible, intellectual nature. It is a deep feeling in the heart, but one in which an intellectual truth becomes embodied or incarnated as a personal reality in people.[13] This is, of course, hard to swallow for modern consciousness, for which intellect and feeling are radically dissociated, indeed opposites. Which is why it is fundamentally abstract.

Jung says: "It was clear to me that in this fashion we were to incorporate him [the Lord Jesus] into ourselves. This seemed to me so preposterous an impossibility that I was sure some great mystery must lie behind it, and that I would participate in this mystery in the course of Communion [...]" (p. 53). Here we have several contradictory tendencies in one sentence: first, there is obviously an inkling that the Communion was about something noetic, a *mystery* accessible only to the intellect, to a deep soulful understanding. But this inkling is immediately put down as a "preposterous impossibility," a judgment in which the modern positivistic, cynical ego or "No. 1" personality expresses itself, which in turn shows that in reality the child status has indeed already been left. And in the contradiction between "the great mystery that must lie behind it," on the one hand, and his denigration of it as a "preposterous impossibility," on the other hand, we see (not a child's but) a regressively childish mind at work. A real child has no difficulties with mysteries and miracles. For the imagining child the impossible is precisely not preposterous. No, in Jung's reaction it is already the thoroughly modern adult mind that construes the mystery of the Communion in a downright positivistic way as the literal incorporation of the Lord Jesus into ourselves. It is the thoroughly modern mind for whom the satisfaction derived from the ritual has to be seen as a merely emotional satisfaction. The positivistic construal of a soul mystery amounts to a mystification. And a mystification on the theoretical side requires as its counterpart on the feeling side an insistence on and craving for the great ego experience, for a "high." This shows that Jung demanded from the Communion celebration something that might rightly be expected from circus performances,

---

[13] Cf. James Hillman's idea of "The Thought of the Heart." (*Idem, The Thought of the Heart.* Eranos Lectures, Vol. 2. Dallas [Spring Publications] 1984.)

thrilling movies, or a Woodstock Festival, and above all from certain hallucinogenic drugs, but was totally out of place at this religious ritual. Jung was barking up the wrong tree. The Communion ritual was of course aimed at the educated, intelligent, illumined feeling of the soul, not at the abstract, fundamentally blind and dumb emotionality of the modern ego.

What formerly had been the actual achievement of the ceremony (namely, the *soul's* fulfillment through the performance of an event of truth), on the new level of modernity as well as of the post-childhood situation of a modern adolescent inevitably had to show itself to be an empty claim. And, seen in terms of the boy Jung, this claim has to be judged by us as an idle wish, an illusionary demand of his as "No. 1," a demand that *deserved* to be disappointed. We could also say that it was "No. 2" who was here indirectly unmasked as being "no more than words," as being no more than the split-off personification and hypostasis of the ego's or "No. 1's" *idle demands, subjective fantasies,* and *private hobby*, which decades later would even receive their external objectification in material reality in Jung's Bollingen tower.

Interestingly enough, the mature Jung as a psychological theorist did not go the way of the hunger for emotion. He saw through the emptiness of subjective emotions.[14] He insisted on substantial contents, on "the objective psyche." We just need to compare his psychological analysis of the transformation mystery of the Roman-Catholic Mass, a topic most closely related to that of his first Communion, to his report about the latter in *MDR*. In his later essay of 1941, Jung is absolutely uninterested in what feelings the Mass evokes in people, how they understand it, and what they get from it. He merely describes its objective psychological truth, the cold truth of the soul, a truth that is absolutely self-sufficient and deeply gratifying because it is enough for it *that it is true*.[15] Here he obviously is speaking from the standpoint of the soul, not that of "civil man" (but also not as "No. 2"! Rather, he is merely speaking as a psychologist, i.e., on a "scientific" or "scholarly" level, as a theoretician. His insights

---

[14] See above all Jung's decisive distinction between drug-induced "so-called religious visions" and actual religion in *Letters 2*, p. 382f., to Betty Grover Eisner, 12 August 1957. The former have "more to do with physiology" and are a "dangerously simple 'Ersatz.'"

[15] This truth is not ontological. Just as the truth of all ritualistic reality, it exists only *ex opere operato*. It is performative. It has to be *made*.

about the Mass are not elements of the immediacy of existential experience—which is what "No. 2" is about—but come about through a special *methodological* point of view—the standpoint of soul—applied by the *conscious, mature, modern* personality C.G. Jung who as such is beyond the dissociation between "No. 1" and "No. 2").

Here we may also be put in mind of what Jung himself once said. "... people have still not got it into their heads that the psychology of religion falls into two categories, which must be sharply distinguished from one another: firstly, the psychology of the religious person, and secondly, the psychology of religion proper, i.e., of religious contents" (*CW* 11 § 751). The former type is personalistic psychology, the "psychology" concerned with the *psyche* of the human animal, the latter psychology proper: the psychology of the *soul's* self-articulation.

Now it is, however, significant that this later insight and his later capability to take the standpoint of soul did not make him, as the author of that part of *MDR*, in any way revise and revoke his adolescent condemnation of the Communion ritual in his own Church, although this Communion ceremony was *mutatis mutandis* the expression of the same soul truth, only greatly reduced both in internal complexity and potency. Old man Jung, writing or dictating his memories, much rather upheld his early highly emotional verdict, in no way distancing himself from it as from a youthful folly, namely his refusal to leave his child-mentality behind—as if his later insights into the truth of the Mass had no bearing whatsoever on the psychological evaluation of his own Zwinglian Communion tradition.

Either his appreciation of the Catholic Mass as a true transformation mystery, as truly symbolic, would have had to lead to an at least milder view of the Communion and of the bread and wine of his real community and tradition. Or, conversely, his disparagement of the Communion would have had to lead to a disparagement of the Mass, too. For the bread in the Mass probably tastes just as flat; and what is empirically and experientially happening in it is not anything emotionally spectacular (in the sense of "things of fire and unearthly light"), either. Jung applies double standards: the ritual that was obligatory for him was declared to be devoid of soul validity; the foreign ritual, by contrast, could be appreciated as a wonderful truth of the soul. I submit that the reason—one reason at least—for this difference is that it was precisely the fact that the Mass did not come to Jung with a living claim on him that enabled him to see its deep soul value. In modernity the soul cannot be anything obliging in actual lived life (with the one exception of neurosis: the very point of neurosis is that the neurotic has to live a soul program as a compelling and unquestionable necessity; he has to *be* it). Jung can only find the soul in what is already historically irrelevant from the outset.

For the psychological view, the disappointment Jung experienced from his Communion ceremony was not a mistake. Rather, it came to Jung as his psychopomp. It had the psychological purpose of expressly initiating the boy Jung into the (historically speaking) new, modern truth into which he had been born and as which he consequently already existed.

But instead of letting himself be—*logically*—dis-appointed, dis-illusioned, in his reaction he stayed merely on the (*emotional*, ego, or childish) level of disappointment and resentment. And thus he refused to be initiated into the modern situation, the modern soul truth. Instead of letting the experience come home to him and realizing that *he* (his expectation, his demand of an exciting happening, or as he put it: of an experience of "the vast despair, the overpowering elation and outpouring of grace which for me constituted the essence of God" [*MDR* p. 55]) was wrong, he turned his whole wrath against the innocent *ritual* and blamed *it* and the whole Church for being wrong: "'Why, that is not religion at all,' I thought. 'It is an absence of God; the church is a place I should not go to. It is not life which is there, but death'" (*ibid.*). I have to interject here: of course it *is* "death," and that it is "death" is the whole point of it, as of any true ritual, because it is about soul truths and soul is the fundamental negation of civil man, of natural, abstract-emotional life: it is absolute negativity. As a matter of course from a modern ego point of view the ritual must, as Jung complained, amount to no more than words, because the modern ego, and modern born man in general, is incapable of letting the objective soul meaning of the words and actions take real residence in the subject through its feeling of the heart.

The disappointment made Jung discard the traditional particular object or place of fulfillment (the Communion ceremony and, by extension, his church's religious practice at large), but he insisted on holding on to the same old demand for fulfillment. He vehemently rejected the religion of his fathers so as to be able to defend his own illusionary demand of an immediate overwhelming experience of the presence of God. And he could only hold on to his demand by going utterly subjective, solipsistic: I "found myself involved [...] in 'my secret,' which I could share with no one" (*MDR* p. 56, transl. modif.), where "my secret" refers to his belief of, during his twelfth year, having directly and unshakeably experienced both God's terrible, overwhelming will and God's grace through his, the boy Jung's, obedience towards God's alleged demand on him to think a sacrilegious thought (the "Basel cathedral" episode[16]).

Along with the rejection of his traditional religion, Jung also, closer to home, broke on a *psychological, logical* level his inner loyalty and solidarity with his father. From the superior position of his secretly believing to have a direct line to God he, so to speak, threw him, as a poor soul, away into religious-intellectual nonexistence ("He was struggling with a death whose existence he could not admit. An abyss had opened between him and me, and I saw no possibility of ever bridging it, for it was infinite in extent"). By contrast, on the *subjective emotional* level he fobbed him off with his pity and empathy ("I was seized with the most vehement pity for my father," "my dear and generous father") (p. 55).

This "death" (in which his father was allegedly entangled) and this "abyss" (between Jung and his father) are, however, nothing else but a manifestation of the new truth, into which his frustrating experience could have initiated Jung, the new logic of the unbridgeable difference, the logic of the S | O form. But Jung did not allow it to become his new truth—although de facto he of course inevitably lived in it—because he did not let it come home to *himself,* did not *erinnern* (inwardize) it, did not reflect it into the logic of his own consciousness, but instead acted it out on the positive-factual level as a form of his "object relations" (the relation to his father). Despite the fact that Jung said, as we already heard, "I had, so it seemed to me, suffered the greatest defeat of my life," he nevertheless by no means bore this defeat as his own (unwanted) truth (*he* was, after all, in the possession of "my

---

[16] I discussed this in detail in my "Psychology as Anti-Philosophy: C. G. Jung," in: *Spring 77 (Philosophy and Psychology),* June 2007, pp. 11–51. Now Chapter 2 in the present volume.

secret"), but rather projectively made his "father" the carrier of it (to be precise: only his father-imago, his father *the way* he fantasized him[17]). In his own inner scheme, as an element of his self-invention, as part of "*my* fable, *my* truth,"[18] his "father" became for him the externalized embodiment of the defeat and frustration of *his own* (Carl Gustav's) illusion.

In this way—subjectively speaking—the *frustration* or— objectively speaking—the *negation* of the illusion was successfully disposed of, shelved out there with his father, so that in C.G. Jung the *illusion itself* could go on, undisturbed (if not even confirmed) by his disappointing experience. However, it had to go on merely in the form of "his secret" that he could not share with anyone, in other words, as an untruth. Jung's "my secret" was an untruth because, as on principle incommunicable, it (a) stayed isolated only on the left side of the entire S | O relation and could not account for the whole relation (which would be the whole truth), and because (b) Jung thus had the essential other side of his truth only "out there" in his rejected and pitied father imago. Furthermore, it (c) had to be an untruth also in the sense that, inasmuch as it was enclosed and hidden within his chest, it was condemned to remain in the status of an untested, on principle untestable, subjective claim,[19] an uncovered cheque.

But the essential *other* side of his "truth," because it was projected onto his father and thus acted out, externalized, and semanticized, was itself *also* given the form of an untruth (for how else if not in the form of an untruth could it have been disposed of, and how could a split-off half of the whole truth still be a truth?).

---

[17] We have no way of knowing anything about Jung's father as a real person (what he truly thought and felt). We only have C.G. Jung's account of his *perception* of him. Generally we have to say: *Et audiatur altera pars!* But in our context, Jung's real father is of no interest. We are exclusively concerned with Jung's story. And even if Jung's perception and interpretation of his father were completely accurate, it would nevertheless be a projection because Jung made his father embody something that belonged to himself.

[18] See below.

[19] Later in life, Jung himself realized that unless he was able to plant "the results of my experience in the soil of reality," they would remain "*subjective assumptions without validity*" (*MDR* p. 192, my italics). What precisely he meant by planting the results in the soil of reality and whether such planting would indeed overcome the subjective-claim status of "my secret" or not does not concern us here. The main thing for us is that here he realized for once that personal experience as such is fundamentally insufficient.

Truths, in order to be truths, require to be *made* true and *owned up to*: what at first appears as a semantic content of consciousness, a particular experience or insight, needs to be turned into the very syntax or logical form of consciousness itself.

Through his Communion fiasco as well as through the drastic contrast between his experience and that which the people of former ages had in view of the same reality (the bread and wine of the Communion), Jung could have become aware that he was faced with a problem on the level of syntax and logic and that this contrast was due to a fundamental difference between the former and the present logic prevailing for the mind of man. But instead he stayed on the level of semantics: of contents, particular experiences, symbols, images, personal (religious) "secrets."

It was not only that as a private individual Jung pushed the negation of his illusion off onto his father in order to thereby rescue the abstract form of his illusion, his illusion which—in the beginning completely subjective and personal—had as its concretization no more than "*my* secret." On top of it he also deserted his Church, his religious tradition, and his religious community, establishing an unbridgeable abyss between them and himself. And as a private individual he instead took refuge in the *exotic* inner world of absolute privacy (secrecy). The same as what applies to "my secret" also applies to so-called archetypal images from out of the so-called unconscious, such as in dreams. What characterizes all these contents, by comparison with those contents he had grown up with in his own religious community, is their fundamental foreignness, the greater distance that Jung and his real life world had to them, and consequently their psychological *neutrality*, *not-relevance*, and *abstractness*. They a priori come without a real claim. Their "claim" can at best be a subjective emotional feeling of importance ("numinosity"). They are essentially free-floating—colorful balloons, maybe tied with a thin thread of personal associations to the individual, but certainly not rooted and vested in one's lived life within one's concrete social, professional, and family reality and in the context of society's institutionalized traditions. They have a role solely in the segregated sphere of one's private inner, which is objectively *symbolized* by the consulting room that is cut off from social reality. This is why they are on principle neutralized.

All these characteristics—this uprootedness and freefloatingness of "my [utterly subjective] secret" and later of archetypal images—made it easier for Jung to successfully project upon *them* that same old promise of vertical or syntactical (i.e., soul) presence, the presence of God or numinous meaning, which in his real life had precisely been frustrated. The archetypal images and his exotic "secret,"[20] however, are of course just as semantic and merely horizontal,[21] merely positive-factual contents as the flat bread and sour wine of the Communion were *for* the thoroughly modern subject's experience.

From *hic* to *alibi* and the loss of earth

Here, now, we have to realize that the Church creed and ceremonies of his home town were the *real* place of his religious and soul life. *They* and not his secret were the only psychological reality rooted in the real world and real tradition that he authentically belonged to; they alone came with a *real* claim on him,[22] with the expectations of his whole real community, his family, the people he lived with and above all with the *real* claim to *truth* (the *salvation of the soul*); they were essential parts of the psychological soil in which he was rooted. And thus for Jung it is to these ceremonies and religious convictions, that the adage frequently cited by Jung[23] applies: *hic Rhodus, hic salta* (here

---

[20] In the Basel cathedral episode we see most clearly how Jung artfully built up certain ordinary emotions belonging to the horizontal level into the overwhelming "terrible will of God," i.e., into something that intruded from the vertical dimension into horizontal life. See my paper on this episode mentioned earlier.

[21] The exotic is the semanticized vertical on the horizontal plane. The vertical (and this means categorial) distinction, e.g., between Heaven and Earth is replaced by the horizontal distinction between the familiar and the foreign, which is just as positive-factual as the familiar.

[22] Jung, of course, always insisted that we should feel ethically committed to our inner experiences. But the fact that this had to be preached shows that ethical commitment is not intrinsic. The most natural thing is precisely to take them as "mere images." Any commitment felt here is entirely up to the personal discretion of the individual. The religion of his community, by contrast, came as an *objective* commitment, much as its laws and social mores. Here it precisely takes a particular courageous act on the part of the individual subject *to be in breach of* these commitments, while the natural thing would be to comply with them.

[23] Just one example: *CW* 13 § 5. This adage is the Latin translation by Erasmus of Rotterdam of a Greek statement ('Ιδού ή 'Ρόδος, ιδού καὶ τὸ πήδημα) occurring in a fable by Aesop about a sportsman who repeatedly bragged how far he had been able to jump on Rhodes and that he could prove it when witnesses from Rhodes would arrive. One person interrupted him saying this sentence. The point was that he should not put off the proof of his claim till maybe those witnesses would appear, but rather prove it by doing it here and now. (Erasmus actually has: Hic Rhodus, hic saltus.)

is Rhodes, here jump!). And "to these ceremonies and religious convictions" means: at this particular early moment in his life, to his (for him of course frustrating) Communion experience, and to nothing else. Here is Rhodes, here jump!—in other words: demonstrate here and now what you can, or that you in fact are able to do it). In *MDR* Jung even said that this saying was "My motto" (p. 189, transl. modif.). Hegel, too, cited this dictum in the Preface to his *Philosophy of Right* both in Latin and in Greek, adding that philosophy's task was to comprehend that *which IS* (rather than what ought to be). He then also gave a beautiful twist to it by reformulating it as: "Here is the rose, here dance" (the rose representing Reason).

Whether the Communion was edifying or frustrating, whether it "worked" for him or rather "did not do anything for him," is in this regard of no significance. *Here* was the place of decision for Jung, *here* the soul issue had to be resolved one way or another, *here* his soul had to dance, and in this connection we have to remember that for the soul, failure or success, disappointment or blissful elation, negation or confirmation, fairy tale or tragedy, are equally valid options. In either case the soul finds its fulfillment, just as, for example, a mother complex gets on the soul level its due just as much if on the behavioral level you full of anger constantly fight against your mother as if you stay in the most harmonious loving relationship with her. *The Communion event* was his only chance, only *real* chance. There was no other place, no alternative.[24] Generally speaking, we cannot freely choose our Rhodes—satisfaction or money back. For better or worse we are stuck with that Rhodes that happens to be our *real hic*. Here (and here alone) we have to prove ourselves (in psychological, "metaphysical" regards), we have to show who we are, show our speculative potency, our capability to reach, as one fairy tale type puts it, the top of the slippery glass mountain—or not.

In Jung's own writings we have a good analogy to the logical relation prevailing in the *hic Rhodus, hic salta*, an analogy also to its necessity, although in a very different area (not in that of religious

---

[24] With these statements I am not suggesting that his confirmation experience in the literal sense as the one-time event in his youth was Jung's only place. "Place" has rather to be understood as a logical, intellectual "topos" or theme, as the fundamental *issue* that emerged for Jung through this his experience and that cannot be tied down to a particular historical date. For this issue, the Communion experience was merely a concrete exemplification.

experience and speculative truth but in that of honest self-representation). When prefacing *MDR*, Jung pointed out that what he was going to do was no more than "to tell the myth of my life. I can only ... 'tell stories.' Whether or not the stories are 'true' is not the problem. The only question is whether they are *my* fable, *my* truth" (*MDR* p. 3, transl. modif.). Just as in the one case it is indifferent whether the Communion fulfilled Jung's hope or proved hollow (because in either instance it was inescapably *his* experience, *his* Rhodes), so in the other case it is indifferent whether the stories Jung is going to tell are "true" in a literal historical-factual sense or not. The only thing that counts is whether they are truly *his* stories. *Hic* in the one and "my" in the other situation are more or less synonymous. *Hic* is always *my* Rhodes and always *this* particular Rhodes in the fundamental contingency of this my *hic*.

In the psychological use I make of *Hic Rhodus, hic salta*, two things are noteworthy, the notion of jumping and the strange identity-and-difference relation of *hic* and *Rhodus*.

Concerning the first point, we note that *salta* is an imperative. Jump! Jump here and now! It is an assignment of a task to be achieved, an act to be performed. With the metaphor of jumping this saying refers for us to a *general* psychological necessity. In a psychological context we of course have to conceive this jumping as a high jump rather than a long jump, because what is psychologically at stake is the vertical dimension. It is a jump up out of the flatness of the horizontal plane, a jumping that eo ipso for the first time *opens up* the vertical dimension and performs the vertical syllogism described in the above scheme. In other words, it is the jump from the standpoint of the ego to that of the soul, from the sphere in which, for example, gold is *aurum vulgi* to the sphere of *aurum nostrum*, or more generally from the interest and entanglement in the pragmatics of survival in the ordinary world (which includes all the issues of profession, career, relationships, and love life) to the awareness of the absolute negativity of "the soul." It is the truly *humanizing* jump. To the extent that one lives only in the horizontal world, one is only the animal that one is (although as human being an animal that has *logos* [speech and reason]). One becomes truly *human* if one shoulders the task of rising to and holding oneself in an upright position, not so much physically, but logically or metaphysically, or if one "rides up the glass mountain," that is, succeeds in the logical feat of performing what I described as the double syllogism.

I already pointed out that once upon a time, as long as man was still unborn and as such enwrapped in the soul, it was ultimately the soul that sort of "automatically" performed this feat for him, but now I have to stress: only ultimately. Because for the soul to be able to perform this work in people, an active contribution or participation by man was absolutely indispensable; man, the human person, the I, had to be intensely present, make himself present in the drama. In a different but similar context Luther had said: *oportet me adesse*, which I translate as: it is indispensable that I am fully, wholeheartedly present so that the soul *can* do its work, a work that certainly is not the I's work. Similarly, the alchemists knew that, *Oportet operatorem interesse operi* (the adept performing the opus must be *in* the opus, *CW* 12 § 375).

In archaic cultures the human contribution became visible, on the personal biographical level, in the elaborate initiation ceremonies performed there (which were *tasks* and *trials* to be mastered by each subject undergoing them, not simply "experiences" to be had). And the human contribution became visible, on a more fundamental, communal level, in all the communal rituals, above all in those *explicitly* cosmogonic rituals performed in certain tribes. The particular type of rituals I have in mind were perhaps most impressively exemplified in those ancient African tribes in which periodically, e.g., after the king's death, the tribe went through a symbolic end of the world (all fires in the whole kingdom would be extinguished, there was not to be any procreative activity [= the *pars pro toto* stopping of ongoing life itself], all laws would be abolished so that a state of lawlessness resulted [= a symbolic return to primordial Chaos] etc.), *until*, after some days, a new king would ritually with a fire drill on a fire board start a new fire from which embers were carried by heralds to all parts of the kingdom to reignite all other fires, and the world would be ritually *newly created* by man also in various other respects. What we see from this is that the world was not taken as simply given by nature, as a positivity, an ontological entity. It had to be *made*, in order to be a *world* (a human world) in the first place—just as for Jung's Pueblo Indians it was an indispensable human task to ritually help the sun travel across the sky, something that physically the sun can of course do quite well all by itself.

It is clear that the degree of how deep the soul in a particular individual could go in bringing about the vertical dimension depended on the psychological, "metaphysical" giftedness of the individual. Ordinary individuals might not get much further than making the collective belief systems their own in such a way that the pragmatics of life are gilded over for them in a rather conventional way, whereas a select few persons might be able to reach true religious or metaphysical depths. And the task of performing the great public rituals *correctly* also required especially gifted individuals with deep insight and intuition, shamans, medicine men, fetish priests, etc. A ritual could by no means be performed by mechanically going through a fixed routine. True rituals were (had to be) to some extent each new time *creative* productions, despite the extremely conservative nature of rituals.

Something of this sort can be seen to be even more true when, with a big jump from the level of tribal cultures with their initiations and archaic public rituals, we go over to those cultures in the Western world whose ultimate truths were determined by philosophical thought: to the age of metaphysics and Christianity. On the cultural level, each period during that era had to logically establish and justify afresh its own particular access to the vertical dimension, to heaven, to the absolute, according to its specific historical locus. And it had to do so through a "labor of the concept" (be it in theological or philosophical theorizing or in the production of art). Whereas the truth in archaic cultures was historically amazingly stable, those cultures that have their truth in the form and on the level of philosophical thought (which here includes religious, theological thought[25]) are characterized by a succession of ever new stages of truth or thought. These stages are different moments within the coherent nexus of one unfolding discourse going on through the ages. Philosophy, Hegel had said, is *its own* time grasped in thought. Here, too, it is the few psychologically gifted persons who as great philosophers, religious thinkers, artists, or poets[26] are capable of performing the "jump," i.e.,

---

[25] Christianity cannot be thought of without Greek philosophy.

[26] Sometimes, but rarely, this list would have to include truly great, creative political leaders.

of expressing the new form of truth, the new way in which verticality can become real for the new historical locus.

With these comments I have already encroached upon the precinct of the second point to be noted about our adage, *Hic Rhodus, hic salta*, namely the identity-and-difference relation of *hic* and *Rhodus*. This saying performs a negation of Rhodes. At first, Rhodes is an unambiguously defined place, the name of a particular island located in geographical reality, in the Mediterranean: a positivity. But now all of a sudden, Rhodes is supposed to be here, where "here" is *wherever* the speaker and the addressee of this command *in fact happen* to be. Even if the *hic* is thousands of miles away from literal geographical *Rhodus*, this *hic* is now said to be the actual *Rhodus*. Rhodes has changed from being the proper name of an *eternally (once for all) fixed*, literal locality into a designation that always accompanies me to any contingent Here to which I happen to move. It has changed from a geographical term to a word that assigns a task to me. *Rhodus* is now the *name* of the psychological task of performing the jump at wherever *hic* that I happen to find myself at. It has become logically negative.

Like "this," "now," and "I" the word *hic* has no specific, determinate semantic content of its own. It does not say *what* concrete situation it is about. It does not *name* a place. All it says or rather does is point to a locus or situation. As this pointing, the saying of "hic" *is* an act of *placing* me, and at the same time committing, binding me. It is like throwing a spear or shooting an arrow at something, into which the spear or arrow bores itself. Or, more precisely, like the flinging of a harpoon ("with strings attached"). But to which locus or situation the *hic* commits me is left entirely open. At each time, by each I, it needs to be found out, experienced anew. In other words, the referent it points to is contingent.

Lacan spoke about the gliding of the signified under the signifiers. What *Hic Rhodus, hic salta* displays is, however, better described as the gliding of the *referent* under the signifier. The name *Rhodus* stays the same (both the same signifier and the same signified, namely the place of jumping, psychologically the place of performing the feat of establishing a real connection between Heaven and Earth). But the actual place in geography and time, or in cultural history, that it refers to, and what this place concretely amounts to, and where this jumping has to take place, is contingent, without, however, in any way being unspecific, indeterminate, and arbitrary. It is not arbitrary because it refers to this one and only place or situation into which I happen to find myself placed at this moment. It is always this *real* one and only Here of my being, the always already given Here that commits me. No choice. No searching. Passive: the where of my having been situated. The existentialists spoke of man's being thrown into existence. In our context we could say that *hic* means the concrete historical situation into which I have been "thrown" through my birth or through historical time.

Psychologically, *hic* represents what we call, using a mythological term, the moment of the Earth in contrast to Heaven. Usually we *imagine* "Earth." We think of soil, rock, the natural world, of solid ground, all sorts of landscapes, of a flat disk or the globe, and in any case we conceive it as a thing in space and in terms of matter. But psychology has to overcome the externalizing literalism inherent in the imagination and realize that as a psychological term Earth has no material, semantic definition. Like "world," it is nothing ontological, but only—quite abstractly, formally—denotes the *logical act* of pointing to, and firmly *positioning* ourselves in, the concrete situation in which we (passively) find ourselves (cf. Luther's "Here I stand!," pronounced with full risk). Just as "Heaven" in this context is the logical act of a vertical "jump" (or its result), rather than ontologically or semantically a cosmological region high above the Earth. The sky is, at least experientially, a dome above us. But heaven is a logical act, a psychological doing, and psychologically it is a great blunder to project the act upon the sky, the logical performance upon a static thing.

To do full justice to our adage we need to realize that the same negation that it performs concerning "Rhodus" it also performs upon the *hic*. The salient point about the *hic* is that it is not simply the positive-factually *given* situation, just like that. Rather, the given situation turns only into a true *hic* (and into "the Earth") *if* it is in fact comprehended as one's *Rhodus*, one's task of "jumping." Both terms in our saying define each other. The *hic* tells us where the psychologically real *Rhodus* lies that demands of us to perform the jump, and the psychologically real *Rhodus* transforms our given situation into our *hic*. Neither term is a positivity that exists in, and is all along known from, external reality. We are here in the sphere of soul-*making!* The rejection of the *hic* is therefore ultimately the rejection of the task of "jumping" and vice versa.

His Communion experience was Jung's *hic* and as such *his* Rhodes. However, because the Communion turned out a terrible disappointment, Jung flatly rejected it as his *hic*, going to *alibi* ("somewhere else") instead. The failure of the ritual, the negation of the bread and wine as symbols, seemed to indicate to him that any "jumping" was impossible from the outset.[27] There was simply nothing, "even a loss" (he thought), so that all he could do was turn his back on it. But of course, the failure of the Communion did not really exempt him from the task of "jumping," did not release him from this his *hic*. However, this is what Jung refused to accept.

We have to think about this for a while. What does the rejection of one's *hic* involve? Factually it is of course absolutely impossible to leave one's Here. We are stuck in it, whether we accept it or not. This means that a rejection of it must mean something else. It means refusing to let the Here that one inevitably belongs to become one's *Rhodus*, the one and only locus where "the jump" has to be performed, and ipso facto to let the Here become one's *hic*. Such a refusal would allow for two possibilities. One could either altogether cancel the idea of *Rhodus* (and thus the obligation of shouldering the task to jump, the task to establish the vertical dimension), and content oneself with an existence at the positive-factual Here on the horizontal plane. Or one could accept the challenge of the *Rhodus* idea, but dissolve the identity and interdependence of *hic* and *Rhodus* and transfer the then detached *Rhodus*, the *Rhodus* dissociated from the *hic*, elsewhere. The latter was Jung's chosen option. He never betrayed *Rhodus* since throughout his life he adamantly insisted on the vertical dimension, the relation to the Self or to God.

But *this* seeming faithfulness to *Rhodus* IS the betrayal of *Rhodus*, and thus also of "the soul" (inasmuch as soul belongs to the vertical dimension). What we have to realize is that due to the mutual

---

[27] Conversely we could say that precisely when the bread and wine still function as true symbols, there is no need for the human subject's explicit jumping because then it is the logic of a symbol itself that takes care of it for him, transporting him into the vertical dimension.

dependence of the two terms of our adage on each other, *Rhodus*, if severed from one's real Here and attached to some other locus that is *not* one's inescapable Here, is *Rhodus* no longer; the alleged verticality achieved through the transposition of the task of jumping from the Here to "my secret" or, later in Jung's life, to other *Urerfahrungen* ("primordial experiences") is not the true vertical dimension at all. The vertical dimension can *only* be had at one's *hic*. One's commitment and loyalty to one's *hic* are indispensable. Jung felt that he could dispose of his real Here and nevertheless keep faith with *Rhodus*, i.e., with the soul, with the vertical dimension or, as he called it, with "the symbolic life." But this is a psychologically fatal error. Without its rootedness in the *hic* as the only point where what we *psychologically* call the Earth is first constituted and becomes a real presence, the "world-tree," that in many mythologies once pictorially represented the vertical dimension, falls down. It cannot stand upright. Thus its very verticality is felled so that it now lies flat on the Earth parallel to the earth's horizontal surface. The boy Jung's "secret" and the later psychologist's "the Self" stay on the horizontal plane. They are mere *exotic* (i.e., *hic*-less) contents on it.

Conversely, if one attempts to perform the jump at *alibi*, one has also lost one's groundedness in the Earth. Because the literal earth turns, in the first place, into the Earth in a psychological sense only to the extent that it is the place were the real connection to Heaven is in fact established and cultivated. It is Heaven, we might say, that gives birth to the Earth. Without verticality, without Heaven, no Earth. The horizontal plane that is left when the vertical dimension is lost is not the Earth, but something totally different: the sphere of positivity.[28]

The exotic character of "the Self" and of "primordial experiences" in general is one that manifests in their numinosity, and this means, only on the subjective emotional level. This exotic character takes the place of the vertical dimension, which is the dimension of the cold logic of the soul in its absolute negativity. Other than in psychology, projection in geometry means the representation of a three-dimensional body or solid on a two-dimensional plane surface. It is this sense of the word that also applies to what happened when Jung moved to "my secret" and, later, when he designed his archetypal

---

[28] Which, paradoxically, includes the whole universe of modern physics and astronomy.

theory. The vertical dimension is projected onto the horizontal plane of particular motifs, the syntactical meaning onto specific semantic contents, the negativity of "the soul" onto certain positive factual ideas and emotions. The psychological difference between horizontality and verticality is reduced to a difference between different types of elements on one and the same horizontal plane: the "rational" contents and aspects of our familiar public world, on the one hand, versus the exotic contents of our private inner world (dream images, archetypal visions, feelings of numinosity, etc.) or of former ages (myths, symbols, rituals), on the other hand. The former is classed with "the ego" or "consciousness," the latter with "the soul" or "the unconscious" (despite the fact that dreams and dream motifs as well as our knowledge of ancient rituals and symbols are just as much contents of our *consciousness* as anything else we are aware of in our ordinary world). What ought to be the logical (categorial) difference between two dimensions, the semantic and the syntactical, is translated into an intrasemantic difference, a difference between certain traits of items on the same plane. The exotic is the horizontalized vertical.

We already know that the refusal of the *hic* is at the same time the refusal of *Rhodus* as the task of jumping. But conversely, the acceptance of the *hic* as *Rhodus* IS in nuce (i.e., logically, implicitly) already the "jump." All that is missing is its full explication. The copula IS the *act* of conjoining *hic* and *Rhodus*, the logical strength to in fact comprehend the real Here AS *Rhodus*.

Psychological consumerism

But why did Jung refuse his *hic*? Here we have to realize that his disappointment at the failure of the Communion was not a reaction of his after the fact, not a response to what he had experienced. Rather, the failure was set up in advance. "Set up" because, as we have already seen, he did not come to the ceremony unprejudiced as the whole person (*homo totus*), but with his artificially split personality, the duality of "No. 1" and "No. 2." With studied innocence ("I was sure"), he put his hope on the bread and wine—although as "No. 1" he "knew" ahead of time that what the ceremony was supposed to produce was a "preposterous impossibility." As "No. 2," however, he approached it at the same time (1) with a prejudgment, (2) with an anachronistic misunderstanding, and (3) with an excessive demand (of getting a subjective "high" from it). Even as a youth, Jung was an intelligent, insightful person, psychologically and religiously gifted, and on top of it the son of a Protestant minister. Therefore deep down he knew better. He knew all along about the sober manner that the church-goers display. It was obvious that religious ceremonies do not aim at ego emotions. But he nonetheless purposely raised his expectations to the sky against his better knowledge in order to stage-manage an exposure of the traditional religious ceremony as containing no trace of God. The so-called "greatest defeat of my life" was wanted. It is safe to assume that no other youth of his Confirmation class had such high expectations and felt such a disappointment.

As his yardstick for the minimum requirement for this "high," he, as "No. 2," brought along in his luggage "his secret" of an immediate and absolutely inexorable experience of God that he had managed to construe for himself during his twelfth year (in the "Basel cathedral" episode referred to above). And so from the outset he had already decided—i.e., dictated—that the bread and wine ought necessarily to bring about an *overwhelming* experience of God and of a true communion. On both counts he was not open to the experience of what might actually happen and so he was also not able to see his *hic* the way it truly was. He was not in the frame of mind of a curious empiricist who simply wants to find out what happens. <u>This is the prejudgment aspect</u>.

The fact that Jung insisted that the satisfaction of his wish for an immediate and overpowering relation to Heaven should happen through the *literal sensual objects* of bread and wine and the *literal* enactment of a ritual is <u>the anachronistic aspect</u>. He had long been beyond that stage of consciousness. He was not so naive, since a few years earlier he had already given up on the Church: from out of the position of solitary superiority on account of his having "my secret" and of his feeling "outlawed or elect, accursed or blessed" (*MDR* p. 41) he had all along been looking down on the numerous parsons among his relatives and their theological discussions and sermons, haughtily thinking about them: "'None of you know anything about that [the secret of grace]. ...' Everything the others said was completely beside the point. I thought, 'For Heaven's sake, there must be someone who knows something about it ...'" (*MDR* p. 42). From the outset the bread and wine did not have a chance. Jung had blown up the significance of the event beforehand in order to let it fall straight into the trap. Unadmittedly he *wanted* to prove it hollow so that he could feel justified in wholeheartedly rejecting the Church, his official and communal religious tradition, once more as a sham, as containing no trace of God, in favor of his utterly subjective, private secret, his own home-made God.

The third aspect (his <u>approaching the Communion with his demands</u>) is the most important. It means that Jung fundamentally rejected the notion of *his* having "to jump." He did not accept the essential aspect of our human need in religious or "metaphysical" regards to become active, of our having to *make* soul. He wanted to stay passive. He insisted on being overwhelmed. This is why for him God was a priori defined as an overwhelming experience. And throughout his life, Jung exclusively focused on experiences, i.e., on something that came to the passive I. Thus he also derived the word *religio* from *religere* (to observe carefully), vehemently rejecting the other ancient etymology from *religare* (to bind back, establish or reconfirm a bond). He wanted us to observe carefully the images coming from the unconscious: what emerges when we are (literally or in a figurative sense) *asleep*. Jung thinks in terms of "revelations" coming from "the unconscious." His theory of the archetypes conceives them as "ageless and everpresent," as always already given dominants, whose passive victims we are or which are the exclusive source of meaning for us. In a certain sense we could say that he wanted what is essential to be served to himself on a silver platter. Even in the one of two cases where he explicitly stressed our having to become active, namely in our practicing "active imagination," consciousness had to be "switched off," as he put it,[29] and the activity performed in active imagination amounted to no more than provoking the unconscious to present new revelations and manifestations, which again had to be passively received and

---

[29] According to the "Protocols of Aniela Jaffé's interviews with Jung for *Memories, Dreams, Reflections*," Library of Congress, Washington D.C., Jung's scientific question [behind his fantasizing experiment from 1913 onwards] was to see what took place "when he switched off consciousness." Cited by Sonu Shamdasani, Introduction "Liber Novus: The 'Red Book' of C.G. Jung," in: C.G. Jung, *The Red Book. Liber Novus*, ed. by Sonu Shamdasani, New York, London (Norton) 2009, p. 200b.

carefully observed.[30] And in the other case (his idea that we should dream the Christian myth onwards, *CW* 9i § 271), the fact that Jung speaks of "dreaming" shows that deep down it is again conceived as a form of passive receptivity.

Thinking in his psychology in terms of (passive, overwhelming) experience, Jung faced the soul (and thus also already in his boyhood days the mystery of the Communion) as consumer, if not, as I said above, a junkie. His standpoint of passive experiencing and wanting something overwhelming[31] is a regressive return to the innocent child's standpoint. Children experience adults and the world as overwhelming powers. They know that they are helpless without their parents and that they cannot shoulder any responsibility. They are not yet burdened with essential tasks. They expect everything essential to be provided for them. Children crave excitement. Children want to *be* entertained. The standpoint of adulthood—of an awareness of a manly task to be performed, of the necessity of an active contribution by the human being, of having to achieve something, and of soul as something to be *made*—was altogether canceled from Jung's psychological scheme, that is to say, as far as essential, metaphysical, religious matters are concerned (of course not so on the personal behavior and pragmatic level). The task of "jumping" was totally excluded.[32]

With this consuming and observing attitude, Jung operates within a logic of difference and otherness on the horizontal plane. Since in his scheme there was no room for a logical achievement on the part of the human mind and thus for verticality, the difference between "the unconscious" and consciousness (to use Jung's categories) had to remain unbridgeable. A *coniunctio*, a syllogism conjoining the opposites, a real *copula* or *vinculum* was precluded.

---

[30] The fact that what Jung conceived of as pure nature, as spontaneous manifestations of "the unconscious," is nevertheless in truth precisely mental production (fabrications) is another story.

[31] Which must not be confused with scientific empiricism. The latter is a mature methodological stance on an advanced adult level, requiring much self-discipline. Jung's insistence on passive experience is not a scientific move, but much more basically experiential, psychological, and metaphysical.

[32] Maybe it is by way of *compensation* for this fundamental exclusion from his theory of the moment of a human logical, syntactical activity that in his theosophy Jung insisted that God was dependent on man because of man's superior moral consciousness. But this significant contribution of man to the future fate of the world was reduced to the semantic level. And God himself, *for* whom man had to make his active contribution, was syntactically presupposed as a natural given, something to be experienced.

I already mentioned that from the soul perspective the boy Jung's disappointment in his Communion experience was meant to be his psychopomp. Here now we can add that it was precisely the aspect of the *failure* of bread and wine to bring about the expected overwhelming bliss which was his real *Rhodus*. For the soul, the disappointment, the *negation* of his expectations, were precious: indispensable rather than a mishap. For they had the function of propelling him forward. Jung, by contrast, thought that the fact that nothing had happened meant that, as it were, there was no *hic* in the true sense at all. He thought that the negation negated (totally canceled, eliminated, did away with) any possibility of a true *hic*, whereas I say that in truth *his* Rhodes was precisely the failure of the Communion. Here, on the ground of the *negation* of his hope, "the jump" would have had to take place for the purpose of establishing an authentic new access to verticality and the soul—much like the fairy tale dragon that prevents people's access to their water source IS their real *hic* and as such the only entrance to the yonder. Jung refused *his* Rhodes (or his real *hic* as his one and only *Rhodus*) because he essentialized or semanticized the *hic*: he kept insisting on what he thought would be "*the true*" Rhodes, i.e., the soul's fulfillment in the accustomed old style through the sensual objects (bread and wine) as veritable *symbols*—although he imagined "symbols" already thoroughly modernistically, namely as a fulfillment through one's subjective emotional experience of the ritual. He did not allow for the *hic's* contingency and historicity, for the possibility of its appearing as an entirely new, unexpected *hic*. Rather, he codified and eternalized one particular, namely the premodern symbolic or ritualistic, form of *hic* or *Rhodus* as *the* Here and Rhodes.

The fact, however, that he expected this premodern form only in an already modernistically emotionalized, and this means egoic, deformation reveals that it was not *really* the old form of truth. This his own expectation objectively (although for Jung unwittingly) betrayed that *what* it expected was *for it* in fact already obsolete and out of the question; it was a self-contradictory expectation.

In the spirit of the refusal of his disappointment he stuck to his "my secret." He ostensibly clung to the fiction of a "timelessly true" *hic Rhodus* and thereby deserted his very own *hic Rhodus*. In the agelessness and everpresence ascribed to his later theoretical construct of the archetypes the *hic*-lessness is codified.

Ultimately "my secret" means: the *hic* is replaced by the ego, by *my* feeling overwhelmed, *my* numinous experience. (This is what makes it logically fundamentally modern, although semantically it pretends to be premodern.) The real *hic*, by contrast, had been what was communally performed and as such was something that preceded and surrounded him. The religious truth had its place in the official, public medium, e.g., in the Communion ritual, and was supposed to show itself there, and only there. This medium was, as is appropriate for the world of rituals and sacraments, a sensual, bodily, physical one, both in the sense that it avails itself of material objects like bread and wine and that it is a literal ceremonial enactment "in the flesh."

The historical move from sensual enactment to logos and thought and Jung's rescue of the sensual

Above I demonstrated the discrepancy in Jung's evaluation of two psychologically rather similar phenomena, the Roman-Catholic Mass and the Zwinglian Communion as a memorial service, and suggested that one reason for the difference was the negative one that the Mass, as exotic for the Protestant Jung, did *not* come with any real claim on him. Now I have to come to a discussion of a second reason, namely what positively was for him an indispensable worth, on account of which the Mass naturally recommended itself to him.

As long as symbols truly function as symbols, they relieve the human subject, as I pointed out, of having to personally and explicitly perform the jump. The indisputable negation of the Communion ritual that he experienced, the fact that the bread and wine obviously were no longer able to function as true symbols for Jung, makes it evident that in *this* form, in its sensualness, in the medium of symbolic or sacramental acts, it was no longer possible for the logical function that they had, and that they used to perform during earlier ages without problem, to be actually executed, to become realized. The failure of the Communion means psychologically that now the task of "jumping" needs to specifically come home from "out there," from the ritualistic level, to the human subject. What once upon a time was to a large extent done for man by, and actually happened in, the sensible, physical enactment now no longer takes place there. If at all, it now has to happen in and be explicitly performed by *the mind* as its *own* logical feat, as its (objective) thought. Objective participation in the ritual enactment simply does no longer do it. The mind itself, its power to think, is called to the front and has to enter the fray. What formerly happened perfectly well on the level of symbols and symbolic actions is no longer able to reach, persuade, and convince the soul. It needs to be interiorized into the very syntax or logical form of consciousness as the new place of action.

A *form change* of the *public medium* in which this function was supposed to happen was needed, a change in the sense of an "alchemical" process of fermenting corruption, sublimation, distillation. This form change would amount to the removal of the whole ritual *from* the medium of the sensory, from the level of sensual things and physical enactments, *to* the medium of thought, the level of "in spirit and in truth" (John 4:23f.). A form change which would of course at the same time mean that for this logical status the ritualistic, sacramental, and symbolic form as such is once and for all overcome, sublated (inasmuch as rituals and sacraments are essentially tied to the physical level). What formerly used to happen through the material wine and bread as veritable *symbols* would after this fundamental form change still have to happen, however now in an entirely new medium, in the *interiority* of thought. The question would now be: how can that process that formerly occurred on the sensual level of symbolic, sacramental action be truly and honestly performed in thought? How can the mind perform, and in fact *achieve*, an *actual* transgression ("jump") in thought, in its thinking? A transgression, the "same" transgression as ever, from the positive-factual to the infinite, from "Earth" to "Heaven"? How can it in fact conjoin the psychic opposites and make us know the presence of the Universal in the Particular, so that the soul might find its veritable fulfillment?

This was the entirely new challenge of "*Rhodus*" at Jung's *hic*. The new situation, brought about by the failure of the Communion, required a potency of thought, of *logos*, the ability to bring about, without the external help of sensuous things and actions "out there," the achievement of actually carrying out the vertical (and ipso facto double) syllogism in the clarity of the thinking mind. The disappointment in his Communion experience had the important psychological purpose of expressly initiating him into the (historically speaking) new, modern truth: into the fundamental shift of the soul's locus (its *hic*) from the semantic to the syntactical, from the sensible, imaginal, or symbolic to the logical as such, alchemically speaking, from the "physical" to the "mercurial."

Ritual, as the *implicit* form of logical movement—the logical movement still enwrapped and concealed in ostensibly external behavior and projected into physical things (just think of "transsubstantiation"!)—would through this transformation have come home to itself. "Home to itself" in the sense of becoming in fact explicitly apparent *as* the logical movement that implicitly it had of course always been, even during the time of its confinement in the external form of visible rituals and symbols. Alchemy spoke of the imprisonment of the Mercurius in the physical matter.

Such would have been the transformation of the old medium. The new medium, *logos*, thought, is not an *alibi*, not elsewhere, an Other, a different alchemical vessel or a different (exotic) prime matter in the vessel, over against or besides the now negated traditional *hic* (the failed Communion). It is, figuratively speaking, only the alchemical distillation of the same old medium. Just as was the medium of the sensual and symbolic, so also is thought still a medium that addresses and belongs to the generality. And as such it is in itself still essentially a *public* locus of truth, even if *empirically* it may only happen in a few individuals in their physical loneliness. Logically, psychologically, thought is communal.

What Jung did—instead of staying with the general public medium and allowing *it* to undergo its "alchemical, mercurial" form change from sensual, visible objects and performances to performances as logical operations of thought on the home territory of the soul or mind—was to move "in space" from *hic* to *alibi*, from the arena of the generality and of public concerns to the wholly other arena of the subjective privacy of the ego's inner: a move to "my secret." Simply turning his back on the public scene and leaving it to its own devices, Jung opened, so to speak, a "secondary theater of war" in addition to the now once and for all discarded sphere. This secondary theater of war, however, was *declared* to be the primary one, the true place where psychological, metaphysical action was to be: "the unconscious" in man's inner. In other words, instead of allowing the *medium* to undergo a metamorphosis, what Jung did was to exchange the *referent* (or, alchemically speaking: the vessel, along with the prime matter in it).

A true (sublimating, distilling) transformation would have been the form change of one and the same referent or matter. Jung avoided the transformation—by switching from the public sphere, i.e., the sphere of truth, to the ego, the felt experience of the individual personality. All of a sudden the individual personality was the new referent. *It* now was what was supposed to undergo a change and discover "the Self." The ego personality was supposed to find *its* satisfaction (its meaning, its myth, its "wholeness").

But anything like that had never been the purpose of myth, ritual, religion, and metaphysics. Concerning the Christian Communion we can say that in it it was the bread and wine that had to undergo an essential change, in the Roman Catholic tradition called "transsubstantiation." *Truth* was supposed to happen. *The soul* was to find its fulfillment. The personality of the people, by contrast, was to remain the same as always—with the one exception that it of course made a difference whether or not they had participated in the happening of truth and whether or not in this their participation *the soul* had indeed found its satisfaction. But the fulfillment of the ego personality had never been a topic. Jung instituted the ego-personality as the new referent.

Instead of moving, in the spirit of alchemy, from the physical level of ritual movement ("in the flesh") to the (no longer ritualistic) "decomposed and distilled" and thus *purely* logical movement of thinking and comprehending, Jung retained the physical level of the original ritualistic medium, merely removing it from *hic* (out there, the public, communal sphere) to "in here," to the privacy of subjective *imagination* (image processes). The symbols in dreams and "the imaginal" or "metaphorical" of archetypal psychology psychologically *share the same physicalness* with the former sacramental symbols and ritual behavior—while having lost their belonging-to-the-generality and thus their committing truth character. It is of course correct, there *is* a difference between, e.g., dismemberment as a literal fact and dismemberment as an image in one's dream. But the essential difference is not that between physical and imaginal, literal and metaphorical, but between *hic* and *alibi*, objective and subjective, public and private. "The imaginal" is simply the *imagined* physical. But whether something physical is imagined *or* concrete event makes *psychologically* little difference. Dream images as metaphors are just as naturalistic as the corresponding literal behavior or objects. They are *sunken*, sedimented cultural symbols and ritual movements, symbols and movements that on the cultural, public level have become obsolete and therefore can appear as timeless free-floating memory images[33] without any *hic*. Earthless. But ipso facto also without Heaven.[34] Merely fancy balloons up in the "*sky*" of subjective aesthetic appreciation.

I already showed that the mature Jung was committed to his appreciative psychological assessment of the Roman-Catholic Mass. If so and if, on account of the internal impoverishment of the Communion of his own original (Zwinglian) Church and its reduction to a mere memorial service, this Communion had become too poor for him to return to it, one would expect him to have joined the Roman-Catholic Church and participated in the celebration of the Mass. But as it is, his great psychological insights into the psychology of the Mass had no consequence for his own life. "I cannot experience the miracle of the Mass; [...]. I know it is the truth [...]. It is no more true to me [...]" (*CW* 18 § 632). In other words, it is true, but—so what? Real life, on the one hand, and what one knows to be the truth, on the other hand, are two totally separate things—dissociated from each other. The soul truth, that is, truth itself, remains cut off from lived life, without any *Sitz im Leben*. It is an inconsequential antique for Jung, and psychology is in truth, but unadmittedly, a purely archeological discipline.

But an abstract truth that is cocooned in itself and cut off from really lived life is itself no longer true. "True" means really true, hook, line, and sinker. Truth always has to *become* true, be *made* true: by being celebrated in ritual or expressed in great art, poetry, music, philosophy ... *Hic Rhodus, hic salta.*

"I know it is the truth [...]. It is no more true to me [...]": the duplicity of this statement is also the truth of "my secret" and of all archetypal images and experiences in modern dreams or visions. It is not restricted to the symbolism of the Mass. The psychology of archetypal images is a psychology without *Rhodus* and without

---

[33] If not mere tropes as instruments of thought.
[34] I already mentioned that Heaven is not a positivity. It exists only for a mode of being-in-the-world that is firmly grounded on the horizontal Earth, but as such—to express it in terms of the premodern stance—psychologically rises to an upright position, looking upwards. In fact, Heaven is nothing but the substantiated act of looking upwards.

the necessity to actually "jump," a psychology of beautiful words without consequences.

To Jung it seemed, as it were, that the Mass, which "is no more true to me," was his Scylla, and the Zwinglian memorial service, which to him is "wretched," was his Charybdis. But for a psychological view, the Mass was the historically obsolete past and the "memorial service" was, to be sure, not the future, but nonetheless what pointed the way into the future. The transformation of the actual transsubstantiation into a mere memorial service is psychologically a significant moment in the soul's opus of distillation and evaporation, a fundamental *form* change. It is one step in the move from the sensual to the form of thought, that is, ultimately to absolute negativity. The moment that what used to be the Mass has turned into a memorial service, its truth no longer resides *out there* in the physical objects, bread and wine, and in the physical acting out of the ritual, it is already receding into the *form* (not the positivistic locus!) of mind, into *memoria* and Mnemosyne.

Jung dreaded this form change. His whole psychology has the purpose of rescuing the sensual as the locus of truth. Since the way back to the sensual *out there* in the literal physical world (the Mass) was all-too obviously blocked, also blocked for him (this was his concession to his modernity), he simply relocated the sensual from out there to *in here*, in the individual personality. The retained sensualness of the "prime matter" (be it the soul itself or its particular concerns) as something that has been *transported* from the real world into "the inner" is *the inner image*, the archetypal image, the image which for him above all figured as symbol, whereas by his followers it was later, more poetically, viewed as an element of "the imaginal." The point I made apropos the example of dismemberment can be repeated here in a different way: whether a ritual is literally acted out in external (material) reality or happens as an image in the inner of man does not make any difference as to its sensual character. *That*, the sensual character, remains the same in both cases. The historical form change inherent in the soul's move from the Mass of the Roman-Catholic Church to the memorial service in the Reformed Church is replaced by Jung with a change of location. The inner serves him as a refuge from his Scylla and Charybdis and is the documentation of his protest against the living *soul's* further-development, his opting out of the opus of the soul's truly "alchemical" self-transformation in its own historical process.

In Jung's *Red Book* we find the revealing statement, "God is an image: and they that worship him must worship him in the image of the overmeaning" (p. 229b, transl. modif.). If read as an explicit attack on John 4:24—"God is Spirit: and they that worship him must worship him in spirit and in truth"—it is programmatic. For in it, with it, Jung undoes the move to "Spirit" and returns to the sensual, which, under the conditions of his time, a time once and for all beyond the sensual, he can only do by storing the sensual away in a segregated, fundamentally hidden (and imaginary) retreat within the *real* world all around it: that is to say, in the inner, "the unconscious."

But why was it of vital importance to rescue the sensual? What was at stake for Jung as well as, later, for the imaginalists? The answer must be: the sensual was indispensable for them to guarantee their need for preserving the sense of *immediate presence*[35] of, and *direct access* to, the divine. Or, the other way around, the notion of soul had to be kept fundamentally free of any logical negation, departedness, sublatedness, brokenness, reflectedness—in order to retain, in Jung's case, the (psycho-)logical (not psychic or personal[36]) child status, and in the case of imaginal psychology the status of the *puer*.[37] (For us this

---

[35] Part of this is the claim of the everpresence both of the archetypes and of the imaginal.
[36] However, so much of Jungian psychology after Jung has become downright childish, infantile, clinging to the emotional and to wishful thinking. A psychology for *psychological* children whose horizon is defined by pictures, "numinous" feelings, warmth, self-development, "wholeness," and "meaning," just as very much of our culture at large today is one for children, as can readily be seen from television and computer games, but also from most movies, most entertainment, and politics.
[37] As we know from James Hillman's paper, "Puer Wounds and Ulysses' Scar" (in: *Puer Papers*, Irving TX [Spring Publications: 1979] pp. 100–128), the *puer* may certainly have wounds. But he would not be *puer* if he allowed his woundedness to come home to him. The wound remains for him a permanent *psychic* injury and annoyance, but never becomes *psychological*, is never integrated into the very structure of his consciousness, as is shown by his inability to let it develop into a scar as the *sublated* wound. By psychically keeping the wound open, he psychologically rescues his logical in-nocence. The psychological child status, as a status of theoretical (not personal) consciousness, by contrast, remains fundamentally unwounded. Consequently it feels exposed to the overwhelming, irrational-ambivalent Parent (above all, the Father God). This is one reason why for Jung the topic of evil was so essential and why he passionately had to fight for the ontologization of evil and the attribution of evil to God himself as one of God's aspects. "Evil" is the excluded, externalized, and quasi reified wound (or *negation*) in the logic of the child status of theoretical consciousness (quite in contrast to the innocent *puer* who owing to his aestheticizing is not touched by evil).

means that it was not allowed to come home to itself. It was supposed to show itself only in the medium of its Other, the sensual.)

Holding one's place within the negation and the situation of absence

There would have been only one honest and legitimate reaction to the insight (which of course was already the insight of adolescent Jung) that "It is no more true" [where "it" can for us refer both to the Mass and to the "wretched memorial service"], only one honest and legitimate reaction *if* one was not ready, the way Freud was, to throw religion overboard altogether as an illusion. I will describe this honest reaction in two steps.

It would first have been to systematically and openly construe psychology as a purely historical discipline having access to the soul only in Mnemosyne, the discipline of the "fair memory of things that once were" (*CW* 9i § 50)—once upon a time when people indeed were still enveloped by the soul, so that it was the soul that was the true subject in them. This historical research was what Jung, without admitting it, actually performed when he was at his best, such as in his work on the Mass. The fair memory of things that once were would not have to be an idle pastime. Rather, it still could give us much to think about, much to move the soul. And this takes me already to the second step.

The honest reaction would in addition have been to document that precisely our living under the conditions of the logic of the unbridgeable difference (S | O) is our real *hic* and that this *hic* IS our real *Rhodus*,[38] our place to "jump." The honest reaction would thus also have been to document that the soul, that truth, still have a *Sitz im Leben*, only in some new and totally unexpected, not understood way and sense, a way and sense still to be discovered, or rather *produced* by our soul-*making* on the soul's home territory, thought.

---

[38] And as such already the *implicit* S – M – P.

But Jung did not make either of the two aspects of this possible reaction his own.[39]

Concerning the second aspect, it would of course be all-too easy to understand egoically, and thus misunderstand, the "our" in "produced by our soul-making" or "our place to 'jump'"—as if *we* were able to think the double syllogism by command. Thinking in the true sense is not the ego-personality's doing. If, as Hegel stated, philosophy is its time grasped in thought, then the real subject of thought is Time, the objective soul itself in its actual historical process. There is, however, also a place for our active participation—an active participation, of course, on the deep level of the logic of "the soul," not on that of empirical behavior. What in the narrower sense is *our* thinking (or "jumping") is the grasping of the thought as which our real *hic* (our historical locus) exists.

The dialectic of "our," e.g., in "our soul-making" is that it is the unity and difference of the soul's (uroborically) making *itself*, AND of our indispensable contribution, in the sense of Luther's *oportet me adesse* and alchemy's *oportet operatorem interesse operi*.

In the above description of the second aspect, it would likewise be all-too easy to understand, i.e., misunderstand, the phrase "our place *to jump*" in the traditional sense of what "jumping" once amounted to during the age of metaphysics, namely a true opening up of the dimension of verticality, as an actual reaching the top of the glass mountain through the vertical syllogism. In our historical situation of the unbridgeable difference the very idea of "jumping," too, has irrevocably been distilled and evaporated, or, logically speaking, negated. It can no longer be pictorially imagined (ultimately along the lines of the old mythic difference of Mother

---

[39] However, we must not forget that by means of the crutch of "*the* unconscious" and by shifting away "the battlefield of the struggle between light and darkness" from the real-life arena to the fantasized inner (cf. *CW* 13 § 293), Jung was still able to rescue for us moderns the knowledge about the psychological difference. But he did so only by holding on to the old, outdated logical form of the sensual and imaginal. The price he had to pay for the rescue of the knowledge about the difference between the (basically biological) psyche and the soul on the basis of this outdated logical form was that he was not able to uphold this knowledge *in his real life* (*vide* his Communion experience). This knowledge was only a fundamentally neutralized one, which keeps using *semantic* differences (different sorts of images: ordinary reality ones versus mythic ones) to express a difference that is the difference *between* the semantic *and* the syntactical. And, as the perhaps highest price: the loss of truth and the resulting free-floatingness, dissociatedness, and by definition fundamental unconsciousness of the world of archetypal images.

Earth down here and Father Heaven above: the finite natural world and the infinite, transcendent God). It now has its place "in spirit and in truth," in the absolute negativity of thought, although our time is not yet up to what is already its real truth. Our time still seems to be stuck in the negation of metaphysics, without being able to distill this negation into "spirit" as absolute negativity. For the time being, therefore, "jumping" can mean no more than our modest consciously and patiently holding our place in this situation of the unbridgeable difference as the simple negation of a full-fledged "jumping," the "jumping" *as* negated and absent (left blank); our holding our place in Jung's as well as our own disappointing *hic* so that it might slowly explicitly *initiate consciousness into logical negativity.*

However, this would only be a true holding our place in the situation of absence if it is already our holding our place in this our *hic* truly AS our *Rhodus*! This "AS," this tarrying or dwelling with the negative that can still say "This is it" with respect to its situation, would be *our* contribution, *our* addition, *our* "adesse," "interesse," in Luther's and alchemy's sense, *our* soul-*making*. Only with this "AS" would *our* accepting our *hic*, which is the *hic* of the negated verticality, be wholehearted, without reserve; it would be our full presence *in* the absence of presence, without any escape to the *alibi* of wishful thinking, utopian substitutes, or nostalgic consumption of the myths and symbols of former times or alien cultures—nor an escape to the deconstructive mechanics of an unending deferral of "meaning," a serialized perpetual gliding of the signified under the signifier. Only with this our resolute presence in the absence is there a consciousness at all that can be initiated by the absence.

And, furthermore, this "AS"—I indicated as much—would already *be* the *implicit* bridging of the difference and, as such bridging, also the *placeholder in Mnemosyne* of the former verticality, the former Heaven, and thus even already the *implicit* "jump," its first immediacy. But no more.

For any "more," if there should be any, we would have to patiently wait, holding our place in our historical locus. Stay put in it.[40] Perhaps, one day in the distant future *Time* might have moved from our *hic* of

---

[40] No hoping, no utopia.

a merely implicit bridging to a new real *hic* of the fully developed explicit double syllogism. *In patientia vestra possidebitis animas vestras.*

Maybe Jung's father, the way Jung perceived and described him, with all his mental suffering could have served as an exemplary model for such an attitude of patiently holding one's place, even if a merely preliminary model. Jung wrote about his father: the Church and its theological thinking "had faithlessly abandoned him after having blocked all avenues by which he might have reached God directly" (*MDR* p. 93, transl. modif.). What this means is in the last analysis that Jung's father (in the image Jung had formed of him) had been on the way to the ultimate experience of Christ on the Cross, "My God, my God, why hast thou forsaken me," which is the simple negation *of* the still mythically imagined God. As such, it is the preliminary form of the ultimate distillation and evaporation of theism, of the mythic, sensual God-image. It is the necessary prerequisite of the form of absolute negativity. In other words: the preliminary form of what in still imaginal language is expressed as "the coming of the Spirit."

Although the form of absolute negativity is already in fact the existing truth of our time, the consciousness of our time is not yet up to its truth. Nevertheless, for the time being it is on principle already possible, even if only within the niche of the special discipline of psychology (and thus in a merely *methodological* sense), to achieve absolute negativity, to "reach the top of the glass mountain," in certain lucky moments and only within the confines of the eachness of this or that particular "matter" (this one dream, this specific psychic phenomenon) and only for the persons, in their privacy, involved in the soul work on this "matter." But, provided it happens at all, this methodologically produced achievement in the private intimacy of soul work has as such no meaning for the generality.

The communal nature of soul

Concerning the *hic salta*, I have so far mainly emphasized the necessity of a rootedness in lived life and our presence in the disappointing nature of our *hic*. In addition, we also have to consider the other already mentioned aspect of the importance of the community. It concerns the notion of subjectivity itself. A subject exists only by virtue of a community of subjects. Without logically being acknowledged by another subject, there is not a subject at all. The subject is not, like a living organism, an entity having an existence of its own. It is not a fact of nature. There is not first a subject that then is also, or is maybe not, acknowledged by others and integrated into a community. No. Mutual acknowledgment—a psycho-logical act— is the *origination* of subjectivity. Subjectivity is *contra naturam*, existing only in the sphere of *Geist*, mindedness, and this is why the idea of a single, atomic subject is a contradiction in terms. The subject requires other subjects to come into being; it requires language, which is fundamentally communal.

This insight is mirrored in a phrase often quoted by Jung: *extra ecclesiam nulla salus*,[41] to which we might add: *et nulla veritas et nulla anima*. *Ecclesia* has become the Latin word for "Church," but originally it simply meant the community, the assembly of the citizens, the congregation. And in our context we have to understand it in this wider sense of the community of subjects. Truth and soul require a mutuality of subjects. There is no such thing as a soul without a community.[42] As the subject, so also is the soul nothing natural, ontological. It has to be "made." It only comes into being in a social, cultural, linguistic context. An embryo may have a psyche, but it does not have a soul.

Jung only gave an emotionalizing, experiential, and in this sense positivizing interpretation of the state of being *extra ecclesiam*. He said, "[...] then things really become terrible, because you are no more protected, you are no more in the *consensus gentium*, you are no more in the lap of the All-compassionate Mother. You are alone and you are confronted with all the demons of hell" (*CW* 18 § 632). In other words, he addressed the problem on the level of the ego. He was not aware of the logical dimension of the problem and did not see that the community / communality is the *sine qua non* of subjectivity, soul, and truth. He thought that the real psychological threat is that something terrible happens *to* an individual, to an existing subject, a subject that precisely affirms and maintains itself in any suffering it may have to go through. But we have to say that if you get yourself into a situation where all hell is loose, this is *psychologically* insignificant,

---

[41] Cf. Cyprianus, Epistulae 73,21,2.
[42] Not always literal, empirical community. A hermit lives empirically in isolation, but logically within the community and its communal faith. That this is in fact so can also be seen from the veneration hermits generally receive from the community.

because it is only *psychic*, only a (terrible) *happening* or *experience*, i.e., an experience for the ego personality or civil man, and only something semantic. The *psychological* question, by contrast, is what happens to the *logic* of the very subjectivity of the subject, to the logic of soul and truth as such.

By rejecting the Communion experience Jung also rejected once and for all the community of subjects, the *ecclesia*, and opted for his logical isolation. His rejection was total. "The Church was a place that I was not allowed to go to ever again. What was there was for me not life, but death." "My sense of union with the Church and with the human world around me [...] was shattered. The religious view of things which appeared to me as the sole meaningful cohesion with the Whole had disintegrated; I could no longer participate in the general faith, but found myself involved [...] in 'my secret,' which I could share with no one." (*MDR* p. 55 f., transl. modif.) Talking about the "*kirchliche Gemeinschaft*" (the Church community, the community of the believers, the congregation) he said: "I could not connect any meaning with that phrase" (p. 75, modif.). Jung had (logically or psychologically, not empirically) dropped out for good and was from now on defined as a logically solitary individual. "For the sake of God[43] [!, i.e., *ad maiorem dei gloriam*] I found myself separated from the Church and from my father's and everybody else's faith [...]. I had fallen out of the Church" (p. 62, transl. modif.).

Jung's self-excommunication was a deliberate act and had *systematic, programmatic* significance. This move amounted to the renouncement of the possibility of truth as such. But we have to realize that it *ipso facto* also amounted to his excommunication from the land of "the soul" in favor of ego and self, which were already inherent in his early, youthful insistence on "my secret."

If Jung had on this basis continued like Freud, who had no stake in such a thing as soul and its truth, but was satisfied with positivistically studying the functioning of the psychic apparatus, all would have been fine. But Jung wanted, Jung needed "truth," despite his having knowingly and willfully given up the basis for truth. And so, after having banished from real life the *sine qua non*

---

[43] "For the sake of God": really? Or not rather for *his* own satisfaction of still possessing a God, in other words, for the sake of his ego needs?

of truth, the subject's participation in the community of subjects, he sunk this very precondition of truth (the communal aspect, the *consensus gentium*, or what he had called in the cited passage "my father's and everybody else's faith" and "the general faith," and what Hegel one and a half centuries before had called "the faith of the world") deep down into "the unconscious" as "the *collective* unconscious." A communality *by naming* or *declaration*.

Freud's positivism was naive, the empirical, pragmatic, or semantic positivism of the facts of psychic life, human desires and their vicissitudes. Jung's is much more radical: a logical, syntactical positivism. He absolutely wanted to rescue truth, the spirit, the sense of the communal, "the stars" (*CW* 9i § 50[44])—but he "rescued" them on the basis of the not retracted rejection of his real community. This means he could "rescue" them only by positivizing and entombing in "the unconscious" the *very notion* of truth, of the communal, and of spirit, by turning them into natural things or attributes. In fact, this description could even serve as the definition of "the unconscious." The positivization of the *logic* of truth is what Jung clearly expressed in metaphorical language with his statement that spirit "has descended from its fiery heights. But when spirit becomes heavy it turns to water [...]. [...] spirit is no longer above but down below, no longer fire but water" (*CW* 9i § 32, transl. modif.). These sentences speak of what in and by his psychology *was done to* spirit, although Jung of course presents this change as if he was merely describing an objective natural *fate* of spirit which he had observed.

What was done by his "psychology of the unconscious" was the operation of an alchemical coagulation, that is, the logical "naturalization" *of* what is the very opposite of the natural or physical, namely spirit or mindedness. His psychology "naturalized" that spirit that, as fundamentally *sublated* nature, in truth only exists through, and lives in, the real communal life of a people, the most fundamental basis and expression of which is language.[45]

---

[44] "Since the stars have fallen from heaven and our highest symbols have paled, a secret life holds sway in the unconscious." This sounds like the generalization of Jung's early "my secret."

[45] What in psychology we call "the soul," as absolute negativity, has its locus in this real communal life and not *in* each positively existing person as isolated individual.

The downwards process of spirit described (and performed!) by Jung, on the one hand, and what I discussed above as his rescue of the sensual, on the other hand, coincide. They are work at the logical imprisonment of the spirit Mercurius in what for the alchemists would have been the physicalness of the matter—a veritable *opus secundum naturam.*

CHAPTER FIVE

The Smuggling Inherent in the Logic of the "Psychology of the Unconscious"[1]

A famous dictum of Hegel's states that just like each individual is a son of his time, so also philosophy is "*ihre Zeit in Gedanken erfaßt,*"[2] its time grasped and presented in the form of thoughts. The same applies analogously to all great cultural manifestations, to works of art, poetry, music, to fashion, life-styles and so on, but also to psychology. I stand up for the historicity of psychology. The findings of psychology are not like those of the natural sciences, e.g., medicine. We have to assume that the knowledge gained during the last decades about viruses, neurophysiology, and genes is not simply an expression of our time, but is valid also for all times in the past, even though it was not available then. Psychology is different from medicine. Such a psychological idea as "the unconscious" is not a timeless anthropological fact, part of the inventory of the personality. People of the Middle Ages or of Antiquity did not have an unconscious. "The unconscious" is an idea and as such a product and expression of the time that developed this idea.

This, of course, is not to imply that in earlier ages people were always completely conscious. There is a fundamental difference between the adjective "unconscious" and the noun "the unconscious."

---

[1] Public lecture, given in October 2002 at The Praxis and Research Institute for Clinical Psychology and Education, Graduate School of Education, Kyoto University, here printed with a few additions.

[2] Hegel, *Grundlinien der Philosophie des Rechts*, TWA vol. 7, p. 26.

There is no doubt both that *people* of all times were and are to a large degree unconscious and that many really existing feelings, ideas, motivations etc., remain unconscious. The adjective "unconscious" describes either a *state* of people's consciousness or a *quality* of certain contents. "The unconscious" as a concept of depth psychology, however, means something completely different, be it a layer of the psyche, a part of the personality, or a reservoir of images, ideas, instinctual wishes, repressed memories, or an organ, possibly even an agent with a certain subjectivity and intentionality of its own, so that in some quarters one can, e.g., say, "the unconscious has sent me this dream" or ask, "what did the unconscious want to tell me with this dream?" To put it in slightly exaggerated terms, "the unconscious" was not discovered, but invented.

What I want to do in this paper is to look a little bit behind the scenes of this invention. Of course, "the unconscious" is not an unequivocal term; there are in fact several distinct unconsciouses, if I may say so, most notably a Freudian and a Jungian one. In this paper I will restrict myself to "the unconscious" in the sense of C.G. Jung. And since I want to go behind the scenes of this term, I will not start out with Jung's *teachings* about the unconscious, but with a dream that Jung had while working on his early main work, *Wandlungen und Symbole der Libido*, maybe in 1911 or 1912. This dream

> had its scene in a mountainous region on the Swiss-Austrian border. It was toward evening, and I saw an elderly man in the uniform of an Imperial Austrian customs official. He walked past, somewhat stooped, without paying any attention to me. His expression was peevish, rather melancholic and vexed. There were other persons present, and someone informed me that the old man was not really there, but was the ghost of a customs official who had died years ago. "He is one of those who still couldn't die properly." That was the first part of the dream (*MDR* p. 163).

Jung's dream had a second (and as Jung thought) "far more remarkable" part. In it the dream-ego found itself in an Italian city, that reminded Jung of Bergamo. It was noontime, between twelve and one o'clock. It was summer, the blazing sun stood at the zenith, and everything was bathed in an intense light. Many people came towards me, and I knew that now the shops were closing and people were on their way home to dinner. In the midst of this stream of people walked a knight in full armor. He mounted the steps toward me. He wore a helmet of the kind that is called a basinet, with eye slits, and chain armor. Over this was a white tunic into which was woven, front and back, a large red cross.

One can easily imagine how I felt: suddenly to see in a modern city, during the noonday rush hour, a crusader coming toward me. What struck me as particularly odd was that none of the many persons walking about seemed to notice him. It was as though he were completely invisible to everyone but me. I asked myself what this apparition meant, and then it was as if someone answered me—but there was no one there to speak: "Yes, this is a regular apparition. The knight always passes by here between twelve and one o'clock, and has been doing so for a very long time [for centuries, I gathered] and everyone knows about it." (p. 164f., transl. modif.).

After the narration of the dream itself, Jung describes how he analyzed this dream. The report in *Memories, Dreams, Reflections* about the dream and about the interpretation that he gave to it at the time of the dream were dictated by Jung and edited by A. Jaffé almost fifty years after the reported events happened. There is no indication in Jung's description that from the distance of his old age Jung felt the need to view his dream any differently than he had done around 1911 or 12.

There exist, however, several different versions of the dream, different in certain not unimportant respects. The notes of Jung's own verbatim report on which Aniela Jaffé's *MDR* version was based[3] is different from the printed *MDR* version, and both are different from the way Jung first reported this dream material in his 1925 *Analytical Psychology* seminar.[4] The dictated notes version represents the two dream parts as two independent dreams separated by a few weeks or months in time, and curiously the first dream part as the *later* dream, the second part as the *former* one. In the seminar version both scenes

---

[3] Sonu Shamdasani was kind enough to make the relevant portion of these notes available to me.

[4] C.G. Jung, Analytical Psychology. Notes of the Seminar Given in 1925, ed. William McGuire, Princeton, N.J. (Princeton University Press) 1989, pp. 38–40.

are part of the same dream. The first part takes place "on a road in the country" and the second part is introduced by the words, "Then the scene changed and I was in a southern town ...." Now, years after I wrote this paper initially, the earliest version of this dream from Jung's "Black Books" (2, pp. 25f.) has also become available as it has been quoted in the "Introduction" to the *Red Book*.[5] Here, as in the 1925 version, both scenes are part of one dream, but in contrast to the later versions the whole dream (also the scene with the customs official) plays at one and the same location, namely "in a southern town."

If my purpose was "dream interpretation" I would have to stick to the Black Book version, as it was recorded right after Jung had had this dream. My purpose is, however, a different one. What I want to do with this dream text is to *use* its images and the internal relation of its contents for elucidating the problematic hidden logic of the invention of the notion of "the unconscious." For this aim, the version as it appears in *MDR* is more suitable since it reveals old man Jung's memory and view of it. Psychologically, the truth and essence of something does in general not show itself primarily in the *prima figura*, but in the final product. I use this dream as an illustration *in the light of* which it is possible to present more clearly and easily complex relations and the logical structure inherent in "the psychology of the unconscious." In other words, I do not take this dream as clear-cut "evidence," nor as literal "origin" or efficient cause. The memory of this dream accompanied Jung through his life. It was a living matrix. As such it reflects certain aspects of the *background of his thinking*. Inasmuch as I use the dream for illustrating a conception, I do not *derive* Jung's concept of the unconscious nor my interpretation of it from this dream. Rather, my interpretation of the logic of "the unconscious" is based on my study of Jung's work as a whole. But the fantasy expressed in the dream *together with Jung's own interpretation* very nicely brings to light an essential aspect of his theory, which otherwise tends to remain invisible.

---

[5] Sonu Shamdasani, "Einleitung," in: C.G. Jung, *Das Rote Buch. Liber Novus*, ed. Sonu Shamdasani, Düsseldorf (Patmos) 2009, p. 200. Engl. transl. of the dream in *idem*, "Introduction," in: C.G. Jung, *The Red Book. Liber Novus*, ed. Sonu Shamdasani, New York, London (W.W. Norton & Company) 2009, p. 198.

After these preliminary methodological considerations I return to the dream itself and to Jung's own interpretive comments. The first association Jung had about the first part of the dream was in connection with the motif of "customs." It immediately evoked in him the idea of the psychoanalytical term "censorship." And the idea of "border" made him think of the border between consciousness and the unconscious, on the one hand, and between Freud's views and his own, on the other. The scrutinizing customs examinations usually taking place at borders seemed to Jung to allude to analysis. "At a border suitcases are opened and examined for contraband. In the course of this examination, unconscious assumptions are discovered," Jung states. Along the same lines of interpretation, Jung saw in the old customs official an embodiment of Freud. He said, "As for the old customs official, his work had obviously brought him so little that was pleasurable and satisfactory that he took a sour view of the world. I could not refuse to see the analogy with Freud."

What do we make of this interpretation that Jung gave to his own dream? In order to get a perspective on this question I want to confront this interpretation with something Jung himself said in connection with a dream of an analysand of his. In that dream the dream-I was about to go to a doctor who lived in a house at the sea. In interpreting this dream during a seminar in 1930, Jung said the following:

> Naturally when she dreams of the doctor, everybody is inclined to think he is myself. She is under my treatment and so that refers to me. Now it is only funny that the unconscious does not say so more definitely. Naturally anybody who analyzed dreams according to Freud's point of view would say that it was I, but I am not sure. If the unconscious wanted to convey the idea that this was Dr. Jung, it would say so; then the dream itself, which we cannot criticize, would have brought me in. But the dream says "the doctor by the sea," and the Lake of Zürich is not a sea. Therefore there is some change in the whole situation and we see that behind the impressions of the daily life—behind the scenes—another picture looms up, covered by a thin veil of

> actual facts. In order to understand dreams, we must learn to
> think like that. We should not judge dreams from realities
> because in the long run that leads nowhere.[6]

In this rather casual comment Jung laid down an interpretation
principle of fundamental importance. It is a truly *psychological*
principle, in other words, one that allows dreams to be viewed from
the perspective of soul, rather than from the perspective of the ego
and its ordinary life interests or other external considerations. This
principle has two aspects.

> (1) In order to do justice to the dream we have to understand
> it immanently, in its own terms and as basically self-sufficient;
> we have to stick to the image. "To understand the dream's
> meaning I must stick as close as possible to the dream images"
> (*CW* 16 § 320). And in his late work, *Mysterium Coniunctionis*,
> Jung therefore advises the psychologist, following an
> alchemical dictum, "Above all, don't let anything from outside,
> that does not belong, get into it, for the fantasy-image has
> 'everything it needs' within itself."[7] [This is the principle of
> self-enclosedness of the image.]

> (2) "Sticking to the image" should not be taken to mean
> reading it in the light of how it appears to the everyday
> mind concerned with ordinary reality, with the factual. We
> are not to read it pragmatically with the utilitarian ego
> interests in survival, success, personal comfort, and profit
> in mind. No, we "should not judge dreams from realities,"
> but should rather see the "other picture" that "looms up"
> "behind the scenes," "behind the impressions of daily life."
> The soul has another, its own agenda. [This is an expression
> of the psychological difference.]

Returning from these general remarks about fundamental
principles of a *psychological* dream interpretation to our dream with
the motif of customs, of the border, and the customs official, we are

---

[6] C.G. Jung, *The Visions Seminars*, From the Complete Notes of Mary Foote, Book
One, Zürich (Spring Publications) 1976, Part One (Lectures October 30 – November
5, 1930), pp. 7f.
    [7] C.G. Jung, *CW* 14 § 749. I have added the not unimportant words "within itself,"
which have been omitted in the *CW* translation, but are part of Jung's German original.

immediately struck by the fact that the interpretation given by Jung in his *Memories* does not abide by those principles that Jung himself had laid down later. It may well be that at the early date when he had the dream, at the beginning of the 20th century, Jung had not developed these insights yet and that therefore we cannot charge him with not having followed his own rules. At the time, Jung was still relatively close to the Freudian approach to dreams and had not completely liberated himself to his own view. He still was used to practicing "free association." But we are here concerned with his late discussion of the dream in *MDR*, and, as I stated, Jung does not indicate that at the time of telling us about this dream in *MDR* he would feel the need to distance himself from his earlier interpretation, to modify or correct it a bit.

But obviously, his interpretation does violate his own principles of dream interpretation. Jung had told us that in the case of the "doctor by the sea"-figure in his patient's dream we should not jump to the conclusion that this doctor must refer to the analyst, i.e., Dr. Jung, because the unconscious could have said so if it wanted to convey the idea that he was meant. In just the same way we must here not jump to the conclusion that the figure of the customs official refers to Freud (who, after all, is a person outside the dream), even if they have some features in common: his expression is peevish and he takes a sour view of the world, just as Freud did in Jung's estimation. The unconscious could have made clear that it is referring to Freud, if it had wanted to.

Just as important is the other problem in Jung's interpretation, namely that he views the details of the dream completely in the light of "the impressions of daily life" and "from realities," rather than going "behind the scenes" to the "other picture" that is "covered by a thin veil of actual facts." The horizon within which Jung perceived the dream is that of his daily professional life as a psychoanalyst (thus his associations of censorship and the border between consciousness and the unconscious) and his personal feelings and complexes, particularly his highly ambivalent, strained relation to Freud and Freudian theory. His relation to Freud at the time was characterized by an exaggerated esteem for Freud, based, on the one hand, on his projection of "the superior personality" or "the father" (p. 163), that resulted in a dependency, and, on the other hand, by corresponding resistances toward him and a critical assessment of parts of his theory. Jung explains that at the time of this dream he was still unconscious of this situation and had therefore not resolved it. He had cast aside his own judgments and repressed his criticisms. And thus it was to his surprise that he dreamed, as he states in *MDR*, "of him as a peevish official of the Imperial Austrian monarchy." And the meaning of the dream, Jung concluded, was "a corrective," "a compensation or antidote for my conscious high opinion and admiration. Therefore the dream recommended a rather more critical attitude toward Freud" (p. 164).

But Jung did not stick to the image. The image itself does not give any hint that it is about Freud, that Freud could be meant and that the dream is concerned with Jung's personal ambivalences concerning Freud the man and his theory. We would do well not to quickly identify the image of the customs official with something that is known to the dreamer from daily life and reduce it to this. The dream is about a customs official, and the actual topic of the dream is a border crossing that, however, turns out to be an unusual one. This essential aspect is completely lost if the dream is viewed in terms of Jung's difficulties with Freud, or rather, it is reduced to a feature *of* the real Freud, to *his* peevishness and dissatisfaction with life. In other words, the *subject* of the dream is turned into a mere *attribute* of a person outside the dream who is now considered to be the real subject. "Freud" is Jung's external whimsical association on account of one single feature that both may have had in common, their peevishness and dissatisfaction with life. This abstract feature that they have in common is the lever with which the quality of "being the *subject* of the dream" is taken away from the customs official and re-assigned to a person outside the dream.

So we have to start afresh and ask who the customs official in the dream is. Just as "the doctor by the sea" in the dream of Jung's analysand referred to the inner doctor, the source of healing in the soul, so here, too, the customs official has to be seen as a soul or dream customs official, one who guards the *psychological* border; and he is not a person who merely happens to have the *job* of customs official, in addition to what other qualities or functions he may have otherwise. In empirical reality a customs official may in his private life also be a good (or bad) husband and father and a member of his town's baseball club. But the soul or dream customs official is *only* this: customs official. He is THE CUSTOMS OFFICIAL as such, the pictorial representation of the *concept* of customs official, its embodiment. As such he does not have a private life nor an individual personality. Empirical reality or ordinary life is characterized by the fact that concept and real being (or behavior), substance and attribute, and title (job or profession) and person are separable; a doctor can be a good physician or a quack, a judge can be a conscientious judge guided solely by the idea of justice or he can be prejudiced, even bribed. Not so in dreams. What distinguishes psychological or dream reality from empirical-factual reality is that attributes or features appearing in dreams have to be read *substantially*, as a substance or essence in itself, rather than as *accidents* or contingent modes of being, modes that exist *in* a substance (e.g., person) and depend on it for their existence. A person in the dream characterized as doctor or judge is generally the true healer, the true judge and nothing else.

In this dream the customs official appears to be peevish and melancholic. Rather than going outside the dream to Jung's subjective or ego impressions from daily life and drawing the 'external' conclusion or syllogism:

1. premise: The customs official gives the impression of being peevish;
2. premise: Freud gives the impression of being peevish, *therefore*

---

3. conclusion: the customs official must be Freud,

and rather than thinking that the fact that the official happens to be in a bad mood today may be because of a quarrel with his wife or because of bad news or because he has a grumpy disposition, in other words, rather than thinking that the official's bad mood is accidental and that he could just as well be in another mood, we have to understand the peevishness of the dream customs official as belonging to his *definition*. As a dream invention, the peevishness must reflect the situation or status that the very concept of "customs official" is in at the psychological moment that this dream is displaying. The (seemingly personal) impression he gives *defines* what he *is*, customs official, not something personal about him. And what this mood is about has to be interpreted solely from the hints contained in the dream itself, solely in terms of the information we get within the dream: we hear that he is not real, he is the ghost of a customs official who had died years ago, one of those who cannot die. We also hear that he walked past the dream-ego (Jung) "without paying any attention to" him.

This last dream motif is very interesting, because it is in sharp contrast to what one would expect of customs officials and what indeed Jung's immediate association was. Jung thought of a scrutinizing examination for contraband of the luggage of those who come to the border. But the customs official here simply ignores the would-be border crossers. Instead of their having to go past him and of his critical gaze, he walks past them. An upside-down world. The customs official is not a customs official in the strict sense at all; he does not fulfill his notion anymore, but he merely still bears this name. This is the reason why he is merely the ghost of a customs official who had died years ago. He is a zombie, one of those who couldn't die properly. And this sufficiently explains his peevishness and melancholy. We must not take recourse to the entirely speculative idea that he is so because his work brought him so little that was pleasurable and satisfactory and that so he went sour, because the dream does not give any indication that this might have been the reason.

What the dream does tell us, and only this counts as explanation, is something completely different: the customs official is in an unbearable, absolutely contradictory position. He is dead, has been dead for years, but cannot die properly; he has to continue to factually walk about, but he cannot really live and do his job either. In conceptual language we might say that he represents the *obsolescence* of "customs official" or of the institution of customs at large that he embodies in this dream, and the idea of the ghost is the pictorial expression for the compromise formation between still existing—yet having lost his function and *raison d'être*. Our customs inspector obviously has to be on duty, but must not do his job—reason enough to be melancholic.

In empirical reality a customs official can go into retirement or die, but then he will be replaced by another one. Because in reality, person and office are separable. The person is subject to all kinds of fates, but the office stays. In the dream, if THE customs official is said to have died years ago, the whole office of customs inspection is defunct.

As we have heard, Jung was of the opinion that the purpose of the dream was to "urge upon [him] the necessity of clarifying" his unconscious projections upon Freud and attain to a more critical attitude toward him. This interpretation continues the complete reversal of roles that has taken place: instead of being, within the dream, *exposed* to the critical scrutiny by the customs official, Jung as ego outside the dream is supposed, so his interpretation suggests, to *take* a more critical stance towards Freud, who is allegedly represented by the dream customs official. The dream, it seems to me, urges a very different necessity upon us: the necessity to think about why there is no customs inspection any more, what the contraband or smuggle (implied by the motif of customs inspection at the border) might be, and why the customs official, despite having died years ago, cannot die properly. Why does he have to walk as a ghost? Why can he not either be truly dead and gone or be fully alive and doing his job? What does this unresolved, uncanny situation of an neither-nor displayed in this dream refer to? What did it want to make Jung aware of? These are the questions that require to be answered, but that did not even come to mind in Jung's discussion.

From here we turn to the second part of Jung's dream. In the period following this dream Jung thought a lot about the mysterious figure of the knight. But only later, he says, was he able to get some idea of its meaning. With this knight from the twelfth century, the time was conjured up when alchemy was beginning and also the quest for the Holy Grail. The stories

> of the Grail had been of the greatest importance to me ever since I read them, at the age of fifteen, for the first time. I had an inkling that a great secret still lay hidden behind those stories. Therefore it seemed quite natural to me that the dream should conjure up the world of Knights of the Grail and their quest—for that was, in the deepest sense, my own world, which had scarcely anything to do with Freud's.

The image of the knight symbolizes what was, "in the deepest sense, my own world": the world of the mystery of the soul and of mythic meaning. And this dream section as a whole shows the direct, unmediated juxtaposition of the modern world and the

Middle Ages and thus it is like an illustration of the juxtaposition of the two extremes contained in a reflection of Jung's a year or two later: on the one side Jung's diagnosis, "No, evidently we no longer have a myth" and on the other side Jung's insistence, "But then, what is your myth—the myth in which you do live?" (p. 171). The modern city with the hustle and bustle of people who are concerned only about their business on the one hand and their comfort on the other and therefore have no eyes for the spectacular apparition of a knight represents the sphere of the practical reality of daily life, the sphere of secularized modernity devoid of myth. The crusader who has appeared here for centuries between twelve noon and one o'clock represents "my myth—the myth in which I do live." Indeed, exclusively *my* myth, for the knight seems to be completely invisible for, i.e., unconscious to, all the others. And yet we hear that "everyone knows about" the apparition. A remarkable contradiction: completely unconscious to all, but everyone knows about it.

This contradiction is what characterizes also the archetypes of the collective unconscious. Ego-consciousness is totally divorced from the archetypal truths, completely unaware of them. This is why Jung speaks of the collective *unconscious*. But at the same time, these fundamentally unconscious contents of this collective unconscious represent the "consensus omnium" (the store of common knowledge about which everyone agrees) and "that which has been believed always, everywhere and by all" (*quod semper, quod ubique, quod ab omnibus creditum est*[8]). The knight in Jung's dream could thus be considered a personification of Jung's notion of the collective unconscious. It is the "*offenbare Geheimnis*" (Goethe), the manifest mystery, in other words, the contradiction of something that despite being a manifest apparition remains to be a mystery that is closed to everyone—except the dream-I, Jung. "The archetypes," Jung once stated, "are ageless and ever-present."[9] In a similar way the crusader is a "regular apparition" (= ever-present) and has always passed by here from time immemorial (= ageless).

---

[8] Cf. Celsus, *De medicina* 3. 4.
[9] *Letters 2*, to Trinick, 15 Oct 57, p. 394.

In this sense, the appearance of the knight in our dream might be seen as the first emergence in Jung's consciousness of the *concept* of the collective unconscious, the first inkling in image form of what later would become an elaborate theory.

In aphorism 125 of *The Gay Science* Nietzsche describes a madman who, holding up a lantern during daytime, goes around on the market place searching for God. In Jung's dream, no lantern is needed. The knight could theoretically be seen by everyone, since he is openly in bright daylight walking among the people. And yet in fact it is as though he were invisible to all except the dream-ego. In Nietzsche's tale, only the madman is searching, but even with the help of a lantern he cannot find what he is searching for. Nobody else misses anything. This is so because in Nietzsche's story "God is dead," i.e., there *is* nothing that could possibly be found. The masses are not missing anything. In Jung's dream, by contrast, the dream-ego is not searching, does not have to be searching, because it in fact has right before its eyes a miraculous apparition that it could not possibly have expected. There *is* here a real presence, an overwhelming richness in meaning; in the knight "my world," i.e., "my myth, the myth in which I live," had appeared to Jung. Even if the apparition of the knight is hidden from the conscious awareness of the crowd, it is right there among them.

We can see here *how* Jung's psychology is, as it were, a reaction to Nietzsche. Whereas Nietzsche diagnosed nihilism and the death of God as the truth of his age, for Jung there is a really existing substance that actually manifests itself in life. But whereas Nietzsche was absolutely serious and raised the question about God and meaning for real life in its totality, Jung reduced and relegated the presence of meaning to a special limited sphere severed from the rest of life, to the sphere of dreams and the unconscious. But because Jung did no longer insist on a meaning and a presence in real life in its totality, but only a presence in the unconscious, the ego in his dream did not have to be a madman as in Nietzsche's story.

The dream-ego in Jung's dream can be the mentally sane observer of this unlikely apparition, because for him it is an apparition only in a dream, only in the unconscious, while the conscious ego outside the dream is allowed to hold on to the rationalistic, scientific world view. It is an apparition that *does not make a difference* for the world of the real people; the two worlds, that of the people (or modern mythless consciousness), on the one hand, and that of the knight (or the collective unconscious), on the other, do not touch despite their simultaneity in one and the same space. They are neatly held apart, immune to each other. Dissociated! Nietzsche's searcher for God, however, has to be mad because *he* has a God in mind that *would* make a difference for everybody, that would be a public, not an unconscious God. Nietzsche does not want to make this split and insists on finding a God and a meaning that is valid also for the conscious mind. And for *such* a God, Nietzsche is implying, only a madman can be searching in *our* time, only a madman can be shocked by the loss of Him. Jung understood this. And because he did not want to become mad *and yet* insisted on still today *having* mythic meaning as a present reality, he had to have two separate compartments insulated from one another, the unconscious for mythic meaning and consciousness for the public scientific standpoint. He had to envelop, encase, mythic meaning in the logical status of unconsciousness ("only a private experience from out of the unconscious") in order to a priori *screen* consciousness from having to take it *seriously*, i.e., "metaphysically" or "religiously" as a public and cosmic truth.

Quite remarkable is the fact that in both dream parts essential information is given verbally, in the first case by some anonymous person, in the second by the voice of nobody. This is information that was not to be had from what the dream-I can see with his own eyes. The customs official, as far as the image itself goes, might just as well have been a customs official who is fully alive. The crusader could, e.g., have been a masqueraded citizen, rather than a "regular apparition." I wonder whether in these voices Jung's own theorizing (theory constructing) mind might not ultimately be at work, however objectified, dis-owned, presented as alien. According to Jung's dream theory, the dream is pure, unadulterated nature (which is, by the way, why in the quotation above from Jung's discussion of the dream of his analysand we have the phrase: "... the dream itself, which we cannot criticize"). About the modern sciences, Jung said that they "try to represent the results of their investigations as though these had come into existence without man's intervention, in such a way that the collaboration of the psyche—an indispensable factor—[*die unerläßliche Mitwirkung der Psyche*] remains invisible" (*CW* 10 § 498). It might well be that Jung's dream theory suffers from an analogous problem, presenting, as it does, dreams as though they had come into existence without man's intervention, obscuring, even denying, the collaboration of the conscious, the theoretical, mind, its *stake* in them.

After having presented and discussed the two dream parts by themselves I now want to turn our attention to the relation between the two parts. The Imperial Austrian customs official at a real border checkpoint is part of tough modern reality, but he is here only a zombie, only "shadowy" (p. 165), of ghostly unreality. The medieval crusader in full armor suddenly emerging in the middle of the mundane bustle of a modern city could actually only be a specter, but appears to be "full of life and completely real" (ibid.). We experience here a complete reversal of values. What is reversed is the relation of what is dead and what is alive, of what is obsolete and what is full of vital strength, of the bygone and actual present. The real is derealized, the unreal presents itself as a vigorous reality.

Furthermore: ghosts usually appear at midnight. The knight from the distant past, however, has his moment at noontime, between twelve and one o'clock. Jung states explicitly: "it was summertime; the blazing sun stood at the zenith, and everything was bathed in intense light." "A fierce sun was beating down upon the narrow streets." As an avid reader of Nietzsche, Jung was probably aware that this time meant the "moment of the shortest shadow; the end of the longest error; the climax of humanity."[10] The fact that it is of all times the noon hour that is turned into the witching hour means nothing less than the victory of the night-world of "Romanticism" over the day-world of the "Enlightenment"; a victory, however, precisely in such a way that no honest fight has been held between the two and the conflict settled. If that had been the case, the oppositional structure as such would remain and it would have only been the roles that would have been reversed (which side is superior, which inferior; or who occupies the superior, who the inferior position); a solution that, however, would have had to have been paid for dearly: by a psychosis.

No, here the victory is brought about through a trick; the *meaning* of both sides has been *tacitly* exchanged, the *definition* of their notions

---

[10] Fr. NIETZSCHE, "Wie die 'wahre Welt' endlich zur Fabel wurde. Geschichte eines Irrtums," in: *idem, Götzen-Dämmerung* (my translation).

has been mixed up: the customs official in his Imperial Austrian uniform belongs to the time and place where he is appearing, namely to the Swiss-Austrian border at the time before World War I, and is an absolutely real representative of modern life—but he is derealized as the ghost of a dead man; conversely, the medieval crusader in the middle of a modern city is absolutely out of place—but he is "full of life and completely real." The real is represented as unreal, and the unreal as real. A revaluation of all values. It is due to a crosswise exchange of the attributes. There are two substances or subjects, the customs official who belongs to the sphere of positive fact, and the knight who belongs to the sphere of the fantastic or mysterious. The attribute or predicate actually belonging to the knight, namely his fantastic quality, is taken away from him and reassigned to the customs official; and the attribute or predicate actually belonging to the customs official, namely the irrefutable realness, is taken away from him and reassigned to the crusader.

This exchange occurs across the "border" separating the first and the second half of the dream. Life and death, reality and fantasy, day and night, the "Enlightenment" and Romanticism exchange their natures. It is precisely the light of the "Enlightenment" that darkens because in the middle of the sober reality of a typically modern and bureaucratic border crossing situation there is the unreal, impossible apparition of a literal ghost, whereas, conversely, the fantastic night world, the world of mystery, appears here in the shape of an empirical figure in broad daylight, as a completely ordinary, absolutely real person walking on the street just like any of the other people.

The customs official and the knight appear in completely separate parts of the dream. Each dream part plays in an altogether different world, so that one might even consider the possibility that they are two separate dreams that only happen to have been dreamed during the same night or even, as indeed Jung falsely remembered, two dreams dreamed weeks apart. The fact that the predicates of the main figures in each part are exchanged across the gap or "border" separating these two parts shows that it is indeed an instance of smuggling, and that the smuggling was successful. But it is an incredibly ingenious smuggling. It remains undetected because consciousness naturally views each dream part in its own terms, assuming its intactness, and would never suspect that the ghostliness belonging to the second part, but missing in it, would show up in the first part as a quality of the customs official and vice versa, just as we would not expect that such a transferral would take place between two independent movies or novels. Consciousness, the dream-I's consciousness as well as ours, is seduced into taking the ghost character of the customs official at face value and accepting it as truly *his* quality, even if an odd one. It seems to belong to his authentic phenomenology, to his definition, as it were. Analogously, the crusader's absolutely convincing vitality and realness, as incredible as it may be, is also taken at face value. After all, they are dream elements, and dreams are known to present strange things. This is simply how the dream comes.

This is a border crossing against which the methods of customs officials are helpless, perhaps in a way that is vaguely similar to how customs and police are powerless against the violation of property rights concerning pieces of music in the Internet— keyword: Napster. Now the customs officials do not know what belongs on this and what on the other side, because either one can occur on either side. What could they still check now? What good would it now do to still search suitcases? The customs official would always come too late. The contents of the suitcases, regardless of whether they may belong on this or on the other side, *are* not the contraband to begin with.

The problem that makes this smuggle indeed undetectable is twofold: (1) The contraband no longer appears in those who want to cross the border, but in the customs official himself, inasmuch as it is his ghost nature that has been taken from the knight in the other part of the dream and pinned on the customs official. (2) The smuggling does not take place at the Swiss-Austrian border at all, not in the part with the customs inspector; indeed, not in the dream at all. Rather it *precedes* both this part and the second part and is *superordinate* to both. In other words, the smuggle now has turned into a *structural, logical, syntactical* one; it is no longer a smuggle of a concrete thing, no longer *semantic*. The smuggle lies in the *logic* of the dream as a whole or in the logical constitution or the general *form* of the mind that dreams such a dream. The literal border, the one between Switzerland and Austria, and the crossing of it and whether one is on this or on that side of it have all become irrelevant. The phenomenological border in the dream is no longer the place where the die is cast.

If we look at the whole dream now, after what we have discovered, it becomes comprehensible why the customs official in the first half of the dream looks peevish and is the ghost of a customs official who had died years ago. He has lost his function. He has become useless. He is absolutely obsolete. The border that he guards is not the critical border at all, and as a living dead man he himself *is* the *personified smuggle* in the first place. Smuggling here is no longer an act, a behavior, it has become structural, institutionalized, an ideology. But the dream as a whole makes it also comprehensible why he cannot die: the rigid border between the opposites, between the rational and the irrational, between the ordinary world of mythless modern reality and the numinous world of mythic meaning has been retained, and with the redefinition and redistribution of the opposites on both sides of the border a smuggling has occurred, and is continuously going on, that absolutely calls for a rigorous customs inspection. The fact that this customs official appears at all in this dream is the trace *within* the dream of the smuggle that is underlying the *mentality* governing this dream. And it is the clue for us (and could have been the clue for Jung) to detect, that is, to raise to consciousness, the actual smuggle that is the actual (even if surreptitious) theme of this dream.

From the beginning Jung was of the adamant opinion that "no arbitrariness can be attributed (to dreams) and above all no legerdemain" (*MDR* p. 162). I agree. Dreams do not lie. They show the whole situation. It's all there. But this particular dream *reveals* the situation *of* a (logical) legerdemain, in the twofold sense that it both presents a deception and invites us to become aware of the deception. As a dream about a successful smuggling, it is necessarily self-contradictory: it has to conceal *and* reveal the smuggling at once, thus showing once more that the fantasy image has indeed everything it needs within itself. The presence of the customs official in our dream who is the zombie of himself is the exact image for and the clear pointer to the smuggle that the dream wants to describe, and at the same time he is apt to pull the wool over our eyes.

Jung and Lopez-Pedraza were right in stating that in interpreting dreams we have to stick to the image. Indeed. But psychologically it is vital that we take the dream image *in its entirety* and not only one half of it: the *literal* dream images. In order that we really stick to the image it is not enough for us to concentrate, as imaginal psychology does, on the content side of it, on the semantic aspect of the image, because then we take, in the case of such a dream, the legerdemain at face value and fall for it, so that we think that what the dream presents is simple *phainomena*, maybe even epiphanies, revelations of archetypal truths. To the extent that this happens, to the extent that we perceive the dream naively, we paradoxically do not stick to the image although, and precisely while, we apparently stick to the image. In order to really do justice to the dream image, we also have to be open to the logic or syntax of it, to the logical structure of the dream, to the abstract formal relation of its individual elements.

Jung's dream speaks of the Swiss-Austrian border. The sequence of this *formulation* represents a movement from the Swiss to the Austrian side. But the fact that the dream-ego encounters an Austrian customs official could suggest that the dream Jung is rather moving from Austria to Switzerland, because normally one first has to cross the customs station of the country that one is leaving and then only pass the one of the country one is entering. Also Jung's own associations point in this direction. He saw the dream as one pointing to the break with Freud, the Austrian, a break which necessitated for Jung to establish himself on his own native ground. The two parts of the dream with their totally different atmosphere support such a view. The second part, as Jung himself states, conjured up "the world of Knights of the Grail and their quest—for that was, in the deepest sense, my own world, which had scarcely anything to do with Freud's." The knight might be seen as a symbolic abbreviation for the collective unconscious as a whole, the realm of the archetypes. The first part, by contrast, does not only, with its drab atmosphere and matter-of-fact topic, evoke much more the Freudian reality principle, but is also associated by Jung himself with Freudian concepts ("censorship") and the person of Freud himself. So we might not go wrong in assuming that this dream indeed tries to show the logical pathways upon which Jung came to himself, upon which he had to move in order to arrive at his own psychological standpoint, at his "psychology of the unconscious" (as he often termed his psychology), and thus at his own conception of the unconscious. "Smuggling," then, should in this context not be taken as a moral category; it is the name for the complex logical moves that are *the condition of the possibility* of such a "psychology of the unconscious."

In this connection it is significant that the part of the dream that shows what was, in the deepest sense, Jung's own world, all of a sudden does *not* play in Switzerland, where the dream-I initially seemed to be headed and where Jung was in fact at home, but in Italy. This inconsistency in the sequence of the dream events, as well as the discrepancy lying in the fact that Jung according to this dream finds his *home* ground geographically in a *foreign* country and temporally in a *bygone* past, are revealing. That it is his home ground can be derived not only from Jung's own interpretative comment to the dream, but also from the fact that this Italian city was somewhat reminiscent for Jung of his actual home town, Basel, without being Basel (p. 164). It is a border crossing to the power of two (a move from the first country to another *and* a move to a completely other country than originally intended) *and* it is, at the same time, the concealing of such a crossing movement, inasmuch as the sudden appearance of Italy seems to suggest a totally fresh start, disconnected from the first scene. This is, of course, in tune with the fact that the customs official in the first scene has lost his *raison d'être* and rather than letting the people pass by him passes by the dream-I himself, thus showing that a literal border crossing is now without any significance. In order to arrive in his own world, i.e., at the standpoint of his own "psychology of the unconscious," a border crossing of an entirely different caliber had to take place, one *not in literal nor in imaginal geography*, not on the phenomenal or semantic level, but *in the logic of the soul.*

What the two regions (that are in fact separated by this fundamental border) are becomes apparent from the different character of the two dream parts. The first half of the dream suggests abstract-functional and conceptual ideas: border, scrutiny, censorship, difference or opposition, contraband, duty to be paid according to the abstract value of goods; there is nothing *substantial* of importance, not even the customs official, since he is more a function than a person and, on top of it, whatever substantiality he might have had is negated by his being (dis-)qualified as a mere ghost. The images occurring here are predominantly images of abstractions and abstract relations. In other words, we are dealing here mainly with formal, structural or logical concerns. The second half of the dream, by contrast, centers around images expressing substantial realities full of highly symbolic meaning: summertime, noon hour, blazing sun, the knight, the red cross, and by way of association the world of the Grail and the Quest. Even the business people streaming home from work for their siesta represent a quality or content, namely the ordinary workaday world. What is predominant here, is the semantic aspect, not anything syntactical or structural. The one place where something logical or syntactical might come into play within this almost exclusively semantic sphere, is with the radical opposition between the modern people and the knight from the twelfth century; but just as in the first half the substantiality of the customs official as a person was played down, so here the potentially syntactic problem of the opposition between modern reality and an apparition from the distant past is annulled since both worlds co-exist here without conflict or manifest difference; indeed, they do not touch, they are immunized one against the other or oblivious of each other.

This latter fact is absolutely astounding. We have here two incompatible worlds, incompatible in two ways: on the one hand, the mundane world versus the otherworldly sphere of mystery and mythic meaning divided from each other *ontologically*; on the other hand the world of enlightened modernity versus the medieval world divided from each other by a radical *historical rupture*. How is it possible that they do not clash? One would expect at least some strong reaction, if not an explosion when they come together in their mutual radical otherness. But they coexist without taking note of each other.

Traditionally, there is a fundamental distinction between two ontologically or logically separate realms, between the sacred and the profane, the day-world of ordinary rational reality and the night-world of spirits, demons, gods, of magic and mystery. To get from the one to the other, always a border has to be crossed. Initiation is one name for the process of such a border-crossing. In the case of a shaman this border-crossing has the form of falling into trance, which is indispensable if he wants to be able to communicate with the spirits. In fairy tales the hero or heroine has to leave their town and venture into the dark forest or behind the seven mountains in order to meet, and prevail over, the witches and demons and find the treasure hard to attain, the treasure that bestows upon them miraculous power. It is always very clear what belongs on this side and what on the other side of the border.

Historically, this clear *positive* separation has been abolished in Protestantism, in which there is no literal division of the sacred from the profane any longer (as it still exists in Catholicism). The relation between the two opposite spheres has here changed into a dialectical, contradictory one, and the ontological separation has yielded to a logical distinction, the opposition itself having been distilled, sublated, spiritualized: each Christian, to give only one example, is within himself at once a part of the secular, fallen world *and* a true priest in the kingdom of God: *simul iustus et peccator.*

In Jung's dream, however, we have neither the clear separation of the opposite dimensions, nor a dialectical relation between *them as* sublated ones. What we do have, rather, is a little bit of both. The positivity of an unambiguous separation of the opposites has been retained: the people on the street in the Italian city and the crusader remain insulated from each other, each enclosed in their own worlds. They are two positivities that despite their sharing the same space do not touch. There is still a clear border and in no way a sublation, no dialectics. But at the same time, the opposites are no longer assigned to ontologically or logically different realms, neatly the one on this, the other on that side, but they share one and the same ontological or logical space, one and the same sphere, that of bright daylight and empirical-practical reality.

This blindness to logical form is the *revolution* underlying Jung's "psychology of the unconscious." The ontological or logical difference between two realms is abolished. This is the function of the first part of our dream: by displaying the customs official as obsolete, as not executing anymore his function of examining the luggage of those who want to cross the border, but rather as passing pointlessly by them, the entire topic of a border separating two logically or ontologically distinct realms is once and for all cancelled and along with it the necessity of initiation or—if we leave the realm of *mythos* and go over to that of *logos*—the necessity of an actual transition from empirical knowing to *speculative knowing*, too. But by ridding himself of the entire border question and the fundamental ontological or logical distinction, the special experiences that previously could only be had on the other side of the border, *after* a border crossing and *through an initiation* and its trials, or *through* speculative knowing, were not given up, too. By forgetting about the border, Jung did not restrict himself to what traditionally was on this side of the border, the so-called "banality" of ordinary life (p. 165). No, his revolutionary move was precisely to have redefined the special contents that originally belonged to the other side (the divine, the sacred, mystery, meaning) as belonging to this side, too, so that the banal and the mysterious, the pragmatic and the deeply meaningful came to be situated in one and the same empirical sphere as *positive empirical facts* ("the archetypes of the collective unconscious"), facts accessible to a psychology that claimed to be a modern *empirical science.*

This is so because now the medieval crusader (the symbol for the general experience of mystery and mythic meaning) and the business people (the representatives in the dream of ego-consciousness) belong to the same positive-factual reality, the yonder. And along with it the border between this side and the other side, has indeed become obsolete, ghostly. From this we can understand that the first half of the dream with the ghostly customs official is the *sine qua non* for the possibility of the miraculous apparition in the second part. The yonder now is empty and as such simply nothing. There is no other side, no otherness. Any other that still exists is now an *empirical* other on one and the same side with the ordinary. To still try to cross the border would be vain, even absolutely prohibited: "metaphysical speculation." Because this, becoming metaphysical, was for Jung, as for his whole age, an absolute horror.

Jung believed here to be able to rely on the philosophy of Kant, the way he understood him, that is, on a Kant, who, as Jung claimed, had "erected a barrier across the mental world which made it impossible for even the boldest flight of speculation to" get beyond (*CW* 18 § 1734). And this barrier was perceived by Jung as a "wall at which human inquisitiveness turns back" (*CW* 18 § 1734, transl. modif.[11]).

In addition to the knight and the ordinary people there is a third position in the second part of Jung's dream, that of the dream-I, that we had occasion to look at briefly when we compared it with Nietzsche's God-seeker. Just as the knight symbolically represents what later would be called the archetypal or collective unconscious and the

---

[11] The translation given in *CW* ("the barrier against which the speculative tendency rebounds") does not convey the precise meaning of Jung's formulation.

people represent ego consciousness, the dream-ego represents and embodies the superordinate *standpoint of psychology*, the standpoint of the empirically-minded depth-psychological observer, who, personally uniting[12] in himself "personality No. 1" and "personality No. 2," is capable of seeing at once both sides, the pragmatic concerns of the ego within its ordinary world *and* the revelations from the collective unconscious. Whereas ordinary consciousness is blind to the archetypal manifestation, the dream-I (as the standpoint of psychology) is open to it. The border and the opposition have obviously been taken into the subject (the logic of consciousness), been swallowed by it. The subject *is* now the border between and the opposition of consciousness and the unconscious. Because the subject *is* the opposition, both worlds can coexist without getting into each other's hair. The subject has itself become the customs official or the border who/which keeps both apart, but at the same time also side by side.

So the dream-I (as the embodiment of the standpoint of psychology) is open to the archetypal manifestation. And it can see the archetype (in our case the knight) *just like that*, simply with his ordinary eyes and everyday mind, the same eyes and mind as those that also the ordinary people have, in other words, without initiation, without trance, without first *in fact* having moved across a border.

This supports my observation that in this dream we witness the cancellation of the necessity of initiation. The empiricist standpoint adopted by Jung means the abolition of the necessity and the possibility of initiation. The psychological empiricist in Jung's sense remains on the side of the Enlightenment, of modernity, of the natural sciences, but by virtue of the redefinition described he is nevertheless capable to have before his eyes *on this side of the border* that which actually could only be reached on its other side: the knight as symbol of the world of the soul's mysteries, a world which now, however, is defined as "purely natural fact." Once upon a time, this world was only accessible through an initiation, i.e., through a real border-

---

[12] The "personal union" does by no means imply that the contradiction would have been canceled, the opposition between No. 1 and No. 2 *reconciled* in the superordinate standpoint. The dream-I simply perceives both of them in their peaceful factual juxtaposition. Just as those two do not touch each other, so also the observing subject remains opposite to them, untouched by them and not entering into an interaction with them.

crossing: the passage across to the other world through logically dying a death. As an initiation the border-crossing would have been an *existential* experience, which, however, as a ritualistic one would always at once have been a *logical* one (a logical transformation of the constitution of consciousness). An existential initiation is no longer possible in modernity, because the locus of such a process has in the meantime been inwardized from the externality of sensuousness, representation, and intuition into the interiority of the *logos*. An initiation therefore would now have to be, as a *logical initiation*, the border-crossing over into speculative-dialectical thought.

Jung, however, replaces the initiation's or border-crossing's having become logical by logically invalidating "border" and "border guard," on the one hand, and by the structural exchange of the valences or attributes of day-world and night-world, this world and yonder, on the other hand. The place of, e.g., the "night-sea-journey" is taken by the encounter with the soul mystery in the middle of the day world. This means that it is not the subject who himself has to cross the border. Rather, the agency of the day-world, the border check, is, as being "unreal" and a ghost (the customs-official), *logically* transported to the side of the night-world, i.e., into unconsciousness, whereas the substance of the night-world as now being a reality full of life in bright daylight (the crusader) is (again logically) taken to the side of the day-world accessible to the empirical observer. This is the archetypal images and symbols coming from "*the* unconscious" *as* contents of psychological *consciousness*!

The border-crossing is thus no longer a logical *act* to be explicitly performed by the subject on his own account, but is, nay, always already has been, performed in the background, unconsciously and invisibly; it is in this dream (and from then on on principle) *to be found* as a finished logical *structure*. It is found, but precisely not taken note of: because only *that* is heeded which shows itself *within* this presupposed structure as a *content*, in empirical or objective form, as images. The actually logical or syntactical is thus itself pushed off to the level of the semantic, where it no longer appears as itself, but only as an *existing (positive) structure*: as an ontological (substantiated) opposition of two oppositional and logically (not empirically) mutually immunized systems of the psyche, consciousness and "the unconscious."

Because the logical-syntactical has been pocketed by the personality (swallowed by it) and it, the personality, in its subjectivity now *is* the logical relation (and therefore does no longer have this relation objectively "outside," opposite to itself in substantiated form as a border and customs-official), it is now free to be only concerned with the semantic, with the contents of the unconscious: the crusader, the Grail, the quest, the soul mystery, the imaginal, etc. The real border-crossing or smuggle is thus the swallowing of "the border" as such, which had the consequence that the structural, logical, syntactical aspect sank completely into unconsciousness and all that was left for one's attention was the contents, the semantic. This, consciousness's becoming unconscious about the formal or logical side, became objectified in the *concept* of "*the* unconscious."

Other than Freud, who still performs his operations upon the semantic content level *before* consciousness, Jung has long arrived on the logical level. He *is* already thoroughly modern; he is operating on this logical level, but he holds the latter down in unconsciousness, in order to consciously be able to devote his attention solely to the semantic, to the contents of the collective unconscious.

Just as for Klages contradiction was located on the objective side in the content and not in the structure of his thought (*Der Geist als Widersacher der Seele*, "Intellect as the adversary of the soul"), so contradiction was in Freud, too, "outside," in the subject-matter of psychology: in the psychic apparatus. *There* there was a censor, and the dreams were not pure nature, but revealed a manifest meaning behind which a latent one was hidden, which had to be deciphered through a kind of criminal investigation, as it were. Jung by contrast had removed from the object of psychology any thought of "intentions to deceive," any contradiction between manifest and latent meaning, any censorship, etc., because—not unlike "the lamb who takes away the sin of the world"—he had taken contradiction and border upon himself, or, worded less personally and more precisely, into the subject of psychology: into the *logic* or *syntax* of psychology or of the psychologizing consciousness. Through this move, the contents or objects with which psychological consciousness had to deal were *released*.

In the dream under discussion here we see the anticipatory solution for that problem that had arisen for Jung a little later through his having reached, as he explicitly stated, a border, a dead end (*MDR* p. 171). It is the same problem that found expression in his much later speaking of the "wall at which human inquisitiveness turns back" (*CW* 18 § 1734, transl. modif.), since what is on its other side is absolutely forbidden metaphysical speculation. Now, after the move that we witnessed in Jung's dream, this border did no longer have to be transgressed because both what is on this side of it (the working people going home for lunch; and what is more "banal" than that?) and what is yonder (the knight from the age of crusades and the search for the Grail), *and along with these the very idea of a border or threshold*, had been pulled over by Jung to the same side *before* the border, into the world of sunlight, that is to say of scientific empiricism, as a mere *motif* of psychic felt experience (*Erleben*), i.e., as something exclusively semantic. This very move of his is *his* transgression of the border, his smuggle, and it is a much more fundamental border crossing than the one where one has to in fact go across a literal border by going past a border guard. I already affirmed that I agree with Jung's assessment that no "legerdemain" (*MDR* p. 162) can be attributed to dreams, but I also pointed out that this dream *reveals* a legerdemain, a trick. His not knowing and not suspecting that his, Jung's, "so disappointingly simple empirical standpoint" (cf. *Letters 2*, p. 573, to Robert C. Smith, 29 June 60) *is* that very border transgression that he wants to avoid at all cost, this is *his* unconsciousness on the theoretical level, but of course precisely as such also the condition of the possibility of the psychology "of *the* unconscious."

Initiation, we heard, is over and out, and after what has just been said it also *has to* be over and out if there shall be a "psychology of the unconscious." Or should we perhaps rather say that this very dream is a dream of an Initiation after all, only of a fundamentally new type of initiation? For the dream-I is one that is indeed being initiated, but this particular initiation is an initiation precisely into initiationlessness, into the standpoint for which there is not and must not be a border and no other side anymore, because even the Other, the world of mystery and archetypes, has to be conceived by it as an empirical reality and as positive fact on *this* side of the former border and thus ontologically or logically on par with the ordinary facts. Is this very dream not the dream of the initiation into the positivism of the standpoint of the empirical observer of the soul's archetypal mysteries *as positive facts*, as, to say it with the imagery of our dream, walking publicly on the street?[13]

An initiation into the standpoint of psychology was necessary, because without it the positivistic, natural-scientific mind would have declared the world of mystery and meaning to be simply nothing but nonsense, madness, absolutely unreal. This initiation had to translocate the mythic and the metaphysical from yonder, i.e., from the status of *truth*, and re-establish it here in the everyday natural world as empirical facts of felt experience and thus it had, by way of one example, to discover a medieval knight as absolutely real walking in a modern city at bright daylight.

The question that arose was, however, how the mythic and metaphysical could be translocated into factual reality without this move having to be classified under the rubric of insanity? Here the notion of "the unconscious" comes in. All the mythic and metaphysical contents had to be defined as belonging to a fundamentally extraterritorial precinct within consciousness: the un-conscious. Consciousness and "the unconscious" share the same world, but due to the one being the negation of the other they are absolutely insulated from each other, just as the knight and the working population in our dream are. In therapy we often speak of "making the unconscious contents conscious." But we have to realize that these are made conscious *as contents of the unconscious*. They never lose their definition as belonging to the unconscious. To express it with the images of our dream: the medieval knight will never take off his armor and become an ordinary shopkeeper in the modern city; and conversely the shopkeepers will not all of a sudden become medieval knights of the Holy Grail. In the first case the unconscious would not have been made conscious, but simply been lost. We would end with the scientific world that knows of no meaning and no mystery. In the second case we would have to speak of an inflation or psychosis. The two structures, knight here and shopkeepers there, will stay forever insulated from each other. Making conscious in the sense of this psychology means something altogether different. It means

---

[13] An example for this conception of archetypal mysteries as positive facts is the interpretation by a Jungian of the case of a young woman who was entranced by sexy-looking sandals as a manifestation of Aphrodite. See my discussion of this interpretation in my *What Is Soul?* New Orleans (Spring Journal Books) 2012, pp. 214 ff.

developing the consciousness of the third party, here represented by the dream-I, in other words, that consciousness that is aware of them both *in* their mutual and inalienable insulation and that at the same time is not identical with either, but holds itself apart from both as the neutral empirical observer.

"The unconscious" is the black box that was never allowed to be opened.[14] This was the price for getting rid of the border, getting rid of the necessity of initiation, and for constituting the mythic and metaphysical *as* positive empirical facts ("archetypes"). Without having to cross the border and undergoing a real process of initiation, mythic meaning as a present reality could only be had in either one of two ways: either in psychosis—or shrink-wrapped in that transparent film that is called "the unconscious." Just as the dream-I was able to *see* the knight, but remained just as remote from the world of that knight as if it had not seen it, so psychological consciousness can see the contents in the transparent film, but never get in touch with them. In fact, it has to constantly keep the danger in mind that the plastic wrapping might have a leak and it might become inflated by these contents. In this way, psychological consciousness (*this* psychological consciousness) is in the position of the Biblical Moses who could *dream* about the promised Holy Land, but was never allowed to get there. So Jung, too, could literally dream of images of archetypal meaning and entertain them as something that the psyche *says*, but he could not subscribe to them on his own account; they had to be for him no more than facts. The logical constitution of his consciousness was not permitted to be affected and transformed by them as *truths*, because if it had become affected Jung would have crossed the forbidden border and have become guilty of making metaphysical statements—"a deadly sin" in Jung's view (p. 70). There had to be the total separation between Jung, the empirical scientist, and Jung, the person who immersed himself in the dream world, the separation between Küsnacht and Bollingen, between personality No. 1 and personality No. 2. So there was in fact mythic meaning, only not for the modern I, that I that was the one that actually needed it.

---

[14] See my "Alchemie der Geschichte," in: *Eranos 54-1985*, Frankfurt (Insel) 1987, pp. 325-395, here pp. 325–357, now in English as "The Alchemy of History," in: Wolfgang Giegerich, *Soul-Violence*, Collected English Papers, vol. 3, New Orleans, LA (Spring Journal Books) 2008, pp. 353–414, here pp. 377–381.

In the last analysis, the smuggling inherent in the notion of the unconscious consists in that it presents a fundamentally *other, reduced* sense *of* the Other while claiming the *same* dignity for it that that Other once had. The logical or ontological difference between two worlds is reduced to an empirical difference in one and the same world (two compartments of the empirical psyche: consciousness and "the unconscious"). Initiation used to be initiation into an absolute *truth*, absolute in that it was (a) the unquestioned public and highest soul value of a whole tribe, and (b) cosmic truth, a truth not relativized by science. Just as initiation is now replaced by personal analysis and private introspection, so truth is replaced by subjective felt experience (*Erlebnis*) on the one hand and an intellectual "understanding" gained through comparative amplification on the other hand.

The boon of this whole construal of psychology was, to be sure, that meaning in the sense of the full weight of the word—the idea of mythic meaning as a present reality—could be held on to. But to this we must add the devastating caveat that his meaning *is* no longer *truth*, but "truth" *shrink-wrapped* in transparent film, in other words, castrated truth, meaning as mere fact and this means as *meaningless* meaning—or: *simulated* truth.

If "the unconscious" is mythic meaning sealed in transparent plastic foil, three inferences can be drawn.

(1) The translocation of the mythic from yonder to this side of the border could only preserve its mythic character under the conditions of ordinary reality, if a sense of border and otherworldliness was transplanted along with it. The transparent plastic that insulates the knight from the people or, in more general terms, the extraterritoriality of "the unconscious" within consciousness is the *empirical* imitation of that border that used to separate the realm of the empirical from the otherworldly. The imported mythic content alone, without some kind of border and separateness, would either have become a banal fact (e.g., a superstitious idea of former people) or, as we have seen, it would have inflated consciousness. It is the insulation alone that allows for the preservation and protection of the mystery and meaning-quality of the contents within the banality of the positivistic mind, i.e., despite their having been transplanted into the banality of the positivistic mind. The medieval knight can carry the mysterious meaning *for* the observing

dream-I only because he, the knight, is shielded from the normal
people and they from him (just as is also the dream-I as observer from
the knight, as we have seen).

(2) But this new type of border is *really* only an imitation of sorts.
It has a completely different function. Rather than dividing the
ordinary world from the yonder, this new border now separates the
semantics of the archetypal image from its syntax, the content or
substance from the logical form. This is best illustrated by my
image of the transparent film into which the archetypal content
has been shrink-wrapped. This wrapping allows us to *see* what is in
it, including the *mythic, mysterious, archetypal or meaning quality* of it.
But that is all. Only to see it. The *logic* of this meaning cannot and
must not come out. Because this would either necessitate an initiation
into this meaning, in other words, a transformation of the logical
constitution of consciousness (because the awareness of the logic of
an experience would inevitably have repercussions on, i.e., affect or
even *infect* the logic of that consciousness that has become aware of
it), or, without initiation, lead to inflation and possibly madness. So
the invention of "the unconscious" as the transplantation of the mythic
and metaphysical contents from the status of a metaphysical or mythic
truth into the status of an empirical *fact* and the status of felt experience
means the reduction to the semantic and the elimination of the
syntactic or logical level altogether. This is why in archetypal
psychology one speaks of "the imaginal." The imaginal is the, as it
were, visible (imaginable) aspect of the *content* that is perceived.
Initiation as the real border-crossing, by contrast, meant nothing else
but that the mind was introduced into the syntax operative in the
semantic contents it was confronted with and that its own syntax or
logical constitution was thereby transformed by it. The real border-
crossing thus is the crossing over from the semantic to the syntactical,
from a particular substance to the logic exemplified by it. As such this
border-crossing is precisely that "speculation" that was forbidden for
modern consciousness and that Jung's "psychology of the unconscious"
was supposed to make once and for all superfluous. With the images
stemming from "the unconscious" and defined as facts, mythic meaning
could be had still today, but, alas, only as additional pieces of furniture
that are placed into one's unchanged apartment. To be sure, these
additions are beautiful antiques, but they make their modern

surroundings look all the more drab and meaningless (Jung: "the banality of ordinary life").

(3) It is not "the unconscious" that is unconscious. In the expression "the psychology of the unconscious" the genitive is a subjective genitive (it is the standpoint of the psychology of the unconscious or psychological consciousness that is unconscious; psychology itself *is* "the unconscious"; psychology is the cultivation of unconsciousness), even while psychology itself of course innocently believes (and wants to impart the belief) that the genitive is an objective one. "The unconscious" as the realm of archetypal contents is rather the reflection of the unconsciousness to which psychological consciousness reduced and stultified itself, by systematically blinding itself to the logic and syntax of the themes it is confronted with and restricting itself exclusively to their semantic or content aspect. It is a sign of unconsciousness—nay, of the *will* to unconsciousness—to believe that one could find mythic meaning as positive facts, nothing but facts, facts that merely have to be feelingly experienced, intellectually understood and possibly ethically applied in one's practice of life, while systematically excluding the logic of the matter.

I want to add two more observations about the image of the crusader.

Jung connected the knight in his dream with the beginning of alchemy and the quest for the Holy Grail. But is it not interesting that the dream did not present a medieval alchemist or a Parzival/Perceval, but a crusader? A crusader is neither withdrawing from the world into his laboratory to proceed with the laborious process of trying to produce the *lapis*, nor does he venture out into the realm of the essentially unknown on a quest for the mysterious Grail or some other mystery. Rather, he goes to a known place, a place that is on the map from the outset, and he goes there as soldier in order to conquer back the empirical city of Jerusalem from the Moslems, into the hands of whom Jerusalem had fallen. To be sure, the empirically real Jerusalem was taken as a symbol of the Heavenly Jerusalem and thus for a highest goal of the soul. But nevertheless it was first of all a positivity (an empirical fact) and thus altogether different from the alchemical Stone or the Holy Grail, which were a priori logically negative, otherworldly mysteries.

Secondly, the image of the crusader, with which Jung's dream is trying to secondarily regain something lost, might reveal that "*loss* of meaning" is his starting point, so that he, the crusader, is not exactly apt to serve as an image for the *primordial* presence of meaning, that sense of meaning that might be able to heal the modern feeling of loss of meaning. And at best he would reconquer literal Jerusalem, which— I am arguing here from the standpoint of modernity to which Jung's dream belongs—as positive-factual reality would remain just as far removed from the Heavenly Jerusalem that is actually sought as any other earthly city. So the very element in Jung's dream that seemed to Jung to express what he said "was, in the deepest sense, my own world" and thus to promise to heal the modern illness of loss of meaning is itself sicklied over by that modern illness; even the counterpart to the "banality of life" is itself not so far removed from that very banality; the knight's difference from the ordinary people is only a semantic difference (an exotic fact, a spectacular sight), not a syntactic or logical one.

As we heard, Jung regarded "the unconscious" in general and dreams in particular "as natural processes"; dreams are the "unmediated expression" of this nature. "I knew of no reason for the assumption that the tricks of consciousness can be extended to the natural processes of the unconscious" (*MDR*, p. 162 with *Erinnerungen*, p. 166). Our dream, for one, gives the lie to this view of the dream as an innocent, artless product of nature in the naive sense implied by Jung. Although I agree with Jung that no legerdemain and no wish to deceive can be attributed to the dream, the simple distribution that Jung wants to establish between a pure, innocent nature as immediate self-display on the side of the productions of "the unconscious" and the reflectedness and deviousness on the side of the conscious mind, cannot be upheld. Already biological nature is full of deviousness and deception (just think of mimicry), although of course an objective, not subjective deception. The mind is on both sides; consciousness is not simply the empirical observer and passive receptor of images coming to it from a pristine nature; it is already—even though unconsciously—*in* the alleged facts themselves that it seems to "find" strictly vis-à-vis itself as unspoilt nature and pristine origin. Indeed our particular dream shows a much higher degree of reflection, sophistication, even artfulness and deviousness, at work in the unconscious production than in the receptive consciousness, which here attempts to hold itself in an innocence that in modernity is no longer adequate, no longer true.

But of course, we always have to keep in mind that this is not a *mistake*. On the contrary, it was precisely the whole point of this dream as well as of the thinking of the "psychology of the unconscious" at large, into which this dream tried to initiate, to *artificially* establish a seemingly *innocent* consciousness that exclusively focuses on the semantics of dreams and other images and remains systematically unconscious of the complexities of their, and the artfulness of its own, syntax or logic as well as of the dialectic or uroboric relation of subject and object, reception and production. "*The* unconscious" in the Jungian sense was invented to have a pure vis-à-vis. And this vis-à-vis was indispensable if (a) there was to be a real presence of mythic meaning under the conditions of the modern situation while (b) the transgression across the border to "speculation" and "metaphysics" was to be avoided at all cost.

But the cost was high, I would say too high. What was the price that had to be paid for having mythical meaning *as* a present reality? It was the repression, the scotomization, of the syntactical in favor of the semantic and thus the self-stultification of consciousness. One's keeping consciousness unconscious about the logical or syntactical in order to be able to have the contents—unsullied by the problems of modernity—as pure nature, as pristine origin (archetypes, *Urerfahrung* [primordial experience]) fulfills the definition of a neurotic structure.

While before I stated, following Jung's interpretation of the knight as pointing to the quest for the Holy Grail or the alchemical *lapis*, that the juxtaposition of the ordinary business people and the knight from the twelfth century expresses the relation and tension between Jung's diagnosis, "No, evidently we no longer have a myth," and his insistence, "But then, what is your myth—the myth in which you do live?," we now have to see that the one side of this pair, the dream image of the Crusader alone, already expresses *in itself* this whole modern contradiction of loss of myth and insistence on myth, just as the knight's Jerusalem reflects the nature of the Jungian version of the soul's mysteries (the archetypes) conceived *as* empirical facts.

* * *

In the earliest *Black Book*-version, the last sentence of this dream reads: "Inside, a voice calls, 'It is all empty and disgusting.' I must bear it." After the grand apparition in the dream itself of the knight, who represented for Jung "in the deepest sense, my own world," this is a surprising end result of this dream experience.

These two sentences and the emotion expressed in them disappeared from all the later versions of the dream. We have to ask: did Jung bear it, really bear it? And, furthermore, is it not perhaps "all empty and disgusting" for the sole reason that he was not ready to *bear*[15] the modern emptiness?

---

[15] Jung's word is *tragen* (to bear in the objective and active sense of carry, shoulder, take upon oneself), not *ertragen* (to bear in the subjective-emotional and passive sense of endure, suffer, put up with).—Also, Jung's word for "disgusting" in the immediately preceding sentence is not an adjective, but, rather unusually, the noun, *Ekel* (disgust), which makes it less a subjective feeling or reaction *to* a condition and more an objective description of it (in the direction of "everything is [disgustingly] rotten" or "only disgust prevails [in the world]").

CHAPTER SIX

The Flight Into the Unconscious
C.G. Jung's psychology project

N ow, at the end of the century of psychology[1] and at the threshold to a future that will no longer be psychological, it is time, and has become possible, to look back upon C.G. Jung's psychology project. It has become *possible* because the psychological century has released us from itself, and Freud and Jung, for example, have become historical for us. But for such a discipline as depth psychology a look back is not merely possible and does not only happen out of an antiquarian interest. It is also indispensable for intrinsic reasons: because it is the discipline of making conscious.

In its beginnings depth psychology had to learn in a painful way that it is not sufficient for the analyst to perform an analysis *upon the patient*. Rather, the analyst himself has to undergo a training analysis. But this is only the first step or first half of analytical self-reflection: its personal aspect. The equally important second half is the critical analysis of psychology itself as the instrument with which, or the spirit in which, the therapeutic work is performed.[2] The theoretical orientation that forms the background of the practical therapeutic

---

[1] This was written in 1999.

[2] About the insight that psychology has to be its own first patient, cf. W. Giegerich, "On the Neurosis of Psychology or The Third of the Two," in: *Spring 1977*, Zürich (Spring Publications), pp. 153-174. Now in *idem, The Neurosis of Psychology. Primary Papers towards a Critical Psychology* New Orleans, LA (Spring Journal Books: 2005), pp. 41–67. In German: "Über die Neurose der Psychologie oder das Dritte der Zwei," in: *Analyt. Psychol. 9* (1978), pp. 241-268.

work must also be critically examined for *its* neurotic structures. Adapting a saying of Marx's we could say: So far the Jungians have only *applied*, that is, *acted out*, the psychology developed by Jung in various ways; the point, however, is to *erinnern* (remember, reflect, see through) it. Jung liked to quote the apocryphal *logion* of Jesus, "Man, if thou knowest what thou doest, blessed art thou; but if thou knowest not, thou art accursed and a transgressor of the Law." But do we *know* what we do when we speak of the collective unconscious, of the numinous, of individuation, of anima, of self, of the thinking *function*? Or is it merely that we trustingly work with these ideas? Have we already *awakened* from the *dream* of the 20th century, the dream that has the name "depth psychology" (or, in our case, more specifically "Jungian psychology"), or are we still enveloped in it in "dreaming innocence" (Paul Tillich)? Do we merely dream it onwards?

In a discipline whose very task it is to make conscious it is certainly not sufficient to take up Jungian psychology as a ready-made and to make it one's base on which to stand and from which to proceed. We also need to know what it is which we take up; we need to comprehend that base on which we established ourselves (where "comprehend" means comprehending its logical genesis). Jung demanded of us as persons that we learn to distinguish ourselves from ourselves and stand objectively vis-à-vis ourselves; as professionals or theoreticians, we Jungians have to attempt to do the same with respect to our Jungian theory, to Jung's work. We have to reflect the end product back into its producedness, the certain, if not trite base or floor back into the process and adventure of its origination, into the state when it was precisely not yet one's always already presupposed solid base or foundation, but the "ceiling" or "roof" above oneself (here: above Jung), and when psychology was still to be erected for the first time, in other words, when it was in its *status nascendi* and thus still merely a *vision* "up there," full of excitement, mystery, if not numinosity.

This is all the more important if we keep in mind that psychology and the reality studied by it do not relate to each other like a neutral mirror and an object in front of it. "We should never forget that in any psychological discussion we are not saying anything *about* the psyche, but that the psyche is inevitably expressing *itself*" (*CW* 9i § 483, transl. modif.). "Being the science of the soul, psychology is what the soul says about itself" (*CW* 10 § 1065, transl. modif.). What this means is nothing else than that psychology, inasmuch as it is the science *of the soul,* cannot be a *science* (in the usual sense). If in psychology the soul does not only speak about itself, but also expresses itself (*sich aussprechen*: express or unbosom itself), then the so-called "science" of psychology is not a purely passive recording of what is factually given, but active formation, construction, generation. "True expression is formative [or creative] perception," Jung said himself (*CW* 4 § 771, transl. modif. The whole sentence is in italics in Jung's German), thereby hinting at the dialectic unity of perception and production, of active and passive. Furthermore, psychology does not have an object vis-à-vis itself that would be clearly demarcated over against it, definable or separable. The alleged object is only generated, pro-duced *in* the soul's speaking about itself. Here Jung's saying comes spontaneously to mind: "The psyche creates reality every day. The only expression I can use for this activity is *fantasy*" (*CW* 6 § 78).

The important insight that follows from this is that everything taught by Jung is not exempt from itself being subject to his insights. The unconscious, the archetypes, anima and self, complex and individuation are not simply factual realities that, according to the usual view (also often presented by Jung himself), have empirically been established by psychology. No, they, too, are likewise fantasy products, *science fiction* in the literal sense, active formation of the phenomenology found as given and distinctions *posited* within this phenomenology. On one occasion already Freud was able to say that "The theory of instincts is so to speak our mythology,"[3] whereby we may leave it open as to how seriously he took this insight and what weight and what consequences it had for him. Jung's entire psychology is not only *about* symbols; it is itself *symbolic action*; it is construction and generation, not, however, construction by Jung personally, by him as ego, but by "the soul," which *through* what he said merely spoke about itself: itself at this one particular historical locus, a historical locus at which it felt it needed to express itself as this psychology. This psychology, which

---

[3] Sigmund Freud, 32nd lecture of *New Introductory Lectures on Psycho-Analysis*, SE 22, p. 95.

he liked to refer to as "the modern psychology of the unconscious," is not, as the empiricist stance would imagine, the scientific *account of* psychic reality pure and simple, merely neutrally describing the "facts" of the soul's life. It is itself an instance of the soul's soul-making, a product *of* the so-called "unconscious," of the psyche's fantasizing activity. It is one fiction in which "the soul" imagined itself under the conditions of this concrete historical locus.

Distinguishing ourselves from our Jungian theory and "looking back" upon Jung's psychology project thus cannot mean to merely paraphrase what Jung taught. Not even giving our own interpretation of it would be enough. Looking back must rather mean analysis or, better, reconstruction of the major aspects and tenets of his work from the nuclear concern as their heart or soul that generated this work. The question is: what were the historical motives that forced it to be the way it then turned out? What now imperceptibly informs psychological consciousness from behind must be transformed back into what is in front of consciousness and is still at stake. The point is to bring psychology home to itself—to return it to the soul's life (which is both logical life and historical).

But in order to be able to reconstruct Jung's psychology, we must first of all methodically leave behind what we believe to know all along about Jung and his psychology, its origin, the relation of Freud and Jung, the concept of the collective unconscious, etc., and what we tacitly presuppose as self-evident. Only this will enable us to allow ourselves to be *given* what needs to be learned.

In such an investigation it is essential always to keep in mind that the analysand of this analysis and the object of this reconstruction is not a person (here C.G. Jung), not what psychologically happens in this person (or in people in general), but (Jungian) psychology, its theory and the cosmos of its conceptions. It is one thing to talk about "the unconscious" (taken as a constituent of the personality) and its genesis, but something very different to talk about the *concept* of "the unconscious" or the *standpoint* of a "psychology of the unconscious" and its genesis, and this in such a way that the theory is in fact not statically apperceived as a doctrinal edifice (product), but as psychic action (production, fabrication). Jung figures in these examinations at bottom only as the real place in which "the soul," under quite particular conditions, spoke about itself. The name Jung must be imagined to be enclosed in quotations marks.

I. The acquisition of the *standpoint* of "the unconscious"

As an old man, Jung told Aniela Jaffé about "a moment of unusual clarity" that he had experienced after the publication of his first major book, *Transformations and Symbols of the Libido* (1912), and after his separation from Freud, "a moment of unusual clarity in which I could see the path I had traveled so far." For us the following report from *Memories, Dreams, Reflections* is much rather a document revealing to us with unusual clarity the hidden logical drama giving rise to the notion of "the unconscious." The text reads,

> About this time I experienced a moment of unusual clarity in which I could see the path I had traveled so far. I thought, "Now you possess a key to mythology and are in a position to unlock all the gates to the unconscious human psyche." But then something whispered within me, "Why open all gates?" And promptly the question arose of what, after all, I had accomplished. I had explained the myths of peoples of the past; I had written a book about the hero, about the myth in which man has always lived. "But in what myth does man live nowadays?"—"In the Christian myth," the answer might be.— "Do *you* live in it?" something in me asked.—"To be honest, the answer is no! It is not the myth I live in."—"Then we no longer have any myth?"—"No, evidently we no longer have any myth."—"But then what is your myth? The myth in which you do live?" At this point things became uncomfortable, and I stopped thinking. I had reached a boundary (p. 171).[4]

Jung reported this from memory as an old man. Thus it is not the immediate recording of an experience coming from the time *about* which it reports. But this does not diminish its authenticity *if*, rather than taking it literally as a report *about* ... and, with a historical biographical interest, reading it for its factual veracity,

---

[4] The page reference is to the Vintage Books edition. I slightly altered the translation given there to bring it more in line with the German original in *Erinnerungen Träume Gedanken*, pp. 174f.

we see it as a self-portrayal, as a text that betrays to us something of the motives behind Jung's thinking, or more precisely, if we comprehend this report as a "myth"[5] (told by Jung himself) which with "unusual clarity" lets *us* look behind the scenes of Jung's "psychology of the unconscious" by revealing, couched in narrative form, not so much the temporal, but the *logical* genesis of his psychology. Seen in this light, this narrative allows us for once to see the hidden drama which is the logical and as such the always ongoing, accompanying origin and driving force (*archê*) of this psychology.

As a parenthetical remark I want to mention at the outset that Jung frequently used the expressions "the psychology of the unconscious" or "the modern psychology of the unconscious" when he in truth implicitly referred to his own psychology. Beside "analytical psychology" and "complex psychology" we could also use "the psychology of the unconscious" as an official name of his psychology. This title indeed captures the heart of his psychology. Of course, the disadvantage would be that this designation seems to apply just as much to the other depth-psychological schools of psychology and thus not to give them adequate expression of their specific difference to Jungian psychology. However, this appearance is due to the equivocal use of "the unconscious." This term in the mouth of Jung is something totally different from the same-named concept in Freud's thinking. Jung did not simply expand Freud's concept of the unconscious by adding the region of the "collective unconscious" to it, sort of as an

---

[5] "Thus it is that I have ... undertaken ... to tell the myth of my life. I can only ... 'tell stories.' Whether or not the stories are 'true' is not the problem. The only question is whether they are *my* fable, *my* truth" (*MDR* p. 3, transl. modif.).—It is crucial to see that in speaking of the "myth of my life" (*MDR* unfortunately has "my personal myth") Jung is not using the word myth in the sense of the now popular personal myth movement, as if it were his aim to sacralize his personal life story by relating it to the larger cultural and universal meanings that once functioned as myths in the original sense. "Myth" has almost the opposite (sobering, even reductive) meaning, as the word "only" in "I can only ... 'tell stories'" (i.e., "I am not in possession of a higher truth or meaning") makes expressly clear. What Jung is suggesting here comes much closer to Nietzsche's melancholy "Only fool! Only poet!" than to "personal myth" in the emphatic (inflated) sense, just as his "*my* fable, *my* truth" clearly alludes to Goethe's "*Dichtung und Wahrheit*." See Sophia Heller, *The Absence of Myth*, Albany (State University of New York Press: 2006), esp. pp. 67f.—When I suggest reading as *myth* the old man Jung's report about his 1912 reflections (reflections *about* the myth in which he lived), I obviously use the term myth in yet another sense, as a subjective story which is intended as a straightforward report about factual events but which, at the same time, inadvertently reveals to us a deeper truth, namely the hidden motives or inner logic behind his theorizing (but by no means a "higher meaning" or "archetypal pattern").

additional storey. *His* concept of the unconscious is not derived from Freud's at all and has its specific locus and logical origin in the living heart of *his* psychology.

It is Jung's vision or conception which generates the concept of "the unconscious," and not the other way around, that the unconscious is a given empirical reality for which Jung's psychology tried to provide an adequate articulation. (As a matter of course, Freud's concept of the unconscious must also be deduced from within the heart of *his* thought.) Here one might object that the term "the unconscious" was by no means something that needed to be *produced* by psychologists, inasmuch as it had been available since the Romantics and had by the end of the 19th century become a much-used concept. Jung could thus have fallen back on this familiar and readily available concept. This is of course also what he did. However, this applies precisely only to the *label* "the unconscious," but not to the *concept* that this label denotes for him. We must not mindlessly insert "the unconscious" like a jetton or ready-made into various contexts. We always have to *reconstruct* the essential terms of a theory from its living spirit and pulsating heart. In the following, the term "the unconscious" always refers to Jung's thought of the unconscious.

The drama that takes place in the short text quoted above can be divided into three acts.

THE FIRST ACT contains Jung's review and assessment of what he had achieved up to this point. His first thought in this narrative is: "Now you possess a key to mythology and are in a position to unlock all the gates to the unconscious human psyche." His taking stock results in a sense of pride and great confidence concerning what lies before him. His way has lead him to a summit: what more could a psychologist wish for than to possess the key with which to unlock all doors to the human psyche? At the beginning Jung feels, as it were, to be in the position of a psychological Saint Peter equipped with the power of the keys. Or, with an allusion to Matth. 4:8, he sees himself, so to speak, taken to a very high mountain from which he sees "all the kingdoms of the world [of soul] and their glory" beneath him. With this result of his reviewing his life up to date, the text could actually end. Jung has arrived. A fantastic career as psychologist would have to be ahead of him.

However, surprisingly the story does not end here. A SECOND ACT follows. In it Jung confronts himself with the spiritual situation of his time. This actually begins with a voice whispering within him: "Why open all gates?" An absolutely astonishing question. If it were indeed a genuine question about the "reason why" rather than the disguised prohibition that it is, the answer to it would be obvious: "Because it is the very task of science and all the more so of psychoanalysis to open all the doors that can possibly be opened." But as indicated, this sentence has only the form of a question, but it does not really want an answer. As the inner *whisper* betrays, this question is simply the way in which the Tempter, who *wants* something, approaches Jung. By comparison with Matthew 4 it is, however, a Tempter in reverse, because he does not want to take Jung up to an exceeding high mountain to tempt him with a splendid career as scientist or therapist (which would here, of course, not make sense in the first place because Jung is from the outset in possession of the power of the keys and on the pinnacle from which the world of the psyche at his feet is open to him). This Tempter wants conversely to seduce him into giving up his power of the keys to all the gates at least to some degree, in other words, to a restriction, a withdrawal. What this sentence really wants to say could be expressed in the following way: "should you, Jung, really venture upon a path of unrelenting questioning, a course of analyzing and thinking without restraints—*or*, should not much rather at least some gates be left unopened? Are there not forbidden chambers that you should respect?" This shows that the Tempter is not Lucifer, the Bringer of Light, of more consciousness, but one who tempts Jung into accepting certain mental taboos and restraints, in other words, into staying or becoming unconscious. Already here we get a first vague idea that he will prepare the way for "*the* unconscious."

This impeding tendency becomes even more obvious when we take the immediately following sentence into account: "And promptly the question arose of what, after all, I had accomplished." In it and in the following sentence the ultimate value of his scientific main work to date is unmistakingly denigrated, that work in which he had acquired through his labors that very key to the understanding of the human psyche. In the last analysis, these statements amount to an (at least partial) devaluation of the scientific impulse as such, of the pure urge for research and for opening as many doors a possible.

The devaluation is performed in the light of the distinction between that which is interesting merely in an historical, antiquarian sense, on the one hand, and present actual reality, on the other hand. The "myths of peoples of the past" that Jung had explained in his book now appeared to him as—in the last analysis—irrelevant, dead, and this on account of another concern, one that is articulated in the question that follows: "But in what myth does man live nowadays?" This is the very modern, almost existentialist concern for *immediate relevance* for us today, a wish for something to be vividly felt, directly, personally felt by oneself as existentially important and vivifying. And the "But" in "But in what myth does man live nowadays?" plays this desire off against the strictly scientific or therapeutic opening of all doors.

One sees here quite clearly that Jung was not first of all the born scientist and psychologist (as which he mostly understood himself), but was *primarily* and *deeply* driven by the question or quest for myth *as a present reality*, more generally said, for a meaning of life to be experienced and *possessed* here and now. The strictly scientific interest of simply *knowing* and *comprehending*, be it the myths of peoples of the past or the psyche of present-day man, had to take second place to this irrenunciable concern. It was not enough as a psychoanalyst to possess the key to all the doors of the soul and to use it therapeutically. There was more and something more important for Jung. First and foremost, one could say, Jung was a *homo religiosus* and only thereafter also a scientist and therapist. And our text passage shows precisely the movement away from the scientist's initial pride in his intellectual-analytical discoveries and methods of explanation to the longing for a living immediate meaning *today* as the main issue. Years later, in 1945, Jung himself explicitly avowed this priority in a letter: "... the main interest of my work is not concerned with the treatment of neuroses but rather with the approach to the numinous."[6]

In this sense the whispered question is crucial. *This* Tempter does not lead Jung astray; he conversely calls him to his destiny, gives voice to his calling. The "Why open all gates?" puts him onto his very own

---

[6] C.G. Jung, *Letters*, vol. 1, S. 377, to P.W. Martin, 20 August 1945. (In *Briefe I*, p. 465; the date given is 28 August. I do not know which date is correct.)

track, which he had not been on before inasmuch as he had still tried to settle under the wings of Freud's theoretical framework, thereby avoiding having "to sew his garment himself" (cf. *CW* 9i § 27). In the whispering voice from within, his necessity, the original thought that the name Jung stands for, comes home to him with its own claims on him, after a time of aberration. And this is probably the reason why Jung experienced this moment as one of "unusual clarity." In a way, the whisper is the Annunciation of the birth of his idea of the unconscious as the new savior, an annunciation, however, not as a splendid revelation from above, but as a dim whisper from below. At any rate it pulled him back from the sphere of a purely analytical, scientific interest and returned him to his own deepest and innermost concern.

The beginning of the next sentence in our text ("And promptly the question arose ...") as well as the following train of thoughts show that the temptation had been successful. This is why now suddenly his initial proud assessment of his achievement so far is reversed, from triumph to contempt. He basically says now that what he accomplished amounts to nothing; his book contains merely antiquarian studies that might perhaps be of academic interest, but are certainly not of any relevance for life today. So what we witness here is the intrusion of *time* into consciousness, time in the special sense of an irrevocable rupture between two times, past and present, formerly and nowadays. The Jung who initially had been in a position to unlock all the gates had dwelled in the continuity of an unbroken time that we might call *tradition*. *As* extending far back into an ancient past, tradition nevertheless *is* so-to-speak an eternal *present*. But this present is over for Jung. We could also say that what we witness here is the intrusion of *modernity*, in the sense of a consciousness that feels itself absolutely cut off from tradition. Or, to be more exact, modern consciousness is one that is driven to actively and continuously *cut itself* off from tradition. Thus Jung here unrelentingly discharges tradition, he *makes* a clean break with "the myth in which man has always lived" and almost brutally sets over against this traditional time his own new present as the time that is characterized by a radical negation, a time in which "evidently we *no longer* have any myth." Even though presented as an insight or a diagnosis, and a painful one at that, we have to see that Jung's idea of the obsolescence of myth is much rather a psychological *move*, indeed, a violent act, the act in which not Jung personally, but *modern* consciousness in him at one strike sweeps away all tradition. The first act in founding modern psychology as Jung saw it is its categorically ridding itself of its cultural and religious heritage.

In his Eranos lecture of 1933 in which Jung introduced the concept of the archetypes of the collective unconscious, we find the most blatant and lengthy expression of this active dismissal of tradition. He says there, for example, "It seems to me that it would be far better stoutly to avow our spiritual poverty, our symbol-lessness, instead of feigning a legacy to which we are not the legitimate heirs at all" (*CW* 9i § 28). And in almost poetic language he tells us what the renunciation of our heritage amounts to: "to dwell with oneself alone, where, in the cold light of consciousness, the blank barrenness of the world reaches to the very stars" (§ 29, transl. modif.). Religiously, metaphysically, or psychologically we arrive at a zero point. But: "We already have inherited this poverty from our fathers" (§ 30, transl. modif.).

It is possible that when speaking of the symbol-lessness that we have inherited from our fathers, Jung also had his personal father in mind. In him, a Protestant minister who, according to Jung, had lost his faith and had inwardly given up, Carl Gustav had had a living example of the spiritual poverty of his time right before his eyes, and, owing to its continued emotional impact, in a very vivid and absolutely evident way. What Jung experienced in his father was more than a single individual's inner problem. His father became for him a concrete demonstration and symbol of the debility and spiritual ineffectiveness of the Christian faith in the modern situation as such. But of course, with his diagnosis Jung also follows in the footsteps of Nietzsche who before him had diagnosed the death of God and nihilism as the fundamental character of his time.

Inasmuch as we have arrived at a definitive answer, "No, evidently we no longer have any myth," this is a second point in our passage at which these considerations of his could actually end. The question posed has been settled. But to our surprise, and with this we come to THIRD AND LAST ACT of the drama that takes place in our Jung passage, this conclusive diagnosis is followed by a repetition of the very question that had just led up to this conclusion, the question: "But then what is your myth? The myth in which you do live?" Jung does not take "no" for an answer. He does not allow himself to be fobbed off with the insight he just gained that myth is lost.[7]

At least it seems that with this question we have returned to square one and that Jung simply ignored his own insight, maybe because the longing for myth, that is, for a "higher" meaning of life and for a "connection of gods and men" was too strong (cf. "My whole being was seeking for something still unknown which might confer meaning upon the banality of life"[8] [*MDR* p. 165]). But as the "then" shows, the seeming renewal of the initial question is itself a *consequence* of the preceding answer. The new question about *his* myth occurs on a higher level and rests upon the accomplished break with all traditional myth; and the notion of myth that we thus arrive at is one that presupposes, and includes within its definition, the debunking of tradition and specifically the concrete present state of religion as it had historically developed. It is cleansed of all remnants of the existing tradition. Traditional myth or religion, on the one hand, and the myth that this passage is after, on the other hand, exclude each other. The text merely uses the same word for both. This is why there is no contradiction between the categorical diagnosis that there is no myth any more and the insistent question, "But then what is your myth?" The first "myth" refers to the really existing faith, religion, or world view of the time, and this "myth" is ruthlessly brushed aside.

In this sense, the idea of "myth" in our text by no means returns, in the sense of a revival or "Renaissance," to an equivalent of what myth was in ancient societies. Rather, it is a typically *modern*, early 20th century fantasy of a new beginning, only retrojected into the past, just as one and a half centuries earlier and under different conditions Rousseau's "return to nature" had neither been a "return" nor really

---

[7] Here I refer back to the very end of the foregoing chapter where—apropos of the last sentence of a dream report of Jung's from about the same time ("Inside, a voice calls, 'It is all empty and disgusting.' I must bear it.")—I raised the question, "did Jung bear it, really bear it?"

[8] The logic of this statement is revealing. The truth about life is that it is banal. It needs something from outside that is bestowed on it to cover up its real banality. This is why meaning has to be *sought*. The search for meaning *malgré lui* expresses its own underlying nihilism. A searched-for myth is a contradiction in terms. Real myth is "the true word" (W.F. Otto) and expresses the meaning that *is*. If a myth has to be searched for it is one that could only be superimposed upon an actually meaningless reality of life and is *ipso facto* untrue.

one "to nature" in the sense of what is given. It had been a fundamentally novel Enlightenment fantasy, a utopian idea. "Myth" is here an abstract notion and a new invention that did not exist before. As the dream of an immediacy undefiled by reflection and history, it is the inherent counterpart to the modern turn against tradition (and the *concrete* present), and at the same time it is the instrument for more thoroughly divorcing oneself psychologically from the historically given. And inasmuch as only this abstract immediacy counts, it does not really matter whether one thinks in terms of a utopian program for the future or a prehistorical origin or an atemporal principle. They are all equally ex-centric.

The consciousness at work here in Jung is not content with historically mediated religion or religiouslessness as it really exists at a given time; he could not be content with it because in the new situation of Industrial Modernity traditional religion and metaphysics had in fact lost their capacity to express the truth of the time. Instead, this consciousness insists on immediate, unmediated access to an origin conceived as *the* origin, "literal," "naked," ahistorical origin, and this is what is asked for in the question the second time around, "But then what is your myth?" And this is also why years later Jung's answer to his diagnosis about the lack of myth today was that we have to have *Urerfahrung*, "originary or primordial experience," and why the idea of *Urbilder* (primordial images) and *arche*types had to come up. "It is a vital necessity for us moderns to rediscover the life of the spirit, that is, to have primordial experience" (*CW* 4 § 780, transl. modif.; Jung italicized this entire sentence). Both the sweeping away of the really existing historical religious tradition and the reaching out for his very own myth (in the second sense of the word) are two sides of the same coin. The driving force behind both is the need to begin from scratch, with a clean slate or with pure, abstract beginnings, which is only the other side of the wish for an eminent origin. The word "myth" in Jung's final question here is utopian; it is defined as the myth that *is* not, but has to be sought; it is a *program* for the future, not a reality, and a counter-program to historical social and intellectual reality at that. This program introduces a split-off alternative to the main development of civilization.

Because of the need for a naked origin and an absolutely fresh beginning, the actual present in its historicity is construed by Jung as an absolutely *exceptional* situation. In other texts we find statements that show this clearly: "This distinguishes our time from all others" (*CW* 10 §161); "This situation is new. All ages before us ..." (*GW* 9/ I § 50, my transl.). To construe one's own present as radically new and to assign to it the status of an exception over against all past history is the constitutive act of modernity, at least of modernity in its Industrial phase (and it is an act repeated by one modern thinker after the other). The idea of the exceptional situation is not only the result of the recognition that, owing to the fundamental rupture that separates the age of metaphysics and Christianity from modernity, traditional faith could no longer satisfy the soul (which it could only have done if it could have expressed the truth of the new situation). It also and at the same time functions as an instrument, as the lever for *explicitly* psychologically heaving human existence out of its actual embeddedness in its tradition and sending it off on a tangent, in search of a naked beginning. In Jung, the act-nature of the idea of the exceptional situation comes out most clearly when he demands of us a "vow of spiritual poverty" and our withdrawal "not only from the sorry remnants ... of a great past, but also from all the allurements of the exotic fragrance of the East; in order, finally, to dwell with oneself alone, where, in the cold light of consciousness, the blank barrenness of the world reaches to the very stars" (*CW* 9i § 29, transl. modif.). Jung *makes* a clean sweep.

But what, therefore, also is an act has to disguise itself as an innocent insight, diagnosis, or discovery about the (unfortunate, fateful) factual state of the present. One cannot lay claim to the absolutely exceptional character of one's own time if one is conscious of the fact that one has oneself produced this exceptional nature of one's situation. It must appear exclusively as history's doing. Here we come to an important point. Despite the real breaking-off of the religious and metaphysical tradition that happened, roughly speaking, with the beginning of the 19th century, the situation that arose thereby was precisely not truly *exceptional*. In actuality, mankind had always had to *make* soul; under the particular conditions prevailing at each respective time it had to re-establish, reformulate, and convincingly justify its faith or access to truth. One's hallowed tradition had to be newly "veri-fied" (made true) by each new generation. A tradition did not simply come with its truth. It is never a kind of consumer good.

Time and again, by each new generation, its truth had to be freshly established and made accessible. Under the conditions of archaic cultures governed by myth and ritual, each qualitatively new time performed in rituals the new establishment of a center and created the world anew out of the prevailing actual chaos. But this ritual new creation of the world was nothing else than the new enactment of the primordial ritual instituted by the ancestors, in other words, it was a new creation in the spirit of what Jung called in our passage "the myth in which man has always lived" and thus precisely the new confirmation and "veri-fication" of the old tradition. In fairy tales, which probably date back to the Stone Age, we already find this necessity of "veri-fication" expressed, for example, in the motif of the dragon that blocks the access to the water of life. There is no life in a tradition if it is merely continued or taken over "just like that."

It is true, with the change to modernity there was indeed a more radical, more pronounced challenge than during many centuries before. But this did not make the new situation *absolutely* exceptional. What in truth is a difference of degree or in intensity should not be absolutized as total otherness or an unbridgeable difference. The new challenge presented by the historical locus of modernity (or the newness of this challenge) must not go to one's head. The moment it is literalized as an absolutely exceptional situation and acted out as the belief in a totally new beginning in the sense of a start from a clean slate and as the wish for an eminent origin, one has become inflated by the new challenge. This is what happened and characterizes all modern thinking in all its many varieties. And Jung, by claiming an absolutely exceptional status for his time and searching for the primordial (*Urerfahrung, Urbild*) is no exception.

The mentality or logic prevailing in this idea of the fresh beginning and the search for an eminent origin is totally different from that expressing itself in alchemy, for example. Alchemy always begins in the middle. For it, the *prima materia*, the beginning, is the actually given mess, the *massa confusa* at hand, the concrete real condition as it exists and results from the history that produced it, and which is at first dismissed (*in via ejectum*) as "nothing" (*vilis* and *exilis*). And the "origin" to be sought, the Mercurius, is precisely not an eminent origin, but is already there because it lies *within* the massa confusa itself, not outside, behind, or prior to, it. In the sense of the "psychological difference" it is there and not there: implicitly present, but explicitly absent. This is why the work of alchemy is one of an ever deeper *Er-Innerung*, an inwardization into the heart of the matter in the sense of sublimation, distillation, vaporization. Similarly, the true origin in archaic cultures determined by myths and rituals had always been *in* the concrete present, in the center, and not in a literal beginning before all time. Each *Now* of a ritual established the center of the world and *was* cosmogonic, was the creation of the cosmos now, in the middle of time. Worlds lie between such a stance and the one displayed in our text. In the latter, the origin is decidedly *not* in the concrete present as it historically came about; it is *not* mixed and messed up with human, all-too-human social, political, economic, intellectual activities and developments. This origin is (is supposed to be) a pure source logically preceding cultural history and empirically informing or steering it from behind or below as the absolute a priori. It is never dirtied by the real conditions. The Jungian version of "the unconscious" and "the archetypes" is conceived as such a pure source, as unadulterated pristine nature. It is not in the middle, but, extrajected from the middle and dissociated from consciousness as it *is*, it is an extreme, and it works from the beyond as which it exists, in contrast to the massa confusa of the given cultural tradition.

The innermost logic of Jungian psychology is a logic of two extremes around an empty middle. The one extreme is the absolutely fresh beginning, and the other is the goal (the Self, wholeness, individuation) to be reached in the future. The absolutely exceptional situation (wholly otherness),[9] on the one hand, and the eminent origin (the archetypes of the collective unconscious), on the other hand, surround the real present, a present characterized by lack and loss. The importance of the notion of a search or quest in Analytical Psychology is, as the illusory attempt to get from zero or nothing to something, the reflection of this centerless (logical) extremism or, as we could also call it, this logic of dissociation.

Today, we are so used to the idea of myth that we do not see how revolutionary and novel Jung's initial question, "But in what myth does man live nowadays?" already was, let alone the later question, "But

---

[9] Psychologically, the idea of the absolutely exceptional character of one's present amounts to a desertion from this present and to a hyperbolical, boundless claim for a better world.

then what is your myth?" This question—asked in 1913 or so, in a
world characterized by factories and mass society, by a positivistic
science and a cultural Darwinism, and centuries after the European
Enlightenment and after 2500 years of philosophy, i.e., of a *reflecting*
consciousness, and 1900 years of Christianity—this question was
preposterous from the outset. Christian faith had not presented itself
or been perceived as myth, neither at Jung's time nor earlier. Where
should *myth*[10] have come from all of a sudden after at least 2000 years
without myth, or with myth only in the totally different sense as a
kind of raw material, an upper-class repertoire of poetic metaphors
for poets and artists and a subject of higher classical education? "But
in what myth does man live nowadays?" could not be a serious,
straightforward question, no more serious than the question would
be why we don't use stone axes any more. It actually has the character
of a catch question: the artificial innocence with which the question
is put and with which especially Christianity is imputed to still have
been a *myth*, as well as the equally artificial shock at the alleged
discovery that we do not have any myth "any more" has the purpose
of setting this utterly novel and modern thing "myth" up as a human
constant, as something without which one simply cannot exist. This
catch question places (or has always already placed) consciousness into
the feeling that a life outside of myth is downright unthinkable.
Thereby it makes a search for one's myth sound imperative, simply
mandatory, and in this way musters, harnesses all energies for the
Urerfahrung that is to lead to the discovery of one's myth. That a life
outside myth is unthinkable was a theoretical premise of Jung's
thinking. He liked to express it in the form of a dictum dating back
to Cyprianus, *extra ecclesiam nulla salus.*[11] The same premise made him
view neurosis "as the suffering of a soul which has not discovered its
meaning" (*CW* 11 § 497) and as a *morbus sacer* (*ibid.* § 521). "Our
concern with the unconscious has become a vital question for us—a
question of spiritual being or non-being" (*CW* 9i § 51).[12]

---

[10] Jung means "myth" in its full sense: as the articulation, in imaginal, narrative
form and on a prephilosophical level of consciousness, of the truth of actually lived life
("the myth in which you do live").

[11] Cf. Cyprianus, Epistulae 73,21,2.

[12] Marie-Louise von Franz could still in the middle of the second half of the 20th
century, in other words, at a time when the first phase of modernity, Industrial Modernity,
had already begun to give room to Medial Modernity, invoke the idea of the "vital

The original question in our text had been in what myth *man* [*der Mensch*] lives nowadays. Similarly, the answer was that *we* no longer have any myth. But in order to arrive at the answer Jung asked the question, "Do *you* live in it?" The question is directed at himself, at the "I," which then has to confess, "It is not the myth *I* live in." This switching from "man" or "we" (i.e., the level of the generality or the social community) to "you" or "I" (i.e., that of the isolated private individual) is another significant move in dissociating individual consciousness from the existing culture and establishing the novel idea of myth as unmediated primordial or existential experience. The Jung of later years knew: "Myth," that is, real myth as a historical phenomenon, "is pre-eminently a social phenomenon: it is told by the many and heard by the many."[13] But our text definitively dismisses the social, public tradition altogether in order, with the final question, to turn to the privacy and subjectivity of the abstract, atomic individual, "But then what is *your* myth? The myth in which *you* do live?"—as if this were not a contradiction in terms. Just as there cannot be a private language (Wittgenstein[14]), there cannot be *my* myth or a myth *in me*. *If* there is a real myth, then the subject whose myth it is is "we," not "I." Or instead of "we" we could also say the transcendental I (Kant): *die Menschheit in meiner Person* (humanity in my person). With a decidedly modernist move, Jung, however, zooms in on the empirical individual in his isolation and abstractness. For Jung the individual is "the measure of all things" (*CW* 10 § 523) and the "makeweight that tips the scale" (§ 586). He wants, as we heard, the individual "to dwell with [it]self alone" (*CW* 9i § 29), in other words, to go the way of introspection. The individual is now the exclusive locus of truth. Truth has become something private. The locus of truth is no longer the tribe, the nation, the culture as a whole.

question." She said, "civilization needs a myth to live .... If our Western civilization has a possibility of survival, it would be by accepting the alchemical myth ...." S. Wagner, "A Conversation with Marie-Louise Von Franz," in: *Psychological Perspectives*, Issue 38 (winter) 1998–1999, pp. 12–42, here p. 15. Apropos this quoted comment the question arises if survival can be a psychological category (does the soul have an interest in our *survival*? Is it not much rather primarily concerned about the "*underworld*"?). And furthermore, can one "*accept*" (take over) a myth in the first place, and if that is possible, would this be psychologically desirable and would it still be truly myth and not much rather an ideology? It clearly is the ego that is expressing itself in von Franz' statement. *She* knows. *She* has the answer.
[13] *Letters 2*, p. 486 (to Pastor Tanner, 12 February 1959).
[14] Wittgenstein, *Philosophical Investigations* §§ 243ff.

Of course, *within* the individual Jung believed himself able to rediscover something transpersonal and universal. But his wording "the collective unconscious" is very revealing. The term "collective" (from *colligere*, 'to gather, assemble') in itself refers to an aggregation of all the abstract atomic individuals. Introspection or immediate inner experience does not lead to something *communal*, a true *we*, nor to a real universal such as the transcendental I. The collective unconscious does not logically, syntactically overcome the isolation of the abstract individual. The individual in his utter loneliness merely finds (is said to find) something that potentially could be found in every individual. In other words, the collective unconscious does not create any more of a communality than the genetic codes that each individual shares with millions of people.

The abstractness of the individual consists above all in the fact that with the turn to the inner the human being conceives of himself, and particularly also of his very essence, as something individual, as a self-contained substrate according to the model of the physical body. The human organism is obviously an *individual* "thing." But not the human person. Now, with the turn to the inner, however, the person no longer knows itself defined by the fact that it is *not* an entity, but a *relationship*—one side of a relationship *and* at the same time, within itself, the whole relationship. Culture, society, language are not only the individual's "environ," out there, all around it. They are also inherent in the individual's very own essence. But the introspecting individual abstracts from its being part of the societal relations of production and its being embedded in a public linguistic, cultural nexus and in the context of an ongoing public discussion. It abstracts from the fact that all this is inherent in *its own* inner essence, thus showing that it takes the separateness of the visible physical bodies as fundamental and the mind as a mere attribute. (Fundamentalism!)

Here again, it would be a mistake to think that Jung was simply born to be a psychologist. No, he had to become a psychologist because for him the locus of truth had receded from the real world into the inner of the lonely individual. Psychology, as it developed here, is the study of the self-enclosed individual. Since myth and man's sympathetic world-relation have disappeared from the world and as our public cultural truth, they have to be sought by each individual within himself or herself. Since the real God is dead, we insist that

God lives in the soul, as the Self, and even if this may not be the real God, then it is at least a God-*image*. We see that in constituting the logic of his psychology project Jung executes that move that about a century earlier Goethe had caricatured thus:

> Laß der Sonne Glanz verschwinden,
> Wenn es in der Seele tagt,
> Wir im eignen Herzen finden,
> Was die ganze Welt versagt. (Goethe, *Faust II*, ll. 9691 ff.)

> ("Let the sun's shine disappear, / When day is dawning in the soul, / We find in our own heart / What the world refuses us.")

In contrast to all previous questions in Jung's soliloquy, the question, "But then what is your myth? The myth in which you do live?" does not receive an answer. Instead, our text ends with the statement, "At this point things became uncomfortable, and I stopped thinking. I had reached a boundary." One could think that Jung is expressing here no more than a temporary helplessness and that at a later point the thought process disrupted here was again continued and carried forward. But no. This is a definitive end. Jung had reached his Rubicon, and *his* Rubicon was one that was not to be crossed. It was the invitation to stop thinking, the invitation to a *sacrificium intellectus* (not on the behavioral level—Jung never literally stopped thinking—but on a fundamental, i.e., the logical level). Throughout his life he insisted on "the barrier across the mental world" (*CW* 18 § 1734) and vehemently condemned those who he believed had gone beyond it, especially Hegel. Far beyond what Jung immediately and subjectively *intended* to say in our text, the statement "I stopped thinking" is objectively programmatic, confessional. The dead end at which Jung arrived may appear to be a mishap, but it was much rather the telos and positive result of his ruminations. It was for him the solution and not a problem, just as much earlier during his twelfth year in the Basel cathedral incident, "Don't go on thinking," "Don't think of it, just don't think of it!" had been his solution for dealing with his unwelcome thought fantasy.[15]

---

[15] *MDR* pp. 36ff. See Wolfgang Giegerich, "Psychology as Anti-Philosophy: C.G. Jung," in: *Spring 77 (Philosophy and Psychology)*, June 2007, pp. 11–51, now Chapter Two of the present volume.

Again, far from having come to an impasse with the "I had reached a boundary," Jung had paradoxically in fact *arrived* where the whispered question from the beginning, "Why open all gates?," wanted to have him. The boundary closes the gate to a relentless thinking that would go all the way. And this closing the gate was the *solution*! Not a dilemma, an aporia! The myth that Jung was seeking had to be found on this side of the boundary, and found through "immediate experience." The (for Jung precious!) idea of the boundary forced Jung (or rather allowed him) to pull back and reverse the direction of his exploration: *from* going forward with a view to a deeper intellectual penetration that his subject-matter, myth (as the in him as modern man really prevailing deepest soul truth), would actually have demanded, *to* looking backwards and within, into "the unconscious" as he was going to understand it. Or, rather the other way around, the boundary is the objectified image in which the subjective *attitude* of "keeping in" and "holding back" congeals. And, conversely, his notion of the unconscious *is* the hypostatized boundary, the reified "stopping to think."

The closing of the gates to thinking *is* the opening of the gate to the empirical exploration and "immediate" experience of "the unconscious." And as such it is the invention of the general idea of "the unconscious." The latter is in truth nothing but a disguised and hypostatized *prohibition* to *think*, the hypostatized *sacrificium intellectus*.

In the beginning of a therapy, when a patient sought help from him, Jung liked to say that he did not know the answer to the patient's predicament either and suggested that they do not think about it but simply observe the patient's dreams (cf., e.g., *CW* 10 § 314, and also *CW* 12 § 37). No doubt, in therapy this is a very helpful move. But for Jung it was precisely not only a practical method; it was also what he himself had done, on the deepest level of theorizing, to the mind as such. Thinking, thinking with speculative depth and strength, was declared off limits and to be replaced by the observation of (what Jung believed to be) "natural facts," whereby "observation" means an *ultimately* mindless registering (an "innocent" passive receiving without a responsive productive participation of the mind). This is the new *program*.

A contemporary of Jung's, though 16 years his senior, Edmund Husserl, one of the most influential philosophers of the 20th century (influential for Heidegger, Sartre, Lévinas, Derrida, to mention only these), published around the same time when Jung went through the mental movements expressed in his soliloquy, namely in 1913, his book *Ideen zu einer reinen Phänomenologie und phänomenologischen Philosophie*, in which for the first time in print he introduced the concept of "transcendental-phenomenological reduction" as the indispensable prerequisite for achieving the right starting point for a phenomenological investigation. The methodological *sine qua non* of phenomenological studies (in the philosophical sense) was the *bracketing* of the "general thesis of the natural attitude," i.e., of the ordinary, straightforward attitude to the world, which consists in consciousness's naive belief in the existence of its objects (*Seinsglaube*), in other words, in taking the existence of what is given to it simply for granted. Through the methodological device of what Husserl called "transcendental *epochê*" (or "reduction") the philosophical mind abstains from making any statement about the being or non-being of what is given in order to raise itself to the height of "pure" or "transcendental" consciousness through this suspension of the ordinary *Seinsglaube* and so to become free for the "intuition of essence" (*Wesensschau*) and the description of how consciousness or the transcendental I *performs the acts of constitutions* of what it encounters (always already has encountered) as its own objects.

Just as Jung pursued with his psychology an ultimate concern, the search for myth and meaning, so also was Husserl a philosopher not merely by profession, but out of an absolute personal commitment. Philosophy had an inner, existential significance and almost sacred dignity for him. Husserl's particular moves were in the service of the goal of turning philosophy into a strict science. We know that Jung, too, aimed at construing psychology as a science. But in order to establish science these two men moved in opposite directions and their efforts exclude each other. Not only had Husserl previously vehemently struggled to cleanse philosophy of all the "psychologism" that it had succumbed to (Mills, Nietzsche), but his phenomenological aim was also to explore and describe the absolute foundations of the world as experienced by consciousness, foundations that are precisely not accessible to empirical observation.

Jung, by contrast, swore by empirical observation and stuck to the ordinary, straightforward attitude to the world and the objects of experience. Whereas Husserl tried to arrive at "pure" or "transcendental" consciousness, Jung believed in the unconscious as "pure," "unadulterated" nature. And in total contrast to any "transcendental *epoché*" Jung precisely vindicated even to psychic phenomena, to fantasies, images, and visions, their *psychic reality*, a reality of which he said that "it has at least the same dignity as physical reality" (*CW* 15 § 148, transl. modif.). He even insisted that "Psyche is the most real thing there is because it is what alone is immediate" (*CW* 8 § 680, transl. modif.) and that it is "*the* category of existence, the indispensable *sine qua non* of all existence" (*CW* 11 § 769). By advocating a belief in absolute immediacy, Jung not only on principle held on to the "general thesis of the natural attitude," but also to what we could call a positivistic stance to the world. And he even transferred or extended it from the things of the world to all those phenomena that people had always been wont to think were unreal, mere figments of the mind: dreams, myths, and fantasies.

And yet Jung, too, performed a bracketing, an *epoché* or reduction, but, in contrast to Husserl, not one that was intentionally performed as a conscious methodological device, but naively, as an unconscious reduction inherent in the ordinary, straightforward attitude. What Jung bracketed was, however, exactly that very thing at which Husserl had arrived through his *epoché*: transcendental consciousness, the transcendental I and its, the transcendental I's, performances of the acts with which it constitutes the objects of its experience. "Pure nature" and "immediacy" is what is experienced *minus* the awareness of the hidden active involvement of consciousness in it. "The unconscious" is the decision not to (or the prohibition to) reflect the "transcendental" production processes, the thinking mind's participation in the production of images, or the soul-*making* that is going on (not in, but) *behind the scenes of* our dreams, fantasies, or visionary experience. Jung's bracketing resulted in his reducing the mind to the empirical I, to the everyday mentality of No. 1 personality. As empirical I Jung, of course, could continue to think. The transcendental I, the only one that might possibly have been up to the substantial metaphysical contents of "myth" and thus the only real addressee for them, was banished and extradited beyond a never to be transgressed boundary. Indeed, that boundary is the division between the empirical I and the transcendental I.

On one occasion Jung criticized the natural sciences for trying "to represent the results of their investigations as though these had come into existence without *man's intervention*, in such a way that *the indispensable collaboration of the psyche* remains invisible" (*CW* 10 § 498, transl. modif., my italics). In his commentary to the "Tibetan Book of the Dead" Jung says, "It is so much more immediate, conspicuous [or obvious], impressive and therefore so much more convincing to see how things happen to me than to observe how I produce them. Indeed, the animal nature of man baulks at our [possibly] feeling ourselves as the maker of what is given to us" (*CW* 11 § 841, transl. modif.). Object-consciousness and the sense of literal otherness and of "positive fact" are due to our animal nature, our existence as biological organism. Another time, late in life, Jung speaks in the same vein of a "light that gradually dawns on one," namely concerning the fact that it is insufficient to look on from outside. "So long as one simply looks at the pictures one is like the foolish Parsifal, who forgot to ask the vital question, because one does not become aware of *one's own participation*" (*CW* 14 § 753, transl. modif.).

So, in the course of one's individuation process, in one's relation to the inner images, i.e., while one is on the experiential, content, or semantic level, Jung thinks it is indispensable that one becomes aware of one's own participation in them. For the analysand empirical observation (and understanding) of the unconscious is not enough, just as psychologically it is immature to see "the world" or reality as factually given and events as happening to us without also becoming aware of their being produced by the soul. So far so good. However, Jung did not realize that on the syntactical level, the level of the logical construal of psychological theory, he himself is like the foolish Parsifal who forgets to ask the vital question: the question about the conscious mind's collaboration, involvement, and participation, and avoids becoming aware that there is no abstract "the unconscious" as "pure nature," but that all productions of the so-called unconscious are production of *homo totus*, the conscious-unconscious unity of the soul or mind. He himself as theoretician has succumbed to the resistance of his animal nature to psychological awareness. Underlying "the psychology of the unconscious" is precisely a fundamental dissociation: the splitting of the whole man, or of the wholeness of man, as the living conscious-unconscious, active-passive, empirical-transcendental unity of consciousness. What is two moments of or in consciousness, Jung positivized and hypostatized as two separate and opposite systems. Now we have "*the* unconscious" as something factually given, as an *object* of observation. What used to be merely an attribute or predicate, is now a noun.

Returning to Jung's late insight we can say that the empirical human being is supposed to provide what psychology itself explicitly refused; the experiential and semantic level is burdened with the task of achieving what was systematically excluded from the logic or syntax of psychology; expectations for something to happen in the future have to make up for what was missed (or rather intentionally prohibited) in the initial setup. Late in life Jung discovered in the alchemical motif of the fish eyes or of the sparks (*scintillae*) that the unconscious was in itself not totally unconscious. He said, "For the eyes of the fish are always open and therefore must always see" (*CW* 14 § 752). But this discovery did not lead for Jung to a fundamental revision or rather revocation of the axiomatic setup of his theory, namely of the dissociation between consciousness and the unconscious. The always-seeing eyes remained an object or content vis-à-vis consciousness, and only the human person in his or her private image process could *possibly* recognize his or her own participation in them (in what is in the unconscious), but not psychology itself. The discovery *by* the theorizing consciousness of a consciousness *in* the unconscious did not lead to an uroboric closing of the circle in psychological theory, to consciousness's self-recognition in the other consciousness and to its acknowledgment of the latter's being itself, to the contradictory insight that what truly appears to be given as objective existence is at the same time produced by that consciousness to which it is given.

Except for the fact that they never took note of each other and therefore also did not fight with each other, one might call Husserl and Jung inimical twins. Each abstracts precisely from what the other highlights. Each presents only one purified half of the picture. And inasmuch as half of the picture is a distorted picture, both are fundamentally deficient.

With regret Jung noted that his father had given up continuing to struggle thinkingly with religious doctrine because he wanted to be able to hold on blindly to his faith. Jung saw this as his having committed a *sacrificium intellectus*. After what we discussed, we have to realize, however, that precisely in this regard Jung was the true son of his father. Of course, whereas his father performed this sacrifice by refraining on the level of literal behavior from thinking about religious matters and, as a consequence, succumbed to resignation, moodiness, and irritability in his personal feeling, in C.G. Jung the *sacrificium intellectus* had become structural, a logical one. He did not have to literally act it out. He could and did think about all kinds of religious topics, the Trinity, the Catholic Mass, the *Assumptio Mariae*, etc., because he had interiorized the sacrifice of the intellect into the logical form of his theory. This sacrifice had become hypostatized as a realm of being, "the un-conscious." Instead of literally having to stop thinking, Jung *thought* the thought of "the unconscious," which in itself is the objectified (substantiated) bracketing and becoming unconscious, becoming ignorant of the transcendental I. Jung's whole psychology is at bottom nothing else than the unfolding in detail of the concept of "the unconscious."

Now I want to put together once more by way of an overview the five logical steps or moments of the drama that we witnessed in Jung's report, that drama in which Jung transported his consciousness to the *standpoint* of "the unconscious" or acquired this standpoint for himself with "unusual clarity." The moments of this movement are:

1. The unconditional superordination of the existential question of meaning over the strictly scholarly, scientific, or medical interest.
2. The radical break with the concrete tradition of Jung's real present,
    a. in favor of an abstract Now with the status of an absolutely exceptional situation, a Now which in itself is the dissociation into a "no more" and a "not yet" around an empty middle, and
    b. in favor of a likewise abstract idea of Meaning through an eminent "origin" (*archê*) not rooted in his real culture and concrete historical time and thus essentially free-floating ("the archetypal").
3. Correspondingly, the rejection of the "we," the public sphere, and the transcendental I, and the withdrawal into the abstract private individual as empirical personality. This is tantamount to a shift away from a focus on *truth* to a focus on *felt experience.*

4. The insistence, against his knowing better, upon a myth or higher meaning of life, which, however, after steps 2 and 3 can now only be sought as the contradiction-in-terms of a "private myth."

5. On the logical or syntactical level the turning back at "the boundary," a stopping to think, the *sacrificium intellectus* and *ipso facto* the systematic exclusion of a conscious awareness of the syntactical level as such, which resulted in what was to become "the unconscious" to be cast out from consciousness and to be set up as literal Other and abstractly *objective* existence (as given, fact, empirical pure nature).

Together these five moments in their succession and unity make up what was to be Jung's "flight into the unconscious."

II. The flight into the unconscious

This phrase, "The flight into the unconscious," is not really my invention. With it I am rather alluding to and modifying another formula, the phrase: the "flight into the concept." This was the title of a book that appeared some years ago about some aspects of Hegel's philosophy of religion.[16] The book title in its turn had been taken from a statement by Hegel himself. About 90 years before Jung, Hegel, like many other thinkers of his time, had come to the realization that the self-evidence of the truth, and the powers of conviction, of Christian religion, the way it had come down, had pretty much disappeared. This was generally sensed, though of course not generally acknowledged. But already then, around 1800, the almost unbridgeable gap between tradition and modernity, above all also the modern feeling of alienation and disunity with oneself, had made itself painfully felt for many. The "Querelle des Anciens et des Modernes" had also already been articulated, for example, by Schiller,[17] Fr. Schlegel,[18] Schelling,[19] and Hölderlin. And as regards religion in particular, the crisis, so clearly elucidated

---

[16] *Die Flucht in den Begriff. Materialien zu Hegels Religionsphilosophie*, ed. by F.W. Graf and F. Wagner. Stuttgart 1982. "Die Flucht in den Begriff" is also a subtitle in the "Einleitung" by Walter Jaeschke to G.W.F. Hegel, *Vorlesungen über die Philosophie der Religion*, Part 3, *Die vollendete Religion*, Hamburg (Meiner) 1995, p. XXV.

[17] Esp. "Über naive und sentimentalische Dichtung" (1795/96).

[18] Esp. "Über das Studium der griechischen Poesie" (1797).

[19] E.g., "Über das Verhältnis der Naturphilosophie zur Philosophie überhaupt" (1802).

by Herbert Schöffler,[20] into which it had come towards the end of the 18th century had become all too obvious in the suicide epidemic in the wake of the appearance of Goethe's *Werther*.

This crisis was not people's fault. It was a fact in the objective soul's historical development. Traditional religion had objectively ceased to be capable of fully and adequately expressing the psychological truth of a new age.

By Hegel's time it had also become clear that all the various attempts of his predecessors or contemporaries to rescue and stabilize religion by grounding it, e.g., in ethics (Kant), in feeling, sentiment, and direct intuition (Friedrich Heinrich Jacobi, Schleiermacher, and some Romantics), in art and aesthetics (Schelling, Hölderlin) had all failed, each in its own way. In fact, they had turned out to be ultimately *false* ways to provide a secure foundation for religion inasmuch as they

---

[20]Herbert Schöffler, *Deutscher Geist im 18. Jahrhundert. Essays zur Geistes- und Religionsgeschichte*, Göttingen (Kleine Vandenhoeck-Reihe) 2nd edition 1967, which contains among others the especially relevant text previously published as a separate booklet, *Die Leiden des jungen Werther. Ihr geistesgeschichtlicher Hintergrund*, Frankfurt/Main (Klostermann) 1938. See also Albrecht Schöne, *Säkularisation als sprachbildende Kraft. Studien zur Dichtung deutscher Pfarrersöhne*, Göttingen (Vandenhoeck & Ruprecht) 1958 and Walter Jaeschke, *Die Vernunft in der Religion. Studien zur Grundlegung der Religionsphilosophie Hegels*, Stuttgart-Bad Cannstatt (Frommann-Holzboog) 1986.— Above all Schöffler and Schöne demonstrated that the golden age of German literature and philosophy in the decades before and after the year 1800 owed its possibility and emergence to the Reformation and "the Protestant parsonage." A majority of the poets and thinkers in Germany and Switzerland during the latter part of the 18th and the beginning of the 19th century were sons of Protestant ministers and/or had themselves been meant to become (and often in fact been trained as) theologians or clergymen, but went into the secular fields of literature or philosophy instead because by that time it had become unthinkable for truly gifted and creative persons to stand up as preachers of the Christian faith. The energy and deep impulse of the Christian message and the Protestant commitment to "the Word" burst the fetters that had hitherto tied it to and contained it in the traditional literal practice of Church life and was now transposed and *released into the absolute negativity* of poetic imaginary works and speculative thought. The psychological truth that in the Church rituals and in the practice of traditional private piety had merely been acted out was in this way inwardized into itself and came home to itself. 100 to 150 years after this battle about the freeing from positive religion had long been fought and the underlying psychological problem historically had been settled, we see in C.G. Jung a belated repeat of the same pattern. A Protestant minister's son, he vehemently broke with the faith of his father(s) and went into a secular field. For him, too, the religious impulse was something precious to be preserved under all circumstances. However, instead of the release of it into absolute negativity which had been the achievement of those earlier generations, now, at the end of the 19th and the beginning of the 20th century, the high time of positivism, Jung wanted precisely to return to religion as a positivity or to return religion to its form of positivity—of course not by going back to the Church, but by seeking it in the crudeness of personalistic psychology, namely, in private numinous experience as hard "fact" and literal event. "I need a situation in which that thing becomes true once more" (*CW* 18 § 632).

precisely prevented what was actually their objective. By trying to give religion a home in moral philosophy, in feeling, in art, it was always only one partial area of consciousness that was addressed and done justice to. What was ascribed to religion was only a *particular* home *besides* modern, rational consciousness, so that, on the one hand, the consciousness of that modern time itself was not reached by it and, on the other hand, religion itself remained excluded from it. Jacobi, for example, had exactly in this sense explicitly described himself as a "pagan in his intellect, a Christian in his heart [*Gemüt*]." All such attempts at rescuing religion therefore merely confirmed and solidified modern consciousness's disunity with itself, its dissociation.

In view of this fact, Hegel concluded that only one way remained to preserve the *substance* of religion in such a way that it might hold out before modern enlightened consciousness. Religion, so Hegel, would have to flee into, or take its refuge in, philosophy ("*in die Philosophie sich flüchten*").[21] As Jaeschke pointed out, this "flight into the *concept*" was (*sit venia verbo*) a *felix fuga*, a happy flight, a forward move. It was not a withdrawal nor a hasty escape into a foreign territory, but on the contrary a move into its own home ground.[22] (The word "flight" has a quite similar meaning in that phrase with which Tolstoy's biographer Henri Troyat described Tolstoy's fight against bureaucracy, the Church, and the military in Russia: "flight into truth.")

A reconciliation of disrupted consciousness *with* itself and a reconciliation *between* religion and reason was, according to Hegel, only possible if Christianity, taking up the challenge posed by present times, would be raised from its pre-modern form and speak across the threshold of the Enlightenment to the height of modern consciousness, for only then would it be put into a position to give true satisfaction to consciousness's needs. Christianity had to develop further. *Not*, however, as far as its substance is concerned. In order to preserve its "absolute substantial content" under the conditions of a new time, its inner logical *form* had to change. And its transformation had to come about through the achievement of freeing the *rational, conceptual* core of Christian religion that had always already been inherent in its imaginal and emotionally moving contents, so that through this

---

[21] G.W.F. Hegel, *Vorlesungen über die Philosophie der Religion*, Part 3, *op. cit.* p. 96.
[22] Jaeschke, "Einleitung," *op. cit.*, p. XXVII.

freeing it would come home to itself and at the same time be justified before the court of thinking consciousness. Through a kind of distilling or sublimation process Christianity had to be transformed into a religion that was not merely comprehended by us subjectively, but that above all also *comprehended itself* within itself objectively. Religion was supposed to attain to a higher form of itself, the form of its self-transparency, thereby fulfilling its telos and completing itself.

In one and the same process, the modern mind would conversely become enlightened about itself. It would on its part be forced to go beyond its one-sidedness, precisely by recognizing *itself* (*its innermost essence* in its highest potential) *in* the comprehended absolute substance of religion. That "flight" therefore required diligent work upon a further differentiation and sophistication of the modern mind and its capacity of conceptual thought, so that, *as* now having become a *thinking*, comprehending and no longer merely representing or imagining consciousness, it would for the first time have come into the position of being, on a thinking level, truly commensurate with the substantial contents with which it was concerned in its religion. Expressed in another way: so that it could on its part truly be adequate to the truths of religion.

The flight into the concept was thus a move forward, an advance both for the mind and for religion.

Viewed from outside, the problems that Hegel and Jung take up and the situations in which they saw themselves seem to be the same. Almost a century after Hegel, over whom the 19th century had long passed, the old *Querelle des Ancients et des Moderne* that in actuality had already become obsolete with the emergence, after Hegel's death, of Modernity (in the strict sense), received through and in Jung once more an unexpected repeat, particularly also the question of the relation of Christian religion and modern consciousness. But upon closer inspection the fundamental differences stand out. It is not the same situation. A watershed lies between the two. Hegel still had had his place in the tradition of Western metaphysics (in the sense of a *prima philosophia* informed by the logic of the copula), which was the thinking of a time characterized economically by the craft and manufacture mode of production. Jung, by contrast, had already been firmly rooted in and governed by the logic of modernity with its logic of the function or the unbridgeable difference, which in economic terms is the time of a thoroughly industrialized world, i.e., the industrial mode of production. This difference is inevitably reflected in the very different type of answer to each of their (only in external respects same) situations.

Hegel's thought in this connection had the express purpose "*to know* and *to comprehend* the religion that IS."[23] The religion that *is*! In an almost alchemical style, this real religion, as it was given by tradition and in the wretched condition[24] in which it in fact happened to be at his time, was supposed to be exposed to a process of reflection-into-itself in the sense of an internal sublimation or absolute-negative inwardization, a process of a deepening into itself to the point of highest intensity. The aim was, to express it in alchemical terms, to make accessible the gold that lay hidden inside the contemptible substance—*Reason* inherent in religion.

For Jung, by contrast, the religion that *is* (the Christianity of his time) was precisely nothing but a heap of rubble that consisted in "the sorry remnants of a great past" and needed to be ruthlessly cleared away as "*false* riches of the spirit" (see *CW* 9i § 29). "We are, surely, the rightful heirs of Christian symbolism, but somehow we have squandered this heritage" (*CW* § 9i § 28). What had become in itself wretched was on top of it supposed to be ruthlessly cast away (*in via ejectum*!) so as to make room for something else within the thus produced *empty* present cleansed of tradition. A distinctly unalchemical stance. This wholly other thing was "*my* myth," and it was, firstly, to be searched for as a new acquisition in the future, secondly to be found only *inside* him, Jung himself, and, thirdly, despite its still being in the future it was at the same time to reconnect him with the "archaic past" that *preceded* his own Christian tradition (or with something fundamentally atemporal, absolutely primordial, namely the world of archetypes). The last aspect means that it was to be the unity of the extremes, future – pluperfect, around an empty middle.

What Hegel was conversely concerned with was precisely *that* Christian religion "in which [Western] man has always lived" (to express it with a Jungian phrase, *MDR* p. 171). This entails four aspects. 1. "In which": that is, contained and surrounded, in the middle of one's

---

[23] G.W.F. Hegel, *Vorlesungen über die Philosophie der Religion*, Part 1, *Der Begriff der Religion*, ed. W. Jaeschke, Hamburg (Meiner) 1993, p. 10.

[24] As far as its spontaneous convincingness is concerned.

real present and concrete reality; 2. "man" as such: the unity of individuality and the universal, *not* the abstract private person; 3. and yet precisely Western man, the man of the Christian world, in other words, a specific man, not the abstract-universal "man at large"; 4. "always" (Jung has *seit jeher*: from time immemorial): the present as the unity of Now and tradition, or the Now as embedded and contained in tradition. Or the other way around: the real tradition that within the Now has been remembered, inwardized, and awakened to a new life.

The difference between the two attitudes can also be expressed in the following way. In Hegel, the whole burden of the transformation lay on the side of the subject, of consciousness, of *our* thinking (our thinking through Christianity). Here the *opus* had to begin. Here a sophistication of the mind had to be achieved. The substantial content of the matter itself (here: of Christianity) was supposed to remain intact, indeed, even for the first time be released into its truth. Exactly the other way around Jung imposed the burden of the change on the objective side, on the contents. What was needed were new archetypal contents acquired through each person's own primordial experience. Consciousness was supposed to perceive and receive these contents. But *it* had precisely to stay intact as far as its own logical form was concerned. In the same spirit late Jung, with respect to the Christian religion he previously discarded, wanted us to build or dream the "Christian myth" *onwards* (*MDR* p. 333ff., *CW* 9i § 271): there was now, just as in Hegel's case, to be a continued attention to Christianity, and yet how different, how oppositely was it to go on! First of all, Jung resorts to a *dreaming onwards*. Consciousness is supposed to be passive, continue in its slumber and merely observe and receive the autonomous apparition of images. Secondly, what was to be achieved was not a transformation of Christianity's form, but of its substantial content, in particular the expansion of the Trinity to a quaternity. Jung did not see in this move the destruction of Christianity, but something like its completion and fulfillment. But fulfillment through a correction, addition, in other words, through an Other, an alternative, not, in keeping with alchemical thinking, "tautologically," "tautegorically": through a distillation of one and the same, that is, not, to put it in Hegel's terminology, through a reflection-into-itself.

Whereas Hegel realized that it was impossible to circumvent the newly developed critical consciousness and therefore aimed at reconciling religion with consciousness precisely on the home territory of consciousness, Jung, who as a *modern* thinker nevertheless still insisted on higher meaning, had to move in the opposite direction. He had to force myth or meaning underground, out of conscious thought, because under the conditions of the logic prevailing in modernity, mythic meaning could not stand up before the public waking mind and its critical intelligence. It had become illegitimate. Thus it had to be logically stored away deep inside the private individual, and it had to be purified, extricated from its concrete inherited and socially real contemporary form (Christianity).

Jung could not, the way Hegel did, move in the direction of an intensification and sophistication of consciousness so that the latter might become capable of *thinking* and thus truly integrate the substantial contents of religion. Jung needed an intensification (indeed, *surpassing*) of the *unconsciousness* of consciousness through the fact that this unconsciousness was now objectified: fixated *as an existing, ontic structure*—as *the* unconscious. For Jung his analogue to Hegel's "the absolute substantial content of religion," namely what he called "mythos" or "meaning" or "symbolic life," had to *flee into the unconscious.* Jung had to logically (not empirically) offer to it a hidden asylum as a last resort: he had to sink it into the underground, into a crypt, and lock it out from consciousness, from the nave in which the congregation, the community, has its place. And he had to do this because under the in fact prevailing conditions of the logic of modernity these contents could not hold out before the *public waking* consciousness. The substantial contents of religion were no longer presentable to consciousness and acceptable as *its own* property. They simply had to shun the light of day, the full light of consciousness. They could not stand up to the *waking* mind and to the claims made by its critical intelligence and scientific standards. Thus they had become impossible, untenable: they had turned into primitive superstition, sheer nonsense, an invention by priests for the oppression of the people, etc.

Because they themselves were no longer presentable to consciousness, consciousness of modern man (if it still had self-respect), conversely, could no longer let *itself* be seen with *them*. It could no longer acknowledge them as its own. It had to disown them like an illegitimate child, disown them even before itself! And it disowned them, first, by logically storing them away deep inside the private individual, and secondly, by declaring them to be contents of the (collective) *unconscious.* By assigning the unconscious to them as their place, consciousness had once and for all renounced them.

For instance, Jung's own dreams and visions, I claim, did not really come from "*the* unconscious." They were his own speculative thoughts, thoughts thought by him not as ego, but as "the whole man," thoughts which, however, were not allowed to appear in consciousness as what they were. They were expelled from consciousness and allowed to reappear in consciousness only after having taken a detour via "the unconscious" and after having been forced into the guise of dream or vision as purely *natural* products.

This flight (a word that Jung himself of course does not use) is therefore not a *felix fuga*, but really a withdrawal into a protective shelter.

The *essential* (religious, metaphysical, mythic) contents were not only not presentable to consciousness and as such something to be disowned, but they were also dangerous. Consciousness itself in its logical constitution was not allowed to be affected and revolutionized by what it experienced from the unconscious. Because if it were, this would mean having crossed the forbidden boundary and become metaphysical. The spark *must not* spring over. For this would have meant the danger of inflation, the danger of psychosis, a danger that for Jung had been most threateningly embodied in the figure of Nietzsche. Nietzsche had not dissociated himself. He had thought without reserve as "the whole man" and taken full intellectual responsibility for what he thought. And thus he also had had to pay the full price when that which he had staked his whole thought upon, the hoped-for appearance of "Dionysus" (i.e., primordial-original productivity) to the longingly waiting "Ariadne" (i.e., the soul), did not happen.

That these *essential* contents threatened the subject with psychosis was something new. It was due to the new situation of *modern* consciousness, born consciousness, consciousness emancipated from the soul. As long as man had still been contained in the soul, as during the times of myth and metaphysics, to entertain, and believe literally in, such ideas as the virgin birth of the hero, a heavenly Jerusalem, the miracles performed by Jesus, or philosophical speculative ideas, neither proposed any difficulty nor any danger to the sanity of the mind (cf. *CW* 9ii § 274). These conceptions were at that time not incommensurate with the form of consciousness, because it was a *heteronomous* consciousness: resistancelessly given over to the soul as the locus of truth, from the outset embracing its, the soul's, mythical or speculative ideas, and open to their "suggestive power" (*CW* 7 § 269). But modern consciousness, born man's consciousness, is, and has to be, on principle autonomous. It has to be its own locus of truth. It stands or falls with its capacity to hold its place in its integrity *vis-à-vis* all such ideas, allowing in only what proved to it its reasonable nature before *its own* court of justice. If speculative ideas nevertheless take possession of consciousness, then consciousness becomes fundamentally *alienated* from itself (itself as autonomous consciousness) in the sense of mental alienation.

For Jung, Nietzsche had been a warning. The danger of "Nietzsche" had to be avoided at all cost. There just had to be a dissociation. Jungian psychology, as a psychology "with higher meaning," had to *be* neurosis in order to prevent psychosis. There must never be a *coniunctio*, a transference, an alchemical *vinculum*, *ligamentum*, or logical *copula*, 1. between the empirical observing and the emotionally affected subject, 2. between the image in the soul and what it *says* that it is the image of, and 3. between the subject and what the experience of the subject is. Because if such a *coniunctio* occurred, if ever the spark sprang over, this would be the forbidden transgression across the boundary, the opening of *all* gates—and thus inflation or psychosis.

Because of the self-dissociation as which the unconscious as such as well as its individual contents exist, there also have to be two completely separate subjects or personal identities between which one has to switch, one for the *content* and one for the *form*, one for the experience and one for the conscious understanding. Jung personified them in himself as personalities No. 1 and No. 2. The person who *experiences* the dream and records it faithfully is one identity. The person who later tries to understand the content of the dream and possibly apply this understanding in practical life is the other identity, and it interprets the meaning of the dream only in the packaged form of a *text* or mere *statement*,[25] in which mediated form it has been smuggled across the border between No. 1 and No. 2 as contraband, without "customs" having been paid. The interpreting subject only *quotes* the meaning of the text from the unconscious, so that it can never itself be held intellectually accountable for the meaning expressed between the quotes. "The dream said that ..." The meaning or revelation that waking consciousness receives from the unconscious dream must be in itself blind revelation, canned meaning, meaning as commodity. In its belonging to "the unconscious," Jung's successor notion to Christian religion, myth, and along with it the whole sphere of the metaphysical and speculative, had logically become bracketed, hygienically sealed. Even if *empirically* consciousness seriously tried to *integrate* the experienced contents, *logically* it was on principle immune to a real integration—because these contents, *qua* contents of the unconscious, would only be "integrated" *as*, so to speak, in plastic foil shrink-wrapped ones. Consciousness was able and allowed to see them as wholes, but not to insight them in their innards: not to think them. There never was to be *real* knowledge. Certainly, there was to be knowledge, e.g., of the idea of the virgin birth, but it had to stay packaged in the form of "only a statement by the soul" or "only a psychological image." It was not allowed to come out of this packaging. You could not take the statement seriously with respect to *what is was about* and *believe* in virgin birth. From inside: meaning or essential knowledge, from outside: mere quotation.

In other words, the contents are permitted to be objects of consciousness, like psychic commodities for psychic consumption (e.g., for having numinous feelings), but are absolutely prohibited from becoming truths. "The unconscious" is the sum total of such conscious, observed, experienced contents that are in the logical status of being sealed. What makes them be contents of "the unconscious" and what makes the unconscious fundamentally unconscious is not that we have no consciousness of them. After all, we of course *know* our dream images, the ancient myths and symbols, the archetypal motifs. No,

---

[25] See for example *Letters 2*, p. 570, to Robert C. Smith, 29 June 1960: "Within the frame of psychic events I find the fact of the belief in God. It *says*: 'God is.' ... *I am concerned with the statement only* ...."

what makes them "unconscious" is the fact that they are logically deprived of an adequate addressee in consciousness, *the transcendental I*, and cut off from their original connection with the latter. The only addressee that Jung's psychology allows for is the empirical I.

Now, after this sealing of the *essential* contents, consciousness could *speak* of them without having to go red with shame. If it dealt with them, it now did not contradict its own principles at all, because what it spoke about was nothing but contents of the *unconscious* and precisely not consciousness's own beliefs. Consciousness could wash its hands of them. *It* merely had had primordial experiences from out of the unconscious. *Empirically* it could without problem occupy itself with them without *logically* getting its hands dirty. Consciousness was, after all, not responsible for the speculative quality of contents that were not its own at all, but had been produced by "the unconscious." It only *had to* deal with them since it was something psychically *real* that had simply happened to it. Jung repeatedly expressed the innocence of consciousness. *He* was merely observing and describing *facts* or *statements* by the soul. One example for consciousness's washing its hands is this. Asked about his idea of God as a quaternity, Jung pointed out, "The whole question of quaternity is not a theory at all, it is a Phenomenon. ... I am in no way responsible for the fact that there are quaternity formulas" (*Letters 2*, p. 584, to Witcutt, 24 August 1960).

The sealing of the unconscious contents in themselves so that they enter consciousness only as "quotes" is only the one aspect of the flight into the unconscious, one aspect that has its perfectly equivalent counterpart in a second aspect, namely in what happens to consciousness itself. In order to make *empirically* accessible those contents that *logically* have been sunk into the unconscious and sealed in themselves so that they might nevertheless provide the desired experience of meaning, consciousness had to be *put to sleep*, both literally (to get dreams) and figuratively, logically, namely, by declaring itself not competent and responsible for all *essential* questions, for anything of a metaphysical, speculative nature. It had to abdicate *as* consciousness, go consciously beneath consciousness. In all essential questions, it had to wait for messages ("revelations") from the unconscious. As waking consciousness it was not responsible for what it as "sleeping" consciousness had dreamed (or for what it spontaneously had imagined, envisioned). It was not allowed to *think* on its own account in the realm of such matters.

This also comes out, on a basic theoretical level, in a prominent element of Jung's teachings, in his fiction of a so-called transcendent function, a topic that allows me to clarify a bit more what is meant by a consciousness put to sleep and what is not meant. Briefly summarized, the theory of the transcendent function is that it is a normal possibility in the life of the psyche that a situation may arise in which the psyche, be it on the personal or on the collective level, is torn apart between two equally valid, equally strong, but opposite (mutually exclusive) tendencies or standpoints. Jung at times uses the terms thesis and antithesis for this opposition. He usually sees the one as the attitude or need of consciousness and the other as that of the unconscious, and so the conflict of opposites is in the last analysis at the same time an expression of the fundamental opposition of the two structural parts of the whole psyche as seen by Jung, consciousness and the unconscious. Provided that these opposites in a particular case are of equal strength and equal justification, the psyche gets into a deadlock. For our human reason there is then no solution in sight. But what appears to be a hopeless tension of opposites turns out, if honestly borne up under, to be precisely productive and constructive. The tension is a source of psychic energy, and so "between the two is generated a third factor as lysis ..." (*MDR* p. 351, transl. modif.). Through their unrelenting opposition the opposites ultimately produce a new content, a symbol in the true psychological sense, in which justice is done to both conflicting standpoints, that of consciousness and that of the unconscious. The one-sidedness of thesis and antithesis is transcended. A new, heretofore unimaginable level is reached, and this is why Jung speaks of the *transcendent* function. Our human reflection and will cannot resolve the tension of opposites. The true solution of such a conflict has to come through a symbol, which is neither rational nor irrational (but both at once) and as such gives true satisfaction to both consciousness and the unconscious. Any merely rational, intellectually produced solution would not be able to do justice to the unconscious and thus would only be a sham solution.

Speaking from the point of view of the therapist confronted with a patient in whom such a situation has emerged Jung writes: "The open conflict is unavoidable and painful. I have often been asked, 'And what do you *do* about it?' I do nothing; there is nothing I can do except wait, with a certain trust in God, until, out of a conflict borne with patience and fortitude, that particular, for me unforeseeable solution emerges that is destined for that particular person" (*CW* 12 § 37, transl. modif.). What Jung here says about himself as therapist applies of course also to the patient himself. He, too, cannot do anything but wait until the transcendent function produces that unforeseeable symbol that truly resolves the conflict by fundamentally transcending that old level of consciousness on which the opposites had to appear in their mutual irreconcilability.

This theory is a perfect case of the flight into the unconscious! I am not saying this because Jung puts his hopes on the unconscious; not because, according to this scheme, qua symbol the solution has to come as an unpredictable, irrational surprise event to a sleeping ("patiently waiting") consciousness, as a kind of a new revelation; because the solution thus has to happen "out there," not in consciousness. The fact that the real action in the soul's life is said to take place *unconsciously* is precisely not the real problem of the fiction of the transcendent function. I fully agree that any true "healing," any true solution of a conflict, any true further development cannot be brought about by "us," on the conscious or ego level by our human will and planning, that it cannot be "made," but has to come of its own accord. It emerges—or does not emerge. We indeed have to wait and see if it occurs and when it does what it is like. Neither can the patient heal himself, nor can the therapist act as healer. The only "healer" is the soul, as I would say in contrast to Jung's "the unconscious." All real changes happen as a matter of course behind the scene of consciousness, in, as Jung occasionally put it, the "hinterland of the soul."

What makes the theory of the transcendent function an expression of the flight into the unconscious is something else. It is the fact that the real resolution of that sort of a fundamental conflict between the psychic opposites that leads into an absolute impasse is expected to occur in a *uniting symbol*, that is to say, that it puts its hope solely on contents as objects of consciousness. In other words, the union of the conflicting and equally strong opposites is to happen "out there" in the form of an "it," an entity, a psychological substance: a "reconciling third." And this means that the subject itself, as I and consciousness, or more specifically the inner logical constitution or syntactical form of consciousness, gets by unscathed. The "in here" is left out. Only *this*, the fact that the solution is shoved outside into the sphere of the objects of consciousness and away from consciousness itself as subject and form, is what turns consciousness into a really, namely logically, psychologically, sleeping one. Only *this* is the sense of "sleeping consciousness" that needs to be criticized, and herein alone, in Jung's *syntactical* move from "unconsciously" to "*the* unconscious," lies the true flight into the unconscious. "Unconsciously": the form of "I," "the unconscious": the form of "it." That "the unconscious" is, as it were, located outside consciousness is not really that "out there" that deserves our rejection, nor that it is experientially conceived as non-ego. The experiential non-ego does not necessarily have to imply that it has the syntactical *form* of not-I. The really problematic "out there" is the *logical* externality of "the unconscious," its substantiated form as an "it."

By contrast, that empirical-practically or *psychically* consciousness has to be a "sleeping one"; that real soul processes occur for the most part unconsciously; that, therefore, we have to "wait, with a certain trust in God, until, out of a conflict borne with patience and fortitude, that particular, for me unforeseeable solution emerges" which is destined for the particular person (or, on a cultural level, for the particular historical locus) concerned, because any real solution is the work of the objective soul and not of people's ego designs—all this may well be unavoidable in a true psychology. However, it in no way exempts psychology from the necessity of taking the logical or syntactical level seriously. This is Jung's basic fault: he stayed more or less exclusively on the semantic level, identifying it, the contents, images, symbols, with "the unconscious," one-sidedly practicing an object-consciousness,[26] and ignored—stayed himself unconscious about—the subjectivity of the soul as subject and the whole question of the logical form of consciousness, of the *unconsciously* occurring syntactical changes, which are changes *of consciousness* itself in its very constitution.

The difference between, on the one hand, what is called metaphorically "objective soul" (in the positivized sense of Jung's "the

---

[26] Just think of idea of "the archetypes of the collective unconscious"!

unconscious") and, on the other hand, ego-consciousness (or ego-personality), must not be confounded and identified with that completely different, namely consciousness-internal *form* difference between the semantic and the syntactical, between the contents of consciousness and the logical form of consciousness. For a true psychology, the objective soul or the hinterland of the soul refers to the (processes or life in the) syntax of consciousness, the logic of the mind, while what has the form of *contents* inevitably belongs to ego-consciousness, *regardless of whether* it is the kind of contents that for Jung were contents of modern ego-consciousness and everyday life, or rather those very different contents that Jung considered to be the property of "the unconscious" as the opposite of consciousness (the mythic, imaginal, religious, metaphysical images and ideas), but which in reality are simply the contents of the essential life of *former ages*. The difference between Jung's opposition of consciousness and the unconscious as the difference between the ego world and the archetypal world boils down to the difference between present and past, current and obsolete contents.[27] In Jung's scheme the sphere of the syntax of consciousness—i.e., the real life of the objective soul—is, by contrast, simply omitted, excluded. In Jung's own language we could say: it has fallen into the unconscious!

The theory of the transcendent function and the uniting symbol is only of historical relevance, with respect to psychological phenomena of former ages. If restricted to that sphere it is indeed helpful, providing as it does a reasonable explanation of how deadlocks due to conflicts between psychic opposites could truly find a solution in pre-modern (especially archaic, but also ancient and medieval) cultural situations. Why? Because then consciousness was still in the status of unbornness. The soul had not yet attained the status of subject. Consciousness had not come home to itself. It did not yet

---

[27] "The past" is pretty much identical with the essential (mythical, religious, metaphysical) life because this is what alone has been preserved in historical memory from the manifold contents of former consciousness, whereas the more trivial and everyday-type contents of past psychic life (by Jung associated with the ego) have in the course of time quite naturally dropped out from our cultural memory. Conversely, the contents of modern consciousness are all of a merely everyday and ego nature (ego ideas, opinions, desires, feelings) because modernity is characterized by the fact that it does not have *essential* contents (inasmuch as *its* essential life does no longer have the form of content). This is why consciousness as concept of Jungian psychology could and had to become falsely identified with "the ego" and its (psychologically) superficial contents.

exist in its own right, but only in its contents; it was completely given over to them, lost in them. The essential knowledge did not yet have the form of I. This was the precondition for myth and for mythic gods: grand contents, objects of worship. But modernity is characterized by the fact that the objective soul has been born out of its own previous containment within itself and thus has reached the status of subject. In our modern, post-mythological and post-metaphysical situation, not only symbols, but also the very form of symbol or image, of object and content, the entire level of the semantic, are psychologically (not empirical-practically) obsolete. Any concrete conflict involving the psychic opposites therefore cannot possibly find its solution in a uniting symbol as a *content* of consciousness any more, such as in dream images of mandalas or other symbols of "the Self" and of wholeness. Uniting symbols may of course still occur, but their problem is that they do not unite today's *real* opposites any more. The prevailing dissociation keeps persisting anyway. The symbols are disengaged from the soul, running idle like the motor of a car in neutral. There may still be experiences of symbols *of* wholeness, wholeness as content, and they may be beautiful to look at and emotionally moving for the experiencing ego, but what as uniting symbols they are actually meant to do they cannot do: to unite the psychic opposites, making us or our world whole, resolving the contradictions of our time by transporting the soul in the sense intended by the idea of the *transcendent* function to a truly new status of consciousness. Symbols and images fundamentally miss that level on which the problems of the modern soul are located. They only reach the ego (its feelings, cravings, its impressibility). With them psychology is barking up the wrong tree. The arena in which today the real action in the soul's life must take place is that of the soul as subject, which does not mean the ego but the innermost syntax of consciousness (which for object-consciousness must remain absolutely unconscious).

After this discussion of the proper sense of what needs to be critiqued in "the flight into the unconscious," and after distinguishing this critique from any sort of identification of the soul with ego-consciousness, we can return to the exploration of the topic of "putting consciousness to sleep." The displacement from consciousness of its one inherent moment, that of unconsciousness ("background process," "hinterland of the soul," unconsciously occurring changes), and the fixation of this unconsciousness as "*the* unconscious," had the inevitable consequence that the remaining "rump consciousness" (so-called ego-consciousness) paradoxically itself went unconscious, although what was left in it was precisely the conscious moment. Although by no means with respect to his (Jung's) own concept of consciousness and his own "psychology of the unconscious," Jung himself spoke of consciousness's turning unconscious, the *Unbewußtwerden des Bewußtseins* (*GW* 12 § 563). The "psychology *of* the unconscious" is *unconscious* psychology, blind psychology, for two reasons. First and foremost because, thanks to its exclusive concentration on contents, consciousness remains blind to itself, to its own unconscious depth, its syntactical form, expelling this from consciousness in positivized form as a literal Other vis-à-vis consciousness, an independent entity, a realm or agency ("the unconscious"). Secondly, because that one moment of itself that consciousness in Jungian psychology displaced from itself in order to sink it into the status of "pure nature" or *not-mind* (and thus to establish it as "*the* unconscious") was precisely the light of reason, the transcendental ego as the subject of all *essential* (i.e., religious or metaphysical) knowing, the syntax of consciousness. The only purpose of the invention of the unconscious had been to discharge consciousness of the intellectual responsibility for all the traditional speculative or essential knowledge that it kept insisting on clinging to, but that under the conditions of modernity and the born soul had to shun the light of day. For this reason the unconscious was erected as a special construction, a *psychological* museum, to store away the necessarily objectified ("projected") syntax of the at that time still merely *implicit* consciousness of former, pre-modern man as "the imaginal" (as archetypal psychology was to say later), much as literal museums house the *physically* existing cultural remnants of the past.

As for the necessity of discharging consciousness of its intellectual responsibility, this stemmed from consciousness no longer being unborn, a pre-modern, a merely *implicit* consciousness that, *as* such implicit consciousness, could still legitimately (and of course also had to) find its fulfillment in objectified form, in symbols, mythic images, gods, archetypal experiences—in contents, on the semantic level. Consciousness had, as a modern one, become explicit consciousness, consciousness aware of itself, which is also to say, consciousness in the form of subject or self (where "self" of course means the logical form of self and not Jung's substantiated "the Self"). Having been born out of itself, the soul can no longer find its fulfillment in the form of object (images, symbols). It can find it only in itself, in the form of subject, through consciousness's analytical self-reflection of itself *as consciousness*, as logical form or syntax.

Of course in the Jungian scheme there *was to be* the immediacy of "primordial experience," but it required that the experiencing subject be split in two and that the meaning that was experienced stayed inside its wrapping. Thus Jung states, "We cannot tell whether God and the unconscious are two different entities" (*CW* 11 § 757). For personality No. 1, which had to be fundamentally blind to speculative matters, they must be different. For No. 2 they are the same. And the total personality who would be the unity of No. 1 and No. 2 is never home; it is obliterated, bracketed, replaced by the instantaneous switching back and forth between the two identities and their two truths, so that the dissociation can go unnoticed and we can have it both ways: we have a God, but without *really, honestly, openly* having to commit ourselves to it seriously, namely intellectually. We have a God, but can wash our hands of Him.

By the same token, No. 2 can indulge in being "the age-old son of the mother" (*MDR* p. 225) only because it is not really, not wholeheartedly serious about it, inasmuch as it always keeps its alter ego, No. 1, in the background. But No. 1 is also not wholeheartedly serious about its scientific or observer stance inasmuch as it always has "the age-old son of the mother" of No. 2 up its sleeve. No. 1 and No. 2 bracket each other, thereby keeping each other in check *and* allowing each other to indulge, each in its own thing, undisturbed by the other. The left hand must not know what the right hand is doing.

I said that for the psychology of the unconscious the *coniunctio* must not happen. But was the *coniunctio*, the *mysterium coniunctionis*, not a favorite theme of Jung's? Did he not show that it was a real image in the psyche? Indeed, Jung stressed the necessity of the *coniunctio*. The thing to realize, however, is that it was precisely only a theme or motif that he studied. It was a content of his teachings, but what his psychology of the unconscious teaches is the opposite of what it *is* and *does*. *Semantically*, the *coniunctio* is one of the most prominent ideas and goals for Jung. But the *syntax* of his theory contradicts its own semantics. This contradiction is, however, not a mistake, not faulty.[28] Jung was, I suggested, the thinker of (the idea of) *the* unconscious. The unconscious, as the bracketing of the transcendental ego, *is* the (systematically produced) unawareness about consciousness itself; this is what "unconsciousness" means. The psychology of the unconscious is possible only *as neurosis*. Thus it is and has to be the exclusive attention to what the empirical ego can solely be aware of, namely the contents from "the unconscious," the images, symbols, myths, etc.; and it has to be systematically oblivious of the logical form or status of consciousness as such as well as to the logical form of its diverse contents. As a subject-matter of a "psychology of the unconscious" the *coniunctio* had to be bottled up, it had to be no more than an *in vitro coniunctio*, a motif *in* a text, an experience *in* a dream. But it was not allowed to escape the bottle and to permeate the structure of the theory or to infect and decompose the logical constitution of the observer's consciousness itself. If that had occurred, the unconscious would immediately have disappeared and consciousness would have had to start to think all on its own responsibility again. Jung would have been back in the position of Nietzsche that he had needed to leave.

Jung's move from thinking to observation of facts means that consciousness is allowed to perceive—with great openness—mythic, religious, metaphysical contents, but must itself stay immune to them. The program of the "psychology of the unconscious" is conscious semantic awareness coupled with logical, syntactical untouchedness. The "What" of experience, the symbols and archetypal images, are allowed in, but they have to remain safely enclosed, indeed, sealed within themselves as ("numinous") semantic contents to be gazed at in amazement and to be used by the individual for producing a sense of higher meaning for itself.

III. Form change: Echo escapes Pan

"To flee into the unconscious (in the sense of taking refuge in it)," "to assign to contents the unconscious as their place"—the problem with this was that the unconscious did not simply exist. "The unconscious" is not a positive fact, an existing entity, a part, a realm,

---

[28] At least, not faulty for Jung. For us, however, to continue this way of thinking would be unacceptable.

an organ of the human being or the like, the way the brain or the lung are parts of the body. Contrary to widespread opinion, Jung was to some extent aware of this fact. For example, when he spoke about the utter newness of the modern situation and its symbol-lessness, he pointed out that "This is why we have a psychology today, and why we speak of the unconscious. All this would be quite superfluous in an age or culture that possessed symbols" (*CW* 9i § 50, transl. modif.). "Whenever there exists externally a conceptual or ritual form in which all the yearnings and hopes of the soul are absorbed and expressed, that is, for example, a living religion, then the soul is outside and there is no soul problem, just as there is then no unconscious in our sense" (*CW* 10 § 159, transl. modif.). Or: speaking of the psychology of "exotic peoples," Jung stated that "... it has become clear to me that anything like a question of the unconscious—a quite notorious question for us—simply doesn't exist for these people. In the case of the Indians and Chinese, for instance, it is overwhelmingly clear that their whole spiritual attitude is based on what with us is profoundly unconscious. It was therefore left to psychopathology rather than, say, theology to discover that for us a very essential part of the soul has disappeared— to wit, the so-called unconscious" (*Letters 1*, p. 318, to Milt, 8 June 1942, transl. modif.).

The unconscious is not a natural, anthropological constant. It is a product of history. This Jung had fully understood and expressly stated. *As far as its content is concerned*, what we call "the unconscious" appears, such as in dreams or visions, in images that in reality are sunken, sedimented cultural assets, in other words, as something that in other times of history and in other parts of the world was precisely part of people's conscious spiritual, religious, cultic life. In this limited sense one can say that these contents *remain* still today, but only as relics of the past, as Jung's "sorry remnants of a great past." But what Jung completely ignores despite his insight is what it means for the *form* of those contents, for the *logical constitution*, that "a very essential part of the soul has disappeared." As far as their form is concerned, the whole world of those mythological, metaphysical, religious contents has *really* disappeared. But by substantiating "the unconscious" Jung denies their *real* disappearance, thereby contradicting his own statement. He uses a reductive meaning of "disappearance," treating the "very essential part of the soul," i.e., man's metaphysical or religious life, as if it were pieces of furniture that had been removed from one's living room into the attic or basement and in this sense had disappeared. For him they are now merely out of sight—unconscious, but still available provided one is ready to go into the attic or basement for them.

Jung is blind to the form aspect. The problem with the disappearance of the "very essential part of the soul" is not comparable to the removal of objects or contents from consciousness. This is not at all the point. The real problem is the "*sorriness*" of the "sorry remnants of a great past," the fact that they don't mean anything any more to, do not do anything any more for, modern consciousness. Jung himself once said, "In the end we dig up the wisdom of all ages and peoples, only to find that everything most dear and precious to us has already been said in the most superb language. Like greedy children we stretch our hands and think that when we grasp it we would also possess it too. But what we possess is no longer valid ..." (*CW* 9i § 31, transl. modif.). Exactly. Disappearance in the psychological sense does not mean that we cannot still "possess" the myths, archetypal images, symbols, but that they are no longer valid. It is therefore *not* really so that an essential *part* of the soul (in the individual) has disappeared, but much rather that *the soul* has disappeared *from* all myth, religion, and the wisdom of the past, so that the latter have all become soulless commodities (which is why it has become possible in the first place for us to "possess" them).

It is as if we had very important digital data stored on a type of media and in a format for which the hardware and the operating system plus the application software do no longer exist. My first word processor program in the early 1980s came on an eight inch 180 KB floppy disk, which is now absolutely useless. The disk drives and CP/M operating system under which it ran have disappeared. Now we use DVD drives, secure digital cards, and USB flash drives and Windows XP or later versions. Metaphorically speaking, the myths and archetypes are eight inch floppy disks. They are still available through our dreams or through myth studies, but they are soulless because the hardware and software is missing that would make them "readable," accessible.

What we call the soul is, to stay within this image, neither the data medium nor the apparatus or program required for it. The soul is not a thing. It is the *act or event* of reading the data by means of the right hardware and software, the act or event of the *mind's* being reached by them, initiated into their content, and *their* finding an echo in the mind, their being understood on a deep level. The soul is logical *life*.

Jung once made the crucial point that, "Heaven and hell are fates meted out to the soul and not to civil man, who in his nakedness and timidity would have no idea of what to do with himself in a heavenly Jerusalem" (*CW* 9i § 56, transl. modif.). The only thing that is missing from this otherwise insightful description is the temporal, historical factor. Medieval man would as a matter of course have known what to do with himself in a heavenly Jerusalem. No problem at all. That was what he was concerned with day and night. And conversely, that Jung's "civil man" has no access to a heavenly Jerusalem is only *because he is modern man*. His inability to know what to do with himself in a heavenly Jerusalem is precisely not due to a "nakedness and timidity" of his. Just as it is not due to a weakness of our new hardware and software that we cannot utilize eight inch floppy disks any more. On the contrary, the new hardware and software are overqualified, too advanced, too sophisticated for eight inch floppy disks. By the same token, civil man has advanced enormously psychologically, become fundamentally "modernized." He is beyond the form of myths, religious images, metaphysical beings. "Heaven" and "hell" are eight inch floppy disks for him. There is nothing wrong either with the old symbols nor with being modern. What is "wrong" is that this incommensurability is not seen and respected. "The soul" is still expected to be in and identified with the old *form* of symbols and mythic images, of religion and ideas of God. The mind has *de facto* advanced, but not wrested its notion of soul from the old forms through which once upon a time soul was *made* and experienced.

We need to understand the special nature of this form change. Of course, Jung, too, was convinced that a form change was needed. But did he have the same kind of change in mind? About a particular old symbol and ritual he said, "I know it is the truth, but it is the truth in a form in which I cannot accept it any more. ... I must have a situation in which that thing becomes true once more. I need a new form" (*CW* 18 § 632). What the new form is that Jung had in mind comes out in a statement like the following, "Only an unparalleled impoverishment of symbolism could enable us to rediscover the gods as psychic factors, that is, as archetypes of the unconscious" (cf. *CW*

9i § 50). Obviously, it is a change from cultural symbols to psychic factors. What once was out there as a public truth, now has to be sought by each individual in his or her inner. But upon closer look, this change reveals itself not really to be a form change in the deeper sense at all, but rather a change of location, because *what* is rediscovered is precisely the same as before, "gods" (or whatever other symbols and mythic images). "That thing" is supposed to "become[-] true once more." This is also underlined by the word "rediscover," which ties in with Jung's statement cited above that for us a very essential part of the soul has disappeared: something has disappeared, been lost, and is found again somewhere else "—to wit, in the so-called unconscious."

A real form change in the psychological sense is something else. It means precisely that "that thing" cannot become true once more. Much rather, such a change is to be described in terms that Jung himself once used when discussing the historical form change from the ancient level of consciousness (called by Jung "world of the Father" and conceived as the world of Oneness) to the Christian one (called "world of the Son" as the world of duality or conflict). He said that in this new situation man "looked longingly *back* to the world of the Father, but it was lost forever, because an irreversible increase in man's consciousness had taken place in the meantime and made it independent" (*CW* 11 § 203). What is lost forever cannot be "rediscovered" anywhere, and "irreversible increase" means that a qualitatively utterly new situation has been achieved. But conversely, the fact that it is lost forever and cannot be rediscovered is not tantamount to "altogether lost, totally disappeared." Change as such, and so also a form change, precisely amounts to the *contradiction* of irrevocably lost and not at all lost, i.e., still there.

In order to approach the idea of a true form change I use a Greek mythological image as paradigm. The lecherous god Pan chased a beautiful nymph named Echo, but in her panic she changed into an echo.[29] In this way she managed to escape—not to some safe place on that same level on which pursuing Pan was trying to catch her, but with a radical, unimaginable leap out of the realm of spatial

---

[29] I had discussed the topic of Pan and Echo (as well as Syrinx) in a different context before in my "Das Bewußtsein, der zweite Schöpfer der Welt," in: *Eranos 55-1986*, pp. 183-239, here pp. 214ff. See also James Hillman, "An Essay on Pan," in: W.H. Roscher and J. Hillman, *Pan and the Nightmare*, New York (Spring Publications) 1972, pp. I-LXIII.

extendedness altogether into non-space, into another dimension, namely, from attractive female body into the intangible and on principle not locatable sphere of mere sound, indeed *reflected, reverberated* sound: echo. Hers was not simply a contingent empirical flight. She had removed herself in an absolute sense. Her flight was a structural or logical one. The goat-legged Pan with his crude sexual desire could not possibly follow her.[30] And even if he

---

[30] In contrast to this statement I must point out that in my cited essay, "Das Bewußtsein, der zweite ..." I showed that there *was* a union between Pan and the nymphs, after all, as becomes best apparent in the parallel tale of Pan and Syrinx. After having lost Syrinx through her metamorphosis into a reed, Pan breaks the reed and makes panpipes (Greek: *syrigx*) out of it on which he plays his mournful tunes. The base sexual instinct *is* transformed, namely into art (music), and in his playing, that is, his blowing into the reeds, he is united with her in a *negative* way or with her *as* negated, absent one. This is as far as imaginal psychology can get, as far as one can get on the mythological, semantic level. There *is* a negation, sublation, a move from literal act to reflectedness—however only such a one that remains under the still prevailing conditions of Pan consciousness and only within it. Even when flute-playing, Pan stays goat-legged Pan! *He* does not change. The negation (loss of Echo or Syrinx) does not truly negate the logical status. It merely changes Pan's mood and behavior: a *personal* change instead of a logical one. This is characteristic of the level of natural man: the impact of the negative experience is cushioned by being *discharged* (subjectively) into *emotion* (e.g., grief) or (more objectively) into the aesthetic sphere (art, image, fantasy) so as not to come really home to and *revolutionize* the very structure of consciousness. The change from "the literal" to "the metaphorical" (so important for the imaginal thinking of Archetypal Psychology) is not a form change in the sense of our present context. Art, although it semantically transcends the base level of crude desire and behavior, logically or syntactically does not achieve a higher level. As mythological Pan shows us, as also, for example, the symbiosis of fierce hero and bard in archaic cultures confirms, the physical and the artistic are two *complementary* modes of human culture on one and the same anima level. It is merely a change of *area* or *mode* within the same status of consciousness. Very high-level works of art were already created on the earliest Stone-Age levels of culture. Japanese fairy tales give beautiful examples of how negation (loss) can be cushioned and rendered logically ineffective through aestheticization (through a kind of "musical," melancholy ending without resolution instead of an either clearly tragic *or* happy end). By the same token, seen *psychologically*, "grief work" is really a defense mechanism, as is its opposite, anger. What our topic, "form change," demands is precisely that "Pan himself" (not his mood or behavior) is transformed, i.e., that the anima or natural level as such is overcome, that the negation truly revolutionizes consciousness itself and lifts it into an entirely new, previously unheard-of logical status. Apparently, on the level of myth this cannot happen. Myth is capable of going as far as to show us a true self-transcendence in some of its mythic *figures* (here: Echo, Syrinx), but not to the point where everybody in a given myth (here: also Pan) relentlessly undergoes this self-transcendence. Because this would mean the self-transcendence, self-sublation of the mythological, imaginal level itself. That in our story unchanged Pan is left behind holding the bag ensures the self-preservation of the *form* of myth (and mythic imagination as such), although it at the same time objectively, but only implicitly and completely unwittingly, already points beyond itself leaving a task for us. *Quod natura* (myth, the imagination) *relinquit imperfectum,*

could have followed her, he would not have found what he was after, a girl that he could rape. She had dissolved as physical, material body, as flesh, and turned into something strictly "spiritual, vaporous." It is a quasi alchemical transformation, a decomposition and sublimation, distillation, vaporization.[31]

This understanding of "form change" in the image of the Pan-Echo story allows for a plausible explanation of the "sorriness" of the spiritual remnants of the past and the lack of validity that Jung had diagnosed. Just as Pan and Echo, in the beginning belonging to one and the same level and as such commensurable, in the course of the story became fundamentally incommensurable to each other, so consciousness's semantics and syntax, formerly commensurable, became incommensurable in the course of history. The old contents are no longer valid because they do not adequately give expression to the logical form of the soul in that status in which it is at this point in its history. Consciousness in its explicit self-articulation— it as Pan, as it were—lags behind the logical status that it—it as Echo, anima, soul—has reached in its syntactical constitution. This is why from a soul point of view the old contents are no more than curiosities or (spiritual) commodities, whereas from the ego or "Pan" point of view, consciousness still pins all its hopes on them, frantically searching on their level for the lost nymph Echo.

If Jung had given his own insight of a new form a truly psychological understanding, he would have seen that it is not a matter, sort of in the spirit of Pan, of rediscovering the gods and other symbols of old as psychic factors in the unconscious. For much like Echo the gods and symbols have, with respect to their *validity*, become distilled, their "bodily" imaginal form has dissolved; they have become integrated into consciousness and reflected into themselves. The move here is from content to form, that is to say,

---

ars (modern psychology) *perficit*. But as 20th century abstract art shows, even art can under certain conditions be expressive of a form change in the syntactical sense and have truly left the anima or imaginal level of consciousness—when it is the art that complements an age that in fact has left this level.

[31] There are of course also other mythic tales about Echo, involving her love of Narcissus, her tricking Hera, and so on. Patricia Berry wrote an insightful paper on these aspects of Echo: Patricia Berry, "Echo's Passion," in her *Echo's Subtle Body*, Dallas (Spring Publications) 1982, pp. 113–126. As I am not trying to present an interpretation of the myths around the figure of Echo in their own right, but merely *use* the Pan-Echo mytheme as a paradigm for my own topic of true form change, I leave all those other features aside.

from the form *of content* to the form *of form*. Just like Pan was left
with simply nothing that he could chase and rape because nothing
tangible was left when Echo had turned into echo, so the
"unparalleled impoverishment of symbolism" which Jung had
diagnosed means that under the conditions of modernity the very
condition of the possibility of symbols, gods, and God as
psychologically valid has disappeared.

   If we apply to our present discussion the opposition of content of
consciousness vs. consciousness itself (or logical form of consciousness),
or the opposition of semantics vs. syntax, we have to say that the first
element in each pair of opposites had *in itself* been subjected to a process
of sublimation and raised into the dimension of form or the syntactical.
As far as *essential* matters are concerned, modern consciousness has now
inevitably *its own form* as its only "contents." These "contents" are not
objects of consciousness for it any more. The gods of old had of course
also always been the self-manifestation of consciousness's syntax, its
logical constitution. We could also say they had been the self-display
of the logic of the mode of being-in-the-world at the corresponding
historical locus. But as long as they had been truly *gods*, they were
not *known* to be the self-representation of consciousness's own logical
form. They were taken as contents (objects) of consciousness: existing
gods, metaphysical beings or substances. They had for consciousness
the form of otherness. (The fundamental otherness of syntax from
semantics, of the logical constitution of consciousness from the things
and events in the world that consciousness becomes aware of, was taken
literally, that is to say, it was itself viewed in terms of the semantic
side of the pair of opposites: as reified, substantiated, ontologized
Others. The latter became objects of intuition and worship, a real vis-
à-vis, as if they were [wholly other] innerworldly entities.)

   When Jung said that in the new situation of "the world of the Son"
or of duality, man "looked longingly *back* to the world of the Father,
but it was lost forever, because an irreversible increase in man's
consciousness had taken place in the meantime and made it
independent" (*CW* 11 § 203), he was unwittingly speaking about
himself and his own time. With modernity, too, there has been an
irreversible increase in consciousness! This process has made it
independent (no longer always already won over for and "sold on" the

soul and its "suggestive power" *CW* 7 § 269). Consciousness has emancipated itself from the soul and come of age. It has been born out of its containment in the soul.

Consciousness has objectively outgrown former modes of itself. It has objectively become aware of the fact that what it is dealing with (in *essential* matters) is only *itself*, the self-explication of its own "nature," its own logical constitution, whereas formerly it had the form of otherness vis-à-vis consciousness: images, symbols, gods, spirits, metaphysical-ontological realities. The increase of consciousness means that the fundamental psychological insight that "the soul always speaks about *itself*," only about itself, has now objectively—on the cultural level (usually not on the individual, subjective level)—come home to consciousness. Consciousness has reached the Spirit stage of itself, which is reflected in the "linguistic turn," the modern mind's fundamental standpoint shift from metaphysics, positivism, and ideology to language. In all *essential* matters, the semantic has in itself become syntactical, seen through as externalized (partial) self-representation of consciousness's own logical constitution. What used to be gods has become integrated into consciousness, absolute-negatively inwardized, reflected into itself.

As a consequence, the *form* of "semantic contents," the *form* of "object of consciousness" is now *ipso facto* only reserved for what is *not* of essential, of psychological importance, but rather only of pragmatic, empirical, scientific, survival, and entertainment interest. "Contents" now have to be either empirical-factual realities, *or* merely fictional contents which are clearly marked as such (fantasy products), *or* sunken cultural assets reduced to the status of commodities. If they are commodities and nevertheless pretend, or are meant to be, more than that, then they are ideological mystifications.

Once, after quoting the following passage from Goethe's *Faust I* in which Mephistopheles offers civilization-sick Faust the advice:

> Right. There is one way that needs / No money, no physician, and no witch. / Pack up your things and get back to the land / And there begin to dig and ditch; / Keep to the narrow round, confine your mind, / And live on fodder of the simplest kind, / A beast among the beasts; and don't forget / To use your own dung on the crops you set!

Jung commented:

> Obviously one cannot fake the 'simple life,' and therefore that
> freedom from this problem that is characteristic of the life of a
> poor man, which really is delivered over to fate, can also not be
> obtained through such an imitation. Not he who has the
> *possibility*, but only he who has the *necessity* of such a life in
> himself is driven by his nature to live it, and he will blindly pass
> over this problem, which he cannot even see because his mental
> capacity is simply not up to it. But if he is capable of seeing the
> Faustian problem, then the escape into the 'simple life' is closed
> for ever. There is of course nothing to stop him from taking a
> two-room cottage in the country, or from pottering about in a
> garden and eating raw turnips. But his soul laughs at the
> deception. *Only what a person really IS has healing power"* (*CW*
> 7 § 258, transl. modif., Jung's italics. The next paragraph begins
> with the phrase "The regressive restoration of the persona").

The phrase "if he is capable of seeing the Faustian problem" means:
once the modern level of consciousness has objectively been reached.
A practical return to nature, although *logically* impossible, is
nevertheless *empirically* not totally infrequent, and even more frequent
is that it is inwardly longed for.

I mention this only because I claim that this also applies
analogously to *essential* (religious, spiritual, metaphysical) matters.
Here, too, the escape into the 'simple life' is closed to modern man—
and yet there is of course nothing to stop him from regressively restoring
the religious persona or from looking for "his personal myth" or
indulging in "the imaginal." But here, too, this is only possible as fake,
as simulation, and here, too, the soul laughs at the deception. To be
sure, we can possibly "possess" and consume the old myths and
symbols to satisfy our emotional or ideological needs. But if like greedy
children we stretch our hands and think that when we grasp them we
would also possess them, they are nevertheless no longer valid.

The validity depends on what we really *are*. The validity is
something that cannot be "grasped" with our greedy hands, because
what is valid is always what we *are*, not what we have or experience or
subjectively believe and feel. Here the question emerges: what does
"what we really *are*" refer to? Certainly not to our *empirical* personal
or collective characteristics and idiosyncracies. It refers to the logical

status of consciousness that has *objectively* been reached at our historical locus. This is the place of our *necessity* (in the sense of Jung's passage). And wherever religion or metaphysics in fact existed as living realities, they also have always been what people actually *were*: the articulation and celebration of people's *real being* in *essential* regards. The "sorriness" of the sorry spiritual remnants of the past and the lack of validity of what we grasp with greedy hands consist in the transformation that happened to those former expressions from their being the expression of a being (a form of being, the truth of this mode of being) into being mere contents or objects of consciousness—free-floating contents because they are cut loose from modern man's real being and necessity and merely belong to his possibility.

Modern man's clinging to these old, now free-floating contents is of course the result of the fact that there has not been, as in most former periods of transition, a transformation of the old contents into new, other ones, but rather a radical change from the form of "contents" to the form of "form." The obsolete contents have not been replaced by new ones, as it was the case, for example, at the end of antiquity with the transition from the many gods of ancient polytheism to the one trinitarian God of Christianity. No doubt, this had also been a considerable change, but one that nevertheless remained on the same level. At that time, there simply was "all of a sudden" a new incumbent sitting on the same old throne of the divine. But now the very place of contents (in *essential* regards) was gone. Not only the gods are or God is dead, but the very category of such a thing as God or gods has dissolved.

"Pan" consciousness experiences this emptiness as a vacuum that wants to be filled. But the emptiness is experienced as such only by that consciousness that did not go along with the historical transformation process, which happened to have been one of the dissolution of the form of content as such. Therefore it is not in a position to become aware of the fact that in actuality *there is no vacuum at all*. It cannot see that there *is* in fact a successor to the form of content. Pan consciousness keeps searching for the anima in crude physical, bodily, tangible form of "nymph," on the old level of consciousness and in the old familiar dimension of spatial extension. Pan consciousness is characterized by the fact that it cannot, or refuses to, transcend itself, and thus confined within the old dimension as its unsurpassable horizon, it is incapable of following the nymph (the anima) to the level of "echo": sound and reflection and now no longer physical but only logical life. This incapability is due, I would say, to Pan's impotence to really love. Real love would give him wings with which he could go beyond himself, follow Echo and actually reach her. But with his goat legs, he can only be potent in the tangible sphere of sexual desire and thus, after Echo's self-transcendence, has to stay empty-handed on the ground.

The phenomenon of "echo" as (a) nothing but sound and (b) merely resounding sound serves appropriately as the mythological, naturalistic image for what in image and mythology cannot be adequately expressed: the soul's absolute negativity.

Real myth, truly living religion, and still "valid" metaphysics had been characterized by the fact that in their *essential* (i.e., mythic, religious, metaphysical) contents, consciousness recognized *itself* and found adequately articulated "what it *is*," its own being or nature, so that what we mean by "soul" came into existence and received its full satisfaction. The *semantics* of faith (of course only unwittingly) truly expressed the syntax or logical form of the consciousness that had this faith, and they expressed nothing but this consciousness's own logical constitution in imaginal or conceptual form (however, in the form of *content* and not yet in the form of form, that is, as consciousness's own logical constitution). The soul, as I said, always speaks about *itself*, now as well as then. When at one point Jung was able to say, "Whenever there exists externally a conceptual or ritual form in which all the yearnings and hopes of the soul are absorbed and expressed, that is, for example, a living religion ..." (*CW* 10 § 159, transl. modif.), he had pretty much the same idea in mind, although his wording is rather psychologistic: instead of the "syntax" or "logical form" of the soul, he speaks of its "yearnings and hopes"—as if the soul were a person who yearns and hopes. Nevertheless, the precious thing about his statement is the underlying conception of living religion or metaphysics as the event, or prevailing condition, of the uroboric closing of a circle, the conjoining of the two extremes of consciousness: its semantics (the objective "externally existing" conceptual or ritual form, we could also add to this: the imaginal form) and its syntax (its inner nature and constitution). In religion or metaphysics the soul ex-presses, externalizes, articulates itself by giving itself (its syntax) the form of semantic contents of consciousness (psychology speaks of projection) and at the same time it comes home to itself by recognizing and knowing itself in this externalization. The Neoplatonists spoke of the dynamic (simultaneous) movement of *prohodos* (emanation, self-presentation) and *epistrophê* (returning into itself).

Of course, because myth, religion, and metaphysics are the modes of unborn man who is immediately captivated by and at one with the soul's "suggestive power," this uroboric self-recognition of the soul happens on that level only *implicitly* for consciousness. But it does happen. Modern consciousness that has become independent, by contrast, is confronted with the task of an explicit awareness ....

Soul is not what we mean by "psyche," the "behavior of the human animal," its faculties, emotions, impulses, desires, mental processes. Soul is in truth nothing else than this uroboric closing of the circle (*and*, of course, the mind's holding itself on the level of the *coniunctio oppositorum*), which is why I speak of the soul's logical life. It is a mistake to see this *coniunctio* as a distant goal that the soul has and that we have to strive for. No, if there *is* soul, the union is its beginning and *sine qua non*. And without it, there is not, could not be, a soul. The idea of the goal in this context is soulless in a fundamental sense because it starts out from and positions itself in dissociation as its presupposition or *archê*, as if there were indeed first the two separate extremes that in a consecutive step would have to be somehow (miraculously) conjoined. It is the other way around. The soul, when it exists, is the happening (nay, the always already having happened) and the prevailing reality of the union of opposites, it is so to speak the Neoplatonists' *monê* (indwelling-in-itself), and its *prohodos* and *epistrophê* in their simultaneity are its *internal* logical life, just as its semantics and syntax are the two extremes *into* which it *unfolds* itself within itself. "Formation, transformation, eternal mind's eternal recreation ...."

Because of the objective soul's ("Echo's") self-transcendence that was not followed suit by the subjective soul ("Pan"), this uroboric circle has been broken. There is a dissociation and incommensurability in consciousness between its semantics (so to speak the "Pan" side of consciousness with Echo's left-behind empty gown: the old remnants, old conceptual, ritual, or imaginal forms that this side of consciousness entertains) and the now actually prevailing syntax of consciousness (the "echo" side of consciousness, consciousness's being in the state of absolute negativity).

IV. "Immediate experience": Pan's flight from Echo

As we have seen, Jung had arrived at three essential insights in this area. He had realized that

- the major symbols of our tradition had once and for all become obsolete, invalid. They were not totally gone, but had become reduced to the status of "sorry remnants,"
- there was no way back because there had been an irreversible increase of consciousness; the "old remnants" fundamentally lag behind the level of consciousness reached,
- a new form was needed, *if* there was to be a new fulfillment. The problem of modernity could not be solved on the level of contents.

So for Jung the solution of our modern psychological predicament was to be sought on the level of form and not of contents. Here lay his task, the task of psychology. How did he solve it? He moved both from our inherited tradition and from the possibility of "digging up the wisdom of all ages and peoples" to *primordial or direct experience*, personal felt experience. He believed that the *directness* and *spontaneity* of individual experience and the *intensity of feeling* (impressive "numinosity") of "*archetypal*" motifs (i.e., the same type of motifs as the old motifs that were to be found in myth and religious imagery), would provide the indispensable *necessity* (instead of mere possibility) and sorely missed *validity* or *truth* that on the cultural level has been lost and therefore heal the real "*sorriness*" of what is so directly experienced as numinous.

Archaic contents + personal direct experience = validity, truth.

This was the formula of his solution.

In terms of our mythological paradigm we can say that Jung tried to accomplish his task *on the side of goat-legged Pan*, not on Echo's side. But the true form change had been the move from Echo the nymph to the wholly other dimension of her as resounding echo and thus as absolute negativity. By "new form" Jung, like Pan the rapist, cannot imagine anything but a new immediacy, a new present reality, a new possession. He wants direct experience, that is, immediate gratification. Jung's theoretical consciousness cannot free itself in this regard from the greed of greedily stretched-out hands, from Pan's desire "to *have*" the nymph. And "the nymph," on her part, as the soul, as "the unconscious," as dreams and archetypes, *ipso facto* stays absolutely natural for Jung, pure nature, empirical facts. Numinosity means impressive emotion. Jung did not follow Echo into her new dimension and thus circumvented the real form change. Echo's (the soul's, the semantics's) self-transcendence, which had occurred through what Jung had called an "irreversible increase of consciousness," led away from nature (the naturalistic), away from emotion and possession. Echo having become echo means reflection instead of nature and fact, Mnemosyne instead of immediate presence, historical presence instead of present reality.

Paradoxically, the fact that Jung's theoretical consciousness was unable or unwilling to free itself from Pan's desire to *have* the nymph—the soul—in the form of an experience of "meaning" is tantamount to refusing to follow Echo—the soul—into her own dimension of absolute negativity and thus missing her. The immediate desire (and along with it the "commodity" form of "meaning") is not subjected to Echo's alchemical process of fermenting corruption and distillation, and thus it *ipso facto* forfeits that very thing that it actually wants to possess. For what is a man profited if he shall possess the soul in the form of direct experience of meaning, when such a crude form of possession is precisely the way to lose the soul? The soul can only be found on her own home territory, absolute negativity, not on crude Pan's level, the level of natural fact and "the unconscious."

Pan consciousness is that consciousness that self-identically refuses to follow its own "object" (soul, "the nymph Echo") self-forgetfully, with abandon, *all the way* into its innermost truth: absolute negativity. As I suggested, possibly out of a lack of love (or, conversely, out of too much self-love, refractoriness, insistence on self-preservation: on *positive* existence). Pan consciousness is naturally positivistic. Having, on the one hand, lost its true object through the latter's self-dissolution into its truth in which it is absolute-negative, and having, on the other hand, its absolute limit at the boundary of the world of positivity, Pan consciousness lands itself in the situation of that "barrier across the mental world" (according to Jung erected by Kant) "which made it impossible for even the boldest flight of speculation to penetrate into the object," or, again, at that "wall at which human inquisitiveness [lecherous Pan's desire] turns back" (*CW* 18 § 1734, transl. modif.). Absolute negativity is absolutely off limits to Pan consciousness. For it, it is like hitting a brick wall. Actually, Echo did not disappear into transcendence, because what she disappeared to was her innermost truth. It was an immanent, "intrinsic" disappearance.[32] Just like the very concrete phenomenon of echo, absolute negativity is not a transcendent yonder. But due to its commitment to positivity, Pan consciousness has to imagine the actually world-immanent inwardness of absolute negativity as a literal Other and thus in terms of spatial extendedness as a meta-physical transcendence beyond a rigid barrier which in turn is only the reflection and product of its own absolute insistence on positivity.

Another way of describing the same situation would be to say: Pan consciousness is totally in the thrall of Jung's "the animal nature of man" which is characterized by its clinging to what "is so much more immediate, conspicuous [or obvious], impressive and therefore so much more convincing" and "baulks at" comprehending what "happens to" it as its own echo (cf. *CW* 11 § 841, transl. modif.).

But whereas real (mythological) Pan, in view of the loss of his object of desire, simply holds his place in melancholy reflection and celebration of the experienced absence, Jung as Pan consciousness turns after the loss of the real nymph to *Urerfahrung* as a *positivized* substitute for the nymph. As the name suggests, immediate experience (together with its source, the unconscious as fact and pure nature) is "so much more immediate, conspicuous [or obvious], impressive and therefore so much more convincing" for Pan consciousness than the soul's negativity. Jung's psychology entails the promise that it is in principle possible to in fact catch and "have" Echo. Pan consciousness is thus not inevitably subject to the fate of Pan whose lust to rape was frustrated. *Having* immediate experience, *understanding* its content, and possibly

---

[32] The logic of the movement into the true inner, true interiority, is the topic of my paper, "The Leap Into the Solid Stone," in my *The Soul Always Thinks*, New Orleans (Spring Journal Books) 2010, pp. 165–172.

drawing ethical consequences from it for one's behavior—this is the modern psychological guise of the desired rape of the nymph.

It may here be helpful to remind the reader that in these passages and in speaking, for example, of "Jung as Pan consciousness" I am not trying to characterize how Jung worked as a psychological practitioner when it was a question of particular psychological phenomena, of dream images, symbols, myths. In his particular work Jung often penetrated in amazing and admirable ways to the true interiority of his respective objects of study. He clearly had a notion of *soul*. What I am here concerned with is much rather exclusively the general syntax, within which all particular psychological work in a Jungian sense takes place, and the constitution of consciousness at work in the theoretician Jung at that fundamental level at which the strategic decisions about the structure of psychology as a whole were made, above all about the concept of "the unconscious."

Jung's insistence on immediate experience is obviously tantamount to a radical rejection of mediatedness. However, even that flight from mediatedness and reflectedness precisely *attests* to the rule of mediatedness and reflectedness. Because in the encapsulation and segregation inherent in the fantasies of "the inner" and "the unconscious" the reflectedness itself has become reified and coagulated. That "meaning" in Jung's scheme can only be gained in the form of an experience of archetypes of the collective *unconscious* shows *malgré lui* that "possession" is only possible under the prevailing conditions of reflectedness, and "immediate experience" only as fundamentally mediated.

Direct experience is only a fake new form. Jung used a trick. He avoided the change from Pan's naturalistic-positivistic level to the level of absolute negativity and simply substituted for it the move from *everyday* natural phenomena (what is now considered to be the sphere of ego-consciousness) to one *special* type of phenomena occurring on the same naturalistic level, namely dreams, visions, spontaneous fantasies (as phenomena said to come from "the unconscious" and having an archetypal character), pretending that this semantic distinction within one and the same positivistic sphere, or the shift from the former to the latter, represented the necessary "new form." The soul laughs at this deception—and, as Echo-turned-echo, weeps at being deserted, betrayed.

For her flight was not at all, as naturalistic Pan consciousness thinks, a defensive reaction for the purpose of absolutely preventing Pan from being able to reach her and of herself staying virginally untouched. Her flight was much rather her *enticing* Pan to follow and meet her on her own level, in her own dimension, the only dimension in which a true *coniunctio* could be possible in the first place. In other words, whereas from an ego point of view Pan with his lust is the true agent, the originator of what happens, and Echo's flight merely a reaction, from a soul point of view this causal sequence needs to be reversed. It is the soul that starts the action. It sends *itself* as the attractive nymph to *itself* as naturalistic Pan to arouse Pan's lecherous desire (or the psychologist's inquisitiveness). The ego is typically deluded, identifying itself with the desire emerging in it as if it were its own and believing this "its own" drive to be the true cause and ultimate origin, although it is already a produced result, the reaction to the attractive nymph, caused by the literal sight or inner fantasy of her.

And why does the soul send Echo to Pan? The soul wants to raise itself *in toto* to a higher level of itself, a level of higher sophistication and sublimation. It wants and needs to pull Pan consciousness up to this higher dimension and truly initiate it into it. The soul-as-Echo, rather than trying to escape, wants and even needs to be reached by itself-as-Pan, however not in the crude naturalistic way in which Pan consciousness imagines such a meeting. This is why the soul appears to Pan as Echo in the first place, that is, as a concrete nymph evoking his desires and seducing him into chasing her. The nymph Echo is the first immediacy of echo as absolute negativity, and echo is the truth of Echo. But Pan failed. His desire was not strong enough to give him wings that might transport him beyond himself. Therefore, his chasing Echo *was* in itself his flight from her: the establishment of an unbridgeable gulf between himself and her. And even the frustration of Pan's desire (his mourning of the loss of her) cements the naturalistic stance.

That what is directly experienced is always something eminently personal, always *my* experience (rather than something acquired through conscious learning or research ["digging up"] and so coming to me from outside), in no way makes the experience articulate what modern man truly *is*, his real being, namely, the logical form of modern consciousness as which man today in reality exists. Rather, it remains merely a content of consciousness without "validity," just as "sorry" a content as the remnants from a great past. Whether dug-up from outside or spontaneously coming from within makes no difference whatsoever as to the question of validity or truth.

So the flight into the unconscious did not at all primarily have the purpose of safely storing away "in the unconscious" traditional mythic or symbolic *contents* of consciousness. No, what it really rescued, by logically removing it "into the unconscious," was the moment of the *validity*, the present reality, the immediate relevancy, the religious-meaning quality of the contents—and thus the logical innocence of Pan consciousness. The most important aspect of the archetypes of the collective unconscious is not their content and the structural similarity of the different types of symbols and mythic motifs the world over. If that were the case they would be nothing but an equivalent to the "dug-out wisdom of all ages and peoples," no more than assembled scholarly knowledge in the area of religious studies, ethnology and the like. What gives the archetypes in Jung's scheme their central importance is much rather the promise of immediate significance and validity that they entail, the idea with which they come, that through their mere existence *and their being experienced by any individual in his or her eachness* they just like that "confer meaning upon the banality of life."

Not *what* is experienced is essential. As far as that is concerned, anything goes. Although Jung had personally certain very specific and adamantly held "religious" tenets, above all about the reality of evil and the indispensability of a move from a trinitarian conception of God to the idea of quaternity, he nonetheless always emphasized that each individual had to have his very own experience (whatever it may be) and credibly insisted that analytical psychology did not subscribe to a particular doctrine. It was, in ideological and religious matters, conceived as neutral. Jung proudly reported that as a psychotherapist he even accompanied modern people who had lost their faith on their inner way back to their original Church creed or religion, no matter whether it was Roman Catholicism, Judaism, Russian Orthodoxy, or one of the Protestant denominations. The only thing that counts is *that* there is an *overwhelming experience*, the factual occurrence of it. The *happening* per se of an archetypal experience is the bringer of meaning as a present reality, and this is Jung's version of the desired "new form."

V. *Mysterium disiunctionis*

"Overwhelming" is a key word. It is a predicate that *logically*, as far as the inner nature of "direct experience" as such is concerned, characterizes this experience—*all* experiencing in Jung's sense— although *empirically* it of course should be applied only to very special, extremely strong experiences. Already the idea that the unconscious is pure nature and presents us with psychic *facts* means that consciousness is logically steamrollered by it. You just have to give in to facts. When the unconscious speaks, consciousness has to shut up. But in the case of religious experience the sense of being compelled was particularly important for Jung. For him, God was "the name by which I designate all things which cross my wilful path violently and recklessly..." (*Letters 2*, p. 525, to M. Leonard, 5 December 1959). "... I cannot conceive of any religious belief which is less than a violation of my ego-consciousness" (*Letters 2*, p. 51, to Victor White, Spring 1952). The I suffers *violence* from the self (*CW* 11 § 233). As early as in his Basel cathedral incidence, the boy Jung felt cruelly forced against his will to think a certain thought, and this overwhelming will he interpreted as proof of his having experienced God.

However, precisely this Basel cathedral experience helps us to avoid a fundamental misunderstanding. The word "overwhelmed" might suggest something like being, as I or consciousness, swept away as if by a tsunami. But this is not at all Jung's notion of the overwhelming experience. A tsunami-like becoming overpowered would mean inflation or psychotic delusion, and this was of course out of the question for Jung. The encounter with an overwhelming will inside oneself did not mean the one-sidedness of the total subjugation of an absolutely powerless I. In the Basel cathedral event we see on the contrary how the insistence of the force felt increases the resistance, the I's counter-will, and this counter-will increases in turn the irresistible power of that force that wants him to think this thought. Both sides get each other worked up. As a result, it is decidedly a proud, indeed *heroic I* that, "overwhelmed," ultimately gives in and "thinks" that terrible thought—as a test and proof of its courage!

Obedience to this powerful will, yes, but obedience as a demonstration of his own strength and courage. Rather than being simply steamrollered, the I *anticipates* on its own account what the overwhelming experience *would* have done, but now cannot do because the sovereign I has pre-empted it through its "obedience." This is the light in which the term "overwhelming" as the nature of experience needs to be understood.

"Obedience" here means: factually performing the act of letting the incriminated thought come out into the open before his own consciousness, but it does precisely not mean to *simply think* it so as to get enlightened by what it says, gain a new insight from it, and become initiated into it. It is a behavior, merely a going through the motion of thinking the thought. This thought is thus "castrated," reduced to an entity, a thing, or to the committing of a deed (the boy Jung in fact viewed it as his having to commit a sin) rather than *being really thought*, thought in such a way that the thought itself, its meaning, would dawn on consciousness, generate an understanding.

Jung's move from "*simply thinking* his own thought to its end without further ado" to "obediently committing the sin that was (allegedly) demanded of him by God" is in addition accompanied by the idea that before he could allow his thought to surface he had to think about this whole problem beforehand. "*I must think*. It must be thought out beforehand." In other words, that terrible thought, when Jung will be ready to let it come, will not be allowed to simply come and will not be met by an open, unprejudiced mind. Rather, it is supposed to be received by an already prepared, biased mindset and incorporated into an already existing explanatory system. Again a pre-empting by the sovereign I. The I keeps itself immune and is not truly reached by the thought. The mind itself as a hearing and understanding mind reserves itself vis-à-vis that thought. Another time and in another context Jung explicitly proclaimed, "Man always has some mental reservation, even in the face of divine decrees. Otherwise, where would be his freedom? And what would be the use of that freedom if it could not threaten Him who threatens it?" (*MDR* p. 220). The semantic content of the thought is allowed to appear in consciousness "as a fact, a content," but it is prevented from affecting the latter's syntax, from really coming home to it in its speculative import. In this "mental reservation" we recognize the effect of "the animal nature of man" (*CW* 11 § 841) which puts self-preservation higher than self-forgetfully and with abandon following the object of its inquisitiveness or desire all the way into absolute negativity.

On the level of will and emotion, the clash of two wills, regardless of which one will in the end have a slight advantage over the other, does not really bring the two sides into contact with each other.[33] The I's pre-empting upholds a fundamental dissociation. The same is true when we move to the mental level. Thinking the thought only in the sense of being obedient and committing a demanded deed logically insulates the I against the thought's import and conversely keeps the thought itself mute and dead. I (or consciousness) and the thought each stay neatly separated on their own sides. No contact. Mutual immunity or innocence.

And yet there is the "overwhelmingness" of experience and the "clash" of wills. Even on the mental level direct inner experience in general is a clashing of two, the subject and the content or phenomenon. The clash, and the violence inherent in the notion of a clash, are necessary in Jung's scheme because (a) direct experience requires that the two sides come together and (b) that each side nevertheless has to stay absolutely immunized against the other. Violence and having to be compelled are the reflection of a radical resistance, of an absolute will to stay innocent even despite the (inavoidable or desired) meeting of the two. "If belief does not come to me as a shock, it would not convince me" (*Letters 2*, p. 51, to Victor White, Spring 1952). But this means that Jung wants shock *instead of* conviction! For Jung God has to be "as obvious as when a brick falls on one's head" (*MDR* p. 62, transl. modif.): in *essential* matters, Jung wants to be knocked down, not illumined and convinced.

---

[33] Jung of course also believed in the "transcendent function," in the "uniting symbol" as the "reconciling third" born out of the clash of the two wills. But this remained wishful thinking, just a beautiful idea. Just look by way of a concrete example at Jung's letter of 20 August 1945 to Olga Fröbe-Kapteyn. Here, too, Jung says, "We are crucified between the opposites and delivered up to the torture until the 'reconciling third' takes shape." However, the fact is that this third never came, that third that in fact would have reconciled Olga Fröbe's specific collision of duties. And it is hard to imagine what a reconciliation (in the sense of the transcendent function and a truly creative union, not merely quantitative or technical solution) between her duties as a mother and her efforts for Eranos could possibly have been. In general (both on the individual and the collective level), the transcendent function remains in psychological reality truly transcendent, otherworldly, quite in contrast to Jung's psychological theory.

Jung needs "being shocked, overwhelmed, and hit as if by a falling brick" because for his naturalistic (or Pan) consciousness an empirical violent impact ("so much more immediate, conspicuous [or obvious], impressive and convincing") has to take the place of the circumvented logical, psychological self-transcendence of consciousness from the Pan level to that of echo, reflectedness, indirectness, Mnemosyne. It has to take the place of the absolute-negative inwardization into "the object." What Pan consciousness needs to prevent at any cost is that Pan actually reaches Echo (which, as we know, could only happen in her own dimension). And the best way to prevent it is by faking the possibility of his reaching her in *his own* dimension instead of in hers—that is to say, through immediate experience. Because then her disappearance into absolute negativity—and thereby absolute negativity's historically *already having become explicit*—has once and for all been successfully obfuscated, and Pan consciousness, while empirically maybe being on an endless quest for the great *Urerfahrung*, logically, however, can stay contentedly in Pan's own naturalistic-positivistic dimension.

The self-contradictory state inherent in the "overwhelmingness" of experience and the "clash" of wills, as a union within which each side nevertheless remains absolutely untouched by the other, is the true nature of what we call dissociation (*disiunctio*) in psychology. Dissociation does not mean amputation, total separation. It means the contradictory simultaneity and identity of union ("-sociation") *and* split ("dis-"). Jung's psychology is a psychology of dissociation in this sense. Jung needed to think a coming together of the two sides in terms of violence, because it had to remain at all costs a *dissociated* unity. Amazingly, that very author who devoted one of his major works, a thick book, to the subject of the *mysterium coniunctionis* did himself not think, and was not willing to think, in terms of a *coniunctio*. Jung's fundamentally disjunctive conception betrays itself most clearly when in his theory concerning the most essential element of his psychology, the individuation process, he bluntly exposes "the I, the empirical, ordinary man, man as he has been so far" to "the violence done to him by the self" (*CW* 11 § 233). For Jung, there has to be an ego-self relation, a relation between the ego and the unconscious, a relation between man and God, but it can only be imagined as violent, where "violence" is the name for the double phenomenon of "being overwhelmed" and "absolute resistance," i.e., the clash of two. Clash means dissociated union.

Whereas *coniunctio* means a union in which both sides *lovingly*, in mutual desire, embrace and permeate each other, we use the word "clash" in everyday life for the *physical* collision of two things that in their *inner nature* are absolutely incompatible. In the case of a clash the physical, factual union ("crashing into each other") is contradicted by the inner nature or the "intention," "spirit" of the things concerned ("absolute rejection"), whereas in the case of *coniunctio* fact and inner spirit coincide and confirm each other. So a dissociation is characterized by the discrepancy between what happens on the physical, behaviorial, semantic, factual, literal level (namely, a union) and what is true in the inner attitude, intention, spirit, logical constitution, syntax (namely, resistance, rejection, "hate").

Our mythological paradigm displays a dissociation, an unbridgeable gulf. The union does not happen, cannot happen, because Pan does not transcend himself and follow Echo to her new level, on which alone a true *coniunctio* could take place because Echo the nymph is in her innermost truth from the outset already echo, absolute negativity, although at first only implicitly. If we imagine for a moment that Pan would be able to hold her on his own level and rape her there, he would paradoxically not be in contact with *her* at all, but only quasi narcissistically with the mirror image of his own positivity (Echo is *echo*!). Without himself having entered the dimension of absolute negativity, i.e., having become negative, Pan cannot even really perceive Echo. But by being attracted to Echo, Pan shows that implicitly he is, unbeknownst to himself, already obsolete, already beyond the logic of Being (or Pan consciousness) and on the level of the logic of Reflection, whose truth, as Hegel put it, is "the *movement of nothing to nothing, and so back to itself.*"

When we call Jung's psychology a psychology of dissociation this is in accordance with our analysis of what "dissociation" means, to wit, that it is a psychology that exclusively focuses on the semantic aspect and excludes any consideration for the syntax or logical form. Only this analysis can explain why Jung did not become aware of the incompatibility between his explicitly advocating a *coniunctio* on the semantic level, while on the syntactical level thinking in terms of clash and violence and opposites. He did not become aware of the categories at work in his thinking—because he was sold on Pan-like direct experience and scorned Echo/echo. He did not *listen* to the echo of the style of his thought, did not let it come home to him.

Direct experience is nothing but the clash of a by definition *blind, not-*thinking consciousness with archetypal contents that in themselves are likewise by definition *insulated* from consciousness. A double immunization. The archetypal content has of course factually to surface in consciousness—but surface only like a shrink-wrapped book. And consciousness has to take note of it—but only as one that does not read. A true coming together of book and mind, mind on the naturalistic level of Pan, must not happen under any circumstances. Because if "the book" were opened, and if the mind, *that* mind, the mind which had refused to follow Echo all the way, opened its eyes to its content, in other words, if the speculative power of the content of the book showed itself and the mind opened itself to a speculative appreciation of it, the "maximum credible accident"—inflation or psychosis—would have happened. All that is allowed in Jung's scheme of direct experience is "amplification": that the mind handles the experienced contents from outside, as an observer, by comparing them as "facts" or "statements by the soul" with numerous other motifs of the same type. "*I am concerned with the statement only ...,*" Jung had said. The experienced contents have to stay safely enclosed between quotations marks and thus in the status of mere citations for which the mind does not take responsibility and which it does not make its own in the sense of *believing* what they say. It is like a newspaper that prints "letters to the editor" but makes it very clear that the opinions expressed therein are not the editor's opinions and rejects any responsibility for their content.

This is why Jung's attempt to heal through direct experience the problem "that for us a very essential part of the soul has disappeared" had to be a flight into the unconscious. "*The* unconscious" is, contrary to how it is presented and imagined, not a realm, a reservoir of images, or part, or organ, but a logical structure, a syntactical stance. It is nothing but that "direct experience" itself, a fundamentally private experience of the individual, in its threefold structure, namely, as the unity of (a) the blindness of consciousness, (b) the sealedness of the contents as mere citations, and (c) this theory's scotomization of its own syntax (as well as of the difference between semantics and syntax in general).

Jung's already cited statement about modern man—"Heaven and hell are fates meted out to the soul and not to civil man, who in his nakedness and timidity would have no idea of what to do with himself in a heavenly Jerusalem"[34] (*CW* 9i § 56, transl. modif.)—is one example of a clear expression of the general incommensurability between the ordinary modern consciousness and the archetypal contents. Jung saw this fundamental incommensurability. However, he did not do anything to overcome it. He neither tried to subject the modern mind to an opus of sublimation and distillation (from "Pan" to "echo," from positivity to absolute negativity), nor did he work with the archetypal images in such a way that they would lose their archaic mythic character and be raised onto a conceptual level corresponding to the modern status of consciousness. Instead, he let civil man, modern man with his everyday consciousness, *clash* with the archaic-archetypal images of his dreams or visions.

Jung criticized Albert Schweitzer for having "run away from the European problem"[35] to black Africa as missionary and doctor, a task that, Jung thought, could have been executed by any other ordinary doctor equally well. It would not have needed such a remarkably gifted theologian that had delivered such important new insights. "Faced with the truly appalling *afflictio animae* of the European man, Schweitzer abdicated from the task incumbent on the theologian, the *cura animarum*, and studied medicine in order to treat the sick *bodies of natives*" (*Letters 2*, p. 140, to Bremi, 11 December 1953). In a way, this criticism can be turned against Jung himself. Structurally, Schweitzer's escape from the spiritual, intellectual predicament of the Western mind to the dark continent of Africa and from soul to body seems to be the same move as Jung's escape from the real world of industrial modernity and modern highly developed consciousness to the dark continent of "the unconscious" and from the sophisticated predicament of the truly modern soul to the primitive[36] outdated

---

[34] Jung's statement applies to ego-consciousness as such. Modern consciousness has by definition no access to such a thing as a heavenly Jerusalem, to archetypal, metaphysical, speculative contents. They simply do not exist for it. This is its blindness.

[35] *Letters 2*, p. 324, to Murray, August 1956.

[36] I do not use "primitive" as a value judgment, since I do not have low opinions of myths at all.

imaginal forms of myths and archetypes as positive facts. In both cases, although in different ways, consciousness goes consciously beneath consciousness and practices an *abaissement du niveau mental.*

At Jung's time, the real soul predicament was certainly not located yonder, down there in "the unconscious." It was (and still is at our time) here, at home, in our real cultural world with all its inherent contradictions, the real world as apperceived by consciousness as the conscious-unconscious unity of the mind, on the level reached by Echo. It has never been on the naturalistic level of Pan. The "Great god Pan" has psychologically been dead and obsolete since the end of antiquity. And since then Echo has been waiting for her mate to arrive, much like (both mythological and Nietzsche's) Ariadne was longingly waiting for Dionysus.[37]

Psychologically, however, we have to understand Pan's death not as literal death. In truth it is his *not-understood* disappearance from sight, from the naturalistic level, his death *as* Pan (as a figure representing the literalism of mythological imagination), a disappearance only because he had begun to be on his way into Echo's invisible dimension after all. Pan had "evaporated." He had precisely not died in the ordinary sense of leaving a dead body to be buried behind. With the rise of extremely sublime Neoplatonism at the end of antiquity and the emergence of Christianity as the likewise and even more sublime religion of the Holy Ghost, Pan had been absorbed into the dimension of spirit and ipso facto dissolved *as* Pan, sublated himself, and entered absolute negativity, just as Echo had previously, at Pan's time, dissolved *as* nymph. Only our consciousness upholds *former* Pan's standpoint when *he* has precisely left it, and this is why we think he has totally disappeared (or, another possibility for post-antiquity consciousness, that he survived in the altered guise of the medieval devil). His implicit transformation merely needs to become explicit, to be known and acknowledged by consciousness.

That, as Plutarch reported, in late antiquity the cry "The Great Pan is dead" resounded was the (not fully understood) reflection of the final *fulfillment* of Pan's destiny, a fulfillment that he could not possibly reach within mythic imagination. Why would Pan have been

---

[37] The similarity of the two mythemes consists only in the soul's waiting for her other, but as to the psychological concern or topic expressed in them the two stories are worlds apart.

attracted by these ethereal nymphs like Syrinx and Echo in the first place? It would have been so much more likely that this cloven-hooved god would have desired more meaty girls. The existence of this one particular mythologem within Greek myth—the fact that the most physical of all gods longed precisely for the vaporous, for logical negativity—shows not only that this one god would ultimately find his fulfillment in his own sublation, but also that within the mythic imagination there was from the outset an implicit intuition that the naturalism of mythic imagination as such and pagan polytheism as a whole was ultimately destined to sublate itself.

The moment that Jung can say that there *exists* a collective or archetypal unconscious as a constituent part of the makeup of the psychic, the form of Pan-consciousness has been reified and eternalized. Then Jung seems to be out of the woods: *he*, it now seems, is not holding on to an outdated form of consciousness. *He* is innocently discovering and describing facts of nature. Pan, the gods, all the figures of mythological imagination are still there. But because they are *only* still there as logically segregated and secreted away in "the unconscious," they do not and cannot bother modern consciousness. "The unconscious" thus gives modern consciousness licence to simulate Pan-consciousness and to believe that what it is dealing with is both real and of *essential* (meaning) relevance.

Jung's flight into the unconscious is a regressive move: it is *his* flight from Echo, his refusal to allow psychology to become initiated into modernity.

(Of course, both in Schweitzer's and in Jung's case, the escapes were absolutely *bona fide* attempts and not meant to be escapes at all but rather the opposite: the only possible solutions.)

Contrasting Jung's project concerning the *essential* questions with Hegel's project of making Christian religion flee into the Concept, we see that on all three counts (the blindness of consciousness, the sealedness of the content, and the exclusion of an awareness of, and attention to, syntax or logical form) Hegel moved into the opposite direction. He saw his task, as it were, in following Echo to her new level. On the one, subjective side his work was aimed at training the mind to truly become able to think speculatively and overcome the ordinary representational and picture-thinking mode of consciousness. The mind had to become much more sophisticated, distilled, vaporized. At the same time, on the other side, that of the object, the speculative rational core of Christianity had correspondingly to be laid bare, a core that so far had remained hidden under its imaginal and as such naturalistic form. And thirdly, on the whole, in his *Logic* Hegel translated, transformed the semantics of the entire traditional metaphysics into its syntax, thereby turning what had been in the "solid" state of distinct substantiations into the fluidity of thought and thus into *one* infinitely complex, living, self-unfolding thought. This also amounted to bringing the whole logical constitution of consciousness and of the conception of the Real to the height of the development that the soul had reached at Hegel's time. It was, as it were, an "alchemical" opus which achieved a new commensurability between consciousness and the substance of what formerly used to be religion because it transformed and sublated both, "sublated" particularly also in the sense of elevation.

Hegel's solution is not the answer for us and could not have been the solution at Jung's time. Hegel still had had his place on the base of metaphysics. But this basis no longer existed for the time that came after him. In part this is because Hegel's philosophy concluded the work of metaphysics, brought it to its completion, so that nothing more remained to be done by it. This in turn meant that it *ipso facto* gave room to the entirely new post-metaphysical logic of modernity, the logic of difference, *disiunctio*, dissociation, which already had made its first appearance during his own lifetime in the philosophy of Arthur Schopenhauer.

But: that we cannot simply adopt Hegel's solution does not mean that we would be allowed to fall short of the level of psychological sophistication reached by Hegel, be allowed in psychology to desert "Echo" and go systematically down beneath it to the naturalistic level of "Pan" which is already known to have been obsolete for ages—because "Pan" himself has left it.

VI. The *logical* generation of "the unconscious"

Above I had written:

> "To flee into the unconscious (in the sense of taking refuge in it)," "to assign to contents the unconscious as their place"—the problem with this was, that the unconscious did not simply exist.

> "The unconscious" is not a positive fact, an existing entity, a
> part, a realm, an organ or the like, the way the brain or the lung
> are parts of the body.

That the brain and the lung exist can be demonstrated. This is
not the case with "the unconscious." It is only a psychic idea, a fantasy,
a fiction. Nobody has ever seen it. It is posited, not discovered (the
way America, the Jupiter moons or body cells and genes were
discovered). And this is why that place, the unconscious, in which
the essential contents to be preserved could seek refuge, had to be for
the first time *generated* precisely through and in that very flight into
it. This sounds like a self-contradiction, and it is a self-contradiction,
but a constitutive one for the soul, which follows a dialectic, uroboric
logic. Just as the soul always speaks about itself, so it also makes,
generates itself. Soul does not have a substrate. It exists only because,
and to the extent that, it posits itself. This also applies to the
problematic guise it gave itself during the 20th century, namely that
of "the unconscious." In Jungian psychology we are so accustomed to
the notion of the unconscious and so used to working with this concept
that we simply take it for granted and *believe* in it as if it were a fact
rather than a psychological fantasy. We most of the time mindlessly
presuppose that it is an existing reality.

One reason may be that this concept proved useful in the
treatment of neuroses. But of course, practical usefulness does not
necessarily mean theoretical legitimacy. Already Jung warned of the
fault of raising a method or technique to the status of a theory. He
blamed above all Freud for having committed this mistake of
"identifying theory and method and making them into some kind of
dogma" and saw in this mistake the main reason why he had to stop
his collaboration with him (*MDR* p. 167).[38] But despite his avid study
of Kant, in whose work he must have come across the idea of the logical
fallacy called "transcendental subreption" (the positing of an *object*
where in truth there is only a function or act performed by the mind,
that is, by a conscious *human being*), Jung was at his time not able to
see where he himself also succumbed to this same error, even if in very

---

[38] Cf. also: "The immediate reason for my dissension was that Freud in a publication
identified the method with his theory, a fact that seemed inadmissible to me, because I
am convinced that one can apply a scientific method without believing in a certain theory.
The results obtained by this method can be interpreted in several ways" (*Letters 1*, p.
211, to Jelliffe, 24 February 1936).

different respects from Freud. "*The* unconscious" became part of Jung's theory and was taken by him to be an indubitable fact, although it is the result of a certain doing.

What is this doing? How is "the unconscious" in fact logically generated? I will develop the process of the logical generation of the notion of "the unconscious" in four steps.

1. Inasmuch as "the unconscious" is not a discovered fact, but a concept generated at a particular time in history, and inasmuch as it in itself refers to consciousness (it defines itself as the negation of consciousness: un-conscious), it is obvious that it paradoxically must be generated *within* consciousness. It is clear from the outset that we are here concerned with psychic reality. According to the usual view "consciousness + the unconscious" together make up the total circumference of psychic reality. And if under these conditions we want to study the *generation* of "the unconscious" and *ipso facto* start out from a state in which the latter does not yet exist, it follows that "the unconscious" must be produced within consciousness, because after the subtraction of our modern idea of "the unconscious," consciousness is the only thing left of psychic reality, and is the name for the latter's all-comprehensive circumference. For psychology, there is nothing outside consciousness. Even in the case of so-called "unconscious material" we are of course, strictly speaking, always dealing with conscious material. Dreams, archetypal images, visions, active imaginings, free associations, etc., but also the myths, rituals, and symbols of former ages and primitive peoples are not actually unconscious, but contents *of consciousness,* not really different from other conscious phenomena such as our perceptions, emotions, intentions, reflections, and convictions. What is truly unconscious (e.g., physiological processes in the body and dreams that did not become conscious) drops out of psychology altogether. It is partly the subject of biology or medicine (the physiological processes), partly it simply does not exist for us (not remembered dreams). Dreams prior to their having entered consciousness are not a topic for psychology at all. Psychology deals with the soul that has *spoken* and been heard, with "*documents* of the soul," with manifest phenomena, with "statements" and texts.

The statement that there is nothing outside consciousness does of course not imply that everything is absolutely conscious. Much is unconscious in the sense of unknown, forgotten, repressed, not within the range of attention, subliminal, etc. Above all, all contents of consciousness are in themselves not conscious through and through. Much of each content remains ununderstood, vague, obscure. The words that we use in our speaking contain in addition to our intended sense many subliminal, unintended meanings. There is an inner infinity to words, and we say more with our statements than we are aware of. The Bible presents us with the idea: "for they know not what they do" (Luke 23:24), and Jung similarly with his insight about certain people: "they knew only *what* they did and not *why* they did it" (*CW* 10 § 144). Hegel pointed out that "Quite generally, the familiar, just because it is familiar, is not cognitively understood,"[39] it is, we could add, much rather taken for granted, taken at face value. Every content, thought, impulse, intention is within itself a conscious-unconscious unity. Consciousness is within itself the unity of itself and its negation.

This becomes even more obvious when we include the question of where our contents of consciousness come from. I don't know the origin of my own ideas and insights, of why and wherefrom a memory popped into my head just now. Even the processes of what Jung called "directed thinking" (*CW* 5, Part One, II) are not *totally* conscious.

Consciousness has its own unknown, mysterious depth. This was already clearly expressed in philosophy long before the idea of "the unconscious" came up. Kant, referring to productive imagination, pointed out that there is "a hidden art in the depths of the human soul,"[40] an insight that was taken up and transformed by Fichte and Schelling in different ways. Hegel, although distancing himself from this thesis of a *productive imagination* in the depths of the mind, nevertheless in his own way taught that the origination of the object that shows itself to consciousness happens "behind the back" of consciousness.[41] Kant and the German Idealists, however, did not need to substantiate their awareness of the unconscious depths

---

[39] G.W.F. Hegel, *Phenomenology of Spirit*, transl. by A.V. Miller, Oxford (Oxford University Press) 1977, p. 18.

[40] Immanuel Kant, *Kritik der reinen Vernunft*, A141, B180.

[41] On this topic of the unconscious depth of the mind see Elke Völmicke, *Das Unbewußte im Deutschen Idealismus*, Würzburg (Königshausen & Neumann) 2005 and Reinhard Loock, *Schwebende Einbildungskraft. Konzeptionen theoretischer Freiheit in der Philosophie Kants, Fichtes und Schellings*, Würzburg (Königshausen & Neumann) 2007.

aspects of the mind into "*the* unconscious," as it emerged during the 19th century and culminated in the 20th century psychoanalytical schools of psychology.

Even in late Jung we find evidence of a more dialectical view of consciousness or the ego. "The refulgent body of the sun is the ego and its field of consciousness—*Sol et eius umbra*: light without and darkness within. In the source of light is darkness enough ..." (*CW* 14 § 129). Consciousness contains its own darkness within itself, rather than as a wholly other outside and vis-à-vis itself. Conversely, late Jung also acquired through his alchemical studies the insight that there is a consciousness in the unconscious. I already mentioned the alchemical motif of the fish eyes or of the sparks (*scintillae*) in the unconscious. "For the eyes of the fish are always open and therefore must always see" (*CW* 14 § 752). So with these two late perfectly complementary conceptions, if we combine them, we arrive at an equivalent of the yin yang symbol (*taijitu*), as found in Taoist thinking (but also as a Celtic and Roman symbol): two opposites, each of which contains the other deeply inside itself (light without and darkness within on the one side and darkness without, but light within on the other side). This is probably as close as an imaginal, pictorially thinking (i.e., not truly thinking) theorizing can get to a dialectical view. But a truly dialectical understanding was not reached by Jung. Just as the depiction of the *taijitu*, so did Jung, too, retain the two opposites as separate structures (despite the fact that *internally* they each experienced a rapprochement to their other), but he did not manage, and also did not under any circumstances wish, to bring the opposites truly together in a *coniunctio*, in a fluid dialectical relation.

If consciousness is within itself the unity of conscious awareness and unconsciousness in such a way that this complex, contradictory unity imparts itself on every content or state of consciousness in different forms of distribution and different degree of its two moments on the implicit-explicit scale, then "unconscious" is an adjective rather than a noun, an adjective that either refers to a state of consciousness (e.g., ignorant, dozing, sleeping, dreaming, projecting, acting-out, inflated, delusional; *abaissement du niveau mental*) or to a state of specific contents (forgotten, repressed, scotomized, subliminal, etc.).

How can the generation of "*the* unconscious" in Jung's sense happen within a consciousness that from the outset is the living unity of consciousness-unconsciousness? The answer is: through a cut, a logical act of splitting, dissociation. *Particular* contents or regions of consciousness at large, such as dreams and fantasy images, mythological and fairytale motifs, religious rituals and symbols are sequestered from the rest of consciousness, declared to represent a *toto coelo* different and separate psychic system and thereby turn into "the unconscious." "The unconscious" is a kind of foreign state with full sovereignty and autonomy. Indeed it possesses a higher degree of autonomy than consciousness. "The Relations Between the Ego and the Unconscious" are thus really international relations, foreign affairs. We speak of an invasion of unconscious ideas into consciousness, their taking possession of consciousness. "The unconscious" is a superpower with consciousness as its satellite state, a state that through careful maneuvering may or may not enjoy a certain degree of independence within its fundamental dependence. We speak of a "hubris of consciousness" when the latter forgets its utter dependence and delusionally believes to be the master in its own house.

The disadvantage of the image of two countries is that it inevitably suggests that consciousness and the unconscious belong to the same level. But Jungian psychology also thinks the difference as a fundamental otherness in terms of verticality and as a categorial distinction. The unconscious is the ground, the primordial origin and source of everything that exists in consciousness. The unconscious is down there, under consciousness. It is what alone is truly creative. Consciousness is fundamentally secondary, derivative. The unconscious is the primordial mother, consciousness her child. Or the unconscious is the ocean, with consciousness being a small island contained within it.

2. The dissociation through which the unconscious is established is a logical one *in the psychologist's mind*. It happens through a classification, on the level of naming only. It is not an empirical cut. The "facts," the phenomena remain what they were before the generation of "the unconscious." It is a decision of the mind to view the phenomena of the mind as divided into two radically separate, oppositional systems. There is nothing in the phenomenology itself that would make this split necessary.

For it is essential to understand that the cut is not made between what, according to the dialectical understanding of consciousness as a contradictory conscious-unconscious unity, are the two moments of the full phenomenon of consciousness. Neither the difference between states of *consciousness* (e.g., waking vs. dreaming), nor that between the states of a *content* (e.g., subliminal vs. explicit) is the guiding principle of this dissociation. "*The* unconscious" is not our *adjective* "unconscious" from above, the only difference being that it is now raised to the status of a noun. No, the division is made within the whole range of *contents* of consciousness themselves, between two different *types* of contents distinguished from each other with respect to their specific substantial content or semantic message. The central criterion is, to express it by way of abbreviation, whether they have an archaic, archetypal-imaginal character (this would make them part of "the unconscious") or not; whether they express a "deeper meaning" (again this would make them belong to "the unconscious") or are merely pragmatic, rational, and part of familiar everyday reality.

Under point no. 1 I discussed, as it were, the *causa materialis* of the construction of "the unconscious," and found out that the unconscious is made from and established within consciousness itself. And I also discussed the *causa efficiens*, namely, that it was a cut or dissociation through with the unconscious was made. Now, in point no. 2, I turn to the *causa finalis*, the purpose of this generation. At bottom, what was at stake with the logical production of "the unconscious"? What was it all about? The entire present section of this paper is concerned with the *generation* of the unconscious. But in order to find out what the driving force and interest behind this generation was, I need to look at the *finished result* of this generation. The result allows us to infer the inner concern that motivated the production of "the unconscious."

To the question of what the nature of "the unconscious" in Jung's sense fundamentally is we must answer that in radical contrast to Freud's instinctual unconscious of *desire* and, later, Lacan's *linguistic* unconscious, Jung's unconscious is cognitive, epistemic, noetic, an unconscious of *meaning* and *knowing*. It ultimately IS a figuration of *essential knowledge*, knowledge concerning meaning, mythic or metaphysical knowledge, speculative ideas. Jung often used the word "revelation" for this knowledge that came to us from the unconscious. However, it is this knowing *in the form* of natural facts, not in the form of *knowing*, as already the name unconscious suggests. It is a knowing that is not allowed to know. Thus it contradicts itself. Its contents are in themselves dissociated from themselves. They are *meaning* safely packaged in the meaninglessness of "facts"; they are ideas, images, symbols coming as "natural events," as "nature." The inner content is immunized against itself through its external form. "Archetypes" are ultimately canned traditional knowledge, bottled up meanings, insights that as facts are in themselves blind. The notion of the unconscious is the notion of the spirit Mercurius, but the Mercurius only firmly enclosed and sealed in the bottle, bracketed, encapsulated. Inside the bottle all gates were allowed to be opened—as long as the bottle itself stayed sealed. The plug on the bottle itself was the one and only "gate" that could not be opened.

With his idea of "the archetypes of the collective unconscious" Jung alone had a decisive concept of the "Un-Be*wuß*ten" (uncon*scious*) *as* a form of *Wissen* (*scientia*, knowing) or, as we could also say, as a form of an implicit (*ansichseiend*) consciousness. But the knowledge that we are here talking about is not factual knowledge about the world as we need it in science or everyday life, but that kind of special knowledge that concerns (mythic, religious, metaphysical) meaning.

Neither Freud, nor Klages, nor Steiner, nor Lacan needed to sacrifice the intellect. Why did Freud not have to (to comment here only on him who also developed a psychology of the unconscious), whereas Jung was forced to sacrifice the intellect? Because Freud's and Jung's "unconscious" are incomparably different. Only geographically did the two live in neighboring countries. Intellectually they lived on different planets. No bridge leads from the one to the other. Jung's notion of the unconscious is by no means an expansion of Freud's, merely adding a deeper "collective" aspect to the Freudian "personal unconscious." Freud's "unconscious" did not have the character of knowledge to begin with. In Freud's "unconscious," being basically instinctual, irrational *libidinal desire*, the mind was confronted with something by definition wholly other than itself, wholly un-noetic, ultimately biological. *This* unconscious did not represent a threat to the mind in the sense that it might seduce it into speculative thinking, and therefore it also fell to the conscious mind to be the uncurtailed locus and organ of knowledge. The mind could legitimately be a neutral scientific observer and theorizer.

For Jung, however, the contents of the unconscious were immediately of intrinsic and deepest importance to consciousness itself. In the unconscious, consciousness discovered its own innermost truth, from which it had been divorced. The unconscious does not merely supply us with additional information about our problems, the way we get important information about the state of health of our body from X-rays and other diagnostic devices; it contains consciousness's *own* Self! "The unconscious" is the exclusive locus and source of what is fundamentally consciousness's *very own* concern and duty: *essential* knowledge and creative production.[42] Consciousness does not have within itself the answers to its own deepest questions. It has them outside of itself in its Other. It cannot provide what it so desperately needs: "... but we stand empty-handed, bewildered, and perplexed, and cannot even get it into our heads that no myth will come to our aid although we have such urgent need of one" (*MDR* p. 332). "You see, man is in need of a symbolic life—badly in need" (*CW* 18 § 625). "Only the symbolic life can express the need of the soul" (*CW* 18 § 627).

If what was at stake for Jung (prior to the generation of "the unconscious") was that consciousness discovers that kind of *essential* knowledge that should be its very own knowledge, then consciousness, in finding and developing this knowledge, actually relates only with what is fundamentally its own. It is a self-relation. Consciousness learns in this knowledge what it, consciousness itself, truly is (in contrast to Freud's scheme, in which consciousness learns through analysis about what *I, the empirical human person*, truly am). It is immediately apparent that this invites, indeed requires, dialectical, speculative thinking. If psychology—the study of the soul—is primarily concerned with the question of meaning, as Jung's psychology in fact is, and if meaning is not reduced to a commodity, a kind of drug, a thing to be possessed, but requires, in order to truly exist, the immediate illumination and transformation of consciousness itself, then the neat difference between subject and object has disappeared and we have landed ourselves in a situation of speculative thought.

---

[42] My unconscious is creative, my dreams know, not me. "My" creative work, if any, stems from a primordial experience out of the unconscious, a primordial vision. And only to the extent that I as consciousness become blind, i.e., refrain from thinking creatively on my own, can I partake of the knowledge and creativity contained in the experiences from the unconscious and desperately needed by my ego-consciousness.

3. But for Jung, as for the whole historical locus to which he belongs, speculative thought was a horror. Here Kant came in very handy for him (Kant the way he understood him). "Kant in particular," Jung said, "erected a barrier across the mental world which made it impossible for even the boldest flight of speculation to penetrate into the object. ... Nowadays it is not Kant but natural science and its de-subjectivized world that have erected a wall at which human inquisitiveness turns back" (*CW* 18 § 1734, transl. modif.; Hull translates: "erected this barrier against which the speculative tendency rebounds"). We discussed this already in connection with our Pan-and-Echo paradigm, and here we see that Kant's philosophy served Jung as an *intellectual* justification for his personal emotional need to prevent consciousness's "boldest flight" from ordinary naturalistically experienced reality into the dimension of speculative reflection, self-relation, and absolute negativity. Consciousness's standpoint simply had to remain that of Pan. Human inquisitiveness (Pan's chasing the nymph) had to be frustrated and turn back. The object (Echo, the soul) with its autonomous momentum had to be unreachable. Pan consciousness was not allowed within itself to transcend itself, to break through its own internal sound barrier that held it safely encased within its everyday positivism (which is owing to "the animal nature of man") and irrevocably separated it from echo's dimension of absolute negativity. This was the gift of the "Kantian" wall or barrier.

4. Now we find ourselves in a terrible dilemma. On the one hand, what is at stake for consciousness is *essential* knowledge and "higher meaning," which necessarily would involve consciousness in speculative thought (no. 2). On the other hand, but at the same time, speculation is absolutely prohibited (no. 3). Pan cannot give up Echo, but he must not under any circumstances follow her boldest leap out of the world of positivity into that of absolute negativity. The task is thus to find a way how Pan can, *within* his own natural dimension and *as* a natural experience, nevertheless find that which Echo represents in her own dimension. Consciousness desperately needs meaning, something in itself fundamentally speculative, but it must acquire it as a natural fact, as *naturally existing* knowledge, but not under any circumstances as an achievement by the mind's own speculative work and as something intelligible.

The solution for this dilemma lay in the Kantian barrier or wall itself when it was not left "out there" as something *against* which consciousness rebounds when it wants to follow its inquisitiveness or speculative tendency. Instead, it had to be appropriated by and introjected into the mind itself (in a way reminiscent of what psychoanalysis called the defense mechanism of "identification with the aggressor"). The barrier had to be swallowed.

For Kant, what Jung had called barrier or wall had been the boundary of what for the human mind was "the world" as such. Outside there was nothing but "transcendental illusory appearance." But having become interiorized, the wall has become an "innerworldly" boundary, as it were. Much like the Berlin wall separated East and West, so the introjected wall helped to establish a dissociation of consciousness at large into two fundamentally opposite regions, yonder "the unconscious" and over here consciousness in the new narrower sense as so-called "ego-consciousness."

The "barrier" character, interiorized into the concept of consciousness itself, resulted in a strict negation of consciousness: the *un*-conscious. As the radical negation of consciousness the unconscious was as much a wall from which ego-consciousness rebounds as had been the original Kantian one for the inquisitiveness of the uncurtailed human mind.

But because this boundary was one that had been artificially drawn right through the middle of an organic whole (consciousness at large), it brought with it a strange complementary distribution. What was on the other side of the boundary was now no longer nothing but illusion. How could it be nothing but illusion if the boundary was drawn through the middle of what in the Kantian scheme was on *this* side of the boundary and represented *reality* in contrast to illusion outside the barrier? The new internal boundary separated two "reals" from each other. More than that, that side over there (in the *new* scheme) contained what was of absolute importance for consciousness on this side. What was of *essential* or meaning importance lay yonder, whereas what was over here on the side of consciousness (in the reduced sense) was only of ordinary significance, indeed belonged to the "banality of life." Conversely, the contents of "the unconscious" were, as the name suggests, unconscious, without being known, that is, they were only implicit, and thus could find their own being known and acknowledged only on the other side, in consciousness. The unconscious contents were dependent on consciousness for their own full realization. Dissociation does not merely mean that one country is divided in two. It means that each side is deprived of what it needs. It has what is absolutely essential for it not within itself, but on the other side, from which it is radically dissociated.

The new consciousness-internal boundary separated two kinds of "reals" from each other, we said. We also already know that the criterion by which the border was drawn between all the different contents of consciousness was whether the contents qualified as archaic, mythological, archetypal, religious, or metaphysical ones or not. If they qualified as such they had to be cut off within consciousness from consciousness in the new narrower sense and relegated to "the unconscious." This was more than a formal act of relabeling. This sequestering-off of the symbols and mythological, religious, metaphysical ideas of former ages as contents of "the unconscious" provided them with a special, mysterious status, that of archetypal, numinous images. Without this barrier or wall that now ran right through the middle of consciousness at large, these "archetypal contents," as they were henceforth called, would merely have been curiosities from the past, quite ordinary objects of maybe historical scholarly interest, but otherwise totally irrelevant for modern life, indeed simply forgettable. But because they had become walled off and walled in they now were, as it were, (logically) tabooed. As such they were all of a sudden loaded with special importance, with an inner quality of deepest mystery and numinous intensity, and surrounded by an aura, much as in ancient times the marking off of a *temenos* gave to the marked-off space the status of sacredness— not of its own accord, but through this tabooing segregation performed by the theoretical design of psychology. The result was that within the natural world a simulation of the former mythological or metaphysical realm now existed, a simulation of echo's other dimension *on Pan's level of commonplace reality.*

There is an additional essential effect of the introjection of Jung's "Kantian" barrier or wall into consciousness itself. It even changed the inner nature of this barrier itself. In order to see this we have to start with the situation of the archaic ritualistic and the later religious-metaphysical cultures. In ritualistic cultures initiation was the institutionalized transgression of the border between the ordinary-life sphere and the other world of spirits. Later, during the ages of metaphysics the transgression no longer needed to be literally "acted out" in a personal experiential process because it had been reflected into the very standpoint of these cultures themselves. It had become structural. The standpoint was meta-physical by definition and from the outset. In other words, what formerly had been an actual enactment here and now had become the inherent logical character of the mode of being-in-the-world. Psychologically, the mind, if I may put it this way, was at one and the same time standing with one leg here on earth and with the other leg with God. It lived out of a knowledge about God and the immortality of the soul, about God not only as an otherworldly being or power, but also as the very ground of the earthly world and the human mind itself.

The event of the appearance of Kant's philosophy marked the point in the history of the soul when the realm into which the transgression had led was diagnosed as being the result of a fallacy, of the mind's succumbing to the said "transcendental illusory appearance." The barrier mentioned by Jung marked the outermost extent of possible human knowledge. Now there simply was nothing to transcend *to*. On the one hand, the barrier had the effect of a prohibition (namely not to fall for the transcendental appearance and ipso facto transgress into *meta*physical spheres). But on the other hand, it was simply the objective point where consciousness (the mind at large) came to an end, its own end.

Through the introjection of the barrier performed by Jung this barrier was reflected into itself. It was no longer an external and literal border like a border between two countries that needed to be guarded and that prevented the *inhabitants* on either side from crossing it without permission. The interiorized barrier did not need to be guarded, and it was also not like a wall from which one could rebound. The boundary had become internal to each side, "the unconscious" and ego-consciousness. It now was inherent in their own logic. Each side had the border within itself as its own unsurpassable circumference or self-enclosedness. Because they each shut themselves up within themselves and of their own accord, the border was now no longer something *between* them, that is, external to them: their external border. There was no need any more for a prohibition: the boldest flight of speculation and an initiatory transgression were simply objectively and inherently impossible. Ego-consciousness had positioned itself in an observer standpoint over against "the unconscious," an observer standpoint which, however, had become ennobled by Jung as that of *religio* interpreted by him as "careful observation." As observer, ego-consciousness stayed neatly on its own side. It perceived *that* the soul made a statement of archetypal import and *that* the statement maybe came with the aura of numinosity. It may in addition also have tried to *understand* this statement through amplification and thereafter draw *ethical consequences* from its understanding for itself. But it did not intrinsically, i.e., speculatively, get involved in *what* the statement said. The fact that such a statement had happened, the event of this fact in its virginal intactness, had to be enough for it. Correspondingly the archetypal motifs that "the unconscious" presented were, as we already know, in themselves sealed; they came to ego-consciousness as *on principle* inaccessible. The interiorized barrier means that each side is within itself immunized against the other.

The barrier does thus not have the function of keeping the Other out, but of locking each side within itself. Before, I spoke of the clash between the blindness of consciousness and the sealedness of the contents of "the unconscious." But now I have to give a different understanding to this clash. It is not *between* them, but the simultaneity of each side's clash against its own *internal* outer encasement. They clash, but not with each other. They never touch. No *coniunctio*, not even in the form of a full-fledged clash. And thus no event of truth. *Mysterium disiunctionis*!

The interiorization of Jung's "Kantian" barrier from the borders of consciousness right into the middle of consciousness between the thereby resulting two split-off halves of ego-consciousness and "the unconscious" furthermore goes along with a reversal. When the barrier had still marked the external boundary of consciousness, the danger had been the human mind's unrestrained inquisitiveness, its boldest flight of speculation to achieve an event of truth. The place of this forward movement is, in the new scheme of the introjected barrier, taken by the opposite movement of "primordial experience," that is, the spontaneous, autonomous manifestation, if not intrusion, of the unconscious archetypal contents into passive, merely receptive ego-consciousness.

VII. The actual fabrication of "the unconscious"

The theoretical gain from this story is the clear recognition that an unconscious "intention" or tendency stage-managed the fright with the horses ... ... the nocturnal scene with the horses—the starting point of the illness—seems to be only the keystone of a planned edifice. The fright and the apparently traumatic effect of the childhood experience are merely staged, but staged in the peculiar way characteristic of hysteria, so that the *mise en scène* appears almost exactly like a reality.

—C.G. Jung (*CW* 4 § 364)

In the first section of this paper we witnessed how the fundamental principle operative in the generation of the concept of "*the unconscious*" first announced itself to Jung and how Jung acquired the *standpoint* of "the unconscious" for himself. Thereafter we saw that and how the logic of the unconscious indeed determined the basic character of his developed psychological thought as a whole and studied the *logical* generation of "the unconscious." But the link between the first inkling of the idea of "the unconscious" and the finished, fully worked-out psychology, that is, the concrete practical realization of the concept of "the unconscious," is still missing.

Normally a theory is constructed in the mind and as a body of thought, as an extended fantasy, in which the mind stays consistent with itself. And the object that the theory is about is something external to the theory itself, which is why a theory can be true or false. It is true if and to the extent that the theory does justice to the object, and false if it does not. Not so for psychology. In psychology, the soul speaks about itself, and its speaking is the generation of itself and thus also of the very object that it is speaking about. The soul makes itself in and through its speaking about itself. Psychology, as the soul's *explicit* speaking about itself does not have a given object external to itself. This applies also and particularly to the psychology of "the unconscious." "The unconscious" is not a factual reality. It is a construct, it is posited. Here the simple correspondence of theory and object could not suffice. More and something special was required.

In order to be able to credibly entertain the theory of the unconscious, the mind had, on the one hand, to prove the existence of the unconscious. Otherwise it would not have been a theory of *something*, but merely a piece of fiction. On the other hand, because the unconscious was something mental, indeed a fantasy of the soul, the mind had to within itself *produce* that unconscious which it was about. The proof of its existence had to consist in making it real, in establishing "the unconscious" as a psychological reality. This required actually making consciousness in certain regards unconscious. The *sacrificium intellectus* as the founding act of "the unconscious" could not be a mere free-floating fantasy image of such a sacrifice; this sacrifice of the intellect had to be actually performed. In technical imagery we could say: it could not stay a computer program, it also had to be actually installed. However, it could not be performed merely as one's subjective *behavior* of "stopping to think," the way the boy Jung in the Basel cathedral incident had literally said to himself, "Don't go on thinking," "Don't think of it, just don't think of it!" This would have been a mere momentary acting out, and "the unconscious" would have stayed contingent and dependent on whether or not the human subject practiced this behavior of not-thinking. The notion of "the unconscious" had to become independent of the subject and its actual behavior: something permanent and objectively existing. This means it had to become structural, syntactic, a constitutive element in the make-up of psychic reality. Only then could it be the factually existing, objective *form* of whatever contents—and as such receive that kind of ontological dignity that the proof of the existence of "the unconscious" required.

   How could this manufacturing of the unconscious be executed? How could such a *real* transformation of the logical constitution of experience be carried out? Inasmuch as "the unconscious" was by definition *essential* knowledge *as the opposite of knowing*, namely as "the *un*conscious," and inasmuch as it was something mental *as the opposite of mind*, namely pure nature and empirical fact, the mind had to within itself alienate, dissociate itself from itself. The unconscious had to be created as a condition of the mind itself, namely as its *having gone under*, consciousness intentionally resigning as waking consciousness and as creative, speculatively thinking mind, intentionally discharging itself of any intellectual responsibility for the contents it entertained. The mind had to within itself reduce itself to a passive, innocent receptor/mere observer and radically divorce itself from its own, the transcendental I's, ideas, molding these ideas in such a way that they appeared to be objects vis-à-vis itself and as pure nature, an independent reality, a stream of *events* that came to, or rather came over, consciousness all of their own accord, as if they were aliens intruding from outside (from what Freud called *inneres Ausland,* internal foreign countries, or from a kind of internal outer space).

The mind had by itself to bring about the partial eclipse of itself. But of course it had to do this in such a way that it would be absolutely unconscious concerning its own authorship in creating this eclipse as a state of itself. This self-contradiction was indispensable. The production in actuality of the notion of the unconscious through a self-induced eclipse had itself to be unconscious from the outset. The mind had to feel absolutely innocent about its experiences. All awareness of a collaboration of the human mind itself in the images it experienced had to be expunged. The moment there would have been the least suspicion that the notion of "the unconscious" owed its existence to its, the theoretical mind's, own doing, the moment it would have been seen through as his *construct,* this notion would have collapsed. And the moment the images in Jung's dreams and visions would have been realized to have been his own thoughts merely bracketed and pushed down into unconsciousness, they would have lost their status of empirical fact, pure nature, and revelation. This means that the establishment of the concept of the unconscious had to occur in the form of a *petitio principii.* The *sine qua non* of the production of the unconscious was that this production a priori occurred on the basis of and within the result that it was supposed to produce.[43]

How is such a "crazy," self-contradictory thing as the mind's self-alienation possible? There is only one *real* way: through a ritual. And the particular ritual in which the concept of the unconscious was to be made real had to have the *form* of psychosis, as an *objective* self-alienation.

Now we can return to Jung. The realization of the *idea* of "the unconscious" through the production of it *as a natural reality* occurred in the years of crisis after Jung's separation from Freud. This crisis has

---

[43] This is of course a consequence (and an expression) of the fact that the soul's logic is a uroboric one.

often been understood as a prolonged psychotic (or at least pre-psychotic) reaction, and various traumas have been presented or rather invented as the cause of this reaction: the trauma of object loss (the loss of Freud), the trauma of an early childhood abuse, etc. These explanations are not only implausible as well as terribly naive. Jung was not a baby at the time of his separation from Freud, but in his best years, quite successful on his own, and the separation had clearly been a calculated risk long before it happened, which means that the psychological bill had thus already been paid by Jung beforehand; in general, he was far too robust a personality—a personality, as he himself said, of almost brutal strength—for the loss of Freud's friendship to have caused him to lose his mental balance. But quite apart from rebutting these accounts on the same empirical level that they purport to address, it needs to be recognized that such explanations are *clinical* and not psychological. They take the crisis literally, at face value, and do not see through it. The same needs to be said about the opposite interpretation that sees in Jung's crisis in analogy to a "shaman's illness" his personal initiation into psychic reality. With this view the crisis is also not seen through psychologically. One also succumbs to an illusory appearance, only a different one from the first.

We should honor Jung as a great psychologist by taking his crisis as a psychological one. Seen psychologically, Jung's crisis was neither a psychotic *reaction* (caused by an event or condition such as the loss of Freud or childhood traumas), nor was it *his* personal crisis. The psychotic crisis was *arranged*, an *arrangement* in the sense of Adler and Jung. It was created, invented, not by Jung as ego-personality, but by the soul as the "whole man" for its own *purposes*. This means two things:

- *logically* it was not a clinical illness, and yet semantically it indeed had the *form* of a clinical condition, the form of psychosis. Already the "state of disorientation" (*MDR* p. 170), with which it all began, was, as it were, "artificially" produced in the service of "the soul's" project. It was not an event, a fact of nature—poor Jung being helplessly so overwhelmed by his sudden loneliness that his ego simply could not cope. The state of disorientation was the *posited* beginning of a ritual, an *opus* of "the soul." This is the one aspect of a *psychological* view.

• The other aspect of a psychological view is that the crisis was not really his, Jung's *as person*, but the crisis *of psychology*, a necessity of psychological *theory*, although it, of course, played itself out in the man Jung, and this again for a particular purpose. *If* we wanted to say that it was Jung's, then it was the crisis of the thinker or theoretician and his cause, not that of the man. In this crisis "the soul" struggled to give itself a new definition, to house itself in a new building yet to be erected, namely in the idea of "the unconscious" as mythic meaning wrapped up as pure nature, empirical fact.

Before his crisis, Jung had still tried to evade his own fate by hiding under the wings of Freud's theory, in the hope that "the soul" could be fobbed off with this abode and leave *him* alone. This hope had proved to be in vain. During the work on his *Wandlungen und Symbole der Libido* it became clear to him that "the soul" demanded its right, demanded that Jung himself accept his fate to *be* the place in which the new structure of "the psychology of the unconscious" had to be erected. This had been *his* vocation.

The traditional locus of mythic and metaphysical knowledge had always been the objective mind or objective soul. This knowledge had always been out in the open, in proverbs of deep popular wisdom, in mythic and religious tales publically told or preached, in publically enacted customs and rituals, in complex metaphysical theories, in art and poetry. It had never been in people's "inner," as Jung had also known (I already quoted his: "Whenever there exists externally a conceptual or ritual form in which all the yearnings and hopes of the soul are absorbed and expressed, that is, for example, a living religion, then the soul is outside ..." *CW* 10 § 159, transl. modif.).

But in modernity, as again Jung had realized, "the struggle between light and darkness [has] move[d] to the battleground within" (*CW* 13 § 293). The individual personality had become the locus of meaning. Formerly the battleground had been conscious thought (in the wider sense that includes pictorial thinking and the entertaining of ideas) as a communal one. The battleground had been the *common land (Allmende)* of the mind. But meanwhile, as a result of the soul's history, it had left the communal sphere and withdrawn into the privacy of the individual. And this was tantamount to a shift in mode, namely, from knowing and truth (truth and knowledge are by definition public, communal) to felt experience.

This fundamental shift in the history of the soul that came about with its entrance into modernity (around 1800) had only "implicitly," in the objective logic or syntax of modernity, become a reality. It also needed to become "explicit" and semantic. What had become the logical truth of the individual also needed to be taken over by the *empirical* personality of the individual and established in it as a positively existing self-definition and way of experiencing itself. It had been Jung's calling to explicitly catch up with the implicitly already real development.

A *personal* crisis was now indispensable because the establishment of the unconscious as nature required that the locus of traditional mythic and metaphysical knowledge be transplanted from the mind or logos into the personality in its empirical, almost biological reality. It had to be "bottled up" in the empirical personality. The idea of the personality and of "the unconscious" as a part ("layer" or "region") of the personality were required because "the unconscious" could not merely intellectually, through an act of *definition*, be claimed to be pure nature; it had to be proven to exist as nature, i.e., to be actually rooted and anchored in the naturally existing person, as his interior. If this relocation was to be real, then a real (empirical, natural) process of the person was necessary. Or, the other way around, the personality had to be established as the really existing "bottle" which contained the spirit Mercurius encapsulated within itself (a bottle which is, after all, hermetically sealed).

So Jung's crisis was the empirical process in which the factual logical translation of "mind" as essential knowing from the public sphere to within, from "fire" into "water," from "up above" to "down below" (*CW* 9i § 32), in other words, from the ideality of real *thought* into naturally existing (*vorhanden*) bundles of meaning in the empirically existing personality was executed and through which "the unconscious" was established.

At the same time, despite this sinking of the spirit into the personality, "the unconscious" had to be established as a non-ego that objectively stood face to face with the I or consciousness, if it was not only to be factually *prevailing meaning*, but also "meaning" in the logical status of a fact of nature and objective existence. It was not allowed to be ego-syntonic, my own thought or conviction. It had to be a true *object*, an Other (even if of course an internal one).

Only because of the historical shift from the public sphere to the inner of the personality do we have a psychology today, as Jung told us. Psychology in Jung's sense is actually the world of myth, theology, and metaphysics that has been sunk into the crypt of the personality and thus been rendered harmless,[44] and at the same time it has been dissociated from the I. Because it was essentially a matter of sinking the mythic-metaphysical contents from the logically negative status of mindedness (of the logos) into the positivistic status of empirical existence (nature) and, furthermore, because these contents as in actuality noetic, spiritual ones could only receive the status of *empirical-factual* existence (*Vorhandenheit*) through the empirically existing personality, Jung could not become a theologian, a prophet, a founder of a religion. He had to become a psychologist. Theology and religion not only invite but require the speculative mind that opens "all the gates." They inevitably address the whole man. This was of course anathema for Jung as the founder of the psychology of the unconscious.

And because the translocation into the personality was supposed to become *real* and for this reason needed to be established as a psychology construed as a natural science rather than as a doctrine of wisdom, an empirical, natural process in the personality was required: *the ritual of a self-sacrifice.*

I said that Jung's crisis was not a clinical illness, but nevertheless had the *form* of psychosis. In medicine the word simulation is used in a moral sense and refers to a kind of deliberate fraud. In computer technology simulation has a very different meaning (cf. flight simulator). It is in this latter sense that I say this crisis was a *simulated* psychosis, a simulated *personal* crisis, or, in symbolical parlance, a *simulated* descent into the underworld; it too was "bracketed" from the outset. It is stage-managed, the same way hysterical symptoms are stage-managed.[45] It had to be a simulation

---

[44] Speculative thinking and thus a real *coniunctio* had, as we saw, been categorically excluded.

[45] (Note added March 2011) When I wrote this in 1999 or 2000, Jung's *Red Book* had not yet been available. Since it has appeared we can see more clearly that Jung's

or hysterical-like *mise en scène* because only such a simulation performs the miracle of perfectly uniting authenticity *and* a feigned condition, innocent receptivity *and* intentional fabrication, whereby authenticity and innocent receptivity are what is in fact empirically experienced by the subject and semantic, whereas the feigning and the deliberate fabrication are logical or syntactical and remain unconscious. Throughout his crisis Jung remained a dissociated personality, the duplicity of fantasy producer and innocently experiencing and observing consciousness. A genuine psychosis would have been an ordinary illness, a mishap, and not a ritual that relocates and transforms the entire logical constitution of the idea of soul. And yet a (simulated) *psychosis* was needed in order to forcefully and thus credibly[46] establish the neurosis as which the psychology of the unconscious exists in the personality as its new logical structure.

The deliberate, voluntary, or active moment of the simulated psychosis comes out in Jung's statement that "From the beginning I had conceived my voluntary confrontation with the unconscious as a scientific experiment which I myself was conducting" (*MDR*, p. 178). An experiment is something arranged. The actual execution of the beginning of the ritual or "experiment" can be pinpointed. Jung tells us, "It was during Advent of the year 1913—December 12, to be exact—that I resolved upon the decisive step. I was sitting at my desk once more, thinking over my fears [of succumbing to psychosis]. Then I let myself drop. ..." (*MDR*, p.

---

thesis of having been overwhelmed by a kind of volcanic eruption, though probably *subjectively* true, is not borne out by the *Red Book* as the document of this "eruption." My "simulation" thesis in combination with the ideas contained in Jung's own insight about the *mise en scène* character of hysterical neuroses (the simultaneity of the subjective truth of the feeling of being helplessly overwhelmed, on the one hand, and of an arrangement in Adler's sense, on the other hand) is confirmed. Toshio Kawai, in a paper "The Red Book and pre-modern cultures: The dead and sacrifice" read at ISAP, Zurich, in March 2011, says that he was not so impressed by the contents out of the unconscious, but much more by the fact that consciousness was holding its place. "... all images and visions are, however tremendous they might be, very clearly seen and grasped. And the clearness of images must be due to a stable standpoint of the observing ego. That is why Jung could have images and visions which are not confused. This does not indicate a psychosis at all. The content could be extraordinary, but the structure, syntactic is unshaken and still intact." This one could not expect if it had indeed been a volcanic eruption. For other observations concerning this issue see also my "*Liber Novus*, that is, The New Bible: A First Analysis of C.G. Jung's *Red Book*," in: *Spring 83*, Summer 2010, pp. 361–411 (now Chapter Seven of the present volume).

[46] Here we remember what we discussed above concerning the function of the "overwhelmingness" of experiences.

179). This is the *sacrificium intellectus* become real, however not merely negatively and behaviorally as a conscious abstention, a conscious "stopping to think," but positively as Jung's logical self-sacrifice, self-stultification, his reducing himself as "the whole man" to the empirical I, the ego in the form of a systematic, structural *abaissement du niveau mental.*

It is important to see that this "sinking the mind" was structural, logical, syntactic and not semantic. It was not a particular *technique* of lowering the threshold of consciousness such as it is practiced when applying the method of active imagination. Of course, there was that, too. If it had only been the application of a technique it would still have remained on the semantic level. It would have been a contingent behavior. Rather, this going under of the mind was its logical reconstitution as exclusively empirical ego that now was suddenly "*confronted*" with its *own* thoughts of consciousness, however, only with them as they that appeared incognito as ideas of "*the* unconscious."

As such this crisis was the *rite d'entrée* into the psychology of the unconscious. Jung himself referred to this extended founding ritual (it extended over several years) as his "experiment with the unconscious," a "scientific experiment" (*MDR*, pp. 178, 181, 193).

For the purpose of the project in whose grip Jung was, it was indispensable that he acquire for what in truth were *his own* images and thoughts the status of "*psychic objectivity, the reality of the psyche*" (*MDR* p.186). They had to *happen* to him as coming from a non-ego. He had to be their (logically innocent) victim. Otherwise those images and thoughts that were not allowed to be consciously his own and were pressed into unconsciousness would have had to be seen either as irrelevant, silly figments of the imagination or as symptoms of a psychic disorder, maybe even madness: alienation. One of the emerging imaginal figures, Philemon, taught him "that there are things in the psyche which I do not produce" (*MDR*, p. 183). *This* was the accomplished self-alienation of the mind, and this self-alienation was—in addition to the sinking of the "battleground" into the personality—the second purpose of Jung's crisis.

The third goal was to acquire for the alienated, disowned images the status of an independent truth *besides* public truth: *psychological truth*, so that such images could be considered to be images of mythic meaning, although they could no longer be held as one's own *conscious* thoughts or beliefs because they were no longer sustained by the logic prevailing in modernity. Without psychic objectivity (i.e., dissociation from oneself) and without psychological truth (i.e., the dignity of mythic meaning) those images and ideas would, as I pointed out, have had to be seen either as nothing but symptoms of a psychic disorder, maybe even madness, or as idle speculation, or ideology-formation. And without being (only) psychological (only *psychologically* true), they would have been a priori untenable.

Summarizing the different moments of Jung's crisis as the ritual to be performed by Jung, we can say:

- On the one hand, it needed a process of an empirically real, personal inner experience for sinking the actually mythical, religious, metaphysical images and ideas from the sphere of intelligibility into the empirical personality, thereby turning them into *psychic* events. "The unconscious" and the psychology of the unconscious could not have been established and made fully plausible through a process of conceptual argumentation, since such a process would have been suprapersonal and would have belonged to the sphere of ideas.

- On the other hand, this process, despite being a fundamentally personal one, nevertheless had at the same time to be alienated from the personality. It had to be dissociated from the personality's experiencing and thinking center, the I, the *homo totus*, so that the images and ideas would not appear as merely personal, purely subjective events in a psychologistic sense. In order to ensure that they would possess the status of objectivity despite the fact that they emerged as personal experiences, they had to intrude into consciousness with elemental force. This means that the process had to take on the form of an existentially highly pressurizing crisis, indeed, the *form* of a *psychosis*, so that the images and ideas would be equipped with the unquestionable authority and innocence of a natural event and consciousness would not have to shoulder the intellectual responsibility for them. For if the latter had been the case, it would have laid itself open to the charge of being involved in illegitimate metaphysics, mysticism, or mere ideology.

• Thirdly, despite its existentially pressurizing character and its intruding into consciousness with elemental force the psychosis could not be more than a *simulated* psychosis. In other words, it had to have the character of a *ritual* enactment or a ritual display and not that of a truly natural event (a real illness), so that the images would not *on the empirical-factual level* threaten the mind with alienation in the clinical sense of madness. Conversely, it was supposed to be capable of achieving two things:

    a) It should be able to function as a justification with general validity of the concept of "the unconscious," although, as we have seen, the process had to be an empirically real experiential process and was not under any circumstances allowed to be a justification through rational argumentation. Only to the extent that the psychotic process was not a natural event but a ritual was it capable of interiorizing the alienation or neurotic dissociation *into the objective logic or syntax of psychology* and establishing it *as* this logic of psychology—*as* the psychology *of the unconscious* or of the "*non-ego.*" Only if it was an enacted ritual was it capable of keeping that structural *neurosis* that had been installed into the office of "the psychology of the unconscious" free of the blemish of being nothing but a natural event (a personal illness) or a subjective misconception and instead providing the process with an objective logical significance (for the constitution of psychology).

    b) It should equip the experienced images with the status of *truth* so that the experience itself would obtain the character of a *revelation*, and so that, furthermore, at a time when, e.g, in art Jung's contemporaries painted the falling apart of the "natural" image of the world, the mind might nevertheless still have access to *mythic meaning*— even if only in the bottled, canned form of a commodity—and so that, finally, it might delight in feeling like the "age-old son of the mother," "the son of the maternal unconscious"[47]—even if only by way of *simulated* immediacy.

- And yet fourthly, and with this we've come full circle, the truth thus gained of the images and ideas cannot be hypostatized because it is merely an inner, merely a psychological (psychologized) truth based on personal experience. It remains severed from the general truth (which at Jung's time had its place in the natural sciences), essentially bracketed and enclosed in the psyche, so that, conversely, public consciousness on its part could also remain immunized against it.

It took a number of years for Jung to truly sink his thinking mind into unconsciousness and firmly establish his methodological position there. But once he had succeeded to solidly, i.e. *logically*, base himself on the ground (or in the dogma?) of the newly acquired, newly produced concept of "the unconscious," he could emerge from his crisis. For now he as psychologist was firmly secured in his standing as being *not* the whole man, *not* an artist, *not* a philosopher, *not* a prophet or founder of a religion, in other words, *not* the unity of empirical *and* transcendental I, but only the empirical observer *of* unconscious images as pure facts of nature.

"My entire later work," Jung wrote (*MDR* p.199, transl. modif.), "consisted in elaborating the material that had during those years burst forth from the unconscious .... It was the *prima materia* for a lifetime's work." The elaboration had above all two main emphases. On the one hand, Jung saw himself confronted with the task of proving that generally in modern individuals analogous experiences to his own ones spontaneously occur, so that the *existence* of meaning in one's inner might be safeguarded—even if not as a general, then at least as a

---

[47] *MDR*, p. 225.

collective meaning. On the other hand, even the ancient phenomena of the history of religions and of intellectual history had to be re-interpreted as formations stemming from the unconscious, so that "the unconscious" could be established as the true *naturalistically understood factual origin* of all higher meaning.

* * *

As all depth psychology, Jungian analysis has the goal of *making conscious*, which is the opposite of "the unconscious." This process of making conscious can of course refer to people's personal conflicts and complexes, their repressed emotions and memories of traumatic experiences, in other words, to the sphere of what Jung termed the personal unconscious. But it can also refer to the deeper soul processes in the context of what Jung called the individuation process, that is to say, to the symbols and images of archetypal meaning, above all symbols of transformation, of the Self, mandalas, to mention only the most marked ones. What I am going to say now about psychology's goal of making conscious refers only to the second possibility.

What *empirically* is the slow process of making unconscious contents conscious, a process that ever anew goes on in each new analysis with each new patient or analysand, is *logically* or *psychologically* precisely the continued *ritual* of the fabrication and solidification of "*the* unconscious." It needs the endless number of analysands to give to "the unconscious" a broad base in society as part of people's actual self-interpretation and self-experience. For it is only through this making conscious, i.e., through the exploration of the concrete manifestations of "the unconscious" (the *essential* contents, the contents of metaphysical and speculative significance), that "*the* unconscious" is in practice and definitively assigned to them as their true home and origin in the first place. At the same time "the unconscious" becomes more and more firmly established through this process and is erected as a wholly other, separate counterpart of consciousness. The process of making conscious in analysis *is* the process of the (logical) expatriation of these contents from consciousness. It *is* their bracketing, their being sterilized and enclosed in quotation marks, their being locked in the status of belonging to the foreign country of "the unconscious."

All the countless dreams and visionary fantasies serve the purpose of bit by bit consolidating "the collective unconscious" as a firm existence with a rich inventory.

We are familiar with the socio-political phenomenon that people from poor or politically oppressed countries strive to enter one of the rich countries of the industrialized West. Once there they can be accepted as alien residents and eventually even become naturalized. The analytical process of making the images and symbols conscious goes in the exactly opposite direction. Specific contents, which innately are in truth the native thoughts of consciousness *as* conscious-unconscious unity, which, however, due to their metaphysical, speculative quality no longer fit into the logic of modernity, are *within* consciousness all of a sudden declared to be aliens and are deported, a process whereby the psychic foreign country into which they are deported is created for the first time. The psychology of the unconscious is therefore a kind of self-fulfilling prophecy. It—logically, formally, not empirically, materially—itself creates what it is about. It thus is— again: logically—not really discovery and cognition, not an uncovering, but a formation and fabrication.

Not to know about the difference between analytical psychology's empirical activity and the logical import of this activity, that is to say, not to know that its effort of making conscious is in itself the production of "the unconscious," *is* "the unconscious," or the veritable unconsciousness of psychology.

CHAPTER SEVEN

Liber Novus, that is, The New Bible
A First Analysis of C.G. Jung's *Red Book*

A fter first finishing Jung's Red Book, an enthusiast might exclaim, to apply the words of Heinrich Heine (1830) from another context: "What a book! As great and wide as the world, extending its roots into the unplumbed depths of creation and towering up into the blue mysteries of the sky .... Sunrise and sunset, promise and fulfillment, birth and death, the whole drama of mankind, all is contained in this book ...." But for those who read it with the mind of an analytical psychologist the exclamation point at the end of the initial phrase, "What a book!" will soon change into a question mark: What *kind* of a book is the Red Book? In his Introduction, the editor clearly states: "It is nothing less than the central book in his [Jung's] oeuvre," "the single most important documentary source" (p. 221b). The validity of the second description can readily be granted. But is the Red Book really a *book*, and part of Jung's oeuvre? It is a most curious and puzzling phenomenon.

The book which is not a book

What makes a book a book is not that it is so many pages bound in one volume, which is only the meaning of "book" as a physical object. It is inherent in the notion of a book that it is aimed at an audience, a public. Jung never published his Red Book, and not only for external reasons, such as that it was not completely finished or that he feared hostile reactions. On the other hand, he time and again did toy with the idea of its publication. And the text of the book itself clearly operates with the idea of a public and frequently explicitly addresses an imaginary ye: "what I must proclaim to you" (229b)[1], "You coming men!" (230b), "Believe me: ... I give you news ..." (231a f.), "My friends, ..." (232b), which corresponds to the fact that for long stretches the diction is preachy. About the *Sermones ad mortuos* Jung said to Aniela Jaffé, that they "formed the prelude to what had been his to communicate to the world" (346n, tr.m.). At one point we hear, "Therefore I say this to you, my friend, so that you can tell your friends, and that the word may spread among the people" (254n, tr.m.), a clear indication that *within* the fantasy expressed in the book there is a rather strong wish for promulgation and having an effect, which also comes out in the statement, "What is agonizing, however, is the thought that this must occur solely for me and that perhaps no one will be able to gain light from what I bring up from the depths" (267n, tr.m.).

Jung's lifelong wavering and hesitation, which resulted in the Red Book's remaining secreted away for almost half a century beyond his death, is, I think, a clear sign that he had a distinct (and correct!) feeling for the nature of his Red Book, namely that it is an "impossible" book, because of its internal contradiction. In its character it is prophetic preaching and yet at the same time it refuses to be a doctrine for the generality. A recurrent theme is: "I do not want to be a savior, a lawgiver, an educator unto you. After all, you are not little children any more" (231b, tr.m.), a sentence that itself objectively contains the said contradiction inasmuch as its semantic message ("no teaching") contradicts its syntax (the preaching to a ye), whereas the quote cited above about the agonizing thought that "this must occur solely for me" expresses the same contradiction as a subjective emotion. If one really would not want to be a teacher or educator of others, one would not formally address others. One would leave them alone, solely minding one's own business—perhaps as Blaise Pascal, without

---

[1] I quote indiscriminately from all versions of the material given in the main text as well as in the footnotes (Black Books, Drafts, etc.), since I consider all of it as being part of the same matrix. Numbers in parentheses refer to pages, the letters "a" and "b" indicate left and right columns, respectively, of the English Red Book; "n" stands for footnote, "tr.m." for "translation modified."

breathing a word to anyone, sewed his hand-written record of a powerful visionary experience which he had on 13 November 1654, the *Mémorial*, close to his heart into his clothes, where it was found by his servant only after his death.

Jung suggested that his patients prepare their own Red Books. According to Christiana Morgan he told her, "I should advise you to put it [the material of her active imaginations] all down as beautifully as you can—in some beautifully bound book" (216a). And he added: "for you it will be your church—your cathedral," where the "for you" indicates that we have to read "YOUR church—YOUR cathedral," because it would be exclusively hers. The "church" that Jung has in mind and that is embodied in the Red Book is one that by definition has no congregation, but only one single member, the one isolated atomic individual whose personal Red Book it is. It is utterly private, subjective. And this is why it is not a book in the way Augustine's *Confessions*, Dante's *Divina Commedia*, Nietzsche's *Zarathustra* are books. They, too, may be based on personal experiences, but are unambiguously intended for the generality (even if Nietzsche's book is already a bit on the retreat, explicitly conceiving itself as *A book for all and none*). But Jung's Red Book is exclusively his, neither for all, nor for none. It has no message to be shared, communicated: "It is my mystery, not yours. ... You have your own" (246b, tr.m.). "No one besides you has your God" (329b). Ideally, if there are four billion people in the world, each one should solipsistically have *his or her own* equivalent to Jung's Red Book.

Now that the Red Book has been published after all, it can nevertheless not become public property like other books. And the literal preaching internal to its style is in itself contraceptive, fundamentally self-contained, like a tempest in a teapot. It cannot, indeed ought not, reach the reading public. If we as public were nonetheless truly reached and felt that it contained a message for us, we would have misunderstood and *misused* it.

We have to take this insight still further. One main reason why Jung hesitated to publish his Red Book, as we learn from Cary Baynes' notes, is the "difficulty with the form" (212b) that he saw. He could not find "the appropriate form" (213b). "[S]ome of it hurt (his) sense of the fitness of things terribly." He "had shrunk from putting it down as it came to" him (*ibid.*). And decades later he told Aniela Jaffé that he had immediately realized that the material expressed in it would still need to be brought into a suitable form (214a). That Jung was aware of the fact that the problem of the Red Book was one of form confirms the view that he had a fine sense of its true nature. But what is this problem of form? It can become clear through a confrontation of Jung's book with art.

Reflecting about the nature of what he was doing, Jung was certain that it was not science. But then a tempting voice tried to convince him: "That is art," to which he replied emphatically, "No it is not" (199b). The Red Book is not science, not art, but also not *Dichtung* (a poetic work) (213a), nor of course philosophy. This view of Jung's that it is not art and not poetic literature is not so much an observation or assessment as a programmatic statement: his *refusal* to let it be or become art. We have to ask: what is at stake with Jung's adamant warding off of the possibility that his Red Book might have, or might take on, art character? What was to be prevented at all cost? Asked the other way around: what would its turning into art do to the Red Book? What is it that the artist, by which I do not mean here a human being, but rather the art-producing "soul" in a human being, achieves?

If we take a portrait as an example, what turns it into a true work of art is that within itself it successfully manages to perform a radical reversal. Whereas empirically the starting point of a portrait is the real model out there, the work of art deprives this model of being its origin and source and internalizes the source of authority and conviction wholly into the work itself. The portrait as a work of art has its truth not in any likeness with the "original," it is not a copy of the original (as in Plato's idea of art), but it is its own original, containing its truth within itself, and this is why it glows from within. It is, as Hegel saw it, the self-manifestation of the absolute in sensuous form. The mystique of Leonardo's *Mona Lisa* is not derived from the real person depicted; its truth does not depend on any (in this case presumably existing) likeness with her. Rather, the art work has its ground solely in itself and thus has made itself independent, cut itself loose, from its "referent" so that it turned into a *self* that stands on its own and speaks for itself. The art-making process is the "soul's" or "mind's" performance of this "alienation": the dispossessing of the external real of its authority and the making over of this authority to, and sinking it unconditionally into, the art work. (This sinking "origin" and "authority" into the art work itself is an example of an "absolute-negative interiorization": the creation of an interiority that is not a positivity, does not exist as a positive fact. And this is why art is one instance of soul-making.) The actually portrayed person, rather than merely being literally portrayed, is, together with any likeness that the depiction may have, truly reborn, originally recreated within the painting and by virtue of it, from within its own intrinsic origin, so that any still existing likeness has been reduced to a sublated, secondary moment in the painting's self-display.

If we think of a literary work like Dante's *Divina Commedia*, it is conceivable that its starting point was inner experiences. But this is precisely not what gives Dante's work its greatness. On the contrary, its character as a cultural property of mankind results from the fact that the substance of those experiences was relentlessly released *from* the solipsistic privacy of his personal inner experiences and their factual-event character and released *into* its form *as* fantasy, *as* poetic imagination. The fantasy content was relentlessly let go of and in this way allowed to find its own center of gravity and source of authority solely within *itself as* imaginal or fantastic. At the same time it was freed from its empirical rootedness in the author's subjectivity so that it could truly come into its own, which is tantamount to saying that it was allowed to create itself anew solely from out of its fantasy-internal truth and necessity. This is a truth that it only *obtains* through the art-*making* process which, as we have seen, consists in its being dispossessed of its alleged origin or groundedness in empirical experience and unconditionally interiorized into its fantasy character itself. The psychological difference does not reserve itself. Any great artist lets his experience as well as his subjectivity (the fact that it is he who had this experience) completely go under into the very *form* of fantasy, putting all his eggs in this one basket. Art-making requires taking a plunge. The fantasy (the idea, the image) is precisely allowed to be "nothing but" fantasy. Only this unconditional releasement of the fantasy into itself, into its fantasy character, for what it may be worth, allows it to come home to itself and have its truth exclusively within itself and to be determined solely by its own internal logic. And only through this going under of the artist's subjectivity into the fantasy as self-sufficient and an end in itself does the art-work also obtain true objectivity so that the generality can experience it as its own. Dante's work does primarily not belong to Dante. As a work of art it has truly (not only literally, externally) been *published*, that is to say, its own internal form is such that it is given over to all. This is a manifestation of the psychological difference.

Art comes into being through the relentless interiorization of the positivity of the empirical experience and its "realistic" content into the negativity of the form of mere fantasy. Art-making is the relentless working-off of the *duality* of subject (author) versus object, experience (content) versus representation (form), origin or cause versus result, in favor of the singularity of the work of art that has everything it needs within itself. Dante's work speaks for itself. It comes to us with its own authority. And this is so precisely because it has logically once and for all left behind both its empirical starting point as an experience in a human subject as author and this subject itself. If they, the allegedly "original" experience and the person of the author, nonetheless figure in his work, then only as being freely recreated from within the fantasy according to its own laws. Dante's work is not a report about inner experiences from "the unconscious," not his "individuation process." It is the self-unfolding of a self-sufficient fantasy from out of *its own* internal necessity. (And we could even say that the empirical starting-point, the subjective experience, was only the first and rudimentary immediacy of what only in the finished work of art comes fully to light.) This alone is what gives it both its aesthetic beauty and its power of conviction for thousands of readers, making it truly speak to and deeply move even modern readers, readers who in their own convictions may be fundamentally removed from his early-14th century Christian world-view and cultural and practical life-conditions.

C.G. Jung performs the exactly opposite move to what I described as the art-making process. He preserves the initial duality, dissociating the positive-factual event of a vision here and the general fantasy character of the vision over there. As we hear, he "objected to presenting any of it [the Red Book material] as Dichtung [poetic fiction] when it was *all* Wahrheit [truth]" (212b f.). In other words, he tears fantasy (the form of fantasy) and truth apart as two separate, opposite realities, which comes out all the more clearly because of his allusion to the title of Goethe's work which shows both to be precisely an intricate, inseparable unity: *Dichtung und Wahrheit*. In Jung's Black Book 7 we find the statement, "You concern yourself with the form? Has the form ever been important, when it is a matter of revelation?" (211b, tr.m.). What he experienced is seen as revelation, that is, as a priori *coming* (or *intruding*) *as* truth. It is something that therefore does not need to *achieve* the status of truth by being transposed into the form of art (or any other "symbolic form" in Cassirer's sense), indeed it should not receive such a transformation. About Blake's productions Jung remarked critically, "they are an artistic production rather than an authentic representation [i.e., a mere documentation or "report *about* ..."] of unconscious processes" (*Letters 2*, pp. 513-4). This tells us that for Jung the art-making process distorts that true authenticity which for him resides only in the immediacy of the original experience itself (*Urerfahrung, Urerlebnis*; "the most immediate experience" [*CW* 11 § 396]). The ground of the truth and authenticity of a vision is kept external to its representation, such as in the Red Book, by being declared to have been an experience as factual event. "There was nothing of conscious structure in these fantasies, they were just events that happened" (*Analytical Psychology* 97). Happenings! The positivity of "events and experiences" (*MDR* 182)! The *facticity* of their occurrence!

But all art *is* of "conscious structure" through and through, otherwise dogs would be able to appreciate a statue or painting as art rather than as a mere thing. Fantasies, if they are consciously released into their fantasy character and not deliberately construed as reports about factual events, are in themselves thoroughly illumined, *as* art works events of consciousness.

As we already heard, Jung insisted, concerning his fantasy material: "No, it is not art! On the contrary, it is nature" (*MDR* 186). This is, by the way, diametrically opposed to the thinking of the alchemists, for whom *quod natura relinquit imperfectum ars perficit*. According to this view, truth can only come about through the human processing of what is naturally given as mere raw material, as factual prima materia. Truth is the end-product of a long opus *contra naturam*. What is naturally given is ipso facto precisely not (yet) true. Art *creates* its own origin as and within the work of art. But Jung wants to identify truth with factual existence, as if it were a piece of nature: "An elephant is true because it exists" (*CW* 11 § 5). Ultimately Jung's concept of psychic truth boils down to sheer overwhelmingness, brutal power: "the overpowering force of the original experiences" (360), "quite simply experiences" (365a), "The unshakeableness of the experience"

(338b). Jung is here a positivist and, in a sense, existentialist. His word truth has nothing to do any more with truth in its authentic sense.

Jung is here committed to a logic of externality and otherness. For him, the Red Book as an object has its truth, origin, and reality not in itself, but fundamentally outside of itself, in the literal experiences that gave rise to it. Because the event of the overwhelming experience is what really counts, he could not radically release the fantasy substance itself of his experience into its own, into logically being fantasy, having the form of fantasy, being art (or, another possibility, being philosophy or *Dichtung*). He needed to emphatically reject the notion of art for his Red Book because what he wanted to cling to and preserve at all cost was the so-called "original" experience external to and underlying the Red Book: the experience which for him was supposed to be the sole locus of truth and authenticity. Unthinkable that he could have released the substance of his experiences from the facticity of the experiences as well as from himself as the subject who had such experience into the negativity of the form of fantasy. Rather than *à corps perdu* plunging into the fantasy world *as* fantasy world and thus as a mental, conscious reality, as speculation, that is, rather than relentlessly releasing his experience, and himself going under, into "the soul," his whole project was precisely to extract from the fantasy the positivity of a literal external cause of it—ultimately "the primal world of the unconscious" (*MDR* 200) and posit it as its a priori. "The unconscious" is the objectified, literalized, externalized—and thus killed—soul: "the soul" by definition deprived of its "being of conscious structure" or its being thought.

The clinging to the factual event of one's experience over against the fantasy character of what has been experienced is at the same time the self-preservation (or initial self-institution) of the ego (the structure or definition of the subject as "the ego" in the sense of personalistic psychology). The I is not willing to let go of itself and go under into its fantasies, so that they might be released into their inherent truth. This is why Jung described this period of his life as (*his*) "Confrontation with the Unconscious," focusing, rather than on the *work* to be *produced*, on the crisis he had to go through and on his tormenting doubts as to his own sanity. And it is why he tried to substitute for the suggestion that what he was doing was art the following theory about the telos of the process: "Perhaps my unconscious is forming a personality that is not I" (199b). This is already *in nuce* the dogma of Jung's psychologistic "personality cult," as one might term it. He circled around *himself* (which might, e.g., be contrasted with mental-illness-plagued van Gogh's dedication to his painting). The creative impulse, which without doubt was at work in Jung, was diverted from its own direction towards the production of truth (in *works* of art, literature, philosophy, music), i.e., towards soul-making, and abused for egoic purposes (self-development). The truth is not allowed to come home to *itself*, but is forced down into the human being as (a new) literal personality.

Cause and telos are in Jung's scheme dissociated and set up as literal and external (past event or future entity, respectively). Art, poetry, philosophical thought (in other words, soul), by contrast, would be what is in between those two: *presence*, because owing to the absolute-negative interiorization of the experienced fantasy into itself, into its truth, into its own internal ground and *archê*, it contains both its cause and its telos only within its absolute negativity.

Because the Red Book has the mystery and truth that it is about fundamentally outside itself in Jung's factual "original" experience, on the one hand, and in the "new personality" to be formed in the positively existing civil man Jung, on the other hand, it is really an *unwritten* book. In Plato scholarship one distinguishes between Plato's exoteric written dialogues made available to the general public and his "unwritten doctrine" (*agrapha dogmata*) made known only orally to the esoteric inner circle of his disciples. Jung's book is esoteric in a much more radical, namely absolute, sense. Plato logically fully *released* his unwritten doctrine out into the open, and thus logically "published" it, even if only orally to select disciples; he could do so because he obviously had relentlessly abandoned himself to the inner truth of his thought experience. Potentially he could therefore also have written down his *agrapha dogmata*. But Jung's Red Book is the paradox of his "*written* unwritten (and on principle unwriteable) truth": literally, factually written, but logically unwritten. It merely *points to* the mystery that is *per definitionem* solely his mystery and not ours. "The myth commences, the one that can only be lived, not sung, the one that sings itself" (328b, tr.m.), we read at one point in the Red Book. The authentic locus of his truth is now the positivity of *Existenz*, real life: "first and exclusively and solely in one's own person" (*CW* 7,

p. 5, tr.m.), in man whose nature is now no longer comprehended as his *theoretical* I (classical metaphysics) or his *poietic* soul (Nietzsche), but as what Heidegger would later term his mere *Dasein*.

Just as the authentic locus of the Christian truth is not the church as cathedral, but the human heart, so the authentic place of Jung's truth is not the Red Book, which, as we know, he considered his church, his cathedral. His truth has its authenticity only in the factual events of his "immediate experiences" themselves.

Jung's paintings and calligraphy are only secondary illustrations for the external purpose of satisfying his wish to show his *subjective* esteem. If they were art, they would shine from within themselves. The historistic imitation of a medieval illuminated book is the telltale sign that what the Red Book contains has its worth not in itself, but only in the feeling of the man C.G. Jung. "I always knew that these experiences contained something precious, and therefore I knew of nothing better than to write them down in a 'precious,' that is to say, costly book and to paint the images that emerged through reliving it all ..." (360). Decoration. Ego work. It had to be ego work because the fantasy had not been released into its truth, into the *form* of truth. Which is why its truth could not shine forth from it of its own accord. And the fact that the calligraphy and, to a lesser degree, the paintings imitate medieval forms of expression clearly reveals that the visual aspect of the Red Book is not the self-expression, i.e., not the intrinsic form, of the material presented *itself*. Superimposed. An accessory. Inauthentic. Thus Jung's cited critique of Blake ("an artistic production rather than an authentic representation of unconscious processes") reflects upon his own production, if we understand it in a different sense from his. (This is quite apart from the fact that the idea of an *authentic* representation of unconscious processes is in itself fallacious. Authenticity is never the gift of the unconscious processes themselves, of raw natural events, which inevitably come in the state of *imperfection* and *inauthenticity*. If at all, authenticity can only be the *produced result* of the artist's or adept's *ars*).

The Red Book has meanwhile been published. But published only the way art works can nowadays be *technically reproduced*. We can never get behind the reproduction to the "original"—because Jung's own volume is in itself not, and was not supposed to be, the original. Dante's *Divina Commedia*, by contrast, does not need a costly leather binding. Even if it comes to us in a wretched, cheaply printed paperback copy we have nevertheless the original: because as art and philosophical thought it has its illumining and heart-warming truth absolute-negatively within itself, a truth that freely communicates itself to anybody capable and willing to abandon himself to it. It is everybody's mystery, not only Dante's.

Pitfalls for the superficial observer

Madness. In his *Nachwort* (1959) Jung wrote about the Red Book, "To the superficial observer, it will appear like madness" (360). But he remains a superficial observer himself to the extent that he ascribes the not-madness only to the fact that he was secondarily, after the fact, able to capture and contain the overwhelming power of the original experiences. What we have to realize is that the material is not psychotic from the outset. Clinical categories and a psychiatric, diagnostic approach are misplaced. We need a psychological, "final-constructive" approach and to comprehend the whole process as part of a systematic soul opus. About a certain traumatic experience of a hysterical patient Jung wrote: "The fright and the apparently traumatic effect of the childhood experience are merely staged, but staged in the peculiar way characteristic of hysteria, so that the *mise en scène* appears almost exactly like a reality" (*CW* 4 § 364). By the same token, the *apparently* psychotic character of some of Jung's material must be seen through as an *arrangement* (in Adler's sense), as staged, but staged (a) *as* not staged and (b) of course not staged by the experiencing ego personality, but by "the soul"—just as that patient's fright was of course not staged by her ego-personality, but by her neurotic "soul" for *its* neurotic purposes. What in Jung's case "the soul" needed to stage for the benefit of the experiencing Jung through the seemingly psychotic character of the images was the appearance of the *absolutely overwhelming* power of the experiences. It was needed to produce the sense of the absolute immediacy of authentic psychic experience. But with this notion we have already entered the sphere of the second pitfall.

Immediate experience, volcanic eruption, being unintentional. To the superficial observer it might appear as if the fantasy material came to Jung as immediate experience (which was of course also Jung's own view). That he saw it this way shows that he did not look at what happened from the standpoint of soul, but from that of only one half of the whole: the experiencing ego personality. He identified with the latter and therefore took the overwhelmingness that the experiences had for the I at face value, the same way his hysterical patient had taken her fear at face value. In the case of this patient Jung had been able to see the whole picture, but not in his own case.

Psychologically it is a grave mistake to privilege one element of a dream, fantasy, or psychic experience, for example the I, taking it literally by setting it up as a given existing outside the fantasy, in "reality," and thus as already known from "reality," and taking all other elements only as products of fantasy or reactions to the "given reality." The I is just as internal to the fantasy as they are; it is an imaginal, "fantastic" I and needs to be seen through. A dream or fantasy within itself *invents*, just as everything else in it, so also the experiencing I in the particular form that is necessary for *this* fantasy. As psychologists we always have to take responsibility for the whole psychic phenomenon.

However, that Jung here took the I simply for granted "without questions asked" is not so much to be viewed as a failure of his, but rather as a necessary ingredient of what the soul wanted to create with the whole process Jung underwent. Conversely, his *extrajection* of the experiencing I from out of the fantasy character of the experience— his identifying it *tel quel* with himself as the real person that he was—shows that his understanding of it was not a psychological one, but one that paradoxically stayed *fantasy-internal*, enveloped in the external impressions that the fantasy wanted to produce. We could also say that his interpretations of his experiences do the fantasy experiences' bidding and are thus a continuation of them, although in the medium of conscious reflection.[2] They are additional *psychic* phenomena in the same vein, rather than *psychological* interpretations.

The unmediatedness thesis is contradicted by a number of features. As Shamdasani pointed out in his Introduction and as any reader will see right away, much of the content of the Red Book is directly derived from Jung's reading (200b). It is the work of a scholar and in fact largely took place in his library (203a). The Nietzsche imitation in

[2] Following a suggestion by Greg Mogenson (personal communication), this, Jung's sense of fantasy, could be referred to, in keeping with his idea of "overmeaning" (see below), as: overfantasy.

style, and partly in intent, is striking. The Red Book at one point says, "the soul is everywhere that scholarly knowledge is not" (233b), a radical disjunction! If that were true, then the Red Book would not be an expression of soul since it is steeped in learnedness.

Another point is that the process recorded in the Red Book was started as an experiment, as Jung himself said repeatedly. Experiments are performed by the scientific mind. There was certainly spontaneity within this experiment and for the experiencing subject. But the experiment itself as a whole was a deliberate technical undertaking. Jung uses phrases like: "when I switched off consciousness" (cf. 200b), "I used the same technique of the descent" (*Analytical Psychology* 63), an "insane asylum of my own *making*" (*ibid.* 24, my ital.), "But if we *turn* the God *into* fantasy" (283a, my ital.), which betray an element of purposeful design and artifice.

The experiences were also by no means unintentional. It is the "superficial observer" and fantasy-syntonic I in the Red Book that says, "It has happened thus to me. And it happened in a way that I neither expected nor wished for" (338b, tr.m.). In truth, however, there is from the outset a powerful will or craving underlying it all, which shows itself time and again in the Red Book. "I wanted my God for better or worse [i.e., at all cost]" (289a, tr.m.). "And what wouldn't you give for a single look into the infinite things that are to come? Would they not even be worth a sin for you?" (246a, tr.m.) "And I felt it again to be absolutely certain that my life would have broken in half if I failed to heal my God" (281b, tr.m.). "... an unspeakable greed seizes you ..." (270a). There are, more theoretically, apodictic-dogmatic presuppositions like "We need the life of eternity" (253b) or "We lack nothing more than divine force" (281b, tr.m.), which are hardly reconcilable with the truly empirical stance of an unprejudiced experimenter. In general the text is soaked in the rhetoric of wanting, longing, expectation. We hear from one figure of "the excess of my desire" (342a, tr.m.), another felt seduced "desirously stretching my hand after the divine mysteries" (275b). The attitude demanded in the Red Book concerning one particular psychic phenomenon ("joy"), but applying to psychic experience at large, namely that it "should neither be made nor sought; it should come, when it must come. ... [i]t comes and exists of its own accord, and is not sought here and there" (341b, tr.m.) is not corroborated by the Red Book experience as a whole. It is not so innocent. There was from the beginning an unspoken and apparently subjectively unconscious "quod esset demonstrandum," in other words, a hidden agenda, a strategic goal—obvious today but unconscious to Jung, an agenda whose *spelled out execution* occurred in Jung's years-long fantasy process.

Shamdasani rightly characterizes the Red Book material as "dramatized thinking in pictorial form" (200b). The material is in itself highly reflected. *Malgré* Jung's self-stylization, it is a work of speculative thought, thought, however, not presented in the form of thought, but sunk into the form of, and disguised as, spontaneous immediate experiences (and their interpretation). Jung lets his own thought play itself out in dialogue form, as an interplay between different figures, one of which is the I. No doubt, subjectively it probably was overwhelming and in part surprising *for* the fantasizing Jung. But part of the whole project was precisely to create the appearance of a "natural event," spontaneous occurrence, true revelation and to impress the I accordingly in order to take it in. But *we* as psychologists must not be deceived by this superficial impression staged for a particular purpose.

Taking together the strong will as driving force behind the Red Book and its character as dramatized thinking, we could call the process that unfolds in it *wishful thinking* (in the strict, literal sense of this phrase).

Going *in medias res*. The superficial observer, if he is a Jungian enthusiast, might thirdly want to delve directly into the symbolism of the images presented in the Red Book and of the narrative of the successive events, in order to mine them for meaning or wisdom, using the whole process as an authentic model of the individuation process. But the psychological task is to see through. Not to indulge. We are analysts. Not consumers of mysterious images and ideologies.

Gnosticism. In view of names like Abraxas, Phanes, Pleroma and numerous corresponding ideas known from the Gnostics in late antiquity, the superficial observer might jump to the conclusion that these figures or phenomena, just like that, represent the ancient Gnostic ones of the same name. But we must not naively take them at face value. In modern authors we must not identify sight unseen the ancient names they use with the same-named ancient mythological phenomena. Richard Wagner's Valkyries are not a revival of ancient Teutonic Valkyries. Nietzsche's Zarathustra is not identical with the ancient Iranian sage. And Nietzsche's Dionysos must not be confused with the ancient Greek god by the same name.[3] Psychoanalysis developed the notion of "screen memories." While our case is not one of screen *memories*, the familiar names are nevertheless similarly masks (though not disguises!) representing something unfamiliar, an idea, phenomenon, or reality that in each case needs to be inferred and reconstructed exclusively from the modern text and its modern context. It is fundamentally new wine that ferments in those old bottles. The figures just mentioned are natives of the 19th century. It is a hermeneutic principle that we must not presume any elements in a work (or, for that matter, in a dream) to be already known from outside the work or dream and mechanically insert into it this "known" ready-made meaning. Everything must be understood in terms of its own time. We need to see that the issues debated and at stake in creative works (and thus also in the symbols and figures that appear in them) belong to the particular historical locus that gave rise to those works.

The same applies to Jung's Red Book. It is a child of its own time and on a deep level it is exclusively concerned with the burning deep intellectual issues of his age. It is not a historical study or a book about ancient mythology and the religious speculation of the Gnostics, nor their resumption or revival. In order to find out what the mythological or Gnostic names known from ancient times in fact represent in the Red Book, we must therefore not consult books on ancient mythology and religion, which, although they may give us certain superficial hints, on the main lead astray. We have to look at their actual phenomenology as well as at the function they have within the Red Book.

An example in point is the motif of the dead who come to Jerusalem in the *Septem Sermones* context. This sounds highly "mythological," and Gnostic. We are tempted to think of the dead in terms of the underworld and the ancestor cult of ancient cultures, of

---

[3] Jung felt that Nietzsche, a classical philologist, misnamed Dionysus. He suggested that the god in fact experienced and meant by Nietzsche was much rather the Germanic Wotan. Thus on the one hand, Jung is aware of the fact that the name must not be taken at face value. On the other hand, by simply foisting *another archaic* God on him he changes the particular object of reference, but retains the same logic of "external referent" that also prevails in the other case of seeing in the 19th century figure a veritable archaic reality.

Biblical times, of long-bygone ages and a mysterious exotic world. But when we hear that the dead are those who "repudiated Christian belief and hence turned into those that Christian belief likewise rejected" (348b) and that they themselves insist: "We are not miserable, we are intelligent, our thinking and feeling is as pure as clear water. We praise our reason. We mock superstition" (353a), we realize that they are by no means, the way they are represented in the Red Book's mythologizing style, the dead of former ages, but in truth very much alive. They represent the *Inbild* (envisioned quintessence) of conventional modern man at large as a product of the Enlightenment, Jung's contemporaries (including his own father), who are merely interpreted by the Red Book as fundamentally dead souls who waver between their anti-religious convictions and their deep unsatiable craving for religious meaning and inspiration. The dead are the image for *contemporary collective consciousness*, the embodied "spirit of this time."

Jung's Red Book is a work of thought. It is the soul's (or the historical locus's) attempt to provide an answer to the "spirit of this time." In particular it is "Jung's" wrestling with the spiritual situation of contemporary Christianity and at the same time, as it were, *his* "Answer to 'Nietzsche.'" About the anchorites one of the texts states: "they were those who drew the most inexorable conclusion and consequence from the psychological necessity of their time" (267n, tr.m.). This is precisely what the Red Book wants (tries) to do, too.

I said it is a work of thought, indeed, speculative thought. It is not primarily a work of spontaneous inner experience. What it is ultimately and really about is "the last and simplest things" (229b), "the last mysteries of becoming and passing away" (230a), "the infinite things of what is to come" (246a, tr.m.), "the divine mysteries" (275b). Religion and metaphysics (in the colloquial sense of the word).

"It all began then; the later details are only supplements and clarifications of the material that burst forth from the unconscious." To the superficial observer it might seem that Jung's *Collected Works* are, as it were, the outgrowth of the experiences recorded in the Red Book. This is Jung's own thesis ("The first imaginings and dreams were like fiery, molten basalt, from which the stone crystallized, upon which

I could work" [219b], from *Erinnerungen* p. 203). And when
Shamdasani, as we heard, said that the Red Book is "the central book
in his [Jung's] oeuvre," he seems to support the idea of the seamless
continuity between, and unity of, this book and Jung's oeuvre.

Now it is obvious that many of the ideas and positions known
from Jung's published work in fact already occur in the Red Book,
e.g., the idea of psychic objectivity; of the singular importance of the
individual; Jung's special concept of the self; and even his major
"theological" (better: theosophical) conceptions published in *Aion* and
Answer to Job. On a surface level, semantically, there can be no doubt
that the Red Book material represents the nucleus of the psychology
laid down in Jung's published oeuvre.

So while historically speaking the Red Book is the source of Jung's
"written psychology," logically this "written psychology" is, however,
ashamed of its factual origin in the experiences underlying the Red
Book. This comes out most blatantly in the fact that when Jung used
Red Book material (dreams, visions, or mandala paintings) in his
published works, he time and again felt the need to do so anonymously,
camouflaging his own products as those of other people, of his patients.
Incredible for a psychologist who prided himself on his empiricism,
and doubly incredible considering the repeated motif in the Red Book
of being forced to speak (229b): "But you should speak. Why have
you received the revelation. You should not hide it" (211b), "it also
gave me the courage to say all of that which I have written in the earlier
part of this book" (336b). "[Even if my experience of God were a
deception] I would nevertheless have to *confess* to this experience and
recognize the God in it. ... And even if the God had revealed himself
in a meaningless abomination, I couldn't help but *avow* that I have
experienced God in it" (338b, tr.m., my italics). But the point is
that Jung did not have the courage to avow: to make the Red Book
available. He did not speak. He hid behind the front of alleged
patients. At best he dropped, late in life, some cryptic hints to his
personal experiences such as "I do not believe, I know." And when
diagnosed by Martin Buber as a Gnostic on account of his *Septem
Sermones*, Jung, rather than owning up to this production of his
(so precious to him), dissociated himself from his text, brushing it
off as "a sin of my youth ..., which consists in my once having

perpetrated a poem" (*CW* 18 § 1501). Jung blamed Buber (and other critics) of simply being ignorant of "clinical experience," when in reality the basis of his views was not clinical experience at all, but his own subjective fantasy experiences, his speculations.

As a responsible scientist Jung would have had to present those mandalas etc., as material stemming from his own subjective experience. More than that, precisely if he felt that his scientific work was basically the elaboration of his early personal experiences, he would have had to present all of the Red Book material. An empiricist has to put his cards, all his cards, on the table. Scientifically, self-experiments do not have much value as evidence. They are, as it were, "uroboric," simply displaying the experimenter's subjective presuppositions, predilections, and ideological needs. In his "spontaneous" experiences Jung is merely "incestuously" dealing with his own *projections* (not "*revelations*"[4] from "the unconscious"). Even the experiences in the consulting room are not really conclusive in an evidential sense because, as, e.g., Jung himself rightly wrote to James Kirsch on 29 Sept. 1934: "With regard to your patient, it is quite correct that her dreams are occasioned by *you*. ... As soon as certain patients come to me for treatment, the type of dream changes. In the deepest sense we all dream not *out of ourselves* but out of what lies *between us and the other*" (*Letters 1*, p. 172). Science needs blind or even double-blind experiments, not ones in which test subject and experimenter are the same.

Why did Jung feel the need in his oeuvre to deny (not the content of those dreams, painted pictures, and convictions, but) the fact of their having their real origin in his own subjective fantasies (fantasies which, after all, were so precious to him that he needed to put them down in an expensive leather-bound volume and spent years on their calligraphic presentation)? Why did he behave much like Peter, who also denied what he loved dearly, the Lord? The answer is that something in Jung must have been keenly aware of the fundamental discrepancy, indeed incompatibility, between his fantasy experiences and his "scientific" work as a psychologist. This is why he had to supply

---

[4] Whereas "projection" only formally (neutrally) denotes that something (e.g., an unconscious presupposition or prejudice) has been "thrown" out so that it now appears to consciousness "out there" in objectified form, "revelation" is primarily a religious term implying (ultimately divine) authority, truth, and higher meaning.

a false origin to his own material when using it in his works (similarly to how sometimes important witnesses against Mafia bosses are provided with a new identity by the police), namely an origin in his professional work as an analyst who merely objectively reported what he encountered in his consulting room during many years of clinical experience. The inclusion in his work of his private images and ideas involves a real uprooting of those images and ideas from their own ground and their transplantation into a very different ground or discourse, we could say, from the sphere of Jung's "personality no. 2" and its *speculative thought* to that of "personality no. 1." Jung rode two different horses. There is a logical discontinuity between his experiences and his oeuvre.

"I am much amused that you think I have 'become professorial.' Evidently I have successfully deceived [!] even your eagle eye. One must have a good exterior [*eine gute Exoterik*] 'dans ce meilleur des mondes possibles,'" Jung wrote to Hermann Hesse on 18 Sep 1934 (*Letters 1*, p. 171). Like Plato's esoteric "unwritten teaching" versus his exoteric written dialogues (but in very different ways and for different reasons, see above), Jung's Red Book world and the world of his published oeuvre are heterogeneous: his Red Book is *absolutely* esoteric because it is not even addressed to an inner circle of disciples, but only to himself. It is not psychology, not a contribution to psychology as a theory, but only psychic raw material. As such it can of course become an object of psychological examination, but only with a view to learning what was going on in, and what it meant for, the one individual C.G. Jung—and, of course, in the case of a great man like Jung, above all for the historical locus that expressed itself through him.

Psychology, by contrast, in its logical form inevitably belongs to the generality. In it, universal reason is addressed. The psychologist enters the field not as the private individual that he also is, but as a member of the scientific community and thus as his (personal) attempt to be in the logical status of consciousness-as-such. This is why we have the notion of the "psychological *equation*." The logical form of a psychology and a psychologist's style of speaking have to be such that they within themselves accept the task of justifying themselves precisely before the "spirit of this time," whereas the Red Book says: "No one and nothing can justify what I must proclaim to you. Justification is superfluous to me, since I have no choice, but I must" (229b).

Compulsion. No *logon didonai*. Of course not, because it is (allegedly) merely a natural event. Explicitly conceived as a revelation coming with brutal force, it is of merely solipsistic significance. A revelation can be neither questioned nor criticized, no more than an oak tree or a thunderstorm. It is the way it is, and as such it leaves no room for the psychological equation's equal sign, which makes only sense if there is a duality of a human person and the theoretical claims it makes.

In his oeuvre, however, Jung objectively spoke in the logical form of psychology. As psychologist he felt responsible for the groundedness and general comprehensibility of his statements (which is also why he disguised his personal material as material coming from patients). As psychologist he spoke from the standpoint of consciousness-as-such, as a member of the scientific community. Whether he was successful or not in doing this, whether his grounds stand up to criticism or not, is another question, of no concern in the present context. What counts in our context is the logical form of the discourse of his oeuvre.

As important as the Red Book is *for historical* "Jung studies," *as psychologists* we are well advised to dissociate ourselves from the Red Book and instead base our work on Jung's published psychology, and *critically* so at that. We have not become psychologists in order to listen to revelations and to adopt a pseudo-religious ideology of "the self" (or each develop our own one). Psychology is not about the self in the first place. It is the study of "the soul," the discipline of absolute-negative interiority. (I gave an example of absolute-negative interiorization above in what I said about art. The Jungian self presupposes a "positivistic" interiorization into the human being, which ends up with "*the* self" as Other, as an It. Soul-making, by contrast, is the interiorization of whatever phenomenon into *itself*, its own logically negative [mercurial] depth.) The fact that Jung himself abruptly discontinued this project altogether and, further, that when decades later adding an "Epilogue" he stopped in the middle of a sentence, can serve us as a supporting symbol of the necessity of such a dissociation from the Red Book. In *MDR* Jung even explicitly dissociated himself from the Red Book in favor of his scientific work:

"Therefore I gave up this estheticizing tendency in good time, in favor of a rigorous process of *understanding*. I saw that so much fantasy needed firm ground underfoot, and that I must first return wholly to human reality. This reality consisted for me in scientific comprehension" (p. 188, tr. m.).

The project

Utopia. Now we are ready to look at what the Red Book is actually about and wants to achieve. I already called it Jung's "Answer to Nietzsche." The 19th century as the first phase of *modern* thinking had been the century of the great utopias. After Feuerbach's dream of primordial "conversation" in the sense of "man's community with man," Kierkegaard's dream of the solitary individual's "leap into faith," Marx's dream of a "communist society," the last in the row was Nietzsche's hope for a fundamentally new possibility of creativity, true *poiêsis* (in contrast to simulated creativity, the merely reified and *represented* productive potential of man). Nietzsche *imaged* the event of this new creation of creativeness as Dionysus's coming to Ariadne, to the potentially creative, but to begin with deserted, soul. However, Dionysus's Parousia did not, could not happen.

With the fundamental collapse of Nietzsche's hope the potential of utopian thought—as true *thought*—was exhausted, the utopian dream in thought was over; great philosophical thought was once and for all cured of it.[5] This fundamental disappointment gave room to a radically sobered stance. The early 20th century thus saw the triumphant progress of mathematical logic and Wittgenstein's critique of language, on the one hand, and of Husserl's phenomenology as strict science, on the other hand. Husserl's thinking was the philosophical ancestor of the thought of Heidegger, Sartre, Lacan, Levinas, and Derrida, to mention only a few. The *utopian* impulse could now survive only where it withdrew into the lowlands of thoughtless and literalistic political ideology and practice (communism, fascism), where "ideology" means historically decidedly obsolete thought that is

---

[5] On this whole theme of 19th century utopian thinking and on Nietzsche in particular see especially Claus-Artur Scheier, *Nietzsches Labyrinth. Das ursprüngliche Denken und die Seele*, Freiburg/München (Alber) 1985 and *idem*, "Einleitung," in: Friedrich Nietzsche, *Ecce auctor. Die Vorreden von 1886*, Hamburg (Felix Meiner) 1990, pp. vii–cxxiii.

nevertheless held on to dogmatically as a doctrine and subjective belief system to be literally put into practice by *empirical man*.

In this post-Nietzschean situation Jung started his own work. As we see, he could neither take the self-negation of Nietzsche's vision for an answer, nor could he, like Rudolf Steiner, Alfred Schuler, Ludwig Klages, etc., develop a nostalgic *Weltanschauung*, nor become a political activist. He remained a *thinker* and yet insisted on taking over the heritage of Nietzsche's utopian vision and carrying it further, even if in radically altered form. After the collapse of Nietzsche's vision he could rescue the utopian impulse into the new century only because he believed to be able to "correct" and surpass the Nietzschean position and at the same time to transport *essential thought as such*, or the locus of truth, away from its home ground to a fundamentally *new arena*.

But before we can get to this theme of how the utopian project could be continued *as* "thought" even at a time when it had become historically obsolete, let us look at how the utopian character shows in the Red Book.

The new. What is to come. The dominant orientation of the Red Book is toward the future. Already the title Jung gave it, *Liber novus*, emphasizes its utopian character, and the title of its "Liber Primus" makes it explicit once more: "The Way of What is to Come." Unlike Thomas More's *De nova insula U-topia* (1516) or Bacon's *Nova Atlantis* (1626), the predicate "novus" in Jung's book title does not refer to an island or other geographical place. It qualifies "book." Now it is so that every book that is written comes as a new book. *Novus* cannot mean this triviality. The attribute 'new' must be used in an eminent sense. It must indicate that this book is in competition with *the* previous book and enters the scene with the claim of surpassing it and taking its place. *Liber* is the Latin translation of Greek *biblion*, from whose plural *biblia*, the book of books, we have our word "Bible." When Jung told Christiana Morgan that if she made her own Red Book, "for you it will be your church—your cathedral," he could just as well have said, "your Bible." It is fitting that a book which teaches that rather than "Christians" we all ought to ourselves be "Christs" and which claims to bring to completion the mystery of the Christ (left incomplete by Christ himself) calls itself *Liber novus*.

Throughout the text of the Red Book the commitment to the future is determining: "I read the gospels and seek their meaning which is yet to come, ... their hidden meaning which points to the future" (272a f.), one character, Ammonius, says; "You engender and give birth to what is yet to come" (234b); "My friends, if you knew what depths of the future you carry inside you! Those who descend into their own depths behold what is to come" (241n, tr.m.). "[T]hen your God rises from the radiant cradle, to the immeasurable height of the future, to the maturity and fullness of the coming time" (234a). Time and again we hear of the "new God," or of the "newly appearing God" (301n).

Relentless dismissal of the present. In order for the utopia to have a chance, the prevailing reality has to be logically cleared away. Already Jung's earliest visions are visions of the destruction of old Europe. In the name of "the spirit of the depths" the Red Book states, "for the spirit of this time had nothing to give me any more" (252n, tr.m.). The I of the Red Book has broken with the present, opted out of its own time. To be sure, there is also this isolated statement: "Do not ask after the morrow, the present [*das Heute*] shall be sufficient unto you" (238b, tr.m.). But this is precisely what is not practiced in the Red Book. Its true spirit is expressed in that other statement: "We love only what is coming, not what is" (357b).

Part of the rejection of the present is the vehement anti-Enlightenment impulse. "[T]he enlightened live there. ... They're actually dangerous since they cook the strongest poisons from which even I must protect myself" (282b). "[W]hat you call poison is science" (278b) "'Have you no Gods anymore?' I: 'No, words are all we have'" (279a). "This is also the fate of the Logos: in the end it poisons us all" (280b). "Judgment must fall from you .... Utterly poor, miserable, humble, ignorant, go on through the gate" (246b, tr.m.).

The dismissal of the present also includes the diagnosis of the death of God and its inexorable acceptance. "The dear old God has died, and it is good that way" (333b). "The one God is dead— yes, truly, he died" (357b). "He probably does not know—we have no more prayers. How should he know about our nakedness and poverty?" (271a). I already quoted: "'Have you no Gods anymore?'

I: 'No, words are all we have'" (279a). "Science has taken from us the capacity of belief" (278a).

By the same token, Christianity is rejected, with a strong affect. Christ is once derogatorily described as "the pale God of Asians [der bleiche Asiatengott] who was nailed to the wood like a chicken marten" (242b, tr.m.). Numerous biblical adages are parodied or reversed, just one example: "for thine is our power and glory" (345b, tr.m.). Christianity is viewed as deceptive, as making us blind. "Do not let the teachings of Christianity deceive you!" (234n). "Your Christian shrouds have fallen, the veils that blinded your eyes" (341b); "then you will be free and beyond Christianity" (235b). "We want to continue living with a new God, a hero beyond Christ" (242n).

Right at the beginning we hear that "God is an image, and those who worship him must worship him in the image of the overmeaning" (229b, tr.m.), which is a slap in the face of Christianity: the reversal of John 4:24 ("God is Spirit: and they that worship him must worship him in spirit and in truth").

> Here I have to insert a comment on this translation. Jung wrote *Übersinn* where the English translation says "supreme meaning." *Übersinn* is a neologism of Jung's and is clearly modeled after Nietzsche's *Übermensch* (overman). It implies a meaning that is "over," "beyond," "in excess of" meaning. If, for this crucial, recurring Red Book term, "supreme meaning" is used as the translation for *Übersinn*, the shock of "overmeaning" is eliminated, the concept is rendered harmless, even wonderful. But what the Red Book has in mind is outrageous, which also comes out in the genesis of "*Übersinn*": it is said (*ibid.*) to come about through the "melting together of sense [*Sinn*] and nonsense [*Widersinn*]" (lit. "counter-meaning," i.e., the diametrical opposite or violation of meaning, absurdity). The use of "supreme meaning" renders the sentence following the one just quoted unintelligible: "The supreme meaning is not a meaning and not an absurdity [*Widersinn*, counter-meaning] ..." (230a). This is wrong on both counts: a supreme meaning is of course still a meaning (the highest one, at that), and it is of course *not* an absurdity, since if it were it would not be supreme meaning. But the "overmeaning" is, as the Red Book rightly says, indeed *not* a meaning; because it exists as the "melting together" of meaning and its very opposite so

that its meaning character is destroyed. For the same reason, but in opposite direction, it is also not an absurdity (*Widersinn*). The overmeaning is—at least allegedly—catapulted beyond the whole level of the opposites of meaning and absurdity.[6]—It is probably not possible to imitate in English Jung's play with the words *Sinn, Übersinn, Widersinn, Unsinn.* But since these words are of terminological significance, it is problematic that the English translation does not consistently use the same English word for one and the same Red Book term. It translates *Sinn* one time as *sense*, at other times as *meaning*, and *Widersinn* likewise sometimes as *nonsense* and at another time as *absurdity*, and also obliterates the difference between *Widersinn* and *Unsinn.*—Another problem with the English translation of this passage is the plural of "in the *images* of the supreme meaning" for Jung's singular "im Bilde des Übersinnes," which is reminiscent of Gen. 1:27 (God created man ... "in the image of ...").

Jung's substitution of image for spirit and truth is of course a most momentous move. It amounts to a programmatic attack on the negativity of logos. It on principle opens the way for the positivity of the image, that is, for Jung's naturalistic stance, for the mere factual event of the emergence of an image *as the successor to truth*. Later we read: "It is not to be thought; it is to be viewed. It is a painting" (357b). The thinker Jung *thinks* the departure from the inwardness of thought proper and replaces it with the factual experience of images as pictures vis-à-vis the viewing subject, thereby regressively returning to an objectifying thinking (and the subject-object split).

In the Red Book the radical cutting off of the present is integrated in a larger conception of a succession of historical stages of consciousness, where the caesura between them is marked by the death of the gods of the old stage. "But this is the bitterest for moral men: our Gods want to be overcome .... When the God grows old, he becomes a shadow, nonsense .... The greatest truth becomes the greatest lie ..." (242a, tr.m.). "Everything that becomes too old turns into an evil,

---

[6] This conception would actually require to have been worked out in terms of a dialectical logic, the logic of sublation. But as a prophetic and religious thinker, Jung is content to dogmatically assert the overmeaning just like that as a fact without bothering to *think* it and this means to get really into it by reconstructing its logical genesis. The way it comes in the Red Book it is an unthought claim.

this is therefore also true of your highest. Learn this from the suffering of the crucified God that one can also betray and crucify a God, namely the God of the old year. When a God ceases being the way of life, he must fall secretly. The God becomes sick..." (241b). This is the notion of the death of symbols, known from Jung's published work (*CW* 6 § 816). Compare as well: "then the symbol is ripe to be destroyed, for it no longer covers the seed, which, you see, is about to grow beyond the shell," Jung wrote to Hans Schmid (6 Nov 1915, quoted in the German version p. 335n, my transl.). Christianity's "teachings are good for the most mature minds of bygone time" (234n). "We have outgrown that childhood where mere belief was the most suitable means to bring men to what is good and reasonable .... we need knowledge more than belief" (335b). "Mankind has grown older and a new month has begun" (356b). "[T]he world has acquired a new face. A new cover was thrown over it" (357b).

Hyperbole in goal and style. Since, on the one hand, "the spirit of this time had nothing to give me any more" (253n, tr.m.) and, on the other hand, the entire orientation goes towards the future, the question arises: what is hoped for from the future? What is the real concern around which the Red Book circles, the goal for which it strives? The goal is surprisingly not to find or recover the soul, not to explore its depths. It is nothing psychological, not soul-making, psychologizing. The real purpose is to overcome the nihilism and godlessness of the present. In other words, the goal is Meaning and God, where God means what grants Meaning, and Meaning is the fulfillment experienced through *having* a God to be worshiped. But the Red Book does not content itself with meaning plain and simple. No, right from the outset it reaches out for the overmeaning (229b, tr.m.). "That [the overmeaning] is the God yet to come" (*ibid.*). Just as meaning has to appear in its excessive form of overmeaning, so at the end of the Red Book the idea of God appears as Overgod ("a God above [*über*] God" [349a]). Nietzsche had said: "Dead are all the gods, now we want the overman to live." The Red Book says, as it were, "the spirit of this time has nothing to give me any more, now we want the overmeaning and the Overgod to live." Jung follows Nietzsche and departs from him at the same time by not seeing salvation in the overman but in a new religiousness.

Why overmeaning? Why is meaning not enough? Because meaning, even if it were a different one from the one known heretofore, is discredited as part of "this time." It might be a new alternative all right, but it would nevertheless still belong to the *same old status* of consciousness, the level of the opposites. What in the Red Book is striven for, however, has to be really, *absolutely*, new, an unheard-of, fundamentally new level of consciousness: "... if you also live what you have never yet lived" (233b): never yet! "If I have ascended to the highest and most difficult on the one hand, and want to win through to a redemption at an even higher level ..." (293b, tr.m.). "... only my other leads me beyond myself" (*ibid.*). Even the superlative, the highest and most difficult, is not sufficient. It, too, has to be superseded, outstripped. Still higher: the absolute extreme. It has to be mind-blowing and world-shattering. The Red Book will not make do with less. It reaches out (not for "the absolute" in the sense of classical metaphysics, but) for absolute extremes. Hubris, inflated claims: the belief to be in contact with the "spirit of the depths" and to have been "forced down to the last and simplest things" (229b), "reaching deep down, down to the kernel of the world" (276b). A Titanic vision: "I hate this pitifulness of the God. ... You force the gates of Hell .... You storm Heaven ..." (285b). The Red Book even claims to be able to go back before Adam and Eve and the Fall: "you free yourself from the old curse of the knowledge of good and evil" (301a).

After having been confronted with such a volley of ideas, one is flabbergasted to also find the isolated statement in the Red Book: "I shun far-flying ideas" (249a, tr.m.).

The style of the Red Book is also hyperbolic. Its diction, modeled after Nietzsche (the "Zarathustra form," so Jung according to Baynes [212b]), is stilted, pretentious, unctuous. We experience here how far we are psychologically removed from the early 20th century, when such a style was obviously still felt to be a possible literary form, whereas for us today it is hard to bear. Of course, we also heard that the style of the Red Book already "hurt (Jung's own) sense of the fitness of things terribly" (*ibid.*). But at least the later parts of the Red Book become less bombastic, less inflated (in style!, not in content), and more didactic, theoretical.

Because the Red Book moves into the future and at the same time tries to go way back before Christianity ("thereby you take a step back before Christianity and a step beyond it" [296b, tr.m.] and even back before the Fall), we see that its thinking is around an empty center, a lacuna. What has validity and (alleged) reality for it is two absences, pre-Christian truth, on the one side, and what is to come, on the other. "I lock the past with one key, with the other I open the future" (250a). The present in between has been cast to the wolves. In this regard there is a structural similarity between Jung's stance and that of Schelling who also had to pay the same price of an emptied-out present for entertaining the idea of an infinitely fulfilled past and an infinitely fulfilled future, even though on the very different basis of the premodern logic of classical metaphysics.

One could view the longing for an overmeaning as a compensatory reaction to the experience of the emptied-out present. But it is also possible to see it the other way around. Diagnosing an emptied-out present not as innocent cognition, but as the strategic act of denying that it has any meaning, of depriving it of any meaning. The thus extracted meaning is both retrojected into a lost past and projected into and heaped upon the future where it reappears as a surplus, excess, as overmeaning. The fact that the whole process described in the Red Book gives the impression of being will-driven seems to favor the second view.

The newness of the new. The talk of an overmeaning would itself be an empty claim, a mere word, if what makes it "over-" could not be spelled out. But the Red Book does not let us down. It tells us that overmeaning [*Übersinn*] is the "melting together of sense [*Sinn*] and nonsense [*Widersinn*]" (229b). This is truly mind-blowing. We have long been familiar with the idea of the union of opposites, and indeed, what the Red Book has in mind is just that. But it is easy to think of this union as if the opposites to be united were merely two conflicting, but nevertheless equally legitimate tendencies or values or two opposite natural forces (e.g., the masculine and the feminine), two enemies, two mythic figures or metaphysical principles at war with each other, such as Shiva and Vishnu. This would be a semantic or ontological opposition. But the Red Book leaves this harmless idea behind. What it has in mind is the union of a concept and the negation or denial of this *very same* concept: it is the union of *logical* opposites, namely contraries. One and the same term is at one and the same time affirmed and denied[7]: *Sinn* and *Widersinn*! Reason and unreason (314a), differentiation and nondifferentiation (347a), "the fullness and the emptiness" (347b), "truth and lying" (350a). "The highest truth is one and the same with the absurd [*dem Widersinnigen*]" (242a). "To the extent that the Christianity of this time lacks madness, it lacks divine life" (238a). As such, this idea of the union of opposites is nothing less than a fundamental attack on the law of non-contradiction and thus on logic itself. We always have to understand the Red Book ideas of the overmeaning and overgod as well as of the union of opposites in this absolute sense, in terms of logical contraries.

What the Red Book is therefore indeed capable of is demonstrating the concrete content of the notion of overmeaning. What it is, however, not capable of showing is why a reader should find this overmeaning meaningful, rather than simply nonsense and hypertrophy. Be that as it may, we see again that the Red Book, far from being a "Modest Proposal," hyperbolically reaches out for absolute excess. It *has to* do that in order to let "what is to come" be an absolute break with the present and to let the Red Book be truly *Liber novus*, the New Bible.

The familiar Jungian idea of the union in God of good and evil, of Christ and Satan, that is also discussed in the Red Book must also be understood in this radical sense. But the moment good and evil are personified and mythologized as Christ and Satan, we are back in the innocent imaginal or ontological thinking of the opposites construed as entities or principles. Then this idea of a union might be shocking for our customary moral convictions, but not mind-blowing. With this conception we never arrive at the intended radical idea of overmeaning and overgod. The Red Book attempts to seize the ultimate.

The new arena. The utopian style of thinking had become historically obsolete after Nietzsche. In order to nonetheless come up with a new utopia on the level and in the sphere of thought (rather than as sociopolitical ideology and party politics), the only possible way was to provide a radically new arena not merely for this particular

---

[7] Here we see again how indispensable a dialectical approach would be to give validity to these ideas.

new utopia but, much more radically, for *essential thought as such*, for the locus of truth. So far throughout history, the "arena" or "stage" of thought and truth had always been a fundamentally public one, out in the open so to speak, and fundamentally communal. On the stage of mythological consciousness the arena had been the common visible natural world, the cosmos, the *truth* of which was *thought* in the guise of polytheistic mythic gods and *daimones*, where "thought" had not yet come home to itself (to the *form* of thought), but still occurred in the form of visionary seeing and phainomenal image. Since the emergence of philosophy, that is, of thought's having taken on the form of thought, its arena was the mind, reason, *nous, intellectus, Vernunft,* the *theoretical* I, whose ultimate truth was transcendent (the divine intellect). In this arena, utopian schemes had no chance any more.

But no place existed other than the two mentioned ones that Jung could have availed himself of as a new arena. The *place* for a new arena, if it was to be, therefore had to be newly invented and produced. The only way to create this place for the arena was to revolutionize the very *notion* of "place" and "arena" by forcing the entire substance of the previous arena through the eye of a needle and making it reappear on the other side. This eye of a needle was the atomic, lonely individual, the empirical I. And the new arena thereby established or rather fabricated was each person's *inner world*. Here we get the explanation for why Jung had to reject the idea that what he was doing was art and why instead of releasing his ideas into fantasy and truth he had to aim at the human personality.

The new locus of truth that was needed could not simply be discovered and made use of by Jung, the way America was discovered and then settled by millions of Europeans. He had to fabricate it, and fabricate it as he was making use of it. The Red Book says correctly: "There are no paved ways .... We build the roads by our walking" (299a, tr.m.). Those roads are not already existing entities, indeed they are nothing ontological at all. They are logical roads. By the same token we would have to say: "there is no existing inner, not an existing 'the unconscious.'" There was not an unconscious for Jung into which he ventured forth (or could have ventured forth). Only our "superficial observer" could believe that the Red Book records Jung's "Confrontation with the Unconscious," or his descent into "the unconscious" understood as the modern equivalent to the mythological "underworld," for the purpose of his self-exploration (as, however, Jung himself represented it). The inner had to be fabricated by and in the extended process of moving "into it." Jung's "moving into it" is, however, in reality a process of piece-by-piece interiorizing into himself the spiritual world that has come down to us as our cultural heritage and that was previously out in the open, fundamentally communal. And, mind you, into himself not as the theoretical I of old, as mind or existing thought (which *as* "his" individual *thought* would nevertheless still be part of the public, cultural discourse), but into himself as *positive-factually existing* isolated individual, as *Dasein*, as Heidegger would later call it. And in the Red Book we have the record of this extended fabrication and interiorization process.

The construction of the inner is therefore at the same time also the record of the establishment of literal, empirical, civil man (what we call "the ego") *as* the new stage for truth, since the inner is *empirical man's* inner as the new hiding-place of truth, its last retreat.

For the interiorization to really produce this inner "space" as the new arena of truth, it had to produce it as the one and only arena, the true one, truer than the former arenas, the mind and the mythic cosmos. It had to be their successor and replace them. And it could only become *the* arena *for the new essential thought as such* if one succeeded in making the interiorization nearly total (complete) and correspondingly reinvented even the old forms of mythic and religious-metaphysical thinking as deficient ("still unconsciously-projected") forms of the newly established unconscious. The task was the logical translation, translocation of the locus of truth into the inner, the unconscious.

In other words, what was needed was a kind of *Umstülpung* (usually meaning a "turning inside out," but here: "turning outside in") of the whole traditional intellectual world. What had always been either the natural or the mental cosmos all around us had to be reflected into the human individual (in its positivity) to be "reborn," "reproduced," *simulated* there as an inner world in the individual's so-called (and only thereby created) "unconscious." And then, in addition to this turning outside in, it necessarily also had to be fundamentally radicalized in the direction of overmeaning as the union of meaning and absurdity

and of the overgod as the union of good and evil (because, to avoid
appearing as rehash it had to offer something semantically absolutely
unheard-of). Except for this fact it was a kind of internalized mirror-
image of what human culture in its so-far known history had produced
before as general ("collective") cultural ideas.

What the Red Book is about and what it achieved has its place in
the history of thought. It is a grave mistake to see it primarily as Jung's
personal self-exploration, i.e., as belonging to his private biography
only. No, it was an achievement for the generality. But of course,
because its purpose was to interiorize the arena of essential thought
or the locus of truth into the subjectivity of the positive-factual
individual, it necessarily had to *present* itself as Jung's personal process.[8]
What this process may show about Jung's psychic makeup is, however,
no more than a by-product. The Red Book circles around big questions
of general importance, about the arena of truth, about Meaning and
God, good and evil, the ultimate mysteries, etc., and, above all, it
establishes empirical-factual man in his literalness as the locus of truth,
truth now comprehended as *Urerfahrung* (original experience).

The Red Book has the emphasis on the future, on engendering
and giving birth, in common with Nietzsche's *Zarathustra*. But the

---

[8] My assessment that the Red Book must not be seen primarily "as Jung's personal
self-exploration" seems to contradict my earlier statement that "it is utterly private,
subjective." The point here is, however, that inasmuch as Jung's task is to *think* the idea
of absolutely personal experience, his Red Book takes place on the level of the generality;
but since *what* he has to think is the idea of *absolutely personal experience*, the Red Book
has to be utterly private.—But the private self aimed at is itself only the *general abstract
form* of self: the Red Book more or less completely omits details from Jung's personal
childhood and his private life, his relations to his parents, wife, children, his love-life,
his personal complexes and subjective emotions, etc., that would be such an essential
part of any ordinary analysis.—This is also a point where I can at least briefly mention
that the same dialectic prevails with respect to the question of whether the Red
Book is art or not. But now we have to realize that
inasmuch as Jung *relentlessly abandons himself* to the thought or fantasy of the utterly
private inner in himself (and precisely also to the fantasy that "It is not art!" but the
creation of another literal personality in him) and releases this fantasy *of* the *not*-
fantastic but *positively real* I into itself, the Red Book is, after all, "art" (of sorts; or
literature/philosophy): "art," of course, only on the level of what Mogenson termed
"overfantasy." Or, as already hinted at above, it is, *malgré* Jung, indeed "an artistic
production rather than an authentic representation of unconscious processes," namely,
the artistic production precisely *of* the fantasy of "an authentic representation of
unconscious processes." Though this be madness, yet there is method in it. What in
Jung was indeed an *artistic production* of this "authentic representation of the unconscious
process" is, after Jung, in all the many Jungian analyses focusing on the individuation
process no more than a literalizing re-production or better *simulation* of an "authentic
representation of an unconscious process."

two books or worlds are set completely apart. What Nietzsche was struggling with was what would be the conditions for the possibility of a new true creativeness as such and of a new tragic age (in other words, truly philosophical problems in the sphere of absolute negativity and generality that involve the very *definition* of man and the world). The Red Book, by contrast, starts out from empirical man as a fixed given, a positivity, you and me. When it talks of engendering and giving birth, etc., it means experiential processes in an always already presupposed positively existing man, the concrete individual as *Dasein*, literal man.

The interiorization process is psychologistic and not psychological because it amounts to a reflection into the positivity of the human being as civil man and particular atomic individual. A psychological interiorization, by contrast, would be a reflection of each psychic phenomenon into *itself*, its release into its truth, and not a reflection into the empirical person. The turning outside in that the Red Book performs involves (a) a shift from the universal (general) to the particular, (b) a shift from the negativity of "spirit and truth" to positivity and literalism (the literal individual, on the one hand, and the factual event of the experience of images, on the other), and (c) a prolonged, step-by-step process of sinking the *form* of thought into the *form* of the individual's *Leiben und Leben*, its existential experience "in the flesh." This is a process which to a large extent has the nature of painful suffering and torment (up to the point of near-madness) and is accordingly experienced as "cruel," a very frequent word in the Red Book. The torment was absolutely necessary to really, and absolutely convincingly, install the new arena in factual, bodily felt existence, in man as mere *Dasein*.

Just as Jung's "roads" which we only build by walking them are logical roads, so "the unconscious" is not a literal region or layer in the psyche of people, but a logical arena which comes about through the logical translation of cultural truths from the public, universal realm of consciousness into the factualness of literal events, namely existential experiences of images as facts occurring in empirical man. This sinking essential thought both "into the flesh" of the atomic individual and into the *form* of factual events is, as positivization and imprisonment, (d) *logically* making essential thought itself unconscious. Following the Red Book's dictum about the paved ways, we have to say: there is not an unconscious. We construct it by expelling thought from the realm of consciousness and making it (re-)appear as images, i.e., as objects or 'psychic facts,' that is, by sinking it from the theoretical I of classical metaphysics into the literal, civil man of modernity. But of course, although it seems paradoxical, since this transformation is a positivization, "the unconscious," which is actually a logical status in which thought or truth and particular contents may exist, must become ontologized and thus give itself out as if it were indeed a part of the personality.

We already heard examples of the individual as the exclusive eye of a needle (e.g., "It is my mystery, not yours. ... You have your own" [246b, tr.m.]. "No one besides you has your God" [329b]. "... first and exclusively and solely in one's own person" [*CW* 7, p. 5, tr.m.].). Now I want to give a few statements from the Red Book that show the idea of interiorization or swallowing. "Within us is the way, the truth, and the life" (231b, note the twisting of John 14:16!). "But you find manifold meaning only in yourself" (273b). "The God develops through the union of the principles in me" (254b, "in me"!).

The *totalitarianism* of this interiorization (its in principle all-inclusiveness) comes out, e.g., in the following quotations. "I am my own priest and congregation, judge and judged, God and human sacrifice" (327a). "You are an image of the infinite world, all the last mysteries of becoming and passing away live in you" (230a, tr.m.). "All [!] the darkness of all [!] former worlds crowds together in you" (308a). "You are the will of the whole [*der Gesamtheit*]" (337a). "... that the spirit of the depths in me was at the same time the ruler of the depths of world affairs" (230b f.).

Apart from these more global and programmatic statements, the whole process with the sequence of experiences described in the Red Book is about the step-by-step integration of all sorts of aspects of being, all regions of the world, all elements and facets of human existence into the thus created inner. Over long stretches the book appears to be much like a subjective recapitulation of what one might find in textbooks of religious and mythological phenomenology (rituals and ideas), with the only difference that rather than in dry theoretical form this phenomenology comes in animated personalized story form and is serialized. Night after night Jung produced a new episode devoted to a particular religious, mythic, or moral topic on the stage of *the* inner represented by his inner. Just as *within the show* the I is its "own priest and congregation, judge and judged, God and human sacrifice" or, with reference to Luke 2, "the mother" [who conceived the God] *and* "the careful father" *and* "the shepherd" (284a), *in reality* Jung is, *malgré lui,* simultaneously producer, stage, all the actors, and the experiencing (and reflecting) audience of the show.

The inner, which at Jung's historical locus was still entirely subjective (the human individual was the *medium* [eye of a needle]), later found its *objectified, technical* realization in television. Television is also the interiorization of whatever topics are to be found in the world, but an interiorization no longer into the human subject as medium, but objectively into mediality as such. Here the inner ("the unconscious") has finally become absolute, come home to itself. It has come of age, having completely emancipated itself from a childlike, youthful dependence on meaning (let alone overmeaning) characteristic of the first (industrial) phase of modernity, so that for it anything goes program-wise, as is appropriate for the second ("medial") phase of modernity. In retrospect we can comprehend Jung's systematically induced experiences as his private television shows *avant la lettre,* in which the subjective imagination takes the place of our technical apparatuses.

The Red Book gives us the rare chance of witnessing "live" the primary construction of the unconscious in Jung's sense. It might be tempting to go through the whole book and describe what all is interiorized and how each element contributes to the whole, but as this is not possible here, I will just list a few individual features without much commentary. I must also mention that the *manner* in which the various realities are internalized is very different. One form is a kind of (alleged) seeing-through. Another one is "to kill" the reality to be integrated. Again another is identification. Then there is imaginally living through something, and there is also distancing oneself from it. "I unsuspectingly absorb what I reject" (279b). There is fighting with it, literally taking possession of it, giving birth to it, and planting a seed ....

The socio-political reality of World War 1 is interiorized by being explained as stemming from internal problems: "But people see the outer quarrel alright, but not the one within, even though it alone is the wellspring of the great war" (253n, tr.m.).—"You should carry the monastery in yourself. The desert is within you" (230b).—The Red Book interiorizes the power to murder: the murder of the blond hero (241b ff.). The hero needs to be gotten rid of since he represents the I's ambitious orientation towards goals in the outer world.—"No one knows what happened during the three days Christ was in Hell. I have experienced it" (243b; what an incredible claim!).—The I is identified with Christ and deified after the model of the hellenistic figure of Aion (252a, f.). "In this deification mystery you make yourself into the vessel, and are a vessel of creation in which the opposites reconcile" (252n, quoting *Analytical Psychology*).—"I was smitten by the romantic [i.e., romantic infatuation]. The romantic is a step backward" (263a).—"The knowledge of death came to me that night" (267a).—"I will also not let him go, the Bull God, who once wounded Jacob's hip and whom I have now lamed. I want to make his force my own" (281b).—The capacity of sacrificial murder: "The sacrifice has been accomplished: the divine child, the image of the God's formation, is slain, and I have eaten from the sacrificial flesh" (291a). "But through the sacrificial murder, I redeemed the primordial powers and added them to my soul" (*ibid.*).—"I am just now ... about to reintegrate into my being human all the ancient wisdom that he who thinks in the spirit of this time lacks, in order to make my life whole, rather than entirely casting this ancient knowledge off even more, as the spirit of this time always demands" (253n, tr.m.).—To the soul's question: "Do you want to accept all this [namely: "all the superstitions hatched by dark prehistory," e.g., "dirty pouches filled with teeth, human hair and fingernails, timbers lashed together, black orbs, moldy animal skins"]?" the I responds: "I accept it all, how should I dismiss anything?" (305b, tr.m.).—"I caught the sun ... and carried it in my hand" (287a).—"If I accept the lowest in me, I lower a seed into the ground of Hell. The seed is invisibly small, but the tree of my life grows from it and conjoins the Below with the Above" (300b): here we see the interiorized world tree, the swallowing of cosmogony.—The urge for the totalization of the swallowing also shows *ex negativo* in the statement: "I have overthrown all the Gods, broken the laws, eaten the impure. ... However, I am not ready, since I have still not integrated into myself that one thing which chokes my heart" (285b, tr.m.).

God "was born as a child from my own human soul, which had conceived him with resistance like a virgin" (244b). "I am the mother, the simple handmaiden, who conceived and did not know how. I am the careful father, who protected the handmaiden. I am the shepherd who received the message as he guarded his herd at night on the dark fields" (284a, tr.m.). The experiencing I of the Red Book as the *theotokos*, the origin of the god, who on his part formerly used to be thought of as the origin and principle of the world. But not only the mother of God. The whole manger scene is interiorized.

Especially also Christ is interiorized, in the manner of identification: "You should all become Christs" (234b). "You ... can only overcome the old God through becoming him yourself and experiencing his suffering and dying yourself" (254n). If for Nietzsche man was something that was to be overcome, for Jung it is God who needs to be overcome. We see here the same Nietzschean dynamic applied to a different content. The Red Book blames the Christians for waiting "for redeemers who should take the agony on themselves for you, and totally spare you Golgatha" (254a). "To be Christ oneself is the true following of Christ" (254n). The mystery of Christ was incomplete. It needs to be completed by the individual in his singularity and positivity.

This shows that at the level of Jung's thought we are no longer dealing with the deep image of exemplary man as the "suffering God-man in the shape of a servant" that was so prevalent during the 19th century (examples are to be found in Kierkegaard, Marx, Alexandre Dumas père, Stefan George, Courbet ... ; also Nietzsche's 1889 postcards signed "The Crucified"). The latter was also an identification, but much more psychological (an identification not of literal empirical man with Christ but of the deep image or concept of man that belonged to the generality, which means that empirical man as such in his individuality was not immediately identified, but remained subject to the logic of *imitatio*). The Red Book wants a much more concretistic and immediate, an "existentialist" identification: the individuation process. And whereas the 19th century idea did not go beyond man's com-Passion with Christ, the Red Book radically rejects all *imitatio Christi* and sees as the task to be performed through this identification the completion of the mystery allegedly left unfinished by Christ, that is, our surpassing Christ.

Small wonder that all this culminates in the idea of the self (in the special Jungian sense, substantiated as an Other) which is pictorially represented in numerous mandalas. Small wonder—because the whole so-called "experiment," the project of the Red Book experiences, had from the outset been nothing but the *detailed thinking-through of the (dogmatic!) concept of "the self"* (in Jung's sense), a thinking-through, however, not in the *form* of thought, but in the form of systematically produced imaginal visions and existential fantasy experiences. The self is the Red Book's initial programmatic presupposition (the exclusive focus on the lonely individual) *and* its final goal (the fulfilled self as reflected in mandalas). The self as the concept of successfully *totalized* interiorization into the empirical individual had to be spelled out, to be gone through experientially with all its ramifications and consequences (going through torment, madness, through all sorts of aspects of human nature and all typical places or imaginal regions of the world, through hell, deserts, etc.). This is so because the Jungian self is not so much a given entity, not an anthropological constant existing *depuis la fondation du monde*, but the product of its slow and detailed production through the interiorization process, and as such a modern invention and a specialty of Jung's. The self as the image of totality (the swallowed world of the mind, or the world of the mind reconstituted as an "inner" one) can come about only as the result of a fabrication process.

And here we see again that the Red Book, as a book devoted to this totalitarian self, is not a book of psychology. The soul is not its real topic or concern, but occurs only as one of the figures or voices in this dramatized thought on its way to fulfilled interiorization. What the Red Book is about is really *a metaphysic of "the self"*—however, a metaphysic of self not for its own sake, but in the service of the ultimate purpose of (after "Nietzsche") rescuing God, rescuing the God concept in and for modernity by giving Him a new hiding-place and a radically new definition.

This comes out especially in Jung's Copernican Revolution. From time immemorial man had always expected his *Heil* (heavenly grace, bliss, salvation) from the gods or from God. But the Red Book, in keeping with its interiorization project, reverses this relation. It lets the I ask concerning the gods: "Can I help? Or is it superfluous that a man elevates himself to being a mediator of the Gods? Is it presumption or should a man become a redeemer of the Gods, after men are saved through the divine mediator?" and asserts point-blank,

"the Gods need a human mediator and rescuer" (358a). Earlier the
Red Book stated: "Thus my God found salvation" (283a). Obviously,
in this text "Gods" and "God" are threatened in their very existence.
This is a reflection of the post-Nietzschean situation. The experience
of the death of God is irrevocable and, as we have seen, had been
relentlessly accepted by the Red Book. But on this very basis it starts
its rescue and restoration project by means of the production of the
self. The atomic individual is not only the one who engenders and
gives birth to the new God, but also, radically new, the new Savior,
Savior *for* the Gods. An inverted world.

The price for the metaphysic of the self is that it can (a) only come
up with an a priori "pocketed" God (as the only way how the [retained,
unchallenged] enlightened-nihilistic ego can rescue the religious
impulse for itself) and that "the self" is (b) fundamentally dispersed,
atomized. Each self is imprisoned within itself, it has its *idios kosmos*.
"No one besides you has your God" (329b). There is no possibility of
a shared, communal religious truth any more. What now is shared as
a public truth is only the nihilistic stance, the modern ego. There is
only one single point where, according to this utopia, there might
possibly arise a new *communis opinio* concerning the religious impulse,
namely solely about this isolatedness itself (the atomized metaphysic
of the self): the belief that each individual in his metaphysical
loneliness has to develop this metaphysic of the self in himself.

The process recorded in the Red Book, I have to stress again, has
not much to do with Jung's personal self-exploration or his "realizing
himself." If it is an example of the individuation process in Jung's sense,
then individuation means *objectively* the realization, in each individual,
of the metaphysic of *the* self, not subjectively each person's *empirical-
subjective* self-cognition and self-realization.

The construction of psychic objectivity

Such a radical and totalitarian swallowing by the human individual
would inevitably result in an inflation of consciousness up to the point
of psychosis—*unless* the human individual would, paradoxically, be
capable of reserving itself, distancing itself from its own identification.
The subject has to pull itself out and set itself up vis-à-vis all those
experiences and external to them. Disownment. But is this not

absolutely incompatible with the whole project of a totalized interiorization? How can the essential claim "But if you watch closely, you will see ... that things live your life, and that they live off you. ... Nothing happens in which you are not entangled in a secret manner; for everything has ordered itself around you and plays your innermost" (273a), on the one hand, be reconciled with the move of getting out, on the other hand (irrespective of the fact that "getting out" and distancing oneself may be absolutely vital to avoid going mad)?

Here we have to realize that, far from contradicting the radical interiorization movement, this getting out is the indispensable prerequisite for its completion. The "inner" is "inner" only to the extent that it is "in" some Other outside of itself, "inside" a surrounding vessel or empty container. For there to be such an inner the I has to pull itself out of itself, out of its own subjectivity, and thereby establish itself as an external I, as "the ego," who is set up as innocent observer, *or* victim, of the experiences. This amounts to a fundamental self-dissociation of the I's subjectivity, its split into two. The interiorization of the cultural world into the inner and the I's getting out of itself are one and the same process.

And this self-dissociation is precisely what on principle happens in the Red Book (which is also why the diagnosis of psychosis with respect to its material is a misconception from the outset). We hear: "Thoughts are natural events" (250b). "~~I would have to consider myself mad~~; [; It would be more than inconsistent,] if I thought that I had produced the thoughts of the Mysterium" (250n). If "my thoughts" are events of nature, then they have a separate existence totally independent of the experiencing I, which ipso facto is "ego." "[I]t is nearly impossible for the thinker to differentiate himself from his thought and accept that what happens in his thought is also *something outside of himself*" (255n) (my italics).

An earthquake comes absolutely of its own accord. I am precisely not "entangled in it in a secret manner." A tree stands where it stands regardless of whether I see it or not. Sunshine, rain, and storms happen whether I like it or not. By setting up his thoughts as events of nature, the Red Book construes them as objective facts that merely *happen to* the ego as the innocent victim, and by the same token the I *disowns* its own thoughts, giving them the status of Other, of not being his, the way a man might deny being the father of a child. The Red Book thus established a subject-object dichotomy and operates within it and establishes the I as the untouched container of whatever experiences: as ego.

Underlying the dogma that it would be crazy to think that he, Jung or the experiencing I, had created the thoughts is an ontologizing logic, a logic of things, objects. The Red Book reifies the thoughts of the mystery as entities. Its concept of production or making that it applies to thoughts seems to be taken from the model of manufacturing, such as how a cobbler makes shoes. As long as this is one's schema for understanding "thoughts," one is of course right to say that it would be crazy to claim that one produces them. Goethe said about his poetry, that the poems made him, he did not make them. This view seems at first glance to express the same idea as the Red Book's dogma. But Goethe would not have considered his poems "events of nature." As a matter of course they would have been products of the thinking mind for him. Nor would he have denied that they are *his* productions, and that he was their author. He even explicitly considered all his poetry as "fragments of a great confession," in other words, as fundamentally subjective: his self-expression. With his statement about the poems that made him, Goethe points much rather to the inner dialectic of intellectual, poetic, artistic productivity, namely that it is at once subjective and objective, production and product, active and passive. But this dialectic or contradictory logic is reductively dissolved in the Red Book in favor of an unambiguous placing its two moments over against each other (which is of course necessary for establishing the theory of "the unconscious").

In order to get an understanding of this dialectic let us begin with the more accessible example of life. I do not create my life, and yet it is truly my life, my activity of living, my being and staying alive: my breathing, eating, digesting, protecting myself, etc. My life is not an Other that happens to me or is done to me; life is performative: my performing it. It is fundamentally and exclusively mine and absolutely syntonic with me. Its dialectic consists in the fact that only to the extent that my life lives me do I live my life, and vice versa. The moment it is no longer mine, then my life is gone, i.e., I am dead. Life does not have a separate existence outside living organisms and independent of their actively living. It exists *only* if and as long as it is individually *theirs*. Even my death does not come to me as if it were an Other, like the medieval idea of the Grim Reaper. It is my active performance of my very own finishing my life, my breathing my last.

By the same token, although I certainly do not "manufacture" my dreams the way a shoemaker makes shoes, they are nevertheless my dream thoughts, produced by me, only by me. They are thoughts and not events of nature. They are my thinking, i.e., (1) mine and (2) mental productions, inventions, interpretations, results of the living thinking by me as subject, not the appearance of natural events or existing facts. But here again it is also true that to the same extent that I have and think my dream thoughts they have or think me. "Show me your dreams and I tell you who you are" (Freiherr von Knigge, modified), i.e., I can show you what you are thinking deep down, or better: *as what* thinking, what thoughts, you exist. *You!* There is nobody else.

The anger that may, as we say, "come over me" is nevertheless my being angry. If I kill someone in my rage, it is my raging, my doing, and thus also my responsibility—nobody else's (which of course is contrary to a widespread present-day judicial tendency to consider people not responsible for what they do).

So one has to flatly contradict the Red Book and say that if "the thoughts of the Mysterium" came to me, then I produced those thoughts; it was I who thought or fantasized them. They are not naturally existing things that I merely stumbled across or that mysteriously happened to pop into my mind from who knows where, the way a loose roofing tile may happen to fall on my head as I am walking by. No, those thoughts exist only on account of my *thinking* them (or having thought them), on my responsibility. Conversely, this does precisely not preclude that they are also "objective" rather than ego-concoctions, just as Goethe's poems were, *as* subjective confessions, nevertheless something that "made" him.

To the extent that man is more than animal organism, that is, that he is mind or soul, he IS speculative thinking, the *unity* of himself as actively thinking *and* of his thoughts (or poems, or fantasies, dreams) that think themselves and as such come to him. This is what thinking is. The Red Book's fatal fault is that it tears this unity (the unity of the soul's logical life) apart and distributes its two moments, subjectivity and objectivity, to two *toto coelo* separate ontologized realities, the I and nature, the I and "the unconscious"—and even against the spirit of language to the I and the self (as a real Other).

   In very ancient times poetry was experienced as the singing of the Muse and prophecy as the coming of God's word to or upon the (often resisting) prophet. But psychologically this has to be understood like Goethe's dictum. When we read: "Then came the word of the Lord to Isaiah," then we have to take this whole sentence as a unity, one single soul truth, not as the coming together of two, the word of the Lord here and Isaiah there. Isaiah is Isaiah only as the one to whom the word came, and the word came only to Isaiah. "Isaiah" and "the word of the Lord" are the unfolding of one Biblical reality, one soul reality, one fantasy. The same applies to the Muse and Homer, as well as to the Red Book's I and its "thoughts of the Mysterium." Each is the reflection of the other. They "invent" each other, because they are both figures in the same fantasy. It even applies to Goethe and his poems and to me and my dreams. *Poiêsis*: the Red Book's "myth that sings itself," *our* "thoughts that think themselves" in *our* thinking them, life's living itself in *our* living it.

   We can see the mechanism by means of which the Red Book performs the dissociation of this dialectical unity and reifies the thoughts of the Mysterium as events of nature "outside of the thinker." Repeatedly the experiencing I meets the figures appearing to it with a denial of their reality. It says, for example, "Surely, you are the symbols of the most extreme opposites" (246b, tr.m.), "You are symbols ..." (249b), "I am basically convinced that Izdubar is not at all real in the ordinary sense, but is a fantasy" (282a, tr.m.). But the answer he gets is: "We are real and not symbols" (246b). "But we are just as real as your fellow men. ... you have to accept us" (249b). "You wretch, how can you doubt that I am real?" (262a). According to Jung himself, through these statements he was taught "psychic objectivity, the 'reality of the soul'" (*MDR* p. 183, tr.m.).

   We ask: how does this psychic objectivity come about? Or rather, how is it constructed (for it is artfully constructed)? In a most curious way! Jung enters his fantasies with the categories of external reflection, namely with the distinction between fantasy and reality. *Inside* his fantasies he views them from outside and doubts the reality of their figures. It is as if a novel within itself tried to pull the rug out from under its characters as only imagined, or as if we, while dreaming, turned around to the wild animal or to the murderous criminal chasing us and said to them, "you are only symbols of my shadow." Or as if within a dream we doubted that we really were desperately erring through the labyrinthine halls of a building. This does not make sense. Within the Red Book, within a novel, within our dreams everything occurring in them is real. It is only outside the fantasy, when we have finished the novel, have awakened from our dream, and then look at them as psychic material or texts from outside that we rightly say that they are fantasy in contradistinction to reality and an image or symbol for this or that. But the condition of the possibility of taking figures as symbols when it is a question of *interpreting* fantasy material is that *within* the fantasies, on the immediate, experiential or text level, they are unquestionably real for us. Jung's trick of confounding the level of experience or text and the level of interpretation, the trick of introducing into the fantasies themselves the standpoint of external reflection, means first of all that the subject does not fully enter its own fantasies, namely as I, but only as "the ego." An I that truly enters the fantasy goes under into fantasy and is as such imaginal I, itself an internal part of the fantasy and not "real" in the sense of external reality.

The figures' answer, "We are not symbols, we are completely real" tears, secondly, the very fabric of fantasy asunder. Defining the intrinsic reality of the fantasy figures in contradistinction to their being symbols gives them a positivistic, literal reality that is incompatible with the original imaginal reality that fantasies, visions, dreams naturally come with. It is what construes them as natural objects. Years later Jung said, "we cannot go back to the symbolism that is gone. No sooner do you know that this thing is symbolic than you say, 'oh, well, it presumably means something else.' Doubt has killed it, has devoured it" (*CW* 18 § 632). But here this very doubt is surprisingly the starting-point within this fantasy. The killing of the innocent truth and conviction of the fantasy has already occurred. The spiteful assertion, "we are completely real" thus comes as a secondary reaction to this doubt and cannot really undo it. All it can do is establish a dogma *against* the already attained better judgment, against the higher standpoint of reflection.

The I's doubt is an absolutely essential ingredient of the establishment of the inner as the new arena of truth. The fictions must not be innocently released into their fictional or fantasy character. Their immediate sense of realness must be dissolved. The I is not allowed to simply swing itself onto Pegasus in order to let itself be carried wherever

Pegasus wants, in the same way as the Red Book is not freely released into fantasy, as I showed above. This possibility has to be once and for all prevented in the Red Book by the intrusion into the fantasy itself of the critical reflection that the fictional figures are merely "symbols of" (this or that). The purpose of this operation, however, is by no means the undoing of the fantasy world. On the contrary, it has to supply a springboard for an all the more radical fictionalization: critical reflection is needed to prevent this fictionalizing from wasting itself on nothing but fictional *contents* (figures and happenings)—this would be one's riding on Pegasus—and to force it instead to reach out even for *the very form (logical status) of fiction or image as such*, so as to now set it up as absolutely real in a naturalistic or positivistic (already reflected) sense. Fantasy has to *simulate* the character of hard-core reality for its fictions ("But we are just as real as your fellow men" [249b]), much like the new 20th century *technical* medium of movies simulates reality so convincingly as to fool everyone.

The inner has only truly become the new arena of essential thought and truth if in its logical form it succeeds in *simulating* nature, reality, positivity, and is no longer innocently *fantasy*. Only now can we fully appreciate what the Red Book's turn against "spirit and truth" in favor of image aims for ("God is an image, and those who worship him must worship him in the image of the overmeaning"). For some it may seem paradoxical, but the *attack* on the reductive "*nothing but* fantasy" idea IS the fight *against* fantasy proper, against mythic or poetic imagination, and *for* the inner or *the* unconscious as a "second" (reflection-produced) *positive-factual reality* that is supposed to have the same, or rather a higher, dignity than the "first" reality.[9]

This "psychic objectivity," *this* "reality of the soul" is reactionary: set up in contradiction to its own underlying denial. It is not our precious psychological concept of psychic objectivity, but a psychologistic and ideological one. In other words, here we are again at a point where we have to make a clear cut between the Red Book and Jungian psychology. Although the psychological concept of the reality of the soul has, in Jung, its biographical origin in the Red Book experiences, its logical origin for us has to be fundamentally different.

---

[9] Cf. "It is *psychic reality* which has at least the same dignity as physical reality" (*CW* 15 § 148, tr.m.).

Psychic objectivity as a concept of true psychology means that precisely and only as symbols, as dream or fantasy figures, as *not* "just as real as your fellow men," i.e., as logically negative, are they real. And not completely (i.e., positivistically) but psychologically real. But they are symbols and fantasy only if they are *imaginatio vera*: if they are the self-display of the inner logic of actually lived life rather than *active imaginations*, deliberate fantasy concoctions.

The Red Book's notion of psychic objectivity is all the more discredited in one very telling, but bizarre episode. "[O]n the border between morning and evening" (280a) the I in search of the East meets its own opposite, a God coming from the East, Izdubar. The latter is lamed through the encounter with the scientific, enlightened awareness of the I coming from the West. The I wants to help its God, which can happen only in that world that the I comes from, but to expose him to that world would be deadly for Izdubar. So the I comes up with the following solution: it first reduces him to a fantasy that he can carry on his back, and later it shrinks him to the size of an egg that he puts into his pocket. "Thus I enter the hospitable house where Izdubar is supposed to find healing. / Thus my God found salvation. The salvation occurred through his being subjected to the very thing that one would have to consider absolutely fatal, namely that one declares him a figment of the imagination. How often has it been assumed that the Gods have been brought to their end in this way. This was obviously a great illusion: since this is precisely how the God is saved. He did not pass away, but became a living fantasy .... But I loved my God, and took him to the house of men, since I was convinced that even as a fantasy he really lived ..." (283a, tr.m.).

Here we see the other side of the same coin. The simulation of positive realness has become so certain of itself that it now can be playfully ironized. Before, the predicate "symbol" or "fantasy" had had the function of derealizing a fantasy experience (although only for the higher purpose of thereby in the end precisely establishing "psychic objectivity" in its positivistic sense). Now, the derealization through the reduction of the God to the status of mere fantasy has the opposite function of precisely rescuing the reality of something that is already known to be historically obsolete, and of smuggling it, in this immunized (encapsulated) form, into the world of modern consciousness. Both moves are manipulative, tricks (the Red Book:

"Out of love I devised the trick" 286a), and show the presence of (fantasy-external) ego reflection within the fantasy itself. The second one, with its image of pocketing the God reduced to the size of an egg, thanks to its crude literalism also (involuntarily) caricatures the entire Red Book procedure of interiorization or swallowing. The pocketed and only *as* pocketed rescued God has been reduced to a commodity, a Marxian fetish. Again we see that this type of "psychic objectivity" is unsuitable for a true psychology. The rescue of this God is phony because it is only secured at the price of keeping it concealed from the very consciousness into which it is transported (the world of Enlightenment), in other words, by a *sacrificium intellectus*.

The positivistic objectifying is carried to its extreme when it is directed at the I itself, so that the I appears as an Other, a thou or it. "The taming begins with you, my I, nowhere else. Not that you, stupid [in the sense of dull, dumb] brother I, had been particularly wild ..." (334b). "I felt my I squirm in pain" (336b). It is inherent in the concept of I that it can never be a "you" and a "brother." Both "brothers" are one and the same. The I is in itself self-relation, self-reflection and not the relation of two separate entities or beings. The phrase "my I" is a meaningless combination of words because it pretends that the one I owns the other I as its property. But by means of it, the uroboric unity of the I, its by going away from itself precisely returning to itself, is split into two. The objectified "you, stupid brother I" amounts to a fundamental disownment, the I's deliberate self-alienation and self-cloning. Both this stupid brother and the I who has such a stupid brother (as an Other) should rightly be called "the ego." The ego is the I's self-dissociation, the split of the uroboric, dialectical unity of subjectivity or thinking into two, who are not even really "brothers" because their relation is hierarchical. The one looks condescendingly and contemptuously down upon the other.

Only by the I's having pocketed *itself* and converted the very notion of I into a thou or it, an object, has the opus of swallowing been truly completed: become absolute. And now it again comes out for us that the interiorization is not merely a shoving of things in from outside, but also the reverse (namely externalizing) movement of the I's getting out of its being living thought, subjectivity, the soul's life, and its expanding itself to such an extent that it can become the positive-factual container for the whole world (including the I itself) as its object or content, indeed, for the whole world as likewise totally cut off from living thought: as "images" of "the *unconscious*." "Unconscious" means: everything in "the unconscious" is, in its *logical form*, just as "dumb," just as mindless as the ego's "stupid brother": nothing but images to be observed and, on top of it, fundamentally private, by definition incommunicable (even if they are factually communicated, as in the now "published" Red Book). It means basically what we heard from Jung earlier: "There is nothing of conscious structure in these fantasies, they are just events that happen."

We have to see this objectification (disidentification) very critically, because it means the eviction of subjectivity or the soul from itself as living speculative thought and the reifying of what it is concerned with. The epitome of this eviction is the concept of a substantiated self as an Other. But at the same time, we must guard against throwing out the baby with the bathwater. The capability to see oneself objectively, to distinguish oneself from oneself (without reifying!), and to appreciate psychic material in its (true) psychic objectivity is indispensable for true psychology.

* * *

After this analysis of the character of the Red Book itself I want to add a few words about the published versions. Production-wise, both the German and the English editions are superb volumes. Sonu Shamdasani's introduction and annotations deserve high praise. They give valuable, very helpful background information, especially because they also use much unpublished material not accessible to the general public. At times Shamdasani also adds his own critical judgment to his introduction, such as when he rightly notes: "However, from an evidential standpoint, given the breadth of his learning, Jung's own material would not have been a particularly convincing example of his thesis that images from the collective unconscious spontaneously emerged without prior acquaintance" (220a f.). But at other times he simply adopts at face value Jung's self-interpretation, where a critical comment might have been in place. One example: after relating 12-years-old Jung's thought of the destruction of the beautiful Basel cathedral through an almighty turd falling from God's throne on its roof, he continues, "He felt alone before God, and that his real responsibility commenced then. He realized that it was precisely such a direct, immediate experience of the living God, who stands outside Church and Bible, that his father lacked" (194a). This sounds as if there had in fact been "a direct, immediate experience of the living God." Here one would have expected a word of contradiction, especially since this problematic interpretation sets the course for all of Jung's later thinking about "God" and "immediate experience," also for that occurring in the Red Book.

In addition to noting the changes between Jung's "Black Books," the Drafts of the Red Book, and the Red Book itself, to explanatory comments on certain names, symbols, psychological ideas occurring in the Red Book, to parallels between Red Book ideas and passages in Jung's other works, the notes also identify Jung's numerous unreferenced quotations or allusions. Considering the huge number of allusions it is small wonder that quite a number of them escaped the editor's attention (just two examples, in addition to the above-mentioned "God is an image, and those who worship him must worship him in the image of overmeaning" [229b]: "We asked earth. We asked Heaven etc." [285a]: Augustine, *Confessions* 10, 6; "Bear ye each your own burden" 324a, tr.m.: Gal. 6:2). A few seem not really to the point or even a bit misleading (also just two examples: "the spirit of this time," a phrase expressing Jung's cultural criticism, has nothing to do with the "spirit of the times" quote from Goethe's *Faust* [229n], which is concerned with the totally different topic of historical hermeneutics; "the ram that should bear our sin" [241b, tr.m.]: the more appropriate reference would be John 1:29, because with the Leviticus passage Jung's anti-Christian sting is missed). "*Ecclesia catholica et protestantes et seclusi in secreto*" (320n) means "the Catholic Church, the Protestants, and those who are secluded in loneliness [or secrecy]" rather than "A church both Catholic and Protestant shrouded in secrecy." But these are small flaws in an otherwise highly scholarly and helpful apparatus of notes.

In the German version, the translation of the English Introduction and notes is accurate and reads quite well (minor errors notwithstanding: e.g., omission of "at Herisau" in the sentence "In November, while on military service ...," [210b German ed., 209a Engl. ed.]; "The Comparative Study of the Individuation Process"

[219a] does not mean here "Die vergleichende Studie zum..." [220a], but "Vergleichende Erforschung des...").

It is, however, a pity that, concerning the English edition, in such a handsome, costly volume the English translation of Jung's text leaves much to be desired. The translation is unreliable. It does not consistently convey the sense and feel of the Red Book text. Of course, not all mistakes are of equal importance, some may be oversights, as can easily happen, but they all contribute to a loss of precision over against the original. Often they even distort the meaning and seem to reflect an insufficient understanding of the particular German sentences. Just a few examples, mostly from passages quoted above: "*demütig, unwissend*" is not "unknowingly humiliated" (246b), but "humble, ignorant." "Höre auf" means "Stop," not "Listen" (342a). "*Ich will ... sein*" means "I want to (be)" instead of "I will (be)" (231b and elsewhere). There is a difference between "I would prefer not to tell you" (275b) and "*Ich liebe es nicht, mit dir zu sprechen*" ("I do not like to speak with you"), as also between "May each go his own way" (231b), a hope or wish, and "*Ein jeder gehe seinen Weg*" ("Each shall [or should] go his own way," an imperative). "*Ich wollte meinen Gott auf Gnade und Ungnade*" means "I wanted my God at all cost/ unconditionally/for better or worse," but not "for the sake of grace and disgrace" (289a). In the phrase "*Das Gesetzgeben, das Bessernwollen ...*" the second noun should not be rendered as "wanting improvements" (231b). "*Bessern*" in this context means to reform (people!), to improve them (above all morally), and we can be sure that somewhere in the back of Jung's mind there was the memory of the relevant passage from *Faust*, "I do not entertain the illusion that I would be able to teach something to improve and convert people [*die Menschen zu bessern und zu bekehren*]." In the sentence (and paragraph) beginning "But if you watch closely, you will see ..." (273a) it should read "that things live *your* life," not "*their* life." It is not completely wrong to translate "*aus dem, was ich emporschaffe*" with "from my work" (267n). But what an abstraction, what a flattening! What the German suggests (a bringing up from the depths through his efforts) is lost. Above I already pointed to the same flattening that occurred with the translation of *Übersinn* as "supreme meaning," but in that case it is also a fatal mistake.

* * *

I began with the Heine quotation: "What a book!" I hope that it has become a bit clearer *what* kind of a book the Red Book is. It is a new publication, but it should not be *Liber novus* for us. Its value is twofold: it provides us with a rich source for gaining insight into the formation of and deeper motivation behind Jung's thought and, beyond Jung, into one episode of intellectual history, and it is a mine of interesting symbolism and theosophic speculation.

References

C.G. Jung, *Das Rote Buch. Liber novus*, herausgegeben und eingeleitet von Sonu Shamdasani, Düsseldorf (Patmos) 2009.

C.G. Jung, *The Red Book. Liber Novus*, edited and introduction by Sonu Shamdasani, New York and London (Norton) 2009.

CHAPTER EIGHT

The Opposition of 'Individual' and 'Collective'—Psychology's Basic Fault Reflections on Today's *Magnum Opus* of the Soul.[1]

Not everything painful is a truth. But very often truth is painful. I consider it the job of psychology, of psychoanalysis, to try to bring out and say the truth. Of course I do not know whether what I will say to you today will actually be the truth; this is not for me to decide. But at least I do know that it will be painful.

Let me begin with the motto of this lecture series, "The rescue of one's own soul consists in the rescue of the world." As the author of this statement[2] I may be entitled to subject it to a self-critical reflection. And I must subject it to a critical reflection in order to dispel right from the beginning a possible misconception concerning my basic stance, and a possible expectation concerning the general line of

---

[1] This article is a modified version of an oral presentation to the Guild of Pastoral Psychology, London, May 2nd, 1996. It was the last of a series of lectures on "Collective Consciousness and the Individual—'The rescue of one's own soul consists in the rescue of the world.'"

[2] In my paper "Once More: Jung, Hegel, and the Subjective Universe," published in *Spring 1987* under the title "The Rescue of the World: Jung, Hegel, and the Subjective Universe" (now in: W.G., *The Soul Always Thinks*, Collected English papers vol. 4, New Orleans LA [Spring Journal Books] 2010, pp. 53–61) I had (on p. 60) used this phrase as part of longer complex statement in response to a statement by Jung from *GW* 10 § 536.

thought for the following exposition that the quotation might have awakened. Listening to the sentence today, I am not happy with the word 'rescue' and the concern it expresses. To be sure, despite truly exciting new developments in the sciences and technology, there is enough in the world that urges upon us a desire for a rescue of the world: terrorism, starvation of millions, brutal social injustice and political suppression in many parts of the world, wars, millions of refugees, unemployment, epidemics, the stupidity of much of television entertainment, to mention only a few unbearable vexations. Nevertheless, as I see it there are two problems with the intention of rescuing. First, the idea is grandiose. Is not the mere toying with the wishful idea of rescuing the world *hubris*? Who are *we* to expect to be able to contribute something to the rescue of anything, let alone the *world*? Rescue, *sôtêria*, salvation, is a program of an order far too large, a program suitable exclusively for a *sôtêr*, a Savior.

Secondly, it seems to me that the project of rescuing also contradicts the very impulse of psychoanalysis. One of Jung's analysands had the following dream. She was told to descend into a pit filled with hot material and submerge herself in it. She obeyed, with merely one shoulder left sticking out of the pit. Then Jung came by and pushed her all the way into the hot material saying, "Not out, but through." Aniela Jaffé tells us that when Jung reported this dream in a seminar he did so with obvious delight.[3]—This is a very simple and clear illustration of the depth-psychological impulse. The psychological instinct vis-à-vis a predicament, a pathology, a symptom, inasmuch as it is a truly *psychological* instinct, is not to try to get out of it, nor to wish to 'correct' it. The soul's longing is for consciousness to enter ever deeper into the predicament, to the very heart of the matter, not because of a morbid masochism, but to keep with the alchemical insight that the mess we find ourselves in to begin with *is* the prima materia to whom the psychological eros and the entire Work are dedicated. In this sense one might even say that it is not the world nor we who need to be rescued *from* the predicament; on the contrary, it is the predicament or the pathology itself that needs to be rescued or saved, in the sense of the Platonic demand to *sôzein ta phainomena*, to 'save the phenomena.'

---

[3] Aniela Jaffé, *Aus Leben und Werkstatt von C.G. Jung*, Zürich and Stuttgart (Rascher) 1968, p. 111.

The dream of Jung's analysand shows that the analyst's first allegiance is to the *opus*, and not to the wishes of the empirical person. We see that the dreamer's proclivity as empirical person or ego personality is to get out of the pit. But the Jung of this dream does not lend her a helping hand. The implicit notion of psychotherapy underlying both this dream and Jung's delight with it is that psychotherapy is not a helping profession in the usual sense of the word. Its intent is not to set right, to cure, to better, be it the world or individual people. Such intentions are subjective wishes stemming from ourselves as ego personalities. There is, of course, nothing wrong with such goals. They are very natural and very human. And very often psychotherapy indeed has a curing effect. But as already Freud realized, the curing effect is a mere by-product (even though a desirable one) of the analytical work, not its immediate purpose. The immediate purpose of psychotherapy is "analysis," that is, gaining cognition, doing justice to psychological phenomena by penetrating to their innermost core and by comprehending them. Thus, although our wishes to be cured, to be free of our symptoms, to improve and to grow are legitimate interests of ours, they are not the goals given for the project called psychology or psychotherapy. If, as a book title states, we've had a hundred years of psychotherapy and the world's getting worse—was it to be expected that it would become better? And more importantly, would such an expectation be a *psychological* expectation? No. Psychology has no stake in changing the world for the better, nor in hope, or despair. It has a job to do. This is its commitment. He who wants to enter the field of psychology must therefore cross a threshold, the threshold that divides *our* feelings, needs, and desires from the "objective" intentionality that is psychology's own.

Actually, my critique of the word 'rescue' in my sentence of several years ago does not imply a change of mind on my part. For I had not been speaking with my own tongue at the time. Rather, I had picked up a statement by Jung and tried to examine it on its own, not my, terms. And the title under which my paper was published, "The Rescue of the World," did not come from me either. It was the editor's choice. In the statement referred to, Jung had said (*CW* 10 § 536) that the rescue of the world consists in the rescue of one's own soul. So it was Jung who in this case brought the fantasy of rescue into play. All I tried to do was to put Jung's version of the relation between the rescue of the world and that of one's own soul to a mental test. And the result of this test was not a simple reversal of Jung's dictum into the opposite. My answer to it was more complex. I suggested that Jung's statement could only become true if reformulated in the following way: "the rescue of the world consists only to that extent in the rescue of one's own soul that the rescue of one's own soul consists in the rescue of the world." In other words, given that we operate within a fantasy of rescue, neither the rescue of the world nor the rescue of one's own soul may claim priority. I tried to express the dialectic governing the relation between one's own soul and the world.

And with this key word, dialectic, as well as with my above comments on the difference between the 'subjective' intentionality of us people and the 'objective' intentionality of the project called psychology, I have given you a first indication as to where I stand intellectually and why I think that the simple opposition between 'individual' and 'collective' is psychology's basic fault. There is one more point that should be mentioned in order for you to have an idea of where to place me. My work as a psychologist is mainly inspired by a twofold commitment. *Traditionwise*, I feel committed to Jung, and *systematically* I feel committed to the task of giving an answer, *my* answer, to life, to our situation, to our reality. There is no real conflict between these two commitments. This is so because, as I see it, Jung himself felt committed to the same task of giving *his* answer to life and reality as they were conditioned in our 20th century.[4] His entire *oeuvre* was the result of his wrestling with the problematic, indeed with the predicament, that the modern situation had brought about for the soul. Even if there is no real conflict *between* my two commitments, there is a tension *within* the first commitment, within my feeling committed to and by Jung. The tension is between the letter of his written work, on the one hand, and the vision driving his thought from behind, on the other hand. One could say that it is the tension between the manifest *oeuvre* and the latent *magnum opus*, between written doctrine and living project. I can characterize my relationship to Jung by saying that I try

---

[4] Cf. Jung's statement, "The meaning of my existence is that life holds a question addressed to me. Or, conversely, I myself am a question which is addressed to the world, and I must provide my answer, for otherwise I am dependent upon the world's answer." (*MDR* p. 318, transl. modif.)

to measure the *oeuvre* against the *opus* or the doctrine against the vision and, where necessary, to defend the intentionality of the vision against the limitations of some of the formulations. In this way, I believe a deep indebtedness and faithfulness to Jung and a great freedom vis-à-vis any of his particular convictions can go together.

It needs no long discussion to agree that Jung, when he spoke of the process of individuation, did not intend to advance a one-sided individualism. Even though the telos of individuation is the development of the Self, the Jungian Self must not be viewed as solipsistic, nor set in contradistinction to mankind, or to the world at large. "This self, however, is the world," Jung once said (*CW* 9i § 46, transl. modif.). About the archetypes he stated that they behave as if they belonged as much to society as to the individual (*CW* 10 § 660). And we only need to remember that with his theory of synchronicity Jung gave expression to his vision of a possible unification of psychology and physics, in order to realize that his thinking was trying to, and was able to, encompass both at once, the individual *and* the world as the collective, as well as the individual *and* the world as nature or cosmos.

Whether it was that later Jungians were not able to fully grasp this comprehensive notion of Self and individuation, or that Jung's conception was not fully convincing to them, or, a third possibility, that the way Jungian theory and practice had developed in fact did not support this comprehensive sense—at any rate, during the last decade or so there have been a number of voices within the Jungian field expressing a need to shift the emphasis away from individuation and to the world. James Hillman programmatically entitled one of his lectures "From Mirror to Window." Psychotherapy as it has evolved is seen under the image of the mirror because it takes place in the *temenos*, or the closed vessel, of the consulting room and predominantly works by means of self-reflection. Hillman wanted to break the mirror that returned the glance of the individual back to himself or herself, back to what is going on within oneself, and to open the window of the consulting room so as to allow us to perceive what is going on in the real world around us, the world with its beauty as well as its deformities, and to try again to ensoul this world. Psychotherapy was thus given a much wider scope. On the one hand, it was to attend directly to such close-by realities as public transportation, community politics, fashion, the architecture that we surround ourselves with and live in, and, on the other hand, psychology was directed to the large-scale idea of an anima mundi, the soul of the world. In keeping with the concept of the anima mundi, a return to the notion of the *cosmos*, as opposed to the modern sciences' abstract notion of the *universe*, was demanded; in other words, psychology was given the task of working towards the development of a new cosmology.

The ideas that I sketched out very briefly, far too briefly, immediately speak to the soul: cosmos, *anima mundi*, ensouling the world. They simply feel good. They evoke deep longings and hold a precious promise. The only problem with them, I think, is that they are psychologically anachronistic or atavistic, as regressive as the World Council of Churches' idea of some years ago of Safekeeping the Creation.[5] And this is why they even detract from the real psychological necessities of today and lure us away from the soul's real situation. Can a consciousness that has gone through the process of Christianization return to a notion of the world, the earth, nature as a locus of soul, a locus of theological or metaphysical significance? The very purpose of Christianity is to overcome this world, and the deepest longing of the Christian soul is for a new world. Christianity is a truly *incisive* event in the history of the Western soul. With it the veil in the temple was rent in twain from top to bottom; and the earth did quake, and the rocks rent (Matth. 27:51). This implies a revolution of consciousness. More than a revolution of *consciousness*: a *real* change, a *real* severing has taken place. There is no way back, just as there is no way back behind puberty to the innocence of childhood, or behind the Reformation and the French Revolution to a truly medieval frame of mind. Of course, we can always disown what happened, deny its reality. We can pretend that what happened was in fact not a psychological *event* as real as an earthquake, but merely a false *opinion* or deluded belief system on our part, a wrong human view of things, our lack of respect for planet Earth. False opinions or attitudes can be corrected more or less at will.

---

[5] This is a strange idea because it seems to mindlessly equate "the Creation" which is to be the object of our safekeeping with the earthly physical world in its present-day form. Does this mean that the world at the time of the ice age, the world at the time of the dinosaurs, the world at the time when the Himalayas were still ocean ground, were not the Creation? And does it consequently mean that this slogan amounts to the program of trying to *freeze* one particular moment in the earth's history?

But such arguments are excuses. By means of them we can, to be sure, play "Middle Ages" or even "Paganism" in a way similar to how veterans replay the battles of World War II. This is always possible, but if more than a pastime, it is an escape.

Two thousand years ago it was said that the hour cometh, when ye shall neither in this mountain nor yet at Jerusalem, worship the Father (John 4:21). The world as natural world does not hold anything sacred anymore. We may deplore this, but this does not change the psychological situation. When in 724 Boniface cut down the Holy Oak of the Teutons, he presented us with an image displaying objectively that the transition from paganism to Christianity is literally an incisive event, with no return.

That this transition was not merely a mental change of attitude and belief, but also a full-fledged revolution really and irrevocably changing the *status of nature* is made clear in a passage from Chaucer, from "The Wife of Bath's Tale," written at the end of the 14th century.

> When good King Arthur ruled in ancient days
> (A king that every Briton loves to praise)
> This was a land brim-full of fairy folk.
> The Elf-Queen and her courtiers joined and broke
> Their elfin dance on many a green mead,
> Or so was the opinion once, I read,
> Hundreds of years ago, in days of yore.
> But no one now sees fairies any more.
> For now the saintly charity and prayer
> Of holy friars seem to have purged the air;
> They search the countryside through field and stream
> As thick as motes that speckle a sun-beam,
> Blessing the halls, the chambers, kitchens, bowers,
> Cities and boroughs, castles, courts and towers,
> Thorpes, barns and stables, outhouses and dairies,
> And that's the reason why there are no fairies.
> Wherever there was wont to walk an elf
> To-day there walks the holy friar himself
> As evening falls or when the daylight springs,
> Saying his mattins and his holy things,
> Walking his limit round from town to town.
> Women can now go safely up and down
> By every bush or under every tree;

> There is no other incubus but he,
> So there is really no one else to hurt you
> And he will do no more than take your virtue.[6]

Although written on a comical note, this text must nevertheless be considered a document that reflects the actual experience of a revolutionary historical change that has taken place concerning the logical status of nature or, we could also say, the *nature* of nature. There is a clear sense of a fundamental loss. What is lost (and irrevocably lost) is the natural world *as* ensouled, *as* animated, *as* spirited by all sorts of fairies, goblins, and little people. In nature you can no longer come across these spirits. Nature is no longer a place invested with autonomous meaning and appearing in a personified way, in actual figures. It no longer speaks. Chaucer's is one of very many testimonies to this fundamental change, just as conversely there are countless reports by pre-Christian peoples and by folks little affected in their depths by the Christian revolution that in nature elves and fairies, spirits and the dead had actually been encountered. The Chaucer passage attributes this change to the influence of Christianity, which had in fact fundamentally changed the constitution or the logical status of the world. It had deprived people of the possibility to experience nature in the way they had experienced it in pagan times, not, however, by blinding *them*, but by metaphysically depleting nature itself.

I do not see how after this change one could still try to seriously entertain the idea of an *anima mundi*. This idea is an archetypal truth, no doubt. But it is a truth that has its legimate place in ancient cultures. It is part of *historical* psychology. In our world it is wishful thinking, an expression of nostalgia. I fear that for psychology it has no more than that logical status which—and here I use a provocative comparison—soap operas have for the masses. It may be that the psychological task that we call the *magnum opus*

---

[6] Geoffrey Chaucer, *The Canterbury Tales*, tr. Nevill Coghill, Penguin Books, 1981, pp. 299f. I became aware of this passage through a paper by Heino Gehrts. The Chaucer passage may remind us of Jung's statement, "Well, after all we managed—for first time since the dawn of history—to swallow the whole primordial animatedness of nature into ourselves; not only did the gods descend (or rather were they dragged down) from their planetary spheres and transformed into chthonic demons, but ... even this host of demons, which at the time of Paracelsus still frolicked happily in mountains and woods, in rivers and human dwelling-places, was reduced to a miserable remnant and finally vanished altogether" (*CW* 10 § 431, transl. modified).

remains the same throughout the ages. But what obviously does not stay the same is the *level* on which this task is set for us. Christianity catapulted the psyche onto a very different niveau, and it is on that niveau on which the psyche actually is today that we have to face *our magnum opus*. Today the psyche is no longer on the niveau of antiquity and of pagan psychology.

Of course, we should not connect any value judgment with this observation. Whether this change is good or bad is irrelevant, inasmuch as it is real. It did occur, and thus changed the situation totally.

So it seems to be psychologically the wrong move to directly try to ensoul the world again, just like that, or to expect to experience nature again as divine. It would be a nostalgic re-enactment of a historical psychological situation. I cannot see how we could strive for a new cosmology, a new re-mythologization of nature.

And we do not *need* a new mythology or psychology of nature either. Why? Because we already *have* our psychology of nature. Our real and legitimate psychology of nature is called physics, a term that here includes all natural sciences (sciences of *physis*), just as our real psychotherapy of nature or the world is called technology. The psychological job that physics in the wider sense as the modern psychology of nature has is to prove that there is nothing divine in nature, no elves, nymphs or spirits. Nature is nothing but a kind of machine, a system of abstract, formal laws, a set of mathematical formulas. This is the Christian soul's truth about nature. Therefore, to play the soulful cosmos against physics' abstract universe does not help the soul; it contributes to the neurotic split prevailing in our modern situation. It is an act of splitting to set psychology and psychotherapy against physics and technology, just because physics and technology do not fulfill our *old* ideas of what is soulful and what not, ideas developed formerly when the psyche was still at a very different niveau. The soul has emigrated from the cosmos and moved on to the universe. And, it would seem, it has not done so just as a joke or by mistake. As far as the natural world is concerned, all the *passion* of the soul seems to go into physics and technology. *This* is where the real action is. And it would seem to be a grave psychological wrong *to withhold from that which is driven by so much soul passion the predicate psychological or soulful.*

Of course, I do not wish to suggest that the world as physics presents it to us is soulful in the same old sense of the word, and I do not want us to strive to discover this old kind of soulfulness in physics, because I agree it cannot be found there. This is the very point: The very meaning of soul and soulfulness has changed. The soul is no longer where it once was. And as painful as it may be, it is our job to follow suit in our thinking and acquire a new definition of what is soulful today by allowing ourselves to be taught by the real movement of the soul itself. It is our psychological job to finally *own* and acknowledge physics and technology as inalienable parts of our soul work. This would require that our consciousness undergo a revolution with respect to its categories and that we learn to see the soul where we least expect it and so far have loathed to see it. How else could the neurotic split be overcome? How else could what has been held cut off from the soul for so long be brought home? But we hold on to the old notion of soulfulness and therefore necessarily deny physics' view of nature as the legitimate expression of today's soul work, insisting in its stead on a new cosmology, a new conception of nature in terms of the *anima mundi*. We thereby deepen the split and disown an essential part of today's *magnum opus*.

In my view the road to the *anima mundi* is closed. Nature is 'out,' at least in any psychological, theological, or metaphysical sense, and that it is 'out' is the very point of the message that our psychology of nature, physics, holds for us. Inasmuch as the attempt to re-mythologize and re-ensoul nature was a move away from Jung's emphasis on individuation, do I now with my critique of the world-soul simply return to the very psychology of individuation that world-minded Jungian colleagues tried to leave? I am afraid that the idea of the process of individuation, if critically examined, proves to belong just as much to a *historical* psychology as does the psychology of the anima mundi. Today, the real life of the psyche is not in the individuation process. It is somewhere else. The logical status of individuation is that it is psychologically obsolete, truly a thing of the past. This does not mean that the process of individuation does not exist or occur anymore. It only means that even when and where it occurs together with the deep fulfilling experience of meaning, it occurs only *as* disconnected, disengaged from what psychologically is really going on in our age and *as* suspended within that self-contained bubble that we call our personal psychology.

Individuation has lost its metaphysical *raison d'être* in much the same way as had that old African chief whom Jung once asked about his dreams. The chief replied with tears in his eyes that in olden times chiefs used to have dreams, and thus knew whether there would be war or sickness, whether the rains would come, and where one should drive the herds. His grandfather had still dreamed. But since the white man had come to Africa, nobody had dreams anymore, Jung reports in *MDR* (p. 265). One didn't need dreams any longer either, because now the Englishmen knew everything! Jung added by way of commentary that the medicine man who had formerly negotiated with the gods or the fates and advised his people had lost his *raison d'être*. The authority of the medicine man had been replaced by that of the District Commissioner. Jung said that this man was not in any way an imposing personality, but rather a whining old man. Nonetheless, or perhaps for that reason, he was a visual and impressive representation of the subterraneously spreading collapse of an obsolete and forever irrevocable world.

So far I have merely *claimed* that, as far as its deeper psychological or metaphysical *raison d'être* is concerned, individuation is 'out,' just as much as is the attempt to return to the anima mundi. Now I have to *show* that it is indeed obsolete.

What we are witnessing at present in our world is a gigantic revolution that makes the Industrial Revolution look harmless. In the entire economy a radical and extremely powerful process of restructuring, downsizing, of rationalization is going on. It is a process that renders hundreds of thousands or millions of employees redundant and assigns to those remaining ones the logical status of a collective maneuverable mass. Parallel to "just-in-time" production, there is a tendency to "just-in-time" employment ("MacJob"). In Germany, people with limited-term contracts are sometimes referred to as "Durchlaufmaterial," which might be rendered as "transit material." The term is an allusion to the "Durchlauferhitzer," the continuous-flow water heater, suggesting that as far as their status in industry is concerned, they are considered as an amorphous and continuously replaceable substance as is water, and no longer as so many human beings, each with their individual identity and personal dignity.

This is a process that is not the evil doing of individual managers. It is nobody's fault. It is a development that engulfs us with compelling necessity, and has to be likened more to an elementary force of nature than to a deliberate human act.

Of course, one might say that people had always been a maneuverable mass, just think of the statute labor for feudal lords, of the slaves of antiquity or the masses who where forced to build the Egyptian pyramids. But the slaves or serfs were not real people in our sense. They did not have their freedom and their "metaphysical" dignity in themselves: the Pharaoh, the King, their Lord more or less exclusively embodied and carried their dignity (majesty) and freedom for them. So the enslavement did not really happen to the self, to the "metaphysical" core of humans. It only struck those humans who in this form of society represented what was merely "empirical" or "accidental" about human existence. But the process that today gives people the status of no more than a maneuverable mass happens precisely to people who are *defined* as having their "majesty," we call it human dignity, in themselves, as a constitutional human right. This is what today gives this process a logical, not merely empirical, significance, inasmuch as it hits the "metaphysical" self.

Empirically speaking, this process affects only individual people, even though they can be counted by the millions. But psychologically or logically *their* being affected by this process is to be seen as a symbolic expression and concrete visualization of a much deeper and otherwise invisible (irrepresentable) fundamental change in the very status of humans as such. Above I spoke of this process as a gigantic revolution. Now, when it is a question of comprehending its meaning, I can specify and say that it is a Copernican Revolution. Just as in astronomy Copernicus dethroned the earth from its hereditary position as the center of the cosmos and turned it into a mere satellite of the sun, so today the human being is dethroned. Not only individual people are being made redundant. This is only the literal truth. The psychological truth is that this empirical phenomenon tells us something about the fact that we humans are being made metaphysically redundant. The relation between the production process and the human being is reversed. The human factor is becoming secondary. Ideally, industry would like to be able to do completely without humans, leaving it to the welfare services to take responsibility for them, and to work only with robots and totally automated processes. Unfortunately, in empirical reality this is not possible, you still need people to design and program the robots. But this empirical need for humans is only a tribute to circumstances, not an expression of the truth of the age. In truth, or psychologically, the human being has already lost its *raison d'être*, the same way Jung's African chief had. The economy is no longer there for the well-being of humans, but humans are there for the well-being of the production process and count only to the extent that they are needed for the advancement of production. It is expected of people that they accommodate to what the production process demands; they have to display the highest degree of mobility and readiness to retrain for new jobs. In this way it is brought out into the open that from now on humans, as a maneuverable mass or as transit material, have to be subservient to the objective needs of the production process, which is the only thing that really has a *raison d'être* because it is authorized by, and of course in turn subservient to, the supreme value of today, that of *maximizing profit* in the context of global competition. Profit maximization means "profit for profit's sake," totally abstract. It means *Money's* absolute demand to become multiplied, not simply people's wish to increase their fortune. Profit maximization in this sense is the sun around which humans have been assigned to revolve, by no means because of the personal greed of those who profit from this profit, but because the Copernican Revolution has redefined the role of humans as mere satellites. Money's *objective* need to become ever more for its own sake, completely detached from subjective human wishes for wealth and from any longing of thereby becoming able to fulfill *concrete* wishes within a social context (a villa, expensive cars, designer clothes, etc.), has forced people (together with their naturally also present subjective financial interests) into its service, although very often people mistake these objective wishes that they are forced to have with personal wishes of their own, while those idealistic people who are not part of the financial and industrial sector commit the same mistake by condemning the powerful pull towards profit maximization as modern society's exclusively materialistic attitude.

This sun is, just as the sun was for Plato, *to agathon*, the highest good, the *summum bonum*. It is the only, exclusive value prevailing today; it has no other values, no other suns, before or beside it. It is an end, nay, *the* end in itself. It is our real God, our real Self, and also the real *soul* and *spiritus rector* of (or in) the real. This Copernican Revolution is not bloody, but what is happening because of it is nevertheless tremendous, terrifying. Its violence is logical or psychological, we could also say metaphysical. Compared to it, the French and the Russian Revolutions were cozy.

In such a context where the very goal of the process we find ourselves in is to objectively render the human being, and individual identity as such, metaphysically or logically redundant, the process of individuation has no place. To still advocate it is the wrong move. It entirely misses the point. The process of individuation is totally disconnected from what is really going on. Not individuation, but *globalization* is the soul's *magnum opus* of today. And globalization means the elimination of personal identity as something in its own right and the logical subjugation of everything individual under the one great abstract goal of profit maximization: Profit must increase, but I must decrease. The process of profit maximization (together with the need for companies and individuals to stand up well in global competition) brings about the subjugation of all of life, indeed of Being, under the logic of money.

Here it becomes necessary to remind you that with these statements I am not giving you *my program*. I am not describing what *I* think would be good and right and desirable and should be done. I am merely trying to formulate the program or logic inherent in the powerful 'autonomous' movement of the soul.

But this is a point where violent objections tend to stir in us, objections that apply just as much to my above assertion that *psychologically* or *logically* nature and the anima mundi are "out." The main objections are two. The first is based on the testimony of our personal feeling and experience. Very frequently, our personal feelings contradict my analysis. They refer to our dreams, to our inner experience such as it might occur in a deep analytical process or to the feelings aroused in us by nature. We may have experienced a deeply meaningful process of individuation. In nature we may have felt a divine presence. Both these kinds of experiences may have come with an undeniable sense of reality and conviction that is not invalidated by any rational argument.

The second objection is of a more theoretical nature. It operates by means of the distinction between inner and outer, individual process and the collective life, a distinction that comes with a valuation. Psychology tends to side with the inner personal life, and disregard or depreciate objective social and economic development. All psychological importance is assumed to rest with our archetypal inner experience, our dreams, the imaginal, while what is going on in the world at large is regarded as part of the collective consciousness, which implies that it is of a psychologically more superficial nature and thus of less weight and meaning. From this standpoint one can agree that there is obviously the process of globalization that I described, but one would flatly deny that this process is today's form of the *magnum opus*. On the contrary, one would see in it a kind of defense against the *real magnum opus* of the individuation process, our being one-sidedly caught up in materialistic, merely external ego concerns devoid of any deeper soul meaning.

Both these objections, as mighty as they are, must be seen through as psychologically dangerous traps. Why is this so?

I will first look at the second objection. The opposition of one's inner life and collective consciousness, as generally understood and used, contains an equivocation or is the contamination of two different oppositions that should be kept apart. The one opposition is phenomenological and positive (positivistic). For it, there are two kinds of experiences or two *realms* of experience. On the one side there are our dreams, feelings, and visions, which even if they are archetypal in nature, nevertheless are strictly individual and personal. To be sure, I can share them with others, but I also *have* to explicitly share them if I want others to know of them, because they can only learn from me what I experienced in my dreams. On the other side there are those processes that are publicly visible or truly common knowledge.[7] So this opposition very matter-of-factly distinguishes between two realms of experience according to the *source* of knowledge or the locus of the experience.

The second opposition is one of feeling or valuation. As such it is not positive (positivistic). It requires a certain sensitivity. Phenomena

---

[7] I leave aside here the truly *common*, i.e., communal knowledge which, as archetypal soul truths, is *a priori* shared, be it wittingly or unwittingly. I leave it aside because this knowledge precisely *precedes* experience.

are distinguished as to whether they are felt to be of deeper significance, more soulful, full of meaning, and to be a part of the true mysteries of the soul—or whether they seem to be more superficial and to have to do with practical workaday concerns, with one's orientation and survival in practical reality, with the human-all-too-human. Here the *magnum opus* of the soul has to be distinguished from the ordinary labors in the service of our ego needs and desires. Another formulation for this difference is the distinction between the archetypal and numinous quality of experiences versus the commonplace, rational, empirical, profane quality of life phenomena. This opposition assigns phenomena a different logical *status* according to their feeling value or their significance for the soul. Highly momentous political events may be of little soul significance, while deeply archetypal events may be very inconspicuous and go on unnoticed by the public.

In traditional Jungian psychology the positivistic and objective opposition of experiences that sets off those experiences which are held to be exclusively accessible through the individual from those belonging to the public domain has been confounded with the nonpositivistic and nonobjective opposition of two kinds of statuses or feeling values *we* assign to, or withhold from, experiences. The status of a *magnum opus*, of an archetypal mystery of the soul, was reserved for individual inner experience, and by the same token what happened in the outer world of social, economic and political developments was denied such predicates. By definition it had to be psychologically insignificant, if not downright soulless.

But is this *a priori* identification of the numinous with the inner experience of the individual tenable? It is not. Because it positivizes a distinction that cannot be positivized inasmuch as it depends on our original feeling appreciation vis-à-vis each new phenomenon. There is no *a priori* reason why the archetypal, why the *magnum opus* has to appear in the privacy of the consulting room or in some other alchemical vessel, and why it could not take place in the world out there, in what belongs to the public domain. Here I would like to introduce a phrase coined by Goethe: "das offenbare Geheimnis," the "apparent (or manifest, blatant) mystery." What Goethe had in mind was not a mystery or secret that had been revealed. He meant something that even though it is public knowledge remains a mystery. Perhaps one could say that precisely because it is in the limelight, it is not recognized as a mystery; it becomes the Stone rejected by the builders. The mystery character is obscured because the phenomenon is so exoteric, so apparent. The exoteric as the best concealment, the best shelter of the esoteric mystery of the soul. This parallels Jung's view that the ego, which allegedly and fictitiously is what is best known and most apparent, in reality is an unfathomably dark body (*CW* 14 §129). But above all we can think here of Heraclitus who in fragment 72 (DK) says, "They divorce themselves from that, the logos, with which most of all they are in continuous contact, and what they daily come across, that appears to them as alien."

Indeed there are good reasons to believe that there has been a fundamental change in the history of the soul. I presented two stories suggesting this, the Chaucer passage and Jung's report about the African medicine man. This change is not only a radical rupture, it is also a reversion. At the time of the forefathers of that medicine man, the *magnum opus* came from inside. It occurred through dreams, visions, meditation. It was a situation where in order to become aware of the mysteries of the soul, it was best to go into some kind of seclusion, into the desert, become a hermit, a monk. But now, not only the Africans of seventy years ago, but also we in the Western world live under the new rule of the "District Commissioner," who renders the world of the medicine man obsolete and irrevocable, and, as we know, the District Commissioner is not guided in his decisions by dreams, by meditation and other inner experiences. The change from medicine man to District Commissioner is a change of the locus of the soul, a reversal of the origin of inspiration, which no longer comes from inside but from outside. Now the real *magnum opus* takes place all around us in the tremendous public changes, in the globalization, rationalization and automation we experience today. This is the new locus of the movement of the soul, the present form of the mystery. And it is a real, an absolute mystery because we generally do not have the slightest inkling that, appearing so blatantly and so profanely, it could be a highly numinous archetypal process.

Here the first objection I talked about above comes into play again. Especially if we follow the insight that the difference between the deeply meaningful and the psychologically superficial depends on our feeling appreciation vis-à-vis each phenomenon, is not the individuation process with its deeply moving imaginal experiences something that immediately comes with a sense of highest soul value and deep conviction, whereas the process of globalization is conjoined with a feeling of soullessness, meaninglessness? This is certainly so. But it also is a trap. Because whether our dreams and imaginal experiences come with conviction and rich feeling or not is not the question at all. Of course the experiences that are part of the individuation process are deeply moving and fulfilling. There *is* a sense of undeniable reality. But what we are here concerned with is the shocking, exacting insight that all these experiences *together* with the intensive feelings that they evoke belong to the world of the African medicine man in us, and that this world as a whole, that is, together with our personal feelings of its reality and fulfilling meaning, has been ruthlessly rendered obsolete through the advent of the District Commissioner, a District Commissioner who in our case is the overwhelming pull towards maximizing profit.

The narrator of the Chaucer passage and Jung's African medicine man were honest and humble enough to admit the obsolescence of the world of elves and dreams, *despite* their feelings of deep appreciation and meaning that this world evoked for them. They acknowledged that elves and dreams, as meaningful and fulfilling as they may be, now have the status of no more than, we might say, "psychological antiques." Antiques, too, are invested with much soul value. But as antiques, they are *known* to belong to a world that is irrevocably gone.

We are not so honest and humble. All we want to see is *our feelings*; we want that the images produced by the individuation process arouse in us deeply fulfilling personal feelings of meaning and conviction. Because *we* feel this, we insist that they must still be true. We refuse to raise the question of the actual logical status in which our experiences, together with all the feelings they evoke, stand. We refuse to acknowledge that the real development has overridden and constantly overrides the meaning of those experiences. The individuation process as a whole belongs to historical, archeological psychology. Its images are not unreal, but they represent the reality *of* the past, of what, having once been at the forefront of life, is now historical in us. The images do not represent the reality of the present. Our whole personal psychology with all our feelings of meaning is 'sunken history,' it is the collapsed or condensed and interiorized actual living conditions of former ages. By stubbornly insisting on *our* feelings of the deep meaning evoked by the individuation experience, we as modern people are, as it were, playing 'African medicine man of old' or 'shaman'—without, however, admitting that we are merely *playing* those roles and without realizing that *our* feelings are decidedly *ego* feelings fired by ego desires for a deeper meaning. In a way, we are like tourists watching a show of tribal dancing or a shamanistic séance, and because we are deeply moved by it in our personal feeling, we take this feeling as a mark of truth, closing our eyes to the fact that we are witnessing a mere tourist attraction. To be sure, this show *is* the display *of* a former truth, but this display *itself* does not have the status of truth anymore. Here I am reminded of a statement by Jung about the Catholic Mass: "I know it is the truth, but it is the truth in a form in which I cannot accept it any more. ... It is no more true to me; it does not express my psychological condition. ... I need a new form" (*CW* 18 § 632).

The dreams of the real medicine men of old dealt with where the herds had to be driven, whether there would be war or illness, rain or drought. As Jung put it, they "negotiated with the gods" about the fate, the real (also political, economic) fate, of their whole people. There is nothing comparable in the individuation process of today. Generally the dreams in today's individuation processes, as archetypal as they may be, are nonetheless only of personal, private significance, which clearly shows that the meaning that they undoubtedly have is suspended, idle meaning, similar to the meaning of a personal hobby. It is a meaning that is there, but is no longer *true*, inasmuch as truth would imply a meaning that also encompasses, and does justice to, what is really going on in our modern world.

Jung recovered for our time the notion of the *magnum opus* or the symbolic life (about which he spoke to the Guild in 1939). He recovered it through his study of historical soul processes, such as those in the world of alchemy, and through his finding parallel processes in the personal analysis of his analysands. Because of this formal parallelism, Jung thought that the development going on inside those modern individuals was the same *magnum opus*. But I believe this was a mistake, a mistake concerning the order of magnitude. Jung's newly recovered insight into the reality called *magnum opus* is a precious notion, an invaluable discovery. We should *retain* it—*but* we should withdraw the predicate 'magnum opus' from individual experience, to which Jung had still assigned it. Individual experience of the individuation process today no longer deserves this title. As part of our strictly personal psychology, it may still be The Work, the *opus*, rather than just an ego activity, but it certainly does not qualify as the *Great* Work. It is *opus parvum*, the "little work." It is part of our personal psychology and thus of an ultimately historical psychology. As such, it has both its own dignity and importance, inasmuch as our caring for the past we carry in us is always important, but its status is such that it can no longer be considered "magnum." The true *opus magnum* of today takes place in an entirely different arena, not in us as individuals, but in the arena of world affairs, of global competition, in the arena of the psychological District Commissioner, who in our case, as we said, is the overwhelming pull towards maximizing profit. The individual merely feels the *effects* of the *opus magnum* as those of a blind fate, but remains absolutely disconcerted, helpless, and dumbfounded as to *what* it is that is happening to him and why.

We can get support for the critique of the view of individual experience as a *magnum opus* from Jung himself. When Jung in his *Memories* explicitly refers to the *Faust* work as Goethe's *magnum opus* and when he sees his own work as a continuation of the work on the psychological problematic with which Goethe in his *Faust* and Nietzsche in his *Zarathustra* struggled, he himself sees the *magnum opus* as a non-individual, non-personal Work. Obviously, Goethe's drama is not a report about his personal individuation process. It is concerned with a soul problematic that is the problematic of the Western soul at large (even in Jung's view). The same applies to Nietzsche's *Zarathustra*. And of course the Medieval alchemical *opus*, too, was a decidedly cultural (Jung would have said "collective") project, not a personal one, not one focussing on the individual development of the alchemist as this particular person, even though, naturally, in all three cases (alchemy, Goethe, Nietzsche) the person through whom the Work expressed itself figures in the particular "coloring" of the result.

Psychology is incapable of seeing today's *magnum opus*, the *opus* of maximizing profit, *as* the soul's *magnum opus* of today (or rather, as one, namely the present, *phase* of that ongoing *opus*). Psychology feels it has to disparage it as a *wrong* development, has to deny its origin in the soul, deny that it is the present form of the soul's symbolic life.

Why? Because of psychology's basic fault, which is that it operates with (and within) the opposition of 'individual' and 'collective.' The powerful dynamic of profit maximization in the context of global competition is neither individual nor collective (a term that, strictly speaking, denotes nothing else than a kind of plural of 'individual,' anyway. It denotes a "collection" or amassment of individuals).[8] This dynamic has nothing to do with people. It is of an entirely different order. It is the *logic* of our reality, the logic or truth *we are in* (regardless of whether we are no more than the bewildered victims of this process or, as managers in industry or the like, active participants in, and contributors to, it). Of course, 'logic' not in the sense of abstract *Formal* Logic, logic as a tool for correct reasoning. What I mean is a concrete logic, a reality, a *dynamis*: psycho-logic. It is the real movement of the soul or rather: the soul of and in the real processes; it is the soul's life, which is logical life.[9]

What I said about the dynamic of profit maximization has to be extended to psychological phenomena as such. Inasmuch as they are psychological, they are neither individual nor collective. Those are the wrong categories. They simply do not apply. The soul may show itself in, and play through the lives of, individuals and collectives, but it is not itself something pertaining to the one or the other. With the opposition of 'individual' and 'collective,' psychology still remains subject to the *anthropological fallacy*, i.e., to the assumption that the psyche is a part of humans, a kind of 'attribute' of the 'substance' or 'substrate' called people, so that psychology would ultimately be about human beings rather than about the soul; it would be about what *they* feel, think and desire, about their imaginal

---

[8] Both terms, 'individual' as well as 'collective,' belong to the level of the positive-factual. They are part of foreground reality or the ego-world. The soul has no stake in them. Collective phenomena are the object of study of sociology, not psychology. Statements about collective phenomena are made in the language of statistics and based, for example, on opinion polls. The *psychological* other to both 'individual' and 'collective' is the 'communal' or the 'Universal.' Jung's name "collective unconscious" is a misnomer. What Jung had in mind was the *communis opinio*, just as when he spoke of *quod semper et ubique et ab omnibus creditur*, he by no means thought of the statistical maximum value in an opinion poll, the majority opinion. He thought of something that was not countable at all because it ruled regardless of what *people* said and thought, what they believed or did not believe. Nevertheless, Jung made the severe mistake of using the term 'collective' for something that as soul reality, and thus a logical, absolute-negative reality, was at right angles to the individual vs. collective opposition.

[9] I elaborated this idea in my *Animus-Psychologie*, Frankfurt/M (Peter Lang) 1994.

experiences—generally, about what is going on inside them. Psychology would be a subdivision of anthropology.

But apart from the fact that such a conception of psychology is untenable for methodological reasons, it is also untenable in view of what we experience today. After all, it is the inherent telos and the very point of the process of profit maximization to radically render this conception impossible. This process is all around us, as our *absolute*; it is the medium or element of our existence, much like the air is the element of the human organism's existence, and it is the God to which we sacrifice what we hold most dear.

If, as we have seen, the telos and meaning of the *opus* of maximizing profit is to render people redundant, does this moment of the symbolic life not serve as our *initiation* into what I call the "psychological difference," the difference between human and soul? Do we not have to acknowledge it as our psychopomp guiding us *out of* the anthropological or ontological fallacy dominating the present consciousness and *into* a new form of consciousness? More than 450 years after the Copernican Revolution in astronomy, the process of profit maximization today finally gives psychology (or consciousness itself) a chance to experience its Copernican Revolution. As the human being is dethroned from the central place around which psychological life allegedly has to revolve, the psyche can finally in truth be recognized as what Jung tried to see it: as objective or autonomous psyche, or as I would prefer to say, as the logical life of the soul, a life that is its own end (even though it lives through us and needs us to give expression to it). Jung said that we are *in* the psyche, the psyche is not in us. For him the meaning of human existence was to express and represent the symbolic life; symbolic life was not there to serve people's ends and interests. I think this is what is indeed still happening today in the gigantic revolution I referred to, even if on a fundamentally different level.

But as long as psychology clings to the idea of the individual and the collective, we are blind to it, and while paying lip service to Jung's idea of the autonomous psyche, we reduce the psyche (which after all in reality is the truth we live in) to a kind of human appendix. By operating more or less exclusively within the fantasy of 'individual' and 'collective,' psychology necessarily presses all soul phenomena into these molds. Stultifying itself, it forces its own thought to be and stay ontological (to be inevitably concerned with *ontic entities* and their states, and to systematically hold itself down on that level). Like a balloon tied to the hand of the child holding it, its notion of the soul and of psychological life is not allowed to fly. This notion is put under fundamental *a priori* restraints. It is tied to the notion of 'human being' or "people" and is subordinated to it as its substrate. *It, the notion of the soul and of psychological life, cannot be released into its own* so as to be given the chance of becoming truly psychological.

Now there is no denying that the process of globalization and profit maximization is an absolutely brutal occurrence destroying much of what hitherto has been considered part of a soulful human existence. It violates all our values and expectations. Bringing about the total subjugation of all of life under the principle of money, it ruthlessly sweeps away much, if not all, of what used to give meaning to life. Thus it is not difficult to understand why it is seen as a *wrong* development and as one that psychology is called upon to compensate, e.g., with the personal individuation experience (if not downright to fight against). No doubt, this view is an honorable reaction. However, it is also misguided, for two reasons.

First of all, this reaction succumbs to the moralistic fallacy and has the character of a "defense" in the psychoanalytic sense. It introduces a moral response (a condemnation) at a point where rather our establishing a conscious, knowing relationship to the phenomenon in question would be in place. Thus psychology here does more or less the same thing as what unanalyzed people generally tend to do with respect to the "shadow": because it is "bad," they try to rid themselves of it or deny, repress it. But the shadow first of all needs to be acknowledged and investigated ("analyzed") *without reserve*, prior to any value judgment, in order to become fully known. It would seem to me that the global process we are faced with today first of all needs the same kind of response so that we might get to know *what* exactly the reality is we are faced with here and what its order of magnitude and its psychological significance are. The premature moral condemnation prevents impartial "analysis." It does not give the "shadow" a chance. Thus it misses the very nature and reality of what it condemns. It fights not so much against this *real* "enemy," as it thinks and hopes to be doing; it rather defends against having to face it and becoming conscious of it (and possibly becoming conscious *through* it). But this means that it even misses out in moral regards, in other words, in its own field, because the much needed *proper* moral response is one that comes *after* an uncompromising acknowledgment and psychological comprehension.

What the moralistic defense is ultimately supposed to achieve, however, is to fictitiously prevent the Copernican Revolution we talked about, the shift to the full realization of "the autonomous psyche." Its purpose is a much more fundamental one than to defend against having to face certain unpleasant developments. It fights for something much bigger, much more radical. It fights to retain the very *principle* constituting the modern self-understanding of man; it fights to rescue the logic governing modern consciousness, its *metaphysic of the ego*, and conversely to ward off the insight into the fact that this metaphysic has already been overrun. By calling upon us to take a stand pro or con, the moral defense once more tries to call the "responsible ego" to arms and thus to place itself into the center, as if it were not too late. In this way it tries to supply the long obsolete anthropological fallacy with a (seeming) strength after all.

Now I come to the second reason why the view that the dynamic of profit maximization is a "wrong development" is misguided. From a psychotherapeutic standpoint the question forces itself upon us: could it not be that it is *we* who force this development into soullessness and meaninglessness precisely because we refuse to consciously acknowledge it as an authentic movement of the soul? Much as unacknowledged psychological conflicts may be forced to manifest in the symptomatic form of "soulless" somatizations? By turning a deaf ear to what is happening and by withholding our appreciation from it, we deprive it of the possibility to be connected to consciousness. We force it down into the status of literalism and hold it there.

We must not dissociate ourselves from what is happening, whatever it may be. On the contrary, much as Jung said about God that He needs us for His becoming conscious, this process *needs* us, needs our heart, our feeling, our imaginative attention and rigorous thinking effort so as to have a chance to become instilled with mind, with feeling, with soul. It must not be left as something that happens totally outside of us and apart from our consciousness. It must, as it were, be reborn through the soul and in the soul: in our *real* comprehension, i.e., *in us as* the "existing Concept" (Hegel).

Inasmuch as owing to our longstanding stubborn refusal we are very, very far removed from understanding what is happening to us in this process; for the time being we cannot even dream of a real comprehension. It is probably a task for generations to work towards a situation where this process has fully come home to consciousness. So what "not withholding our feeling appreciation and thinking attention from this process" would mean for us today most immediately is that we allow ourselves to be affected, indeed, wounded, by it; that, even though it pains us, we let it into our hearts, opening ourselves to it. The task is to (keenly and intelligently, not emotionally = sentimentally!) suffer the fundamental loss this process inflicts upon us and to allow it to work on us, as a kind of chisel that objectively and factually, not merely subjectively, works off our inflated egocentricity and subjectivism,[10] our personalistic mode-of-being-in-the-world and along with it the entire "anthropological fallacy." The consciousness, or real Notion, of the "objective psyche" must be *realiter* and objectively acquired through a slow process of painful experiences. It must be more than an "idea" or "representation" in our mind that we subscribe to. It must conversely have inscribed itself into us. We come to a real knowledge only by having "learned the hard way." Subjective understanding and agreeing is not sufficient.[11] The statute of Zeus, *pathei mathos* (which might be rendered as "having learned the hard way" or "conscious through suffering"), is still valid today.[12]

---

[10] It is worth noting that I am not speaking here about a personal or subjective subjectivism. Regardless of whether I or you as private individuals are personally characterized by an inflated egocentricity or not, regardless also of how we subjectively feel, and what we think, about it, this inflated egocentricity and subjectivism is objectively the *logical* character of our being since it is the prevailing truth or logic of our age.

[11] Just think of communism, whose being untenable had *intellectually* been seen through long ago, but whose objective collapse, in the economic reality "out there" and as a form of the organization of a *real*, empirical society, was nonetheless necessary to truly drive this insight home. The alchemy of history makes conscious through *factual* operations (*calcinatio, putrefactio, mortificatio, solutio*, etc.) upon us as the prima materia, not through *our* trying to get rational insights. It brings about the real Concept, one that is not synonymous with "what we imagine or think subjectively about the situation out there." It is the unity of what we think *and* what has *become apparent* as having a real presence 'out there.'

[12] Aeschylus, *Agamemnon*, line 177.

Appendix

In preparation for an online seminar on the above article conducted by me under the auspices of the C. G. Jung, Analytical Psychology, and Culture Website, October 4th-7th, 1998, the moderators of the seminar, Dolores Brien (editor of The Round Table Review*) and Donald Williams, had invited Greg Mogenson to write a response to the theses expressed by me, to which I responded. This first exchange was followed by a second round, and all the material was made available to the seminar participants. Below I present the text of my two answers (in a slightly shortened and modified form for them to be more easily understandable as stand-alone texts) because they introduce valuable differentiations and additional aspects of my view of the role of "the individual." I am very grateful to Mogenson for having made it necessary for me through his insightful critical interjections to tackle this topic anew and to address myself to particular issues raised by him.*

I.

It goes without saying that the individual is indispensable and that "laying [our] infinitesimal grain in the scales of humanity's soul" (*CW* 16 § 449) is crucial. Mankind exists in the form of individuals. Without them, there would be no thought, no art, no social life, no dreams. Just as birth and death, eating and sleeping, working and love-making are constants, so the importance of the individual is a constant. I am not pleading for team work, not for a laissez-faire attitude, I am not trying to do away with individual responsibility and thereby endorse "the banality of evil." My thesis of the obsolescence of the individual is on a different level, which can be seen when in the last passage from my article I add the comment in parentheses, "(even though it [the life of the psyche] lives through us and needs us to give expression to it)." The *parentheses* are to indicate that here, with this comment, I have left the otherwise psychological level of my discourse and shifted to another, the extrapsychological discourse of common sense or everyday consciousness.

Seen from outside, from the perspective of outer reality or common sense, the shaman, the chief, the Pharaoh, the great artist, the alchemist were, of course, individuals. But *psychologically*, they did their dreaming, thinking, and creating not as singular individuals, but *as* the soul of the tribe, as "the whole," as "universal." This alone is what makes a dream a "big" dream, the opus a *magnum opus*, a painting a work of art. The alchemists did not work at *their* self-development, but sought *the* Stone as such, everybody's Stone, the Stone for mankind, and Jung's claim that their's was an unconscious concern for their own Self (only projected outside into matter) is an unforgivable psychologism, and an unfair interpretation of alchemy.

My thesis is that the individual is *logically, psychologically* obsolete. The thesis is not that it is obsolete *as a positive fact*. This difference of the psychological versus the ordinary consciousness sense of "individual" is essential. My whole argument is a psychological one. I am not speaking from the point of view of ordinary reality. This is to say that I attack the *psychological idea* of the individual *as focus and purpose*, not the positive reality called individual. In a way I am trying to return (or advance?) to the truth of alchemy: that what counts is the transformation of the prime matter, not my own; and only to the extent that I dedicate myself to the prime matter's and not my own individuation or transformation process can I, too, experience *my* "redemption," where "my" refers to the extrapsychological notion of me as individual human being and not to the psychological notion of the ego-personality.

Now I want to discuss what I consider the different emphases in the set-up of psychology between two possible different positions. The one position basically operates within the subject-object relation. The Real is then on one side, and the psyche is predominantly the human psyche *responding* to "the traumas of the Real." The "objective psyche is also manifest in the capacity of the individual to image reality," this view says. This sentence has a chance of being true only if it is meant positivistically and not psychologically, i.e., if "individual" refers to the factual or empirical human being, to people, because an empirical person could be a shaman or true artist, etc. However, the capacity of the individual (in a *psychological* sense) to form fantasies is a manifestation of the subjective psyche. The individual's response is the equivalent to the work of sprayers who do not want to see the *reality* of an empty grey concrete wall and thus spray their own colorful designs on it. Psychologically speaking, only on the condition that we do our imaging not as individuals, but as logical "Universal," mythologically speaking: as the soul, the non-ego, is it the objective psyche that manifests in our capacity to image reality. This is a crucial distinction. Of course our young men may continue to dream dreams. But if their dreams are their individual dreams, they have the same status as the dreams and the drug-induced visions of the hippie generation that later turned yuppie. Why today do we have a drug problem as no time before did? Because people want to dream their own dreams, cut off from the soul's *magnum opus*. Only if a young man's dream is not his individual dream, but if he is dreaming the Mercurial dream hidden in today's prime matter, in what is really going on in our time is it a dream of the objective psyche. Yes, *we* must "struggle to differentiate and redeem" the "dark side of the Self," we who, externally speaking, exist only as individuals. But psychologically speaking we must not do this *as individuals*, because as individuals in the strict sense we do not even get near the Self. We pass it by.

I am too much of an alchemist to appreciate the quote from Jung, *CW* 8 §§ 331f., which I find reductive, even nihilistic.

> It is not storms, not thunder and lightning ... that remain as images in the psyche, but the fantasies caused by the affects they arouse. ... Man's curses against devastating thunderstorms, his terror of the unchained elements—these affects anthropomorphize the passion of nature, and the purely physical element becomes an angry god. Like the physical condition of his environment, the physiological conditions, glandular secretions, etc., also can arouse fantasies charged with affect. Sexuality appears as a god of fertility ... or as a terrifying serpent that squeezes its victim to death.

Jung starts out from the fictitious abstraction of "the purely physical element" (as if there were such a thing), which through a secondary fantasy activity is allegedly turned into a god. If this were how it is, such a god would not have truth in him and thus not really be a god. He would not be an epiphany, but a subjective projection, a bumper sticker glued onto the Real. In contrast to the idea that "the *magnum opus* of any age is to fathom and consciously participate in the symbolic life which the psyche makes possible through its autocratic responses to the traumas of the Real with which it is in dialectical [Jung would say, compensatory] relationship," I say that viewed from a mythological or alchemical perspective, the god or the Mercurius does not come from a secondary "autocratic" (!) response to the Real, but is what is contained or imprisoned in the Real itself to begin with. The "autocratic" response to the Real is only anima, only Maya, projection. Likewise, the *effort* to re-ensoul the world with anima mundi is, in my eyes, a typically modern ego effort. If you start out with the idea of the objective psyche, you do not have to work at re-ensouling anything, because the soul is already there to begin with, and it is usually where it is least expected and least wanted. This is why I want to mine the objective phenomena (for example, the phenomena of Globalization, Profit Maximation, etc.) for soul, rather than to "form fantasies" about them. Instead of responding in the sense of a *compensatory* relationship between psyche and the traumas of the Real, I want to listen to what the real process is telling me; I want to be taught by the Real how I have to think, I want to be put into my place, maybe even "baptized" by it. This is how *I* am trying to lay my "infinitesimal grain in the scales of humanity's soul."

I find the idea of compensation in this context less than helpful. In our case it would mean: First we develop an economy based on Globalization and Profit Maximation and then, instead of (psychologically) taking the consequences, we want to cover it up with beautiful fantasies. Would this not be cheating? "Ye shall know them by their fruits." It is the fruits where our truth lies. Yes, let us drink the cup of our own unconscious collective doings to its very dregs. Because in those dregs and nowhere else lies our soul. But by saying this I do not suggest, like the Gnostics, that we should commit any "sins" in order to be able to be redeemed from them. The "sin" (if it is a sin) has already been committed. "To drink the dregs" as used by me is not an appeal to the literal behavior of committing any deeds. It means allowing oneself to be reached by the core of the deeds that have already been done and of what is going on, to both comprehend it and to be comprehended by it.

No doubt, one can back up the view that I cannot accept with ideas of Jung's. But I would want to put the emphasis on another Jung than this one, on that Jung who, e.g., said about the neurosis that we should try "to experience what it means, what it has to teach, what its purpose is. ... We do not cure it—it cures us" (*CW* 10 § 361). As all symptoms, Globalization and Profit Maximation are not what *needs* the psyche's "autocratic response," they *are* the psyche's "autocratic response." It is for us to get their psychological message, to comprehend them and, through our comprehension of them, be transformed by them.

The opposition of "traumas of the Real" and the "autocratic responses to" them seems to create a split. The psychological comes to be placed on one side only, the side of our imaging and the soul's response to the Real, whereas the Real itself on the other side is construed as totally soulless[13] (which is what is responsible for the desire to re-ensoul the world with anima mundi in the first place; if the Real were not *construed* as devoid of soul and in need of our individual symbolizing, no need to re-ensoul it would be felt). In the case of tornados and earthquakes such a conception of the Real may be acceptable. But in the case of Globalization? The latter is a development within our human economic activities and as such not a "trauma of the Real" in the sense that natural catastrophes are. As man-made, Globalization is in itself a product of the soul's symbolizing activity. It does not need *another* symbolizing. It needs our intellectual and feeling comprehension and that response to it that consists in our allowing it to penetrate and transform us or, as Jung put it, to cure us.

II.

My thesis is that today the dissociation, to retain this term, is not an act performed by anybody, but the logical character of our modern world as such. We *find* ourselves *in* the dissociation. The split, the rupture is our *a priori*, and it goes through our world as a whole as well as through the "objective psyche." This is why we cannot speak of the objective psyche or the collective unconscious in the singular any more. Now there are two of them: the *personal, subjective, private* "objective psyche" (or "collective unconscious") manifesting in "our dreams," on the one hand, and the *public, truly objective* "objective psyche" manifesting in what is going on in the economy and technology, for example, on the other. Similarly there is a rent going through the alchemical *opus*, dividing the *opus parvum*, as I call it, of individual analysis and the individuation process (in the conventional Jungian sense) from the *opus magnum* of our cultural process. There are the little "big dreams" of the individual and the big "big dreams" unconsciously driving the development of our

---

[13] The prime example of traumatizing events is literal torture, the infliction of pain that is absolutely devoid of any inherent soul-meaning or spirit. There is not even a "Mercurius" *imprisoned* in it that could possibly be redeemed. The "traumatic" is the one extreme, the opposite extreme would be the "epiphanic," with the alchemical *massa confusa* mid-way between them.

civilization. You cite Jung as saying that our dreams "present the situation as it is." True. But also ambiguous.

The question is, *which* situation? For you "the situation" seems to come as a singular. For me there is a duality of situations. "Our dreams" express only the personal, private situation of each individual, which *is* a bubble (a suspended, relatively self-enclosed cell) within the larger situation of the world. Or do you really believe that "our dreams" and what conventional analytical psychology as a whole has to say are really relevant to, do really touch and reach, what is really going on in our age? Do they represent a contribution to an understanding of these uncanny processes? Are these processes the frame of reference for "our dreams"? Do the latter provide an answer to, or have a handle on, them? I, of course, do not know all the dreams of all individuals, but judging from what I have read of the literature in analytical psychology, which abounds with dream reports and case discussions, I would state that the whole lot of it, including the so-called "big" (archetypal) dreams and the descriptions of beautiful individuation processes, belong under the rubric of "ego-trip." Jung's African chief knew about his obsolescence. He was honest enough not to claim to have any big dreams any more and to be able to provide something like "meaning." In other words, he had accepted that from now on he could act as "chief," if at all, only in folklore shows. As "chief," he was a museum-piece.

But it was not he who had "dissociated himself" from what was going on in the outer world, from the British rule. No, he found himself in this objective split between obsolete traditional culture and superimposed Western civilization and government, and he found himself only on the one, the lower or sublated, side of this split. He was in a bubble. And what really went on, went on above his head. This shows that the dissociation I have in mind is not a horizontal one between left hand and right hand. It is a vertical or hierarchical one. This is why I think the suggestion that for amplification of dreams we should turn to newspapers, not to Greek myths, illusionary for two reasons. (1) You cannot overcome the dissociation that easily. It's too cheap. (2) By doing this, you would even miss out on what dreams and individual psychic life can provide. For it is not true that generally the context of a person's dreams are the forces that are described in my paper. No, the context of today's dreams is the soul's *history*, ancient myth. The consulting room is a museum for psychic antiques. This is what individual psychological work is on the whole all about. And this is what gives Jungian therapy its dignity.

The moment you pretend that it both is responsive to, and has a bearing on, the real problems of the age, it becomes a fraud. The Jungian therapist should know what the nature is of what he is doing when working with a patient or analysand. In the consulting room he should try to be a *good* museum director, as it were. Otherwise he becomes phony and inflates psychotherapy, burdening it with a task that for systematic or structural reasons it cannot possibly achieve. He turns into the sprayer (sorry!). The method of amplification makes sense only if you already know what the individual items used as amplifications mean. Amplification refers to *quod semper et ubique et ab omnibus creditur* (what is always and everywhere and by everybody believed). It serves the purpose of connecting consciousness with the eternal truths. But who today could claim he had a real inkling of what in the depths is going on in our time and thus would be able to use newspaper reports as amplification material? It is all above our heads. It is absolutely new, unheard of. It is precisely not contained in *quod semper et ubique et ab omnibus creditur*. The archetypes have become jobless in the context of these gigantic processes. Their place is in the personal psyche, which is the sublated past (cultural history). There is something totally other going on today.

To my mind it is a deception (sweet talk based on wishful thinking) to state that "the individual, at the logical level, is a universal"—*just like that*. This is the denial of the real plight of the modern soul. And it is a fundamentalism, a mere dogma not in any way borne out by the conditions of life today. Like the African ex-chief, modern man deeply *knows* that he logically is no longer capable of being the Universal. Just look around at our real situation: the feeling of a loss of meaning and of isolation, the addictions, the form of modern art, the character of the prevailing philosophies and theories, etc., all bear witness to the fact that "individual" and "universal" cannot be brought together. At least for 200 years the individual has not been able to *be* the Universal any more, and for that many years this has been the explicit problem so many great minds struggled with. Why does psychology try to ignore this? During this hapless century many politicians and ideologists tried, since this identity of individual and universal was not a given reality, to at least force the identity of the universal and the individual one way or another, with catastrophic results (Fascism, Socialism, etc.). Jung, too, suffered from and struggled with this problem, and I claim that at least the Jung of the conventional Jung-interpretation did not have the logical means to resolve it. If at all, the "individual *as* universal" would only have a chance (no more than a chance) if psychology would go beyond the imagination (the hope for dream images) and advance to thought proper: the logic of the soul ....

You state that "Like globalization, the term 'individual' can also be a symbolic expression of the Real, a face of the objective psyche." Yes and no. Yes: everything that exists is part of our reality and an expression of the objective psyche. This applies to the Individuation Process as well as to the Me-generation and the Culture of Narcissism you refer to. But they, the term "individual," the phenomenon of Disneylands, talk shows, personalistic psychology, etc., are not a symbolic expression of the objective psyche *in the same way and sense* that globalization etc., are. We must not ignore the cleavage separating two very different logical statuses. The phenomena mentioned are the symbolic expression of the one half of the dissociated objective psyche, which has fallen apart into business / the *opus magnum* there and entertainment / the *opus parvum* here. There is the split between the real reality of Industry and High Finance, on the one hand, and the absolutely indifferent entertainment sector, etc., on the other hand. To which needs to be added the additional insight that the entertainment sector *as a whole* is itself a part of big business, which, however, does not alter the fact that the entertainment *itself* is nevertheless split-off, suspended, sublated, dislodged, without "meaning" (in the higher sense of the word). Even those types of entertainment that explicitly try to provide meaning (like the Churches, the New Age movement, etc.) only provide a commodity called meaning, not a real meaning that would truly, i.e., logically, encompass our full reality.

Postscript 2011

In the above paper I demonstrated and substantiated the fact of the obsolescence of "the individual" only briefly, mainly by means of the reference to the type of fundamental changes in economic life that rendered millions of people "redundant." This change in the logical status of the individual, which perhaps best comes out in the terms "human capital" or "human resources," is only one example among many for the general dethronement of "the individual." Just as capital in the literal financial sense consists of absolutely uniform, indistinguishable value units (dollars, euros, etc.), so the term "human capital" has reduced human beings to exchangeable units without individuality, and just as a country's literal resources are the name for the abstract sum-total of raw materials, so the concept of people as "human resources" reduces people to means to an end without human dignity. But the point I wanted to make can of course be corroborated by numerous other observations from our modern world.

We have to distinguish the *psychological* notion of human "individual" (i.e., "individual" as a logical constitution or status of people, as a form of being, a self-perception and self-stylization, people *defined* as "individual personalities" in an eminent sense) from the trivial naturalistic or positive-factual concept of "individual" in the sense that people exist as fundamentally separate beings, individual organisms. The psychological concept of individual entails above all the following four characteristics:

1. The individual is a self-contained unit. It can be imaged as a circle with a definite center as its core and source. It is a self.

2. Essential to it is the distinction between the inner and the outer and the sense of and need for privacy. Jung even emphasized the importance for every individual of having "a secret."

3. In its life-long existence it is determined by an unbroken continuity of its identity and an organic development of its personality, often imagined in analogy to the self-unfolding of an acorn into an oak tree or according to the pattern of a *Bildungsroman*.

4. It has a sense of autonomy and self-determination, for which the said strong sense of privacy and a relative freedom from external influences and from observation by others are essential.

On all four counts the *entire logic of the individual* in this sense can be seen to be over in our present modern world. I will give a few casual hints.

Most telling and truly symptomatic is the rise of statistics since the 19ᵗʰ century. Today the dominant way of thinking about humans is statistical. For statistics, the individual does not count. It disappears in averages and percentages, in abstract numbers. In premodern times one was wont to say, for example, that a village had seven hundred souls. This has become impossible. Opinion polls and statistics are the attestation of the irrevocable sublatedness of the individual, which is, by the way, also the reason why today we have the institution of individual psychotherapy in the first place: as an empirical-practical (psychic) compensation and consolation for the modern truth of the *logical, psychological* irrelevancy of the individual.

We now have a de-centered self. It has even been called a "smeared-out self."[14] Individuals are fundamentally networked. The network comes first, the people second. The network is the true reality, true substance, and individuals are only *accidents* and elements within it. The Internet, the Web, and cell-phones are the technical objectification of this logic of networked-ness. Most telling in this regard is the development towards "cloud" computing. Very often one sees people using mobile phones, e.g., in parks or in cities: they are not relentlessly in their present Here, not where their body is, but both here and with the other person, or rather neither here nor there, at no real locality: in the wireless, immaterial communication. These technical realities are symbolic, that is to say, they reveal to us the inner truth about "the individual" today.

Privacy is being replaced by public self-display (on television, in social networking services like Facebook), sometimes even up to the point of shameless self-exposure. We have self-help groups in which people publicly weep out their grief or lay out their emotions. There is a strong tendency towards externalization: tattooing, piercings, punk fashion, outwardly displaying on one's clothes the labels or logos of the fashion companies, T-shirts with messages, etc. Many people instantly share via cell-phones with others every move they make.

Instant messaging, SMS communication are taking the place of the former culture of letter-writing. Classical writing culture, which involved a delay between thinking, writing, sending, and receiving and allowed for reflection and for carefully considered, articulated self-expression of a personality, is disappearing. On account of their briefness

---

[14] See Charles Ess, "Brave New Worlds? The Once and Future of Information Ethics," in: *International Review of Information Ethics*, vol. 12, 2010.

and instantaneousness, brief instant messages focus on mere *information* and invite superficiality.

The idea of having just one spouse for one's whole life and of establishing one family is succeeded by the idea and reality that a person lives together with a partner for a while and then maybe moves on to the next partner for the next period of his or her life, which results in our modern blended or patchwork families. Children thus cannot develop the same sense of identity with respect to their immediate human context that would be supported by a reality of one family generally prevailing in society, one home, one mother and father, in fact of *the* family, *the* mother, etc. They experience a dispersion of the very notion of "family" and "mother" and "father." For adults, these social developments likewise tend to undermine the sense of the unity of one organically developing individuality, a fact to which must be added the increasingly frequent experience of discontinuous job careers, both in the sense of shifts between full-time, part-time work, and periods of unemployment, and in the sense of having to be periodically retrained for other jobs. Often people are in general supposed to re-invent themselves periodically. In social networks people often entertain additional fictional identities parallel to their real identity, which also undermines the concept of "the individual" and the sense of unambiguous identity and necessary development of the personality implied by the "acorn theory" of personal *nature* and by the Jungian idea of "individuation." Contingency, openness, and polyvalence rather than the idealistic idea of a fixed "code" of character and calling.[15]

Formerly, education was connected with character formation and a person's becoming cultured, for which "learning *by heart*" was symptomatic and symbolic. Education focused on the inner man. One was supposed to become learned, personally carry the knowledge and wisdom of one's cultural tradition within oneself, not as a heap of factual bits of information, but as a possession that was integrated into the personality. Memory! A training in penmanship and manners helped form a personal style and allowed one to ex-press one's character. Now, knowledge is mainly stored outside in the Internet and students

---

[15] On the "code" of character and the "acorn theory" see James Hillman, *The Soul's Code. In Search of Character and Calling*, New York (Random House) 1996.

learn the technical skills of where to look for and how to gather information from the Internet and piece it together into papers and, most important, how to turn their product into good Powerpoint *presentations*. A real reversal of orientation from inside to outside. In addition, we outsource our mental operations to a large degree to pocket calculators and computers. Weather, climate, and economic forecasts depend on model calculations performed by incredibly powerful computers. We get our bearings through our GPS navigation devices and no longer through our own productive comparison of an inner map with our perception of outer landmarks. It all happens out there, not in the mind. We mechanically follow the instructions given to us by the navigation device.

To this we may add that according to Italo Calvino the very form of the corresponding new type of knowledge or consciousness itself has to be comprehended as a *conoscenza pulviscolare*, pulverized and dispersed knowledge.[16] This shows again that we are here not only concerned with changes in people's contingent social behavior, but truly with a change in the fundamental objective logic of how reality is constituted for modern man.

What does it mean for the concept of "the individual" and for man's self-conception as "self-determined individual" that in our technologized world we do not, and cannot possibly, understand essential areas of our own actions or decisions as well as the man-made machines that we use? The technology with which we surround ourselves is so complex (and is getting more and more complex) that we cannot manage it any more without the help of computers. Nobody is able to really understand the complexity of capital flow around the world, which is why bankers, analysts, and rating agencies need special computer programs to evaluate the creditworthiness of countries and banks as well as assess the risk of financial products. Without any real insight of their own, they blindly make their evaluations and decisions on the basis of what those computer programs *tell* them. No single individual is capable of having a full grasp of the source code of computer programs such as Windows. Windows Vista, for example, is said to consist of more than 50 million lines of program code. Nobody could possibly see through such a program in its entirety and

---

[16] I learned this from an as yet unpublished paper by Claus-Artur Scheier.

all its details. In fact, such programs have not even been programed by any human "author." In producing such huge programs, programers rather rely on planning and administration programs for the overview over the structure of the program as a whole, on program libraries which contain specific ready-made routines to be inserted at certain points, and on code generators that automatically produce the code for certain purposes, without the human programer's knowledge *how* these code generators in fact solve the particular tasks assigned to them.

Furthermore, what does it mean for our sense of being concrete individuals and our concept of "the individual" that society as a whole moves more and more in the direction of an undermining of "normal" or even "natural" time structures and rhythms in favor of an eternal present of an unlimited access to everything anywhere (I am thinking above all of online and mobile access to information, games, music, and video entertainment, as well as to the possibility of ordering consumer goods)? Can "the individual" survive the loss of a clear sense of the particular limitations of each determinate Here and Now, of the knowledge of being contained by and subject to a relentless order of time and place—as the external borders that hold its self together and keep it "inside"?

Or what does it do to our self-understanding that modern biology has taught us that we are, as it were, a "walking zoo," a biotope, containing ten times as many bacteria in ourselves than human body cells? Even on the level of the biological organism we are not individuals, but a community.

Having used the phrase "learning by heart," we are put in mind of the fact that modern medicine has learned to transplant hearts. And we have to ask what this fact must mean for man's self-understanding and sense of identity. The very heart of man—the symbol of authenticity and innermost truth—as ersatz, a spare part taken from another person! The credibility of the symbolic meaning of heart and inwardness as such is undermined. The progress of medicine is furthermore such that other organs can also be transplanted, tissue synthesized, children produced through artificial insemination and childbearing delegated; and even our genes can possibly be manipulated. Man can in principle, if not (yet) in practical reality be pieced together from parts taken from different bodies or artificially produced. Furthermore, we know of the possibility of cloning, which as a fantasy and desire captures certain people's minds. All this is the symbolic sign of a change on the deep level of the *concept* of "the individual." The sense of *my* own body as the *reality* and *substrate* of my identity has become questionable.

In his movie *Modern Times* Charley Chaplin depicted the enslavement of the individual by man-made machines that he has to operate. When the Industrial Revolution was still very much at its beginnings, already Goethe realized that this change entailed a development towards the reduction of the individual to a mere appendage of the technical means and apparatuses invented by modern man and that this development came with an *autonomous* momentum. Man as individual was not simply the autonomous inventor and master of machines, but conversely became their servant. We today, in the age of medial modernity, become keenly aware of our dependance on computers and the Internet when, for example, computers fail at our bank or we have no Internet connection. People's minds and behaviors are largely shaped by advertizing, trends, and fads and, of course, by our huge stultification machine, television.

Clearly, the time of the individual is over. Michel Foucault's book *Les mots et les choses* even ends with the vision that Man will disappear like a face drawn into the sand at a seashore, a vision which we may take to refer not to literal man (the human race, people) but to that particular *concept* of man that constituted him as individual personality.

Historically speaking, "the individual" in the sense of an inner self and a *Bildungsroman*-type organic development was also a late, 18th century invention and thus represents only a brief episode, really a fluke, in the history of mankind. At no other time in history and no other part of the world had man ever been *defined* as individual personality in this specific loaded sense. In most societies throughout history, the social group came first and possessed higher reality.

Strangely enough, Jung as psychologist did not comply with this powerful development towards the obsolescence of the individual. Now one could of course argue that most of the phenomena I just mentioned were still unknown to Jung. At his time, computers, Internet, cellphones, GPS-enabled devices did not yet exist. The role of the intact family in society was (in principle) still unthreatened. The old educational ideas and the ideal of a person's life as a continuous organic development of the personality with one more or less steady career and family still prevailed. But this argument does not hold. Even long before these most striking developments of the last few decades, it had become obvious enough that the individual was obsolete. During Jung's lifetime, Chaplin made the movie mentioned above and showed that it was possible to see through to the logic of the time. Goethe had had his insight about the individual already about 80 or 100 years before Jung. Likewise long before Jung, Marx had shown that, under the prevailing conditions of modernity, workers in particular necessarily lose control of their lives and destinies. And during his lifetime, Adorno, who was of course a quarter of a century younger than Jung, had made it very clear that under the conditions of late bourgeois society the individual had lost its autonomy, that it was no longer individuals that steered the course of events, but that the power had gone over to the state, to monopolies, big multi-national concerns, and above all, beyond the direct influence of individuals, to hidden anonymous abstract structures, and furthermore that the socialization forces immediately take hold of people's instinctual life so that the idea of an autonomous I (which was still underlying Freud's theory of an I determined by its own internal economy ["where there was Id, there I shall be"]) had no basis. There were enough obvious signs and theoretical analyses.

One could have expected of a *depth*-psychologist of the rank of Jung, especially of one who when it was a matter of "parapsychological phenomena," was, totally unexpectedly for a psychologist, amenable to the most modern results of physics, that he would also have been sensitive to and psychologically appreciative of the psychological process of the logical obsolescence of "the individual." But in this area Jung only reacted, we could say, counterphobically, a fact to which, above all, his late essay *The Undiscovered Self* bears witness. He decided against the truth of his age and insisted on "the individual" as the irrenunciable and exclusive locus of soul. It was not that he was totally unaware of the obsolescence of the individual: The great danger he saw was what he called *Vermassung*, the restructuring of humankind as a mass (*GW* 10 § 501). But he chose to see this only as a threat. Therefore, a great battle had to be fought by us in defense of the individual against mass society—as if these two formed a neat undialectical opposition: as if the modern "mass" structure was wholly external to the individual and the latter still innocently the pure individual merely confronted with a strictly external threat. A naive dissociation.

That Jung, *once* he had set up the individual-collective opposition as ultimate irreducible alternative, prioritized the inwardness of the individual is, of course, not to be faulted; he was, after all, a psychologist. But that he set up this opposition as basic for psychology is the expression of what in the above paper I called psychology's basic fault. The problem is that the fight against *Vermassung* and for individuality might have been a worthy task of pedagogy, but not of psychology. The really existing individual ("individual" in the naturalistic or literal sense) should, of course, even after the obsolescence of the individual (in the psychological sense) learn to hold its place within the modern structures of society on a behavioral and attitudinal level. This individual, just as it needs to do its own eating and sleeping, also has to take care of its personal needs and its inner life. It has to see to it that it passes through the phases of life with its crises decently. But psychology must not think in terms of pedagogic or sociological categories and is not concerned with people and their behavior. It must not operate on the crude positivistic level of literal or everyday reality, to which the opposition of "individual" vs. "collective" (or "mass") belongs, and it cannot afford to remain blind to the actual dimension of soul: the intangible, irrepresentable "*third of the two*," that is to say, the Universal, the level of the inner logic or syntax of the Real. That dimension within which psychic reality was to have its place was fundamentally underdetermined if it was said to be the inner being of the individual. This is really a reductive conception. Jung's succumbing to this reductive positivistic underdetermination demands an explanation.

In the context of a discussion of the important distinction between (our usual restricted ability to see only) "how things happen to me" and (our usual failure to be able to observe) "how I produce them," Jung explains that it is the *animal nature* of man that baulks at his feeling himself to be the maker of what is given to him. In actuality, the "giver" of all "given" things dwells within us. However, "It is so much more immediate, conspicuous [or obvious], impressive and therefore so much more convincing to see all the things that happen to me than to observe how I make them" (*CW* 11 § 841 transl.

modif.).—By the same token I think it is the seductive power of our animal nature which made Jung cling to our bodily existence as the primary reality and thus prioritize the literal individual, ignoring, in this regard, the psychological difference. That on the level of our animal bodies we exist as separate individual bodies with our very own sensations, sentiments, and images is, of course, "so much more immediate, conspicuous [or obvious], impressive and therefore so much more convincing." And this conspicuous fact seduced Jung into conflating the psychological notion of the individual with the naturalistic concept of the individual as the soul's substrate personality and into grounding the soul in the individual, as "the inner," "the unconscious" in the bodily existing human being.

Strangely enough, in seeing the essential thing to be the individual's personal transformation and individuation and stuffing the *opus magnum* into the individual in its positivity, Jung used the solidity and opacity of the body, the body of the human animal, *as the lens* through which to look into the world of the soul. But only like can see like. In order to approach the soul, you have to have left behind the animal standpoint, the natural, the obvious, the everyday standpoint. The sphere of the soul, the syntax of the Real, is neither immediate, nor conspicuous and impressive. It is probably because Jung did not allow the negation of immediacy and positivity into his standpoint, that is, did not start out from his having overcome the naturalism of our animal nature, that he needed to mystify the soul positivistically as a yonder, a logically inaccessible Other: "the unconscious." But the inescapable negation that his vision was—illegitimately—protected from appeared projected in the *object* of his vision as its "un-."

To what extent Jung zoomed in on the individual can be seen from his advice to his patients as empirical personalities (and modern man at large), "Turn back to what is utmostly subjective in yourself [*zu Ihrem Allersubjektivsten*], to the source of your being and existence, to that point where you are making world history without being aware of it" (*CW* 10 § 316, transl. modif.). This is no longer simply expressive of what I called psychology's basic fault (the positivistic or naturalistic individual-collective distinction). It shows an additional fault, that of an inflated, grandiose idea of the individual.

An important psychological task for Jung was the "dissolution of the mana-personality" (*CW* 7 § 398). But in the present context we see that he merely *reduced* the mana-personality in size to the scale of every Tom, Dick, or Harry. Externally, as ego-personality or civil men, they are of course for Jung, too, ordinary, relatively insignificant members of society. Jung had no illusions about that. But deep down in their *Allersubjektivsten*, in the Self, Tom, Dick, and Harry nevertheless are making world history, *provided* that they "turn back to" what is utmostly subjective in them.

Maybe this provides for us the explanation for why Jung had to succumb to the seduction of "the animal nature of man" and cling to the literal individual in its positivity as substrate in the first place. The ideas of "personal grandiosity," the "mana-personality," "the rescue of the world" through the "rescue of one's own soul," a cosmos of Meaning ("the collective unconscious") were so precious to him that they simply had to be rescued. "The individual" was needed for Jung's anti-modern project of storing these obsolete concerns safely away and providing a secret hiding place somewhere *in empirical reality* for them, because the individual was said to harbor within itself (within its existence as ordinary civil man and ego-personality) an "unconscious" and within the latter "the Self." This made it possible for the dissolution of the mana-personality not to have to go all the way. The grandiosity remained in and through the Self, even after I as ego-personality had thoroughly overcome it. Externally, on the ego or social level, I am just a normal human being, with no airs and graces, but, secretly, deep down inside "in the unconscious," I have an importance of world-historical proportions.

This is not due to the animal nature of man which is so easily seduced by the impressiveness of what is immediately and obviously given. Rather, this is that other seduction that Jung referred to when he spoke of the "suggestive power of the unconscious images" (*CW* 7 § 269). Both types of seduction come together in Jung's setting up the individual as "the makeweight that tips the scales" and "the measure of all things" (*CW* 10 §§ 586, 523). Because Jung insisted that what *in the deep logic* of the modern world and in the development of the *history of the soul* had become untenable was supposed to be rescued at all costs, he had to turn away from the *contra naturam* standpoint appropriate for the soul and *secondarily* fall back on the naturalism of the standpoint of man's animal nature, which provided him with the obvious and safe container for what was to be saved: the individual in its positivity. The individual was only a container, not the manifestation or epiphany of the soul, because the soul that is stored away in it is itself safely sealed in the unconsciousness of "the unconscious."

My own position is that psychology should neither load the responsibility and weight of the *opus magnum* onto the shoulders of the individual, nor throw out the baby, the idea of the individual, with the bathwater in favor of the soul's real *opus magnum* as it unfolds in the arena of our real historical cultural development in medial modernity with its earthshaking scientific and technological advances. On the one hand, I "can no longer in all fairness load that enormous weight of meaning, responsibility, duty, heaven and hell, onto the shoulders of that frail and fallible human being—so deserving of love, indulgence, understanding, and forgiveness" (*CW* 9i § 172, transl. modif.) as which we exist, and I want to keep faith precisely with that individual human being in its—in my own—frailty, fallibility, and neediness. All the new technical and scientific developments do not have to go to our heads. I do not need to personally embrace every new technical possibility and to get enthralled and engulfed by a fascination for it as if it entailed the promise of heaven on earth, nor do I have to personally identify with the logic of modernity and thus forget who I really am and what my real needs as a human being are. But on the other hand, I certainly do want to stay aware of and in contact with the soul's *opus magnum* and respect and appreciate it. I see the obsolescence, sublatedness, sunkenness of what may be of great importance to me as private individual. This is not only my job as psychologist, but also, I feel, my task as a *human* being, a being that is more than its animal nature. But then again, I also keep my distance from it, distinguish and emancipate myself from where the soul is today, from the new logic of modern life, holding my place and staying down to earth as "*only* that!," living my life *only* as this private individual that I am, in conscious recognition of my human-all-too-humanness and my personal needs as a human being. Discrimination. Humility. No identification with and inflation through the "soul," "mana," "Meaning," "the Self," or "salvation," neither in the sense of an appropriation of them into myself by my trying to find within myself my true (Jungian) Self ("the God-image in the soul"!), nor in the sense of my becoming sucked into the true *opus magnum* in its historical-cultural dimension as an enthusiast of medial modernity.

CHAPTER NINE

Closure and Setting Free or The Bottled Spirit of Alchemy and Psychology

B efore I can begin, I must clarify the position from which I speak about alchemy and "which" alchemy I am speaking about. As to the first point: I am speaking as a psychologist and with a definitely psychological interest. And the alchemy I am speaking about is basically the picture of alchemy that emerges from Jung's description of it. So what I can say cannot lay claim to providing a historically and philologically correct assessment of the actual historical phenomenon of alchemy with all its incredible individual diversity and with its linguistic as well as ideational obscurity. My purpose in the first place is not to understand alchemy proper in its own terms and in terms of its own time, the Middle Ages. Rather, I want to see how psychology relates to that alchemy (that foreign body within the corpus of psychology) that through Jung has already been appropriated for and incorporated into psychology. I could also say: I want to look at Jung's version of alchemy and its implications for psychology.

It is of course highly significant, and very characteristic for Jung's work, that Jung felt the need to make something as alien to psychology as alchemy a constituent element of his own psychological theory. The foreignness of alchemy is at least twofold. It is concerned with chemical substances and processes, with matter, rather than with people and *their* feelings, ideas, conflicts, etc. And it is completely obsolete for us, has been obsolete for several centuries; we are divided from it by a fundamental historical gulf; the consciousness that gave rise to alchemy and provided the framework for the alchemical practice in laboratory as well as oratory can at best be reconstructed by us in the mind, but it can never become ours again. The interesting thing for us is to realize that it was, besides other aspects, precisely the foreignness of alchemy that made it so precious for Jung. In contrast to probably all other psychologists, he was not satisfied with clinical observation (with studying what was going on inside people) as the ground upon which psychology was to be based. Jung obviously needed to go away from immediate psychological experience, turn his back on psychology in the narrower (personalistic) sense, in order to find something *really* other that at first sight could not possibly be seen as psychology or psychologically relevant.

Psychology in Jung's view, so we can interpret this finding, *requires* otherness, difference—though not an utterly external other, something totally irrelevant, but its own internal other. Psychology must reflect itself in and base itself on a true (even if ultimately internal) other. For this reason Jung appropriated alchemy for psychology. It was foreign enough to be truly removed from modern psychology and at the same time open enough to be given a psychological interpretation of sorts. The reason for this need on the part of Jung is, so we may conclude, that he was instinctively open to the "psychological difference," to the insight that true psychology cannot be immediate psychology, but must be *sublated* immediate psychology. This is one of the features that sets his psychology apart from all the other psychologies of his time. And the objective, theoretical reason for this internal otherness is psychology's own necessity to overcome all naive empiricism (the tendency to immediately turn to its object) which would unavoidably be fatal in that discipline which is characterized by the fact that in it the psyche observes *itself*. Because such a position of naive immediacy makes it structurally impossible to make, within itself, allowances for the pitfalls of the "psychological equation." Jung was keenly aware of this problem.

At any rate, through alchemy Jungian psychology has, on a theoretical level, its own other or foreign body within itself. It thus exists as an internal tension. This tension can become productive if we compare both extremes, in two directions: (1) does psychological theory do justice to the spirit of its own internal other? Did what it discovered in the latter really come home to and permeate the constitution of the former? (2) Is this other, alchemy, conceived, comprehended, and described by this theory in such a way that the "alchemical impulse" (the inner motif power of alchemy) can really find its fulfillment? Mind you, the question here is not about the relation between historical-factual alchemy and psychology's description of it, but immanently about whether psychology's understanding of what it itself reports about alchemy is up to what is contained in this its own report. Obviously, the two questions are two sides of the same coin.

Jung held that alchemy was a "groping precursor of the most modern psychology" (*CW* 7 § 360), i.e., an unwitting precursor of his own psychology of the unconscious, as well as the historical link that connected his own psychology with Gnosticism. In this sense he thought, as he explains especially in *Memories, Dreams, Reflections*,[1] that his own psychology is the living continuation of an age-old tradition, a new link in the *aurea catena* of historical manifestations of the soul's truth. According to this thesis alchemy was already in itself an implicit psychology, but "hampered by the inevitable concretizations of the still crude and undifferentiated intellect," so that it "never advanced to any clear psychological formulation ..." (§ 361). What in alchemy had still been merely implicit and hidden under the jumble created by a crude, undifferentiated intellect has now, in modernity, in Jung's own work, had a chance to become explicit.

* * *

What is it that makes alchemy, as Jung sees it, a precursor of psychology or even an implicit psychology? It is the sameness of purpose and concern. "But its 'secret,' too, was, just as that to be found in the process of individuation, the fact of the transformation of the personality through the blending and bonding of noble components with base ones, of the differentiated with the inferior functions, of the conscious with the unconscious" (§ 370). Although this statement

---

[1] Pp. 200ff. E.g., "Grounded in the natural philosophy of the Middle Ages, alchemy formed the bridge on the one hand into the past, to Gnosticism, and on the other into the future, to the modern psychology of the unconscious" (p. 201). On the *aurea catena* see *ibid.*, p. 189.

does not come from one of Jung's later works, the thesis it expresses is one that he supported to the end of his life: the thesis that it is ultimately the interest in *the transformation of the personality* that alchemy and psychology have in common.

This is a thesis that invites a comparison, in the sense indicated, between the interpretation of alchemy in Jung's psychology and the report about the factual data of alchemy given by the same psychology. Is what psychology claims to be the inner telos of alchemy borne out by what we learn about alchemy from psychology's own description of its phenomenology?

What the alchemists were striving for was the philosopher's stone, the panacea, the red tincture, the life elixir, the *aqua permanens*, the philosophical gold, to mention only the most frequent names for the ultimate goal of the alchemical opus. It is clear that all these substances, whose description is highly paradoxical in all cases, indeed self-contradictory, do not refer to literal entities to be found or produced in the sphere of positivity. Jung interprets them as "The Projection of Psychic Contents" (*CW* 12 p. 242 ff.) and as mythological symbolizations (*ibid.*, § 342). It is true, his point that they are symbols, we could also say metaphors, is well taken, and his interpretation of alchemy as projections (of some ideas upon matter) *prima facie* makes a lot of sense, too, inasmuch as it is obvious that the alchemist in his experiences sees something in or into matter that cannot really, not literally, positivistically be found in matter. But his thesis becomes highly problematic when we look at *what* Jung says is that which is projected: "In order to explain the mystery of matter he projected yet another mystery—his own unknown psychic background—into what was to be explained..." (§ 345). About projection in general Jung states, "In the darkness of some external reality I find, without recognizing it as such, an interior or psychic content that is my own" (§ 346, transl. modif.). The alchemist "experienced his projection as a property of matter; but what he was in reality experiencing was his own unconscious" (ibid.).

"*His own* unknown psychic background," "an interior or psychic content that is *my own*," "*his own* unconscious"—where does Jung get these ascriptions from? Certainly not from the alchemical texts nor from the spirit of alchemy as it is to be found in these texts. Quite obviously, the alchemists were not interested in their own personal development, their individuation or transformation. It is true, usually each adept worked by himself, but the *arcanum* he sought was never "his own." The *lapis* was explicitly the stone *of the philosophers* in the plural. The red tincture would have been the elixir of life for life as such, not for the adept's personal psychic life. The panacea was likewise not understood and intended as a means for his personal cure or salvation; as *pan*-acea (cure-*all*) it was conceived, much like a vaccine discovered in modern medicine, as something that would as a matter of course have belonged to the generality. The point of a vaccine or of medication or of methods of treatment for all sorts of health disorders is that they are the solution of objective problems that in principle threaten humankind at large, regardless of which individual happened to discover or develop the cure. Medicine as a field of study is not a private, subjective undertaking. Like science it struggles to find answers to general problems and is fundamentally a communal effort. In the same way, the alchemists, as lonely as they may have been in their laboratories, participated in a collective project that extended across the ages, and they all shared the same purpose of finding *the* (not each their own, personal) "philosopher's stone" (or whatever particular symbolic name they might have given to this ultimate goal). In sum, alchemy was trying to find something that had the logical status of objective knowledge, a universal "truth." The (transformation of the) individual was absolutely no theme or concern of theirs, and it could not possibly have come into their focus.

Interestingly enough, the very texts that Jung cites in support of his thesis that what the alchemist experienced was his unconscious clearly show the alchemist's nonpersonalistic, nonsubjective focus and could have opened Jung's eyes to the inadequacy of his individualistic premise:

> ... and you will see with your own eyes one thing after the other appearing by and by on top of the water, how God created all things in six days ... (§ 347)

The prospect was to gain an immediate insight into, and, as it were, to witness, *God's creation work*. No doubt, the general horizon of the alchemical work was cosmic, in a certain sense of the word even "theological." There is no trace of an interest in oneself, no self-centeredness. Alchemy's interest was one that belongs to the wider sphere of a general natural philosophy in the Hermetic tradition. The *Novum lumen* is quoted by Jung, in the same chapter on the projection of the psychic contents, with the following passage:

> To cause things hidden in the shadow to appear, and to take away the shadow from them, this is permitted to the intelligent philosopher by God through nature. ... All these things happen, and the eyes of the common men do not see them, but the eyes of the understanding [*intellectus*] and of the imagination perceive them [*percipiunt*] with true and truest vision [*visu*].

To be sure, it was each adept's personal longing to personally have such experiences and personally see "these things" with the eyes of the *intellectus* (which in medieval contexts is not to be confused with what we moderns mean by the [usually derogative] term intellect [cf. "intellectualism"]; it was the highest faculty of the mind, originally belonging only to God and only derivatively also to man). But just as when we today want to personally see the Egyptian pyramids or the Grand Canyon, or when we wish to personally acquire some of the knowledge produced by the great minds of our tradition, we are not primarily concerned with the transformation of our own personality, but with something in the real world out there, so his own individuation was not the purpose of the adept's hope to see the things he wished to see. His self was no topic. The topic and interest was, to say it with the words of Faust, to get to know and connect with "*was die Welt im Innersten zusammenhält*," i.e., the innermost mystery or logic of the world or, in alchemical imagery, the *mysterium coniunctionis* as the separation-and-union of the opposites. It is the secret of the creation, the creation not as a primordial event in the past, but as its ever-present ongoing living truth. An analogy may be helpful here. Each Roman-Catholic priest has to personally perform the ritual of the Mass every day, but this does in no way imply that his goal in doing this is his own individuation. It is a fallacy to conclude from the personal nature of the aimed-for experience, insight, or effort that the focus of the effort and the content of the experience are one's personal development.

While the transformation of my personality is an absolutely private, subjective concern, ultimately (1) egoic and (2) "practical" (utilitarian: my progress and fulfillment), we see from the above quote that alchemy appealed to the understanding, which is fundamentally communal because it aims for knowing and truth (the "true and truest vision"). But the *person* who possibly happens to become aware of this general truth is *per se* of no importance or interest; only the truth of nature or the world itself is. The alchemist did not search for *his* self, but for *the* spirit Mercurius as the mystery deeply hidden in the real.

So if Jung claims that the alchemist projected "his own unknown psychic background" and that his secret was the "fact of the transformation of the personality," he did not learn this from the phenomenology of alchemy as it presented itself to him in the alchemical tracts that he so diligently studied. Rather, it is a true projection on his part, more specifically: a retrojection of his own modern psychologistic prejudice. The idea of individuation in Jung's personalistic or individualistic sense is foisted on alchemy, smuggled into it.

The same applies to the idea of "the unconscious." Jung asserts that the visionary experiences that sometimes occurred during the alchemical opus "cannot be anything but projections of unconscious contents" (§ 350). We already briefly discussed the theme of "projection," but now have to take up another aspect of it. This idea entails serious presuppositions. Projection implies that there is in me a within which houses the contents that in "projection" are thrown out and then appear to the subject out there, either as apparitions in their own right or as the property of empirical things or persons. By entertaining this concept psychological theory does something very queer and contradictory. On the one hand, it asserts a hidden movement from inside to outside, while, on the other hand, it logically performs what psychoanalysts might call a "reversal into the opposite," namely a movement from outside to inside, by claiming that that which, phenomenally speaking, is seen outside as something real or as the property of something real out there is actually the property of the inner psyche of the subject. But *both* movements are fantasized since we do not actually see that something that "before" was in the alchemist was indeed thrown out from his interior into the external world.

This is very different from Jung's own theorizing, where the ideas of "projection" and of "unconscious contents," etc., are indeed first elements of psychological doctrine and only thereafter "seen" out there in alchemy; first modern concepts, and then said to have already been operative in the distant past. Here the word projection is warranted by the phenomenology of what happens. But as far as the visionary experiences of the alchemists are concerned we could simply leave out this fictitiously assumed and self-cancelling idea of the double movement of projection and stay with the simple phenomenon that something was indeed seen out there.

The idea of projection, not being the result of an empirical observation, serves the psychologistic purpose of *positing* a "within" in the person and of tying to the person, and reducing to personal significance, what for the alchemist (as well as phenomenally, for the unprejudiced observer) is about the inner truth or inner nature of nature. Alchemy is a speculative kind of natural philosophy. The visionary and fantastic aspect of the alchemists' descriptions of their experiences with matter could well be accounted for by the difference between their interest in the inner truth, indeed the *mystery*, of nature and the totally different interest of the modern natural sciences (and the modern mind in general) in the *positivity* of nature, in what we call the facts. If we understand the historical difference between the medieval and the modern mind with regard to their fundamentally different ideas of what is real, we do not have to take refuge to psychologistic interpretations in terms of "projections of unconscious contents." For the medieval mind the truth about nature was *a priori* "metaphysical," essentially mysterious, not positive-factual.

Another problem with the "projection of unconscious contents" idea lies in the notion of "contents." The tacit suggestion here is that what is projected existed prior to the projection, was somehow already a finished entity. The fantastic experience is then merely a removal of ready-made items from the inside storeroom to outside: a theory about the experiences from the point of view of a reifying, positivizing thinking. But why could it not be that the alchemists' experiences were genuine first-time *productions*, on-the-spot inventions? In other words, instances of creative speculative thought? The products of an active, lively mind? Production instead of "projection of contents"? Living thought (as the activity or process of thinking)?

If so, if it is a process of thinking that we are dealing with in alchemy, we do not need the notion of the unconscious implied by the phrase "unconscious contents" (which here means as much as contents coming from the unconscious). The visions of the alchemists are conscious events, products of a visionary or visionizing consciousness, their images and ideas products of a speculatively thinking consciousness, their dreams the products of a dreaming consciousness. In addition to a rationalistic, to an empiricistic consciousness, there are all kinds of other styles of consciousness—an emotionalizing, a fantasizing, a sober, a paralyzed, a pedantic formalistic consciousness, etc.

It is the positivistic mind that posits "the unconscious." The logic leading to this notion is that if what the alchemists believed could be seen in the object did not really come from the characteristics of the object, it must come from some other (positive-factual) place—"the unconscious in them." In other words, the theory of "the unconscious" is *sensualism in reverse*. Sensualism insists that "nothing is in the mind that had not before been given to the senses." The psychology of the unconscious accepts this, except that it adds a second, alternate source from which the mind's contents can come: in addition to the world out there in front of the mind it has also "the unconscious" in the back of the mind. The idea that the mind does not *get* all its contents (either from the sensual world or from an inner reservoir of unconscious contents), but originally produces some of them on the spot and thus is in itself poietic is taboo. The mind must not be a thinking mind. It must be a merely recipient and "*data*"-processing mind.

Whereas the world given to the senses is warranted by our experience, the notion of an "unconscious" *behind* the visions and ideas of the alchemists is a mystification of the phenomenal evidence, a dogmatic invention of a, as it were, "metaphysical" entity within the positivistically viewed world! The mind's activity of speculative and poietic thought is hypostatized as an entity, region, or reservoir behind the mind.

In stressing the production-invention aspect of conscious thought and its momentary nature, I do not want to suggest that the production is the work of that lonely ego-consciousness in which it surfaces. Especially in alchemy we can see how the fantasies and ideas, even those emerging in an isolated adept, are not private concoctions, but collective, often quite conventional, ideas. The creative individual consciousness is not private here, but floats in and is supported by something that is not its own, an age-old intellectual tradition and atmosphere. It is the climate of this whole hermetic spirit, not the adept's ego, that is doing the productive speculative thinking through each individual adept. Jung once wrote that we always dream from within the relationship. "In the deepest sense we all dream not *out of ourselves* but out of what lies *between us and the other*" (*Letters 1*, p. 172, 29 September 1934, to Kirsch). We could extend this statement by saying we always dream from within the real psychological context that we are in as well as from the more superficial or deeper psychological reality level that consciousness is open to. But this applies not only to dream thoughts. It applies to all non-ego thinking. And (a) the less a person has psychologically emancipated himself as a true individual from his social group or intellectual tradition, but is rather in a *participation mystique* with it (as, e.g., the medieval alchemists were with the hermetic tradition), and/or (b) the more a person's roots, through his inner greatness and depth ("genius"), reach down into the foundations of the inner core or truth of that tradition (in that status that has in fact been attained by it in its historical evolution at the respective present), the more the productions of consciousness will not be the merely personal property of the ego-personality. In everything great, in poetry, art, philosophy, in (the rare cases of truly great) statesmanship, etc., it is the *historical locus* (all around the person) that thinks, not the individual as a lonely self.

(Here I must add, however, that concerning a single individual we cannot claim that he or she permanently belongs to this or to that level. A truly great thinker can at times say quite banal things that come only from his or her private ego-consciousness, and, conversely, people who for the most part do not appear to be geniuses may at times produce a single great work or insight that comes from the depth. We may all phase into and out of various depth strata and psychological-intellectual climates, participating in them or being emancipated from them at different times to differing degrees. There is an alchemical text, *Aurora Consurgens*, that has been ascribed to Thomas Aquinas. If we accept this ascription merely experimentally for a moment, we can say that Thomas, when he was in his study or monk's cell, was the great theologian who wrote his *Summae*, but when he went, metaphorically speaking,[2] into his "laboratory-oratory," he at once tuned into or was absorbed by the hermetic tradition and could produce this great alchemical text.)

So, it is always consciousness that thinks; and that *thinks* whether it dreams, muses, fantasizes, is poetically or artistically creative, or whether it thinks in the narrower sense of the word. The delusional concept of "the unconscious" amounts to a mystification, whether it is understood as a reservoir of repressed or archetypal contents or of instincts and desires, or as an agent behind the scene that produces dreams and directs our fate, or as a region of the mind. "The unconscious" is really a *metaphysical* presupposition, a dogmatic concept, in Jung's psychology, *malgré* Jung's oft-expressed horror of metaphysical assumptions and his avowal of a strict empiricism. Unbeknownst it serves a certain *strategic purpose*, although it is consciously intended as a simple naming of an "obvious phenomenon." But this alleged phenomenon does not exist and this is why "the unconscious" is a mystification and a metaphysical hypostasis.

The purpose of the concept of "the unconscious" is first of all to support the idea of "*one's own* inner psychic background," that is, to tie the phenomenology of the soul to the person and enclose, lock it in the individual. This remains true despite Jung's also often stating that *we* are *in* the unconscious, which he then says is all around us, an idea that of course is the very opposite of such an enclosure. But this other idea did not lead Jung to entirely revoke the idea of "one's own unconscious." He pays certainly more than lip service to the idea of the unconscious all around us, but he nevertheless did not unmistakingly break with the unconscious in us. This is underscored by the fact that consistently to the end of his days Jung held on to the idea that the *individual* is the makeweight that tips the scale, that he or she is the one important factor that makes history, the only place where the salvation or rescue of the world can take place (cf. CW 10 §§ 586, 315, 536). And of course his whole focus on individuation and introspection points the same way.

---

[2] Legend has it that Thomas dictated this work on his deathbed (and thus did not produce it in an alchemical laboratory).

* * *

But more important and serious than this locking the soul in "one's own inner" or in the individual person is another kind of enclosure performed by the notion of "the unconscious." The one discussed so far still takes place in the externality of space or in the imagination, and therefore also imprisons the soul only in an external sense; the closure does not get to the soul's heart. By imagining things, the soul leaves its native land and moving out gives itself the form of alienation from itself. Even though our imaginings and fantasies usually happen within the mind and do not literally go out into the material reality "out there," they are nevertheless a kind of mind-internal "projection." But with the second sense of enclosure effected by the notion of "the unconscious" we stay on the soul's home territory and this is why the imprisonment now really hits home. I am referring to the very meaning of the word 'unconscious.' It *logically* exiles the soul from the sphere of knowing and thought and conscious awareness, as from what is its own nature and truth. The concept of "the unconscious" is a true "projection," the transposition of a subjective attitude or function into an imagined "something" out there in objective reality. For ultimately it is the hypostatization or objective representation of *one's will* to hold the nature of psychic reality down in darkness, in undisclosedness, in the status of material nature (in contrast to mind). This concept, rather than innocently naming an observed reality, is a *program* that, however, comes in the guise of an (alleged) fact. And this program is best formulated with Jung's quote from alchemy: *ignotum per ignotius*. It is true, neither for the alchemists nor for Jung was this phrase meant as a program. No, subjectively, consciously, it was perceived more like a resigned admission of our limitations. But objectively it expresses in Jungian psychology a move deeper down into unknowing with no hope of any light. It once and for all denies the possibility of some sort of exit from the dungeon.

In mythology Danae was imprisoned by her father Akrisios, king of Argos, in the darkness of an underground vault. But Akrisios' intention was foiled by Zeus, who having fallen in love with Danae penetrated to her into the darkness of her prison from the height of heaven after having taken the form of a rain of gold that impregnated her and, so we can assume, lit up her darkness *from within*. This is

what happens to the dark in ancient myth. Similarly, the Gospel of John (1:14) tells us, "And the Word was made flesh, and dwelt among us, (and we beheld his glory, the glory as of the only begotten of the Father,) full of grace and truth." "And the light shineth in darkness" (1:5, where, however, in contrast to the course of events in the myth the continuation tells us that "the darkness comprehended it not").

But psychology, in total contrast to Akrisios, is fully successful in locking the soul in darkness and perfectly sealing its underground dungeon. "The unconscious" remains dark *by definition*. There is no better lock than the logical one of a definition. No rain of gold from the heavens could possibly seep into what is defined as the unconscious. The possibility of a true *coniunctio* is *a priori* precluded. How could there possibly be a coniunctio, how could there be some kind of heavenly light to fall into the darkness, if "the unconscious" has already from the outset swallowed and pocketed its own other, the very light of heaven that could possibly penetrate the dark and enter into a union with it, and "heaven" as such into the bargain? "Since the stars have fallen from heaven and our highest symbols have paled, a secret life holds sway in the unconscious" (*CW* 9i § 50). What Jung here states is not comparable to the rain of gold seeping down to imprisoned Danae. The falling of the stars is the equivalent to an abolishment of the very source of that rain, Zeus, and his Olympus. The very place for the light in the system of thought has not merely become temporarily vacant, no, it has once and for all disappeared from this thought, it has become undialectically canceled. There is now a hegemony of darkness. Although the stars may still shine within the unconscious, although a secret life may hold sway in the unconscious, it is now *fundamentally, i.e. logically*, no more than the secret light and life under a totalitarian regime of darkness. Even the *scintillae* in the unconscious, its very own, native sparks of light, remain forever enclosed in it.

Psychology's commitment to "the unconscious" amounts to the systematic closure of that opening and clearance that according to mythology was produced by a primordial culture hero when he stemmed the bodies of the world parents, Heaven and Earth, who had been in eternal cohabitation, apart, lifting up Father Heaven. "The unconscious" as alleged empirical fact is the Earth that does no longer have a Heaven above itself, indeed is not even embraced by Heaven as before the hero's deed: it has swallowed Heaven with the stars and all heavenly light altogether. Now, the whole myth of the separation of the world parents is said to have come from the unconscious as its real source. The latter is the ultimate, all-comprehensive reality.

With the "psychology of the unconscious," the condition for the possibility *a priori* of a *coniunctio* has been abolished. The psychology of the unconscious is a clear avowal of fundamental darkness. A syzygy cannot be, because the unconscious has lost its other. The *ligamentum*, the *copula*, the *vinculum* have been cut. The mind has systematically immured itself in (psychological) darkness by locating soul and truth in "the unconscious" as their authentic and exclusive place and by having rid itself of "heaven above."

But is it not precisely this psychology of the unconscious that in the first place made us aware again of the forgotten ideas and realities of the *mysterium coniunctionis*, of the syzygy, of the *vinculum* as vital and existential psychological problems and that tries to bring a new light to "our benighted present" (*Letters 2*, p. 396, to Trinick, 15 Oct. 1957)? Is it not the purpose of psychology and analytical psychotherapy to make conscious of the treasures in the unconscious? Do we not carefully observe our dreams, trying to understand them and to integrate them into our lives? Did Jung not—in contrast to Freud's wholesale dismissal of the *superi* (the upper gods) in favor of *Acheron* (the underworld)—attempt to reconnect us to the light contained in myths and symbols, in the great soul topics expressed in dogmas and rituals and to bring back the fear of God and gods? Did he not expressly state: "Instead of creating light, we conceal in darkness, instead of lifting up, we expose to ridicule and contempt" (same letter, p. 395) and thereby show what his own outlook and purpose was?

All true. But to no avail. It is all *a priori* superceded by the psyche's fundamental immurement in the unconscious. All our devotion to myths and archetypal images, our "dream tending," as they sometimes call it, our painting from the unconscious, all our attempts at making conscious belong to the sphere of behavior, are instances of acting out, ego-doings. They are empirical, semantic events and efforts that have not got a chance with the fundamental logical-syntactical sinking of all light in darkness. The archetypes are *defined* as archetypes of the collective *unconscious*. No empirical, behavioral "making consciousness" undoes this logical definition of that which is to be made conscious as belonging to "the unconscious."

"It is not a matter of indifference whether one calls something an 'addiction' or 'a god.' To serve an addiction is detestable and undignified, but to serve a god is full of meaning and promise because it is an act of submission to a higher, invisible, and spiritual being," says Jung (*CW* 13 § 55, transl. modif.). Likewise it is not a matter of indifference whether one calls something "the unconscious" or, e.g., "the absolute," for to name it "the unconscious" is an act of repression, a *decision* to have it *logically* locked away in darkness once for all. In our psychological innocence we usually think that what really counts is what we do, that we go into analysis, carefully observe our dreams, devote ourselves to myths and archetypes, etc. But *psychologically*, that is, for the soul, all this is pretty irrelevant. All this happens on the level of the ego and refers to no more than contents of ego-consciousness, its semantics. But psychology only begins where it is a question of the implicit logic or syntax of consciousness, the categories, concepts, definitions, tacit presuppositions that consciousness sight unseen operates with, the *way* it thinks and quite naturally, as a matter of course, apperceives and comprehends its semantic contents, its empirical feeling experiences. For this reason it is indeed a matter of the greatest psychological importance whether we allow ourselves the notion of "the unconscious" or not.

Jung confessed, "Hence I prefer the term 'the unconscious,' knowing that I might just as well speak of 'God' or 'daimon' if I wished to express myself in mythic language." The latter "terms have the great advantage of encompassing and evoking the emotional quality of numinosity, whereas the [former]—the unconscious—is banal and therefore closer to reality. This concept includes the fact that it can be empirically experienced, that is, the commonplace reality the way it is familiar and accessible to us. The unconscious is too neutral and rational a term to give much impetus to the imagination. The term, after all, was coined for scientific purposes, and is far better suited to dispassionate observation which makes no metaphysical claims than are transcendental concepts, which are contestable ..." (*MDR* pp. 336f., modif.) We see very clearly that Jung was aware of the great significance for the soul of which names we use. But we also see two other things.

First of all we see that Jung with full methodical awareness opted for the notion of "the unconscious." And why? Because he insisted on the positivism of the modern scientific outlook as his basic stance: on the systematic exclusion of the metaphysical and transcendental dimension. He presented everything that he said about archetypes and the mysteries of the soul as positive facts, nothing but facts. Logically they were given the status of positivity, while *under* this all-overarching umbrella of a definition, and semantically, they were allowed to be mysteries, gods, *daimones*. What he was doing was, he claimed, natural science. He did not, he insisted, make any metaphysical statements and could get quite worked up when he sensed that what he said was taken as such. The metaphysical, transcendental dimension was *anathema*. Or rather, it was *anathema* only when it was a truly *psychological* question of the names used and the logical statuses, while on the subjective-experiential and semantic level (i.e., on the level of ego-consciousness and its contents) Jung favored a language that acknowledged the numinosity and transcendental nature of the experiences, e.g., "God" instead of "addiction." What he allowed or even demanded with the one hand he sternly forbade with the other. The psychological difference between the psychologically essential logical or syntactical level and the (psychologically already sublated, pocketed) subjective and semantic level was decisively operative in his thinking, but he did not become really conscious of it and what it involved.

We now come to the second observation about the above *MDR* quotes that I want to point to. But before I delve into it, I have to interpret the present findings. If what for want of a better term we call here the "metaphysical" and "transcendental" dimension is, and must be, systematically excluded from psychology's basic notion, "the unconscious," how can Jung hope that we might "create light" and "lift up"? The dungeon is *absolutely* closed, because heaven and the light of heaven have *logically* been done away with. Even his own wording in the quote I just alluded to shows that all is lost: "Instead of creating light, we conceal in darkness, instead of lifting up, we expose to ridicule and contempt." The point has never been to *create* light and to *lift* up. It was the other way around. Zeus let his golden rain *fall* into Danae's dungeon of his own accord, and "people that walked in darkness have seen a great light" (from above); Prometheus stole the fire *from* heaven or from the carriage of Helios and brought it down to earth. Since what in myths is told "did never happen but always is" (Sallustios)—where can Prometheus steal the fire from when the transcendental dimension has been canceled? How can a light fall into the darkness of our existence when the very *source* of any true light is thought to be "the unconscious," the dungeon itself? How, when heaven as the former source of light, of the sun, the moon, the stars, has once and for all been eliminated from our binding *knowing*, our "official" world view, and when consciousness voluntarily settles in the "banality" (Jung) of "the unconscious," in the blindness of the positive-factual? It is the notion of "the unconscious," that is the very way in which *psychologically* (even if not behaviorally) "we conceal in darkness" and "expose to ... contempt." Why to contempt? Because this notion withholds the open acknowledgment of truth from what it comprises. It has already logically stolen that entire dimension wherefrom alone Prometheus could steal the fire or wherefrom a heavenly light could possibly fall into our darkness.

The second observation starts out from Jung's statement that the terms God or daimon "have the great advantage of encompassing and evoking the emotional quality of numinosity." What we have here is a *metabasis eis allo genos.* "The unconscious" is a generic term or refers to a whole realm or region, whereas God and daimon represent individual contents, semantic items. As we have seen, "the unconscious" is a logical term that locks the contents it refers to in the *status* of an *ignotum* and fundamentally unknowable, in the status of contents that our consciousness cannot and must never accept intellectual responsibility for by owning up to their truth (because otherwise the forbidden metaphysical dimension would instantly again come out of the box into which it has been sunk). But Jung reduces and belittles the problem of which names to use to a subjective emotional or experiential issue: "banal, neutral and rational" vs. "evoking the emotional quality of numinosity and inspiring the imagination." We see here confirmed what we saw earlier, that Jung escapes to the semantic level, relegating and delegating what is actually a question of *whether something is true* to the question of *what it does to us in positive[3] subjective experience.* This scotomization of the logical

---

[3] 'Positive' in the logical sense (the sense that underlies the term positivism).

question of truth, stealthily covered up by the reductive substitution for it of the subjectively so impressive category of positive-factual *Erfahrbarkeit* (this is the word I rendered above in the quote from Jung as "the fact that it can be empirically experienced"), *is* in itself the very "the unconscious"—a logical, "metaphysical" self-castration, self-blinding, the soul's self-immurement in irreparable *logical, mental* darkness, no matter how many subjective experiences of light—stars and suns and *scintillae* in the unconscious—one may have and how numinous they may be. The translation of the category of truth and knowing into the category of subjective emotional and imagination-inspirational quality is psychologism pure and simple, psychologism not in the usual superficial sense, but on the very highest or deepest theoretical level, in the very heart of the matter. "The unconscious" is at the same time the lever by means of which this translation constantly is, no, always already has been, performed—tacitly, invisibly, unbeknownst.

In alchemical terms we could express the same observation the following way: Jung locks and hermetically seals the spirit in matter. His is at bottom an *opus contra opus alchemicum*. One of the main general purposes of the alchemical work was to free the spirit Mercurius from his imprisonment in matter. The alchemists maltreated their prime matter, subjecting it to all sorts of destructive and painful operations: pulverization, corruption, incineration, *solutio*, fermentation, etc. The alchemical work was basically one great attack on the image, on the *natural imaginal shape* of the matter in which it came. The intact image and natural form, i.e., the *status* of "natural entity," had to be overcome so that the substance might attain its spirit (or essence) form. When a substance was pulverized or incinerated or evaporated, its imaginable form was gone. You had something else, a vapor, a distillate, an essence, at any rate something that no longer had a figurative shape. And the absolutely self-contradictory nature of the aimed-for end-product, water that was permanent, a stone that was not a stone, shows that the whole level of the natural imagination had in principle been left behind. (In principle only. For it was precisely the dilemma, if not tragedy, of alchemy that what it logically aimed for, and was obviously already claimed by, it made empirically impossible through its own still imaginal style of thinking and by operating within the material-natural horizon of the chemical. Its work was a clear case of "acting out" that work "against nature"—the work of the negation of the natural and imaginal—that could only have been achieved if it had been interiorized into itself instead of being literalized on the level of behavior and if it had been applied to itself instead of being acted out on literal matter out there.)

Jung, by contrast, is a downright materialist, just as above he showed himself to be a positivistic sensualist. *Of course, not on the semantic, but on the psychological, syntactic level.* (On the semantic level and explicitly, he is obviously the opposite. But what he actually does and how he thinks, how his thought is structured is more important than what he explicitly teaches.) He prevents—again I must qualify: not on the phenomenological, practical, and semantic, but on the fundamental-theoretical level—the spirit from escaping, he *logically* stuffs the soul's issues back down into the form or status of "matter," namely the status of *natural events* and *empirical facts* and *emotional experiences*. He does not try to *release* them from their positivity into their truth, in which they would finally have come home to themselves and would no longer be on principle imprisoned in the person ("one's own psychic background"), on the one hand, nor sealed in the logical status of irrevocable positivity, that is, occludedness-in-themselves, on the other. The term "the unconscious," after all, as we heard from Jung, "was coined for scientific purposes, and is far better suited to dispassionate observation which makes no metaphysical claims than are transcendental concepts, which are contestable." On the theoretical level Jung needed and insisted on the unbridgeable gap across which the external dispassionate observer could make his neutral, i.e., intellectually noncommittal, statements about the *per definitionem* "*un*conscious" psychological phenomena that in themselves (but only in themselves, only yonder, on the other side of the gulf, in the private experiential sphere) certainly were, were allowed to be, nay, were *supposed to be*, of a "metaphysical" or "transcendental" nature. The soul phenomena were to be given intensive attention, emotional appreciation, amplificatory understanding, ethical regard. But the one thing they really want was absolutely denied to them: intellectual acknowledgment as belonging to our knowing, the subject's (committedly, not "dispassionately") honoring them as having the status of truths.

* * *

I said that Jung's work was a work against the spirit of alchemy. But it seems that Jung has alchemy on his side when we listen to the following passage from the chapter, "The Problem of Freeing Mercurius," in his discussion of the Grimms' fairytale, *The Spirit in the Bottle*, in his essay entitled, "The Spirit Mercurius." As is well known, in this tale the son who had found the well-sealed bottle in which a spirit had been imprisoned, finally, after some complications, let this spirit out of the bottle and was rewarded for it. Jung is critical of this freeing the spirit. He writes,

> What happens when this Hermes-Mercurius-Wotan, a pagan god, is let loose again? ... The *avis Hermetis* (the bird of Hermes) has escaped from the glass prison, and in consequence something has happened which the experienced alchemist wished at all costs to avoid. That is why he sealed the stopper of his bottle with magic signs and set it for a very long time over the lowest fire, so that "he who is within may not fly out." For if he escapes, the whole laborious opus comes to nothing and has to be started all over again. ...
>
> Be that as it may, the behaviour of the young man—successfully as it worked out for him—must be described as *alchemically incorrect*. ... The golden age of alchemy was the sixteenth and the first half of the seventeenth century. At that time a storm bird did indeed escape from a spiritual vessel which the daemons must have felt was a prison. As I said, the alchemists were all for not letting Mercurius escape, but for his staying inside and for the internal transformation of Mercurius ... (*CW* 13 §§ 250f., transl. modif.)

No doubt, Jung is right that the alchemists unrelentingly opted for the spirit's staying in the bottle. But it is not only a historically correct statement about alchemy. I also wholeheartedly concur *for psychology* with the alchemists and with Jung (who in citing the stance of the alchemists certainly gave us also his own view of things). The fundamentally evasive spirit must be prevented from escaping. The bottle must be sealed.

What does this mean concretely? The way I understand the work of the psychologist, it has to be uncompromisingly devoted to the "matter" at hand, regardless of what it may be: in the consulting room this dream today, this memory from the past that now has come up, this emotional reaction that has become a topic in today's session, and outside the consulting room any issue or image or text that one has taken up as a subject for study. Once it has been adopted as one's topic, our commitment to it must be *exclusive*, for the duration of one's occupation with it. "That's it!" *Closure*. Nothing else must divert us from this topic. Just as, e.g., in dream interpretation we have to "stick to the image," as Jung and Lopez-Pedraza demanded, that is, in a *qualitative* sense be confined in what we say about it by its precise phenomenology, without going off to the level of generalities and abstractions not backed up by its concrete appearance and "feel," so we must also in a quantitative sense dwell with our attention *only* on the matter at hand. The alchemical vessel and the hermetic seal on it are in psychology no longer physical objects, but a mental, methodical attitude, an attitude that, with respect to the fantasy image formulated by Jung, comes across nicely in the following maxim which I have quoted many times in my writings and have to repeat here once more. This maxim or golden rule of psychology can *mutatis mutandis* be applied to any matter.

> Above all, don't let anything from outside, that does not belong, get into it, for the fantasy-image has 'everything it needs' [omne quo indiget] within itself (*CW* 14 § 749, modif.).

The application of this methodological maxim must not occur pedantically and with a literalistic, formalistic mind. The difficulty in making use of it is that there are no positive-factual criteria for the decision about what belongs and what does not belong, what comes from outside (is truly foreign) and what merely supports and enhances what is already there. The decision cannot be operationalized. Rather, it requires that "subtler intelligence" that Jung demanded,[4] an intelligence which is probably "subtler" for the reason (among others) that it contains within itself what Jung might call a differentiated "feeling function" and a good intuitive, inner susceptibility to "the soul" of the matter under psychological investigation.

---

[4] *Letters 2*, p. 410, to L. King, 14 January 1958.

This methodical principle means that anything like free associations, subjective feelings, causal explanations of how the material might have come about, any speculation about better ways how, e.g., the dream ego might have reacted in the given dream, or about what other possibilities or potentials for a (good) ending of the dream there might possibly be would be kept out as extraneous and probably ego-stuff. The phenomenon *is* the way it is. It has to be respected—and stay enclosed—in its being-so. Psychological work requires a discipline and skill in *abstraction* from one's own merely-subjective feelings and personal views and sudden ideas that might pop up in oneself in view of a given motif. Only then can it be hoped that we are open to the self-display and for the logical self-movement of the matter into its own inner depth, its truth.

The purpose of the hermetic closure is "the internal transformation of Mercurius." The matter needs to be enclosed in the alchemical vessel because the work is work on and with the same. One and the same matter is supposed to be interiorized into itself, intensified, heightened. It is a work of the matter upon itself. The carefully sealed "vessel" is necessary so that the matter is prevented from following the natural course, that is, from acting out its own nature, by just being and behaving as would be normal for it. There must not be any external influences on it, but also no effects from it outwards on other matters, no interaction whatsoever. It must not spend itself, *waste* its potential by just "doing its thing." Its self-movement, such as the natural putrefaction of certain materials, must, to be sure, not be prevented, but it must be caught and retained so as to return again to itself, be applied to itself.

As a kind of pictorial illustration of this self-application and the concomitant intensification through interiorization into itself, I mention a Taoist ritual practice in which this self-application is literally acted out in the form of a sexual technique. The purpose of the ritual is to nourish the "life principle" and ultimately to gain immortality. The procedure is as follows. The Taoist first copulates so that "the essence" (the semen) is intensely stirred up. But then, when it is about to be ejaculated, he quickly grabs and pulls the penis in a certain way behind the scrotum while at the same time vigorously exhaling for a long time through the mouth and flashing his teeth. If then he lets the essence go, it cannot come out, but comes back from the penis and rises up (through the spinal marrow), ultimately entering the brain (according to ancient medicine the locus of the soul and as such the place where semen originates in the body). This is a procedure the immortals exchange among each other, but swear not to pass on to everybody.[5]

Let us have a closer look at this practice. The life essence is first stirred up so that it becomes somehow accessible. It is awakened from its dormant state. But then it is prevented from spending and wasting itself for the natural course of events (ejaculation) and its natural purpose (gratification of desire and possibly reproduction). The interaction with the partner is disrupted, intercepted and the self is enclosed within itself. The life essence is forced *contra naturam* to travel back up to its source, the brain as the locus of soul. This reversal of the direction becomes possible through two measures. First, the relentless closure of the outward passage and the prevention of an escape. Secondly, a "displacement from below to above" for the outward tendency and simultaneously an activation of the spirit dimension (breath), in place of the physical, substantial dimension. The intended result of a nourishment of the life principle as such comes about through the self-application of the life principle to itself. And in contrast to normal nourishment of the life principle through something else, through food or joyful experiences, this is a counter-natural nourishment. This practice prevents the life principle from continuing along the lines of the natural horizontality of its movement (sexual intercourse, relation to others, taking in food from outside, etc.) and forces it into verticality, namely to a fundamentally "higher" or "deeper" logical level or status, that of "immortality." Apparently, this revolutionary vertical movement that bursts the horizon of the commonplace is only possible through "self-application." And this self-application presupposes radical closure, the hermetically sealed alchemical vessel.

Instead of fathering a child "out there" and thereby reproducing himself on the same old natural level of life through otherness, the Taoist "fertilized" *himself*, or rather, he forced the "life essence" in him

---

[5] See H. Maspero, "Les procédés de 'nourrir le principe vital' dans la religion taoïste ancienne," in: *Journal Asiatique* (1937) pp. 177–252, 353–430, here p. 385. Cited in Mircea Eliade, *Geschichte der religiösen Ideen*, vol. 2, Freiburg et al. (Herder) 1979, p. 361.

to fertilize and intensify *itself.* We also have to note that his ritual was *not* a psychological one of self-reflection, of moving his *attention* away from his sexual partner as an external other to himself, a shift from the *intentio directa* to the *intentio obliqua.* He did not give birth to an internal child, but was catapulted into a totally new dimension or status. In other words, it was not an achievement in the realm of subjectivity. No, it was the sphere of the objective "matter" itself, of the life essence, underneath his subjective mind, on which this revolution was brought about.

The similarity and difference between this Taoist example and the alchemical opus are obvious. The main difference is that concerning the Taoist procedure Jung could probably rightly say that, although not in a modern psychological sense, it served the purpose of the transformation of the personality, whereas alchemy did not, as I argued, aim at the person of the alchemist. The similarity of the logic of the two techniques is striking. The alchemists, too, wanted to drive the prime matter into verticality, into its own inner depth and truth. The closure of the vessel served the purpose of preventing the natural horizontal development of the matter. When alchemy strove for the stone, the life elixir, etc., it did not seek *another* object on the same horizontal plane of commonplace reality, an object that was merely different because it had miraculous power. Rather, these objects are images for a new logical status, a fundamentally different level of consciousness. Just as the Taoist did not want offspring, but the new status of "immortality," so the alchemist did not want a thing, but a fundamentally, syntactically different level of consciousness, which expresses itself in such terms as fermentations, distillation, sublimation, evaporation. And his dilemma was that what was actually a different logical or syntactical status he had to imagine and express and *think* in the alienating and self-defeating *imaginal,* i.e., semantic language, the language of things, for which reason he had to take refuge to paradoxical formulations ("the stone that is not a stone," "permanent water").

A psychology and psychotherapy in the spirit of alchemy cannot have a therapeutic *program.* No wish for the self-development, improvement, growth, individuation of the personality, no wish for a cure and betterment of the patient, because the alchemical project is not person-oriented. But also no wish for the redemption of the world (which sometimes in archetypal psychology is in truly Manichean manner viewed as a "fallen world") because the alchemical one is not a salvation and Manichean project, despite the fact that its outlook is "cosmic" in the sense of being concerned with the concrete material world rather than with the individual (person). Its intentions are more modest.

(1) While any kind of program, any longing for something else or new, is psychologically a reaching out for the future and thereby stays horizontally on the same old level of consciousness, psychology can be said to turn its back to the open future and its wished-for possibilities. It stays put and wholeheartedly concentrates on and single-mindedly attends to what *is already there*, immediately before it in the retort. In this sense psychology is logically situating itself in the perfect tense. It is, in a way, a looking backwards. What is in the retort is always something that is already an accomplished fact, has already happened. Psychology, psychotherapy have no interest in future potentialities and alternatives to the present. They are committed to the real and the real's own inherent necessity (*Ananke*).

It can and must feel this way because what is in the retort, no matter how corrupt, stinking, perverse it may appear, is for it from the outset defined as being "perfect" in itself, inasmuch as it contains everything it needs *within itself*, even its fulfillment. It does not need any "other" from outside, any correction, any improvement. But what it does need is to be cooked, incubated, absolute-negatively interiorized into itself. It needs its own *vertical* deepening into its truth, its going under or dying into its Concept. "Redemption" or "salvation," *if* one wants to use these terms at all, would here only mean that the phenomenon in the retort finds its fulfillment and freedom through being *released* into its essence—a transformation which the alchemists expressed in the image of the freeing of Mercurius from his imprisonment in matter, i.e., in the material, natural, imaginal *form* of the phenomenon. We could say then that the ultimate goal is that the "mercurial spirit" which had been hidden in and subdued by the material form of the phenomenon finally comes out into the open and takes charge of the phenomenon.

(2) Psychology's commitment is to eachness: to *this* problem, symptom, situation, this dream, image, text, phenomenon at hand, and only this. In this present Now this one phenomenon at hand is

in the retort, and inasmuch as I am a psychologist, I therefore have my back turned to everything else around me and to the retort. This is my methodological stance. As therapist I forget everything else; nothing else exists for me—for the time of my occupation with the present matter in the vessel. Through this absolute closure of the vessel or, the other way around, through this absolute exclusion of what is not in the vessel, this one seemingly insignificant matter in this one small alchemical *vas* is now all that exists for me. It becomes, it *is*, the whole world. Jung said about the *vas Hermeticum* of alchemy, that "it was 'hermetically' sealed (i.e., sealed with the sign of Hermes); it had to be made of glass, and had also to be as round as possible, since it was meant to represent the universe [*Weltall*, the All] ..." (*CW* 13 § 245, modif.). But the point is that we must not think that it "represents" the universe. No, it has become, and now *is*, the universe, the All, through the radical methodical closure and exclusion. There is really nothing outside it, including the literal universe. The *vas* and its content is all there is now.

If we had not also completely forgotten about the literal universe around us, the retort would not be a retort, not be hermetically sealed, because then we would still hold on to something outside of it. The retort *is* only the *vas Hermeticum* if it ceases to be an object *in* the world and instead in itself becomes the whole and exclusive world for us. The seal does not only have the function of keeping the spirit Mercurius imprisoned *in* the bottle; it also, and perhaps more importantly, has to keep everything else, including the notion of the world around it, *out*. The hermetic sealing of the vessel is the imaginal or symbolic representation of the logical interiorization into the vessel, not of the literal world, but of the *notion* of world. This is indispensable. For if the *vas* has not from the outset been absolute-negatively interiorized into itself so that it has the *notion of outside* totally *inside* and the very notion of exteriority is thus altogether gone, how could we hope to interiorize into itself the prime matter contained in it?

Since the whole purpose of the psychological work is the "redemption" of each matter that happens to have been taken up, in the sense of releasing it into its truth or concept, and since in each case the matter is hermetically sealed into itself so that it turns, for the time being, into the whole world with nothing around it, we could call the purpose indeed "the rescue of the world." But we immediately see that this notion does not have the grandiose sense that we otherwise connect with it. The sense of world has completely changed. It is intrinsically connected with "eachness." Instead of its spatial sense, the external sense of infinite *extent* and sum-total of the infinite *manifold* of things, it is now the internal wholeness, inner infinity and totality of each individual phenomenon—*provided that* it is apperceived in the spirit of the hermetic closure described. "World" here, therefore, refers to the *self nature* of the phenomena.

Inasmuch as "world," "wholeness," "self" no longer refer, on the semantic level, to particular entities, contents, or states, but now mean the logical, syntactical character of each individual phenomenon that has been hermetically sealed within itself, all the objections that many Jungians raised, often rightly raised, against Jung's notions of the self and of wholeness no longer apply. Now these notions are no longer the literal mega-notions loaded with "numinous" meaning that they used to be. They have been absolute-negatively interiorized into themselves, distilled, evaporated. One also no longer has to literally play the world out there, "the city," the cosmos against the consulting room. Each phenomenon is its own cosmos, and the literal cosmos and literal "city" as *external* reality is not a topic of psychology.

One sees from these reflections that I myself insist, here concurring fully with Jung, that the bottle with the spirit Mercurius needs to be hermetically closed, and stay closed. If the evasive spirit were to escape, if *ille fugax Mercurius*, the *servus fugitivus*, would go off from the phenomenon at hand to other alternatives, to new possibilities on the same horizontal semantic level, or, again on the semantic level, wander from one idea to the next, as in the manner of free association, or, with Lacan, "metonymically" glide from word to word (*mot à mot*), the whole *opus* of the vertical interiorization of the matter into its own truth through its syntactical, logical transformation would fail.

* * *

And yet, I cannot agree with Jung's rejection of the behavior of the boy of our fairytale who set the spirit free. Here I seem to be guilty of a contradiction. How can I insist on the absolute closure of the vessel and at the same time approve of the spirit's being let out? The answer,

I think, is that precisely this—the overcoming of this contradiction—
is the challenge of our tale as well as of the notion of alchemical and
psychological closure, a challenge that Jung did not master.

Jung's mistake is that he "fell for" the imaginal-pictorial mode of
presentation and took it literally. The problem of a narrative is that it
has to portray as a sequence of events (on the semantic level) what is
actually the logical-syntactical unfolding of the internal dialectic of
one concept. On the level of visualizable behavior the hermetic
enclosure of the spirit in the bottle and the breaking of the seal in
order to release him absolutely exclude each other. On that level we
have to chose, either – or. Because Jung stayed on this level, his
choosing "closure" and rejecting the "opening" of the bottle is plausible,
consistent, one of the two possible choices.

But the problem is that a reading of the story on the semantic or
behavioral level is psychologically inadequate. And this inadequacy of
his interpretation is due to his prior and general failure to really *think
through* the alchemical notion of the hermetic closure of the vessel. His
was a literal, external, dogmatic understanding of closure, closure in
the sense of commonplace practical reality and everyday life, where as
a matter of course formal-logical consistency and unambiguity of the
terms used is required. But "closure" in this fairytale and in alchemy
and psychology is a priori a *hermetic, mercurial* closure that requires a
dialectical understanding. It is not the simple self-identical fact which
Jung took it for. The notion of closure *itself partakes* of the living
mercurial spirit of alchemy enclosed by means of it. You cannot
approach a story about the spirit Mercurius imprisoned in a
hermetically sealed bottle with a positivistic sense of closure. With a
positivistic bottle, stopper and seal, the spirit Mercurius could not be
contained in the first place. He would laugh at any such
incommensurable attempt, or rather, he would not even exist for this
mentality. Jung's mistake is that he comes to a hermetic notion with
a positivistic conception of this notion. The logic of his style of thinking
does not match the semantics that it is applied to.

"Closure" needs to be interiorized into itself, to be applied to itself.
And then it will, within itself, *open* itself to release its own truth, or
rather the truth that it encloses. Within itself: this means that what
narratively appears in our tale as a consecutive (new, other) event on
the same level with the prior fact, the closure, is to be taken as an internal

moment of this (one and the same) prior fact. Our story explains what "hermetic closure" is actually about, what it involves if it is truly comprehended in its depth and ultimate truth and not merely viewed from an outside literal perspective (external reflection).

Instead of being the undoing of the closure (or a revoking of the "don't let anything from outside, that does not belong, get into it"), letting the spirit out is in the fairytale the closure's own internal completion, conclusion, fulfillment. How is this to be understood?

If through the closure the *vas* with its content has to become the All for the alchemist, he cannot just have the vessel opposite to himself as a small object. As an object for a subject (the adept) this object would necessarily be a thing *within* the world, in other words, it would have the real world *around* itself, not itself *be* the whole world. For Jung the hermetic vessel was accordingly only *meant to represent* the universe: that is, it was only a symbol *of* the universe, it was looked upon *as if* it *were* the world.[6] But of course, as such it was not *really* the universe for the alchemist. As long as the alchemical *vas* is merely supposed to represent the All, the hermetic closure is still fundamentally incomplete. It has not gone all the way. This is only the first half of the real closure. It is only the literal, positive-factual sense of closure.

The self-application of the notion of closure to itself requires a second step, namely that what is hermetically enclosed is not only the matter or content in the vessel, but also this enclosing vessel itself, not only the *omnitudo realitatis*, but also the whole *sense* of "closure" itself, the very *notion* of "world," of "around" (around the vessel) or "surroundings." The closure has to be absolute so as to include and enclose *itself,* its own concept. Only then does it include everything without reserve and can it be said to no longer merely be meant to symbolically represent the universe in the sense of an as-if, but really *be* it.

But this closure that has relentlessly integrated every notion of "outside" or "around itself" into itself is *ipso facto* tantamount to the freeing of the imprisoned spirit Mercurius. Pictorially speaking, the surroundings of the bottle are now inside the bottle, which means that the bottle has become infinite, comprising even the adept, who now

---

[6] Archetypal or imaginal psychology explicitly makes this "as if" its own standpoint!

is also enclosed within it and has the bottle all around himself. He thus can no longer be the dispassionate observer of what goes on. And inasmuch as the bottle has truly become the all-surrounding world even around him, and inasmuch as he is hermetically enclosed inside the same world that the Mercurius, too, is imprisoned in, he now has the spirit all around himself and that spirit is now free to roam throughout the entire universe.

Our fairytale tries to present the *whole* dialectic of the idea of the absolutely closed, hermetically sealed vessel. Because it has to do this in a narrative and pictorial form, it cannot fully do justice to what it actually wants to demonstrate. But thought "helpeth the infirmities" of the pictorial representation. What we have to realize is that the second time around the young man no longer lets the spirit escape in the literal, positive-factual sense, but now sets him free from the bottle only within the bottle, which alchemically speaking meanwhile has turned into the fulfilled notion of the All. The freeing of Mercurius from the bottle does not undo the closure but surpasses it, by going through with it all the way. It is its, the closure's, own having become absolute.

It is obvious that Mercurius can only be freed from his imprisonment in the bottle *within* his absolute imprisonment. The absoluteness of his imprisonment in fact is the precondition for there really being a Mercurius at all. If there is no absolute closure, there may be "bottles," but no bottle will contain the spirit, regardless of whether imprisoned or free. Only within the hermetically, i.e., absolutely, sealed bottle can Mercurius be released, and only through his being released does he begin to exist in the first place. Such is the "crazy" logic of the soul. There is not first a Mercurius as a positive-factual entity or being who is then imprisoned and after that (maybe) finally released. Without the absolute closure, there is only positive-factual reality.

You have to pay the full price. There is no other way.

It is naive to imagine that by locking the soul and the Mercurius *positivistically* into the two vessels of psychology (the spatial imagination of the "within" of the person as well as the logical status of "the unconscious") what is inside these two vessels would still be the Mercurius and the soul. With that kind of locking, the soul and Mercurius always have already escaped prior to your locking, and what then will be inside the vessels is at best their semblance, their semanticized as-if replicas. You cannot get away with the half-hearted, positivistic sense of closure. Psychology has to have gone all the way to the end in order to be able to begin.

Our fairytale is thus not really a story about a series of consecutive events. It is the logical explication of one single notion, the notion of the truly hermetically sealed bottle. Closure and release are the same.

Jung *had to* evaluate the behavior of the young man in this tale as alchemically incorrect and forbidden, although the tale itself with its happy end indicated the opposite. He had to construe "closure" and "setting free" as undialectical opposites, as (literalistic, positivistic) alternatives and to choose closure and with some passion reject the setting free. With his *ad hoc* comments about this fairytale and his clear vote "for not letting Mercurius escape, but for his staying inside," Jung at the same time unwittingly revealed the unconscious deepest impulse and principle of his own psychological thought. It is the literalistic closure to which "the unconscious" ("our own"!) and "the psychic background *in us*" owe their existence. He needed the literal closure because the one thing that he really feared was the release of Mercurius, from out of his containment in personalistic experiences and in the status of positive fact (the status of the irrevocably *ignotum*) into the logical freedom of the sphere of truth and mind, which would have involved psychology in "metaphysics" and in the obligation of having to *intellectually* take a stand concerning the content of what was experienced. Outside, all around the psyche, a positivistic frame of mind. Inside numinous, archetypal contents.

So Jung's psychology was a psychology of the *bottled* spirit, in the commonplace sense of bottled—not in the sense of absolute hermetic closure. Other than Freud, he *wanted* the spirit, but the mercurial spirit[7] only safely bottled, as spirit prevented from *being* spirit, and so he trickily substituted our subjective "*experiences* from the unconscious" for what actually should be the official mind's mercurial *truths*. The problem, however, was not, as the reader will understand after what has been shown, the "bottle" and the

---

[7] 'Spirit' must here never be confused with 'spirit' in the New Age sense of "spirituality," "spiritual movements and practices." It is not the spirit to be sought on the "peaks" in contrast to the anima's "vales" (Hillman), but the mercurial spirit in, the internal logic of, each matter, each real situation, phenomenon, symptom.

"bottling" as such, but that the bottle was externally imagined as positivistic bottle which had psychology as its dispassionate, neutral observer outside of itself. And the problem was further that Jung believed and pretended that the personalistic phenomena prioritized and observed by it (i.e., the subjective numinous experiences, dreams, etc.) nevertheless had a mercurial, soul, even religious, significance simply as empirical facts.

No, the "bottle" is not the problem. On the contrary. Psychology can only *be* if it is inside the bottle. If it, psychology itself, is *in* the bottle, the latter is *ipso facto* the bottle whose "enclosing vessel" character has truly been interiorized into itself, too, so that it has nothing outside of itself and therefore has become absolute. And only then can the spirit Mercurius be *freed* spirit. And only the *a priori* freed spirit is the spirit that can be found imprisoned in a bottle in the first place. Psychology needs a sense of *mercurial, absolute* closure to find this bottle. Only like can find like.

* * *

Looking back at the steps of the movement of our thought concerning the topic of closure and setting free we can say that the first step was a methodical decision for an uncompromising closure. As a methodical decision it is an ego move. By insisting on staying with this closure, Jung did not only try to freeze the movement as such, but also, *while* semantically (content-wise) being open to the mercurial mysteries, syntactically nevertheless held on to "the ego." His closure is an ego behavior that is inflicted on Mercurius from outside. It is with the second step that Mercurius is let loose to be all around us and permeate "the world" (whatever "world" happens to be at stake at each present), thereby establishing the logical position of interiority. As I pointed out, this step does not amount to an undoing of the closure. Rather, the ego now gives up its initial idea of having to be in charge of this closure and instead commits, entrusts, the responsibility of closure to the spirit himself as his self-enclosure. The freed Mercurius is he who does no longer have to be enclosed in and restrained by an external vessel because he has come home to himself and is enclosed in himself: in his *concept*, his truth. Only now is he true spirit. What would a Mercurius be who needs to be restrained from outside? This his enclosure in his truth is his freedom, the fulfillment of his essence. This is why he can freely roam through the whole world without becoming dangerous: he will from now on always stay contained in what he truly is.

Here I stop. But it is clear that the movement itself has not come to a full stop, because something has been left behind: the ego with whose methodical closure the movement started. It, too, wants to be released into its truth and freedom. This is why there has to be another step beyond closure and setting free, the step we could call "emancipation." But this is another story for another time.

CHAPTER TEN

Mythic Illusory Appearance–
Blindness to Logical Form[1]
C.G. Jung's *Faust* interpretation,
for instance

E ven if and when, as Kant told us, *transzendentaler Schein*
(transcendental illusory appearance) has been exposed by
"transcendental critique" (dialectic), it nevertheless does not
simply disappear the way logical illusory appearance (that of
fallacious reasoning) disappears once the fallacy at work in one's
reasoning has been seen through. Transcendental appearance is a
natural and inevitable illusion based on *subjective* principles, which,
however, are taken as objective, with the result that impermissible
"transcendent judgments" arise. What I analogously call "*mythischer
Schein*," "mythic illusory appearance," namely the conviction that
a given phenomenon, motif, or experience is a mythic one of
archetypal depth and origin when in actuality it is not, is not quite
as inevitable. It does disappear once it has been uncovered. And
yet, much like transcendental appearance, it is pertinacious, not
because, like its cousin, it is in itself natural and inevitable, but
because there are certain strong anti-modern subjective interests,

---

[1] This revised English version is based on a chapter with a similar title in a German
book manuscript on "The Meaning of Myth Today" that I wrote during the second half
of the 1990s, but never completely finished.

desires, perhaps even "needs" in modern man that give it its power of conviction. *Mundus vult decipi.*

On the very different everyday practical level, we are constantly taught to be aware of the difference between illusory appearance and real being through the modern phenomena of political propaganda, advertizing, and glamorous packaging. Often enough we have to find out that the hopes raised by what the wrapping promises are disappointed by the content, but time and again people fall for the same type of promises of salvation by politicians as well as for the seductive appearance promulgated by "the hidden persuaders" (Vance Packard). Here, too, and not only in the area of myths and symbols, "Consumers want to be persuaded." Why should it be different when it comes to beautiful mythic images that promise higher meaning?

The objective condition of the possibility of one's succumbing to the mythic illusory appearance is an *external, formal likeness* (the "looks") of certain semantic contents or phenomena to elements of actual myths, symbols, and rituals of antiquity, foreign primitive cultures, world religions, alchemy and the like. The subjective condition of its possibility is one's blindness to the specific syntactical form or logical status in which those contents or phenomena, as *modern* phenomena, stand, the scotomization of the intrinsic function and role that they have in their own (textual, social, historical, and psychological) context.

Mythic appearance in this sense is very common in Jungian psychology as practiced nowadays. But it is also to be found in Jung himself. Two quite obvious examples from his work and thought are his depth-psychological interpretation of the Nazi movement of his time as a manifestation of the Germanic god Wotan "from the depth of the unconscious Germanic soul" (in the 20th century!) and his reading of Goethe's *Faust* (especially Part II) as a new, modern representation of the alchemical *opus magnum* or the individuation process. I will use the second example to illustrate the phenomenon of mythic illusory appearance and the corresponding blindness to logical form. But before I turn to *Faust*, I want at least to mention (without discussing it in this paper) that in addition to such specific misjudgments there is also, both in Jung and in his followers, the much more subtle general and large-scale mythic-appearance-like confusion of the *opus parvum* (the personal, merely *psychic* and utterly private inner image and emotional process in modern individuals—as seen, for example, in the consulting room) with the *opus magnum*, the *soul's* historical self-movement in its fundamentally transpersonal, cultural logical life. Jungian therapy, i.e., the *ordinary* work both with patients (for the purpose of healing) and with other analysands (for the purpose of self-development), likes to give itself the aura of a "higher," ultimately "religious" meaning and salvational mystery.

* * *

As far as I know, Jung never presented a full-fledged interpretation of Goethe's *Faust*, but he repeatedly made statements in which he assessed the general character of this work as a whole, what it means psychologically, its historical significance and the psychological problems it contains, in which light it needs to be seen and in which tradition it stands. For the same reason, we will not have to go here into the details of this long work and present an overall interpretation of it. Our theme is not the "meaning" of *Faust II*, not the whole scope of what Goethe intended to express with this rich and many-level work. We can content ourselves with a discussion exclusively of a few *particular* features or aspects of this work, those features on which, however, Jung's claims about it depend, and with comparing and contrasting Jung's view with other views that—notwithstanding differences in individual points or in shades of interpretation—are shared by most present-day *Faust* scholars and supported by what can be seen from the *Faust* text itself as well as what can be known from our knowledge of Goethe's own comments and biography. Jung's view sees *Faust* in the light of an old tradition and thus approaches it with categories taken from that tradition, the other view recognizes in it a fundamentally modern work of far greater internal complexity.

Since my interest is not the *Faust* work itself, but the problem of mythic illusory appearance and blindness to logical form, I will not *argue* for this other view. I only present it in such a way that the higher complexity mentioned can be seen. Even if later scholarship would come to other conclusions about this work, this would not matter so much for our issue. Even if this particular example used by me to illustrate the problem of the logical form difference between *modern* phenomena and *traditional* phenomena and the ensuing problem of a

naive traditional reading of a modern soul phenomenon were shown
to be an unsuitable example, we could still be alerted to the
difference itself that is the sole focus of this paper. If this difference
exists, then there can be two possible ways of seeing one and the
same *modern* text or motif (or dream and inner experience)
depending on whether we take it (what it presents) at face value
without paying attention to its logical form or whether we take its
logical form fully into consideration. Put another way, the first way of
seeing focuses on the semantic aspect, the content and the "looks" of
the phenomenon, as if it contained its meaning within itself, whereas
the second reacts to the syntax which gives a fundamentally discrepant
function and meaning to its content and looks.

    With traditional soul phenomena this distinction is not important,
inasmuch as in them their syntax is usually fully congruous with their
semantics. In fact, in their case, the semantic content is precisely
nothing else but the self-representation and articulation of their syntax.
This is what makes myth and metaphysics—for the empirical view—
fantastic or precisely "metaphysical" because they present the logic of
"the world," of a determinate historical mode of being-in-the-world,
in the form of semantic images and narratives, that is, in that form
that is normally used for describing *inner-worldly* events, things, and
experiences. This is exactly what gives rise to what Kant called the
transcendental illusory appearance. But modern consciousness is
characterized by the fact that for it content and logical form, semantics
and syntax have objectively separated, which is why Kant, who was at
the threshold between the traditional and the modern world and who,
in the form of his *Critiques* explicated this threshold, was empowered
to see through, and had to see through, the problem of the
transcendental illusory appearance. This would not have been possible
prior to the fateful soul-historical event of this separation. Objectively
(though often not subjectively) modern consciousness has become
explicitly conscious of the syntactical as such and in contradistinction
to the semantic. In modern soul phenomena (such as in the *Faust II*
drama), the semantic content therefore no longer has in itself the same
dignity and self-sufficiency as in myth or metaphysics or in traditional
works of art. It does not immediately display the meaning that it has,
or helps to express, within the phenomenon. The content has been
sublated and become functional, subservient to syntax, which has

emancipated itself from the content and external appearance of the soul phenomena and may even contradict them.

The secondary literature on *Faust II* is enormous. Because they are sufficient for making my point, I rely for this paper on only a few major commentaries or discussions in biographies or handbooks.[2] In the following all the quotations from German texts, both from *Faust II* and from secondary works, are my translations without my indicating this in each individual case. Quotations from C.G. Jung are taken from the English *Collected Works*, but here I will indicate each time where I modify the translation on the basis of Jung's original text.

I. The mode of artistic creation

In "On the relation of analytical psychology to poetry," Jung distinguishes two types of poetic works according to his typological distinction between introversion and extraversion. "The introverted attitude is characterized by the subject's assertion of his conscious intentions and aims against the demands of the object, whereas the extraverted attitude is characterized by the subject's subordination to the demands which the object makes upon him. In my view, Schiller's plays and most of his poems give one a good idea of the introverted attitude: the material is mastered by the conscious intentions of the poet. The extraverted attitude is illustrated by the second part of *Faust*: here the material is distinguished by its refractoriness" (*CW* 15 § 111). "... in the one case it [the work of art] is a conscious product shaped

---

[2] Karl Otto **Conrady**, *Goethe. Leben und Werk*. München (Artemis & Winkler) 1994. Ulrich **Gaier**, *Johann Wolfgang Goethe, Faust-Dichtungen*, vol. 2 (Kommentar I) and vol. 3 (Kommentar II), Stuttgart (Reclam) 1999. Dorothea **Hölscher-Lohmeyer**, "Einleitung" and "Kommentar zu Faust II," in: Johann Wolfgang Goethe, *Sämtliche Werke*, Münchner Ausgabe, vol. 18.1, München, Wien (Hanser) 1997. Gert **Mattenklott**, "Faust II," in: *Goethe Handbuch*, ed. by Bernd Witte et al., vol. 2, Stuttgart and Weimar (Metzler) 1997. Heinz **Schlaffer**, *Faust Zweiter Teil. Die Allegorie des 19. Jahrhunderts*, Stuttgart (Metzler) 1981, Jochen **Schmitt**, *Goethes Faust. Erster und Zweiter Teil. Grundlagen – Werk – Wirkung*, München (Beck) 1999. Albrecht **Schöne**, *Kommentare*, in: Johann Wolfgang von Goethe, *Faust*, edited by Albrecht Schöne, Darmstadt (Wissenschaftliche Buchgesellschaft) 1999 (= Johann Wolfgang Goethe, *Sämtliche Werke*, Frankfurter Ausgabe, vol. 7, 2, Frankfurt a.M. [Deutscher Klassiker Verlag] 1999). Gerhard **Schulz**, *Die deutsche Literatur zwischen Französischer Revolution und Restauration*, 2 vols., München (Beck) 1983 and 1989. Friedrich **Sengle**, *Kontinuität und Wandlung. Einführung in Goethes Leben und Werk*, Heidelberg (C. Winter) 1999. Erich **Trunz**, Commentary to *Goethes Werke* vol. 3, Hamburger Ausgabe, Hamburg (Christian Wegner Verlag) 1960. Thomas **Zabka**, *Faust II – Das Klassische und das Romantische. Goethes 'Eingriff in die neueste Literatur,'* Tübingen (Niemeyer) 1993.

and designed to have the effect intended. But in the other we are dealing with an event originating in unconscious nature: with something that achieves its aim without the assistance of human consciousness, and often defies it by wilfully insisting on its own form and effect" (*ibid.* § 116). In a similar way in his "Psychology and Literature" Jung ascribes, by way of example, to *Faust II* the character of a "*visionary* mode of artistic creation." "The material, or the felt experience that becomes the content for the artistic creation, is nothing familiar; it has a strange character, a profound enigmatic nature, as if it had emerged from abysmal depths of prehuman ages, or from superhuman worlds of light and darkness ..." (*CW* 15 § 141, transl. modif.). Jung repeatedly uses in this and the following paragraphs such terms as *Urerlebnis* (primordial experience), *Urvision* (primordial vision), and *Urcharakter* (primordial character) to describe what underlies *Faust II* or other works of this "visionary" type. "Faust" is "a 'primordial image,' as Burckhardt once called it," an archetype, an image that "has been engraved in the unconscious since the dawn of history, where it remains dormant until it is awakened by the auspiciousness or inauspiciousness of the hour ..." (§ 159, transl. modif.) "The re-immersion in the primordial state [*Urzustand*] of 'participation mystique' is the secret of artistic creation ..." (§ 162, transl. modif.), and the poet is "in the deepest sense an instrument and thus beneath his own work" (§ 161, transl. modif.).

Now it goes without saying that any true work of art comes from a greater depth than ordinary, more technical productions that can be considered as ego concoctions. Great artists, like Homer or Hesiod, metaphorically attributed their poems to the singing of a muse, others to some other kind of inspiration, in order to give expression to the non-ego origin and depth of their work. Plato spoke of the *theia mania*, the divine madness, as the source of poetic creation. The Romans contributed the notion of the *poeta vates*, the poet as a seer, to the stock of our ideas of the depth and character of poetry. But the idea of the muse as the actual singer of the epic poem is itself an intra-poetic fantasy capturing something of the internal dialectic of artistic creation, of the poet as the unity and difference of passive recipient and active artisan. The idea of the muse must of course not be taken literally as if there indeed was an external source or origin of the work of art. The human artist, his own mind with its own depths, is the origin of his work, an immanent, strictly human origin and the only origin there is. There is nobody and nothing else.

All the many words starting with *Ur-* used by Jung, together with such words as "prehuman," "superhuman," and "since the dawn of history," suggest, however, that he was thinking in terms of an *eminent origin* and absolute immediacy. The paradigmatic fantasy implicitly informing from behind also his understanding of *Faust II* is the idea with which he interpreted his own inner imaginings during the years after his separation from Freud, namely as absolutely overpowering fantasies coming to him, their innocent victim, like a volcanic eruption, a stream of lava. This fantasy in its turn needs to be seen in the light of Jung's radical dissociation between "nature" and "art." When during the time of those imaginings an inner voice told him that what he was producing was art he "emphatically" protested saying: "No, it is not art! On the contrary, it is nature" (*MDR* pp. 185f.). Art as a product of human making and the voice of nature as something coming to the human subject as an absolutely innocent recipient are for Jung mutually exclusive opposites. By the same token, dreams are in Jung's view pure nature. The human mind, our own thinking, is absolutely *not* implicated in them. "The unconscious is a purely natural event ..." (*CW* 7 § 386, transl. modif.). Dreams are seen as "an unintentional occurrence, just as all natural occurrences," "a natural phenomenon," "direct productions of the unconscious."[3] About "the archetype" he says that it is "pure, unadulterated nature" (*CW* 8 § 412, transl. modif.). "Archetypal statements are based upon instinctive preconditions and have nothing to do with reason" (*MDR* p. 353). Throughout we see here a radically *diastematic* (dissociative) thinking. *Not* art, *not* reason, *not* consciousness, *not* reflection, but pure nature. It is an origination theory in terms of immediacy, directness, purity, and radical otherness (the absolute autonomy of the Other).

Art, however, should be understood in terms of a uroboric logic. The artist, at least the great artist, produces his work on the level of reflection and conscious artistic awareness. But this his reflective mind is *within itself* intently listening to, informed by, and giving expression

---

[3] C.G. Jung, *Kinderträume*, Olten and Freiburg im Breisgau (Walter) 1987, pp. 16 and 20. My transl. Cf. *CW* 11 § 41.

to the truth (the deep logic or syntax) of really lived life at that historical locus at which the artist finds himself. Expression and experience (listening) are simultaneous, intertwined. There are not two, a duality: first a primordial experience as pure nature and thereafter the poetic elaboration of this experience. There is only one thing, the conscious mind, but it is both aspects at once, the artistic labor of processing the truth of the age (by means and in the guise of a concrete plot or *sujet*) *and* within it (*only* within it) the emergence, and the progressive deepening of the awareness of, this truth in the continued process of reflection and production. Even if there is a spontaneous and overpowering onrush of images or ideas, this is nothing "natural," but an event in the thinking mind. Although Jung saw and taught that we are hopelessly enwrapped by images on all sides and that there cannot be an outside for us[4]—when it was a matter of essential "experience" and artistic creation he nevertheless felt the need to tear the mouth and the tail of the uroboros apart, establishing them as a simple linear opposition, a vis-à-vis.

The diastematic, dissociative logic informing Jung's thinking concerning the provenance of certain productions, including the so-called "visionary mode of artistic creation," we can see symbolized in the picture of the alchemists' two distinct workplaces, the laboratory and the oratory (see figure 145 in *CW* 12 p. 291). The laboratory is the place of the emergence of images, the oratory the place of "*scientia* or *theoria*" (*CW* 13 § 482), i.e., the reflection of the images. This *theoria* or reflection, taking place in a separate location, is, as "the second part of the *opus*" (*CW* 12 § 403), also separated in time from the first (image-producing) part of the *opus*. First the images as purely natural occurrences, thereafter their reflection or "amplification." In other words, according to this conception, taken over from alchemy and adopted without the least criticism by Jung, images have their reflection fundamentally outside of themselves. All this is in the back of Jung's characterization of *Faust II* as *Urvision*.

---

[4] The psyche "will never get beyond itself. All comprehension and all that is comprehended is in itself psychic, and to that extent we are hopelessly cooped up in an exclusively psychic world" (*MDR* p. 352). "We are in truth so wrapped about by psychic images that we cannot penetrate at all to the essence of things external to ourselves" (*CW* 8 § 680).

Turning from here to Goethe and to *Faust II* itself, we find that this work is the product of decades of planning and writing. His style of working in old age (when most of *Faust II* was written) was very different from the way he wrote in his younger years (and so also the early parts of *Faust I*). In his youth he produced spontaneously, just as the individual portions, their images and their articulations, came to him. As an old man, Goethe started by making an outline for the whole of *Faust II*. He wrote down notes by way of plans, "schemata," and slowly, one piece at a time, elaborated what had before been sketched out. Usually he thought the next portion through in the evening and began working it out in the morning.[5] To my mind this mode of production is diametrically opposed to Jung's fantasy of *Urvision*. Goethe works with great *artistic* awareness, literally as an artifex, a maker, and is very much in control of the creative process. He is not passively overwhelmed by "visions" from the unconscious. There is a deliberate and very methodical *procedere*. The work is mainly performed by the waking, conscious mind. Whereas for Jung only *Faust II* was an example of the "*visionary* mode of artistic creation," *Faust I* belonging in his eyes to the sphere of our ordinary everyday-life experience, Goethe said exactly the opposite, that "intellect [*der Verstand*] has more claims to it [*Faust II*]" by comparison with the first part.

From a letter by Goethe at the very end of his life (24 November 1831) to Sulpiz Boisserée we learn what Goethe thought the reader could perhaps become aware of through reading this work, namely "what I for many years moved round and round in my head and mind, until finally it took on this form." No immediacy. A long, long processing. Goethe is fully aware of the very peculiar mode of artistic production in the case of *Faust II*. "And through a secret psychological turn, which perhaps deserves to be studied, I believe to have risen to a mode of production which in a state of full conscious awareness created that of which I still now approve, maybe without ever being able to swim in this river again, indeed, what Aristotle and other prosaists might ascribe to a kind of insanity."[6] In other words, the product that at first glance may

---

[5] Trunz, p. 471.
[6] Letter to Wilhelm von Humboldt, 1. Dec. 1831.

appear almost crazy (on account of its strange hodgepodge of images) has been produced by the conscious mind! Goethe thinks he has *risen* to this mode of production, that is to say, risen precisely above the immediacy of any alleged "primordial experience."

What also seems to make the idea of the visionary mode of artistic creation and of *Urerfahrung* in this case rather unlikely from the start is the fact that the Faust material did not come to Goethe from within, but was a well-known traditional one that had been treated severally before him and that Goethe had known from his childhood in its popular puppet show version.

II. The topic and issues treated in *Faust II*

If Jung's view is not tenable with respect to the mode of artistic production, it might nevertheless be possible that through its content and substance, through what it is essentially about, *Faust II* has the quality of an *Urvision*. In *MDR* Jung states, "The second part of *Faust* is, however, more than a literary exercise. It is a link in the *Aurea Catena*, which, from the beginnings of philosophical alchemy and Gnosticism down to Nietzsche's *Zarathustra*, represents—usually unpopular, ambiguous, and dangerous—a voyage of discovery to the other pole of the world" (p. 189, transl. modif.).

> Goethe's secret was that he was in the grip of that process of archetypal transformation which has gone on through the centuries. He regarded his *Faust* as an *opus magnum* or *divinum*. This is why he quite correctly said that *Faust* was his "main business" …. One becomes aware in an impressive way that it was a living substance that was alive and active in him, a transpersonal process, the great dream of the *mundus archetypus*. / I myself am in the grip of the same dream and have a 'main project,' which began in my eleventh year (p. 206, transl. modif.).

Goethe himself commented to Eckermann (17 February 1831) concerning *Faust* that

> The first part is almost totally subjective. … But in the second part there is almost nothing subjective; here a higher, broader, brighter, less passionate world appears, and he who has not come

around a bit and experienced life to some extent will not know what to do with it.

The subject of *Faust II* is not the individual and his subjective conflicts or passions, nor the individual's deeply inner individuation process, but the world! And here again I have to specify, the world precisely not as *mundus archetypus*, as the collective unconscious, as the inner world of a intrapsychic transpersonal, archetypal transformation mystery. But instead: the big wide world out there, the real world as social, economic, political reality, as the sphere of science and art, as the whole process of civilization from the beginning of the early-modern era (16th century) up to the early 19th century.[7]

Interestingly enough, there is a passage in *Faust II* that expressly parodies and attacks the modern turn to one's inner: "Let the sun's shine disappear, / When day is dawning in the soul, / We find in our own heart / What the world refuses us" (lines 9691–9694).[8] Although this is Goethe's critique of the subjectivism of the Romantics, a world-less subjectivism that after his *Werther* time he himself had overcome during his classicist period, it applies equally well *avant la lettre* to the modern introspective search for meaning and for one's self-development in one's "unconscious." Not the soul's transformation mystery, but the character of the modern world and its creation through early-modern man (together with Goethe's assessment, evaluation of it in terms of his general "philosophy" of human existence as a whole and of Nature) are the topic of this work.

Goethe provides a poetic representation of the modern world together with the civilization process that led up to it AND in this poetic portrayal gives at the same time his critical, analytical view of it. *Faust II* gives us an analysis, an interpretation of the world, *his* analysis and interpretation. It is decidedly a work of reflection (albeit in poetic, not discursive, form), of *historical* reflection, in contrast to an *Urvision* and to "pure nature" in Jung's sense. As one scholar states: "The two great poetic vessels that could ... receive and contain Goethe's reflections about his time were ... *Wilhelm Meisters Wanderjahre* and *Faust*, both products of decades of planning and writing."[9] Vessels for

---

[7] Schmitt, p. 213f.
[8] Schmitt, p. 255.
[9] Schulz, vol. 1, p. 494.

his reflections! That the intellect, as Goethe pointed out, has greater claims to it is absolutely right, because this poetic work presents us with the *comprehended* world, with the *Begriff* of the modern world, as well as with Goethe's own *Weltanschauung*—with what he, as he said, "for many years [had] moved round and round in [his] head and mind."

Goethe was a keen observer of what was going on in the world during his age, not only going on on the surface, but in the depths. "Concerning economic theory Goethe was one of the best-informed men of his time."[10] And he was deeply concerned about and touched by the earthshaking shifts that he experienced and that he also envisioned, as still impending ones, namely, by the irrevocable disappearance of the world into which he had been born, a world of human proportions. Far away from any "voyage of discovery to the other pole of the world," *Faust II* is concerned with *this* world, with modern reality, with all the changes brought about by the French Revolution and Napoleon, with the development of bourgeois society and the Restauration, the rise of capitalism, the emergence of paper money and other economic changes in the financial sector, the transmutation of everything into "commodities" whose soul lies exclusively in their monetary exchange value, the difference in literature between the movements of classicism and romanticism, the development, since the Renaissance, of a sphere of aesthetic culture and the cult of beauty, the beginning of the Industrial Revolution, the emerging belief in constant progress, the Greece mania of his own time (Byron!), the technological advances in military operations, etc. In other words, anything but "abysmal depths of prehuman ages," or "superhuman worlds of light and darkness." Not an archetypal mystery, but very concrete *historical* reflection. And therefore also no "secret" (in Jung's sense) of Goethe's and no *opus divinum*, no being in the grip of that "great dream" that would make it one link in the *Aurea Catena*. Only, quite soberly, a poet's *Hauptgeschäft* ("main business," "main project"). Certainly one of the greatest works of art and in this (a figurative) sense "divine," but otherwise completely down to earth and devoted to the Real—even if from a lofty point of view and overarched as well as permeated by

---

[10] Gaier, vol. 2, p. 581.

Goethe's "philosophy" of Nature and the meaning of human life in its highest determination. Although it would doubtlessly be an underdetermination and denigration to call it "literary exercises" (*"ein literarischer Versuch"*), *Faust II* is clearly, and wants to be, a work of literature and poesy and not an *opus divinum*.

So we see that, rather than determining what *Faust II* is trying to say in its own right, Jung simply took Goethe's work and inserted it into his own scheme, using it as evidence of *his* theme, the "transpersonal" topic of the "same" Great Dream that, according to Jung, has since the Gnostics been dreamed perennially (*Aurea Catena*) and that ultimately circles around the mystery of what Jung himself, within his own life-work, called the individuation process. He transported *Faust II* into this wholly different context and thus read it against this alien backdrop he provided. When Jung said, "I myself am in the grip of the same dream and have a 'main project,'" he not only identified his own deepest project with that which Goethe had in *Faust II*, he also conversely subsumed the latter work under his own interest. An act of appropriation. But an innocent act, because Jung with honest conviction believed to see his own topic realized in Goethe's work.

This work, however, precisely cuts the ground from under the feet of any idea of individuation in Jung's sense: because it articulates the demise of the individual as such. Not only are the main persons in *Faust II* no longer, as they still were in *Faust I*, individuals with a persistent identity. They are now functions of the spheres within which they happen to occur. They play representative roles, and each one different roles depending on the spheres in question at each time.[11] In this way they are exponents of historical epochs or of cultural and societal forces, movements, and tendencies.[12] They are fundamentally subservient, "carriers of universal purposes" (Karl Rosenkranz),[13] general types, rather than personalities in their own right. Above all, "The person of Faust is not designed according to the logic of empirical persons,"[14] and Mephistopheles is a "comedian and mimic," who in *Faust II* plays all sorts of roles

---

[11] Schmitt, p. 289.
[12] Schmitt, p. 238f.
[13] Quoted in Schmitt, p. 213.
[14] Mattenklott, p. 397.

depending on the situation.[15] If there is a unity in the character of Faust at all it is only the fact that in all the different facets that he represents he is the embodiment of modern autonomous Man, Man emancipated from all situations of dependence that before had existed as a matter of course.[16] Many other characters are allegorical figurations (e.g., Euphorion), if not literal allegories (e.g., the personified Care).

In addition to this essential feature of having left behind the logic of personality and interest in the human individual (in favor of issues concerning Man as such in his confrontation with suprapersonal historical forces and values), *Faust II* also portrays the new, modern type of public that easily falls prey to the changing fads and fashions (the chorus at the end of the Helen scenes in Act III[17])—because it does not live from a groundedness in its own inner traditional (grown) convictions and values. Most importantly in this context, Goethe had become aware of the completely new situation that had arisen with the era of machines and technological progress, of what it meant for the individual, namely, that man tended to become reduced to a mere appendage of the technical means invented by him and of their autonomous momentum.[18]

Once this status of awareness has been reached, once what is happening to the individual in the modern world has been seen and *accepted* as being the modern reality, what chance could the idea of "individuation" have? When Jung apropos *Faust II* said that he was in the grip of the same dream as Goethe, he added by way of explanation that "My life has been permeated and held together by one idea and one goal: namely, to penetrate into the mystery of the personality" (*MDR* p. 206, transl. modif.). This goal is worlds apart from what *Faust II* is concerned with.

But how was it possible that Jung could misjudge this work so fundamentally? What is there about, and in, the poetic character of *Faust II* that allows for such misjudgement? With this question we have to move on to the next section which is crucial for our topic of mythic illusory appearance and blindness to logical form.

---

[15] Sengle, p. 267.
[16] Schmitt, p. 218.
[17] Schmitt, p. 256.
[18] Schmitt, p. 215.

III. Logical form

Faust II abounds in mythological figures (as also in hermetic, alchemical references). Faust has to ascend deep down to "the Mothers." There is a union between Faust and Helen. "Magic" is practiced. Under these circumstances, what is more obvious than that at least in these regards this work is dealing with that realm that Jung referred to when he spoke of the collective or archetypal unconscious? But in the case of *Faust II* the obvious, what meets the eye, is precisely deceptive. The logical form of this poetic work is such that one must not read the text straightforwardly. A *naive* approach, an innocent perception of the words and images, an understanding of the text at face value, fundamentally misses the extraordinary sophistication, differentiation, and logical complexity of this text (that Goethe had hinted at when he said that Aristotle and other prosaists might ascribe to it a kind of insanity). What is required of any consciousness that wants to do justice to *Faust II* is that it be equally differentiated and un-naive. One must not stick to the immediate appearance, sort of the visual looks and the associations that *they* evoke, but rather focus on the *concepts*, the conceptual *meaning*, that *through* the appearance and above all via the style of language and artistic form are imaginally and narratively presented. Without thought one does not get anywhere here. On the whole, this work is not symbolic and archetypal in Jung's sense, but largely downright allegorical, it aims at conceptual understanding.

Repeatedly Goethe referred to *Faust II* as "these very serious jests."[19] Jests, not *opus divinum*, even if certainly very serious jests. Accordingly, the style of language is a lower one (as otherwise found for example in comedies, not the elevated style usually found in traditional tragedies).[20] There is a lot of irony, parody, mockery. Some parts of *Faust II* are directly comical, grotesque theater,[21] opera-like. But even in those few portions, like in the closing scenes, in which the style is more solemn and a level of mystery is indeed implied, it is nevertheless by no means a mystery in the innocent, naive sense, but has, through its allegorical character, a conceptual nature. In a recent book Paul

---

[19] Letter to Wilhelm von Humboldt, 17 March 1832. Cf. letter of 24 November 1831 to Boisserée.

[20] Sengle, p. 270.

[21] Sengle, p. 273.

Bishop connects this form or style issue directly with Jung's reading of *Faust II*, pointing out that many features of this work make "it impossible to take the action at face value, yet many commentators— Jung and Rudolf Steiner included—seem to overlook the irony and satire, even the comedy-within-tragedy at work in Goethe's text ...." And in a footnote to "take at face value" he adds, "Curiously, both Jung and Rudolf Steiner do precisely this, seemingly unalert to the parodic complexity of Goethe's text ...."[22]

The strictly mythological figures, as in the "Classical Walpurgis-Night" (Act II), have the status of poetic metaphors. They are not themselves mythological, but *figuratively used* figures taken from classical mythology. The mythic images appear only as an illusory appearance, only within modern reflection and modern historical, intellectual consciousness. With the first words that Helen speaks after she has been fetched from the underworld, "I, Helen, much admired and much blamed," she herself tells us right from the outset that she is not an immediate manifestation or epiphany of beauty (which she would have to be if she were an authentic mythic figure), but that she has her life only in people's opinions and ideas. She does not belong to immediate experience, perception, or intuition, but to reflection and reception. When Helen disappears as a bodily form and Faust is left only with her robe and veil, Mephistopheles as Phorkyas consoles Faust saying, "She whom you've lost is not the Goddess any longer, / Nevertheless divine it is ..." (lines 9949f.). The place of the goddess as concrete, sensual figure in imagination and religious feeling is taken by *the* divine, the abstract idea of divine beauty.

This is not only true for the time after her disappearance. Mephistopheles-Phorkyas' commentary on her and the other Trojan women with her is: "Specters!—Like frozen images you stand there, / Aghast to part from day that does not belong to you" (lines 8930f.). Heinz Schlaffer writes, "The insight that ancient figures, which from the 18th century onwards were considered as primordial images of a sensuous, plastic fullness of life, have to content themselves with the status of ghosts is Goethe's provocation to his epoch as well as to his later interpreters."[23] Mephistopheles, so often the voice of truth, states

---

[22] Paul Bishop, *Reading Goethe at Midlife. German Classicism, Ancient Wisdom, and Jung.* New Orleans, LA (Spring Journal Books) 2011, p. 162, with note 220.
[23] Schlaffer, p. 118.

quite expressly, "Quickly free yourself of fables! / The old hodgepodge of your gods / Let it go, it is over" (lines 9680ff.). Homunculus had said earlier: "You only know Romantic ghosts; / A genuine ghost must also be a classical one" (lines 6946f.). What is meant is that Romantic ghosts are relatively harmless because they openly display their ghost character. It is by contrast much more ghostly if the ghost appears as a classical image, we today could also say: in the deceptive form of the genuinely mythic and archaic, the archetypal.

Schlaffer explains:

> One has often noted how rich the two classical acts are in allusions to the present-day situation, but it would be more exact to note that these acts play exclusively in the present. The present-day consciousness merely uses myths and costumes from antiquity for its self-representation and self-deception. The sphinxes solve the riddle of such confounding: "We breathe our spirit-tones / And you thereafter embody them" (7114f.). Projections of modern thought into ancient images determine the sequence of scenes. Modernity's real dream always precedes the dreamed-about reality of classical antiquity. First, still within the laboratory, Homunculus envisions the story of Helen's procreation in the head of dreaming Faust (6903ff.)—Helen is created in the sleep of modern intellect that no longer recognizes itself in its own ideal. Later Faust comes across the same scene— Leda with the swan—in classical "reality" (7256ff.). Initial doubts concerning the degree of reality of what he believes to be seeing—"Is it dreams? Is it reminiscences? / Once before you had already been thus thrilled" (7275f.)—disappear in the face of the sensuous power of the image.[24]

The sensuous power of the image! Jung had spoken of the "suggestive power of unconscious images"—and of our need to free ourselves of this suggestive power (*CW* 7 § 269).

The 2nd Act begins with Faust's study and Wagner's laboratory in order to show that the subsequently represented archaic mythic figures have been *reconstructed* in the spirit of modern philology and modern scientific, historical myth studies.[25] An author from the later part of Goethe's own lifetime, Christian Hermann Weiße (1801-66), wrote

---

[24] Schlaffer, p. 114.
[25] Schlaffer, p. 113.

in 1837 in his book on *Faust*: "Antiquity, just as its artistic images and its ideals, cannot as independent, personal figures lastingly gain a solid, continued existence within a world that is alienated from them. These figures belong to Hades, that is, to memory and to the sciences, in which they, although as shades, nevertheless stand and move about in indestructible personality."[26]

In his biography of Goethe, Karl Otto Conrady writes about the figure of Helen by way of summary:

> The extent to which Helen, too, is seen in terms of the status of consciousness of modernity, she demonstrates through her appearance as a purely imaginary existence. No way leads back to her mythic primordiality; for everything belonging to Antiquity is permeated by modernity in such a way that it can now only be reproduced as remembered time. It is revealing that Helen falls prey to Faust because he as the leader of a better-equipped army defeated the army of ancient Europe[27]; Seismos, the allegory of the French Revolution, makes the classical ground shake to its very foundations. Because Antiquity is thus destroyed as a political reality and the power of its tradition shaken, it can be savored to the full as an Arcadian idyll or historically reconstructed as a utopia. At any rate, it turns into a projection screen of the subjects that take possession of it: Regardless of whether with poetic or scientific means, Antiquity comes into being under the aegis of the present day. Antiquity and the primordial image of its beauty, Helen, is fetched by a modernity that feels, and partially suffers from, what it lacks. It is telling that she cannot return "into the old, the newly embellished / Parental home" (lines 8632f.), but finds her place in the "inner courtyard of a castle": as an object of reflection and contemplation. Enclosed within Faust's museum, she now represents only a reference to beauty; she is reduced to an allegory of allegorical thinking.[28]

What Goethe gives us to understand is that with the destruction of the ancient culture through the incursion of the Germanic tribes and through the earthquake of the French Revolution the continuity of

---

[26] Christian Hermann Weiße, *Kritik und Erläuterung des Goethe'schen Faust*, Leipzig 1837, p. 61, quoted from Schlaffer, p. 115.
[27] This is an allusion by Goethe to the Germanic migrations.
[28] Conrady, p. 1015.

tradition is *in fact* and irrevocably broken. There is no way back behind these real ruptures to something primordial. Whereas Goethe portrayed the brokenness of the continuity of tradition as the objective character of the modern world (the *transformation* of the old world into the modern world), Jung wrote in the context of a discussion of what *Faust* meant for him personally: "Later in my own work I consciously went on from what Faust had passed over: the respect for the eternal rights of man, the recognition of the old traditions, and the continuity of culture and intellectual history" (*MDR* p. 235, transl. modif.). By reading the rupture of the continuity of tradition subjectivistically as Faust's personal wrongdoing, instead of as part of the objective logic of the soul of modernity, he also felt—I would say naively—that through his subjective attitude and doings he could "restore" that continuity, "heal" the rupture. He believed he should and could atone for Faust's crime.[29] Quite well-meaning, no doubt, but psychologically a wrong move. An attempt to tackle a situation that exists on the level of "the Great" with behavior on the level of "the petty," the personal.[30]

What was to be (and has in fact been) poetically portrayed in the figure of Helen was not her mythic image, but the sublatedness and obsolescence of this image. Commenting on the Helen scenes, Jung says,

> What happens in *Faust* probably finds its clearest expression in the Paris-Helen scene. To the medieval alchemist this scene would have represented the mysterious *coniunctio* of Sol and Luna in the retort (...); but modern man, disguised in the figure of Faust, recognizes the projection, and, putting himself in the place of Paris or Sol, takes possession of Helen or Luna, his own inner, feminine counterpart. The actually objective process of the union thus becomes the subjective experience of the artifex, that is, the alchemist. Instead of gaining cognition of the drama, he becomes himself one of the figures in it. Faust's subjective interference has the disadvantage that the true goal of the process—the production of the incorruptible substance—is missed. Instead Euphorion, who after all is supposed to be the

---

[29] Cf. my "Buße für Philemon: Vertiefung in das verdorbene Gast-Spiel der Götter," in: *Eranos 51-1982*, Frankfurt (Insel) 1983, pp. 189-242.

[30] On the distinction between the Petty and the Great see *CW* 10 § 367 ("he who denies the great must blame the petty ...").

filius philosophorum, the imperishable and *incombustibile*, is
burned to death in his own flame—a mishap for the alchemist
and an occasion for the psychologist to criticize Faust ... (*CW* 12
§ 558, transl. modif.).

Here we see very clearly how Jung with a bold presupposition takes a
scene from *Faust* and simply inserts it into his own alchemical and
individuation scheme as the frame of reference for this scene. It is true,
Jung by no means obliterates the fundamental difference between this
scene and what the corresponding scene would have meant to the
medieval alchemist. On the contrary, his very point is that what is
expressed in this scene is a crucial change from the medieval to the
modern situation. Faust is clearly identified by Jung as the embodiment
of *modern man*. However, when it is said that modern man in the
guise of Faust puts himself in the place of Paris or Sol and that this
is a reason for the psychologist to criticize Faust, we see that Jung
holds on to the primordial or archetypal form as his standard and
sees what is depicted in this scene as a *corruption* of the archetypal
truth. For Jung, the one figure, Helen, is in truth still Luna, an
alchemical symbolic figure of archetypal depth, and even if in this
case her counterpart is not, he nevertheless *ought to be* likewise a
symbolic figure of archetypal depth, namely Paris or Sol. The
problem, the fault, of modernity, so it seems, is the deviation from
and corruption of the actually intended archetypal drama through the
substitution of the one symbolic figure by the modern ego-personality.
The result is a terrible failure of the whole *opus*.

What Jung does not see, does not want to see, is that viewed in its
own context and frame of reference, this scene is not about an
alchemical process and archetypal drama at all. It is Jung's *own* need
to assume that "the true goal" of this scene was the production of the
incorruptible substance and that it merely missed this goal because
of a fundamental flaw in the way its starting conditions were set up.
He fails to realize that the moment that the one figure is modern man,
the other figure, Helen, is also a modern figure and not the primordial,
archetypal Luna. The *whole* "drama" of this scene is not an alchemical
one, even if Goethe may have playfully introduced alchemical allusions
and similarities. Neither Faust nor the author of this scene (Goethe)
is here an "artifex, that is, the alchemist." The whole point of this scene
is precisely that such a thing as one's striving for the incorruptible

substance is out of the question. The disaster at its end is not Faust's failing to reach the intended goal. On the contrary, in Euphorion Goethe shows something very different. He portrays allegorically the problematic character of modern subjectivist, Romantic poetry. This scene is a statement of *critical analysis* and *interpretation* about this very real cultural modern phenomenon. It in itself *contains* a criticism, namely, an *objective* (inherent self-)criticism of modern subjectivist poetry, but does not need nor deserve the external criticism Jung felt the psychologist has to raise against Faust (concerning Faust's subjective interference). In the image of Euphorion's absolutely boundless striving for the heights Goethe lays bare the destructive tendencies inherent in this subjectivist poetry of his time to transcend beyond the insight that life has to be lived in self-restraint within the demarcations of the concrete Here and Now.

Euphorion is of course modeled after the classical Icarus. Nevertheless he must not be understood in terms of the puer archetype. This would mean falling for the mythic appearance of this image. Euphorion is not really a puer figure because he is not a figure in its own right at all. The undoubtedly existing puer quality is much rather poetically and metaphorically utilized and repurposed for representing the inner logic of something very different, a concrete cultural phenomenon, namely, as pointed out, Romantic subjectivist poetry. The same applies, *mutatis mutandis*, to the alchemical allusions.

"By identifying with Paris, Faust drags the *coniunctio* from its projected state into the sphere of personal-psychological felt experience ..." (§ 559, transl. modif.). But "personal psychological felt experience" is really not what these scenes are about. Nor is their topic the ancient archetypal *coniunctio* merely removed from the stage of knowing (cognition) to that of inner experience. On the contrary, what we experience in Jung's brief commentary is a projection on Jung's part, the projection of his decidedly *modern* theory of the *coniunctio* AS personal-psychological experience (in the sense of his concept of the individuation process) into *Faust II*. "Goethe's Faust almost reached the goal of classical alchemy, but unfortunately the ultimate *coniunctio* did not come off, so that Faust and Mephistopheles could not attain their oneness" (*Letters 2*, p.453, to Bowman, 18 June 1958). In Goethe's work Faust did not have, and was not meant to reach, this goal. Such is not the point of *Faust II* at all. And since Faust is from the outset not an individual, but a role, or a plural of roles, Mephistopheles is not "his" shadow, just as Helen is not "his own inner, feminine counterpart" (she is, as we already know, a general historical memory visualized and vivified in and by the modern mind at large, a specter; what is important is not she in her own right and as a concrete personified figure, but what she *means*: beauty[31]).

In addition, one can hardly reconcile with the *Faust* drama Jung's assertion that Faust "collides with his dark side, his uncanny shadow" (*MDR* p. 235, transl. modif.). Of course, Faust and Mephistopheles form a complementary pair. But Mephistopheles is not really "dark," "uncanny," not a real devil. For the most part (he has many different aspects) he is quite reasonable, realistic, pragmatic, but also at times a cynic. In the context of this work, the idea of a *coniunctio* between Faust and Mephistopheles does not make any sense.[32]

---

[31] Sengle, p. 272.

[32] On the contrary, it is absolutely essential for *Faust II* that in the end, from the point of view of the death in the last act, Faust and Mephistopheles part company, because only then can the "entelechy of Faust" be absolved (freed) from what is decayable and from the "earthly remainders." Mephistopheles represents after all that limited (almost positivistic) consciousness that insists on dissolution, destruction, and transitoriness as the ultimate truth about human existence (Hölscher-Lohmeyer, pp. 567, 581) that for Goethe himself is precisely not the ultimate answer. Jung may not like or agree with this characteristically Goethean conception of the meaning of life, old age, and death and personally have a different belief, but he should not present the end of *Faust* as an in itself (in terms of its true goal) faulty or deficient ending, namely an incomplete individuation process. This is, however, how Jung views the end. He thinks that Faust's rejuvenation should take place during his lifetime as part of his *empirical* individuation process. Jung's explicit criticism of the ending of *Faust II* is that "[...] Faust's final rejuvenation takes place only in the post-mortal state, i.e., is projected into the future." *CW* 12 § 558. "It is an unconscious reality which in Faust's case was felt as being beyond his reach at the time, and for this reason it is separated from his real existence by death." *Letters 1*, p. 265 (to Anonymous, 22 March 1939). Jung wants the rejuvenation to happen as an empirical experience (even if only as the experience of an event in the unconscious and of an archetypal reality, not as a positive fact), as something semantic. But Goethe is not portraying an individuation process as a particular life-internal semantic experience of archetypal truths at all. What happens after Faust's death presents us much rather in allegorical form with how Goethe *ultimately*, in a quasi classical-metaphysical sense, assesses *Faust's life* as a whole and *human existence as such*, his view and judgment. Nothing is postponed from this real life into the unreality of a merely possible future, because the post-mortal scenes represent an *interpretation* or *reflection* of life, the *ultimate truth* of that real life that Faust had in fact lived. The difference between a reflection or assessment of life and that life itself is a logical difference between two levels, perhaps in some way similar to the difference between language and meta-language. The difference, by contrast, between "what has been reached during his lifetime" and "what is projected into the future" stays on one and the same level, the level of semantics and positive-factual experience, and reduces the logical difference to a temporal one. Goethe is concerned with Faust's "entelechy," his fundamentally "other-worldly" "soul" that belongs to the "vertical" dimension (separated from the ordinary

Applying it to this work means roping the latter in for one's own modern psychologistic purposes.

Projection—Jung's ascribing his own highest goal to *Faust II* and his supplying what happens in it with his own alchemical-psychological frame of reference instead of *its* inherent one—is the one problem. The other problem is that Jung reads this play straightforwardly on the semantic or content level, the level of the plot, of the figures and what they do or what happens (or rather precisely what does not, but ought to happen) to them. He dwells on the foreground, the obvious, the visible. But in this way he misses the logical complexity and subtlety of this work. The essence of this work does not lie in the factual events portrayed alone. It lies in what the action metaphorically or allegorically, that is, indirectly and enigmatically points to, and in the ironic, highly reflective style full of not immediately obvious allusions, indirect citations and intertextual references. *Faust II* is a work that within itself attempts to come to terms with a host of theories and practices of Goethe's time from various fields, as well as with traditions and literary works from a long range of history. In it motifs coming from very different origins are made to mutually reflect, illumine, interpret, ironically call into question, or negate each other, so that through this interplay not any single one can be consolidated into the dogmatically true one.[33] Rather than merely continuing a tradition in Jung's *Aurea Catena* sense, rather than being informed by tradition and making use of traditional motifs and forms, *Faust II* is written and aesthetically composed from a fundamentally historical standpoint, a standpoint that results from consciousness's, so to speak, having turned around and now being able to overlook the whole range of phenomena of its

horizontal one through "death"); for Jung the vertical dimension has disappeared; he thinks on the strictly this-worldly level of horizontal empirical time (the already real time, i.e., the past and the present, and the time yet to come, the future). Jung has his place in the logic of Industrial Modernity, the logic of the unbridgeable difference, whereas Goethe is still rooted in the age of metaphysics and its incommensurable logic of the copula. In Jung Goethe's idea of the entelechy (which, as "vertical," can only show itself "after death") is taken by the idea of the empirical, this-worldly unconscious. It is ironic that Jung does not see that it is actually his scheme which follows the logic that he falsely ascribes to *Faust II*. In his case it is of course not death that separates "real existence" from what is "beyond our reach at the time," but the difference between consciousness and "the unconscious." What happens in "the unconscious" is by definition fundamentally beyond our reach.

[33] Gaier, vol. 2, p. 581.

tradition.[34] The innocent, unbroken oneness with tradition and the immediacy of the creative impulse have been ruptured. The result is a logical distance to tradition, the distance of a reflecting consciousness. Goethe himself confessed that in his old age everything was becoming more and more historical for him and that even he himself was becoming historical to himself.[35]

Far from an immediate expression of a personal inner experience, *Faust II* is at once poesy AND the *reception of* poesy, so that one might even call it *meta*-poesy.[36] It has, we could say, a double bottom, a double meaning. Phorkyas at one point reminds Helen that "Yet one says that you appeared as a two-fold shape, / Which was seen in Ilium but also in Egypt," to which Helen answers: "Do not totally confuse my disturbed chaotic mind. / Even now I do not know which one I am" (lines 8872ff.). The *fundamental* double-sense that here for once is made explicit, this doubled conceptual, self-reflective structure, not only applies to the figure of Helen in particular, but also to the work of *Faust II* as a whole. It is obvious that it is a serious mistake to understand a *meta*-work as if it were a direct first-level work. "... the meaning of *Faust II* discloses itself before us in its whole extent only in a philosophy of its form," Gert Mattenklott tells us.[37]

In this work, at least on one level of it, Goethe portrays in poetic form the inner logic or syntax of modernity together with the logic of its historical emergence. *Faust II* no longer has the structures of the epoch to which it belongs as unconscious conditions behind its back, as what *de facto* but unwittingly determines lived life and thought and

---

[35] Letter to Wilhelm von Humboldt, 1 December 1831.
[36] Gustav-H. H. Falke, *Begriffne Geschichte*, Berlin (Lukas Verlag) 1996, p. 10, writes: "Thomas Zabka demonstrated under the title *Das Klassische und das Romantische* that *Faust II* wanted to unite the two central tendencies of the age and thereby at the same time established a type of reflexive literature that first truly realized what in the poetic endeavors of the Romantics remained insufficient. Hegel attempted in the *Phenomenology of Spirit* quite similarly to combine Classical Metaphysics or Christianity, as the case may be, with the modern philosophies of subjectivity as also the Greek ethical life with modern freedom and thereby developed a radically altered understanding of philosophy. Friedrich Schlegel in the 116th *Athenäum Fragment* had demanded a progressive universal poesy, a poesy which is at one and the same time poesy and poesy of poesy (...). In this sense one can say that philosophy in Hegel becomes self-reflexive, it is always at one and the same time philosophy and philosophy of philosophy." In a footnote to this passage Falke adds, "In the same way Beethoven's Late Quartetts are music and music of music at one and the same time. The emphasis is on the 'at one and the same time.' It marks the difference to postmodernity" (my transl.).
[37] Mattenklott, p. 397.

gives to them its form, but it has these structures in front of itself as a conscious topic and makes them explicit in poetic, aesthetical form.[38]

In closing I want to illustrate once again the problem of mythic illusory appearance using one small example from *Faust II*, an example where I myself fell prey to this mythic appearance and now have to correct myself. In my "The End of Meaning and the Birth of Man"[39] I quoted old Faust saying, "So far I have still not fought myself out into the open. / Could I remove magic from my path, / Altogether unlearn the magic charms, / Were I standing, Nature, in front of you one man alone, / Then it would be worth the trouble to be a human" (lines 11403ff.). With the interpretation in mind that Erich Heller had given fifty or sixty years ago to these lines in his essay on "Goethe and the Avoidance of Tragedy,"[40] I understood the key term, magic, naively as referring to "the sympathetic world-relation, the mode of in-ness," in other words, in that traditional sense according to which it points back to a fundamentally obsolete (archaic, animistic, or medieval-hermetic) practice or mode of being-in-the-world. Thus I inscribed and projected into the word "magic" a meaning I had brought to these lines from outside, rather than having first attempted to find out what the term "magic" means in the context of *Faust II*.

The "appearance" and the immediate associations of this word are indeed deceptive. However, far from referring back to primitive beginnings, "magic" is, as Jochen Schmitt for one has shown,[41] the ironical term in this work for the modern technological approach to reality. In the context of *Faust II* "magic" expresses, and at the same time establishes a critical distance to, modern man's fundamental capability to manipulate through *counter-natural* technological, scientific, but also economic, social, artistic and often truly miraculous means the naturally given conditions of reality. Nowadays we could say that the fact that we can travel via airplanes, that we can manipulate genes, that we have the possibility of in vitro fertilization and communicate via cell-phones and the Internet

---

[38] Schlaffer, p. 5.

[39] Wolfgang Giegerich, "The End of Meaning and the Birth of Man," now in *idem*: *The Soul Always Thinks*, Collected English Papers, vol. 4, New Orleans, LA (Spring Journal Books) 2010, pp. 189–283, here p. 238.

[40] In: Erich Heller, *The Disinherited Mind*, Harmondsworth (Penguin Books) 1961.

[41] Schmitt, pp. 214 and 233.

is "magic" in the sense of *Faust II*: precisely not primitive magic, but (the critically reflected) decidedly modern "technology" in the widest possible sense.

"Critically reflected" does, however, by no means imply "morally condemned." For Goethe, the autonomy of modern man, Enlightenment, and the technological transformation of the natural world (all of which is a result of man's *nature* as a conscious, cognizing being) do not represent a defection from nature but a process *in the spirit of* nature *against* nature.[42] They are precious. We are here reminded of Pseudo-Democritus' Axiom of Nature ("Nature rejoices in nature, nature conquers nature, nature rules over nature").

And as Schmitt further points out,[43] the desire to stand in front "of you," nature, one man "alone" is by no means the wish for a solitary life apart from social reality and societal conventions. This would again be a harmless backwards interpretation, this time a backwards interpretation of the term "nature." No, this wish expresses "modern man's tragic-utopian longing for immediacy within a world of inescapable and continually still increasing mediatedness. Within a situation of alienation from nature, modern man is overcome by a longing for nature"—pure nature, accessible in absolute directness ("I – you") without any connecting, but ipso facto also alienating, means in between. In our time it also shows itself as a longing for the "Re-enchantment" of the world. It is expressive of the feeling of lack that Conrady had mentioned.

We know to what extent Jung was obsessed by the fantasy of "pure nature," "immediacy," *Urerfahrung*, and eminent origins. I only have to mention again the notions of *Urvision*, dreams as pure unadulterated nature, the concept of primordial images, archetypes. And as to "magic"—in *this* regard my wrong interpretation of the *Faust* lines was correct—Jung's deepest longing was for a new true sympathetic world-relation, a new "symbolic life," a new in-ness in Meaning, a new continuity of tradition (his *Aurea Catena* idea), and the discovery of one's true Self—all in all: a new innocence.

---

[42] Hölscher-Lohmeyer, p. 564.
[43] Schmitt, p. 233.

In this longing-driven fantasy lies the powerful seductive pull that Jung's psychology exerts upon its adherents. And to what does it seduce them? To a blindness with respect to logical form—and thus also a blindness to the psychological complexity, in-itself-reflectedness, and fundamental indirectness of the objective soul situation of modernity.

Index

For Product Safety Concerns and Information please contact our EU
representative GPSR@taylorandfrancis.com
Taylor & Francis Verlag GmbH, Kaufingerstraße 24, 80331 München, Germany